WIDENING
CIRCLES

By the same author

REAPERS OF THE STORM (WITH HERBERT STURZ)
YOU YOURSELF

WIDENING
CIRCLES

by Elizabeth Lyttleton Sturz

HARPER & ROW, PUBLISHERS, New York
Cambridge, Philadelphia, San Francisco, London
Mexico City, São Paulo, Sydney 1817

The quotation preceding the text is from Ovid, *The
Metamorphoses*. Translated by Horace Gregory. A Mentor Classic,
published by The New American Library of World Literature,
Inc., 501 Madison Avenue, New York, NY 10022, 1964.

WIDENING CIRCLES. Copyright © 1983 by Elizabeth Lyttleton Sturz.
All rights reserved. Printed in the United States of America. No part
of this book may be used or reproduced in any manner whatsoever
without written permission except in the case of brief quotations
embodied in critical articles and reviews. For information address
Harper & Row, Publishers, Inc., 10 East 53rd Street, New York, N.Y.
10022. Published simultaneously in Canada by Fitzhenry &
Whiteside Limited, Toronto.
FIRST EDITION
Designer: Ruth Bornschlegel

Library of Congress Cataloging in Publication Data

Sturz, Elizabeth Lyttleton.
  Widening circles.

  Includes bibliographical notes.
  1. Argus Learning for Living Center. I. Title.
HV1437.B76S88   1983   362.7'96   82-48136
ISBN 0-06-015109-9

83 84 85 86 87 10 9 8 7 6 5 4 3 2 1

To my mother and all parents who have had to raise their children without proper tools and supportive networks

CONTENTS

ACKNOWLEDGMENTS

Many people shared in the making of this book. The enrollees of Argus Community and Argus Youth provided incidents, commentaries and background materials. They want the world to know not only of their difficulties but also of their capacity to survive and, with help from the outside, to overcome.

Among the staff, Charlotte Bowman, Shirley Brandon, Anthony Daverese, Frances Foye, Beatrice Frank, Mary Fritz, Nydia Guzman, Patricia Ivy, Rhoda Keller, Aubrey La France, Elsie López, Diane Moore, Sudhir Patel, Constance Phillips, Fernando Quiñones, Matthew Silverberg, Joseph Spak, Mary Taylor, Juan Vega and Ru-Mei Wang made outstanding contributions, each in a special way.

Administrators and teachers from the New York City Board of Education, outstationed in the Argus program, have joined with us in demonstrating that the "unteachables" can be taught. Among those who have manifested their belief in the Argus youngsters and in our model are Vita Bogart, Stanley Snitkoph, Eddie Dickerson, Martin Wishnoff, Sandra Eno, Michael Feldman, Ruth Greene, John Cardile, Roy Fields, Frank Valenti, John McGuire and others.

I am grateful to the members of the Board of Trustees—past and present—for their support and help, proffered with generosity and free spirit. Our chairperson, Bertram M. Beck, has fostered Argus in innumerable ways, but best of all with his understanding and compassion. Lydia Katzenbach has given us the benefit of her insight and advice over the years. Mary Conway Kohler has spread her wings over us like a guardian angel. Michael Shimkin and Russell Goings are introducing Argus youngsters to a broader world. Aldo Garcia has heaped good things upon us. Leslie Ross has been with us from our earlier days, bringing enthusiasm and fine judgment. R. Palmer Baker, Jr., helped us to acquire our new building, and W. Clement Stone introduced us to Positive Mental Attitude, a key way of thinking for us. Lorraine Mayfield, J. Allen Strother and Walter Geier have made Argus possible by their support and their wise advice.

A number of foundations and businesses have supported Argus over the years, enabling us to develop in one way or another. The Helene Rubenstein Foundation, the Charles Hayden Foundation, Chemical Bank, the Heckscher Foundation for Children, Morgan Guaranty Trust, the W. Clement and Jessie V. Stone Foundation, the Edna McConnell Clark Foundation, the Exxon Corporation, the New

York Community Trust, the Lavenburg Corner House and the Ford Foundation, among others, have been most generous. We are grateful for their help.

I am indebted to the Ford Foundation for its generous financial support of the writing of this book, and to Mitchell Sviridoff and to Thomas Cooney for their ideas and the latitude they allowed me in my attempt to express the special quality of Argus.

One person remained with me from the beginning to the end of this undertaking: my daughter, Anna L. Chairetakis, who contributed research and editorial assistance, and whose scholarship, intuition and enthusiasm inform *Widening Circles.* Grazie tante, Anna.

I am grateful also to my husband, Herb Sturz, for the precious hours he devoted to reading and editing the manuscript and for his tolerance of my after-midnight and otherwise unconventional working hours.

The late Margaret Mead, whose graduate students used Argus as a research site, encouraged me to write about it. Her faith and her example gave me the stamina to come forward with the best that I can produce.

The generosity and kindness of Joanie Squeri, who typed the manuscript, was a lifeline to me in my struggles. Deciphering my handwriting, piecing together those dislocated bits and producing pages without error were something of a miracle.

My experience at Harper & Row has been a blessed event—from my first meeting by chance with Edward Burlingame, and his persistence in getting me to show him the manuscript, to the work with my two editors, Ann Harris and Sallie Coolidge, both of whom are craftspersons par excellence.

To Daniel Casriel, David Freundlich and the writers and friends whose ideas provided the building blocks for Argus, and the inspiration for this book, I offer my admiration and gratitude, while absolving them from any shortcomings it may contain.

Elizabeth Lyttleton Sturz
April 1983

INTRODUCTION

We are in the South Bronx, an area that is a symbol for urban disease, redlining, arson, violence—and the neglect of a powerful and rich nation. To the north and east and west of us, abandoned buildings; here and there in a blackened window, a staring face. Addicts shoot up in these burned-out hulks, sleep on rotten mattresses, with nothing but the "White Lady" (heroin) to fill their bellies, warm them in winter and keep them "cool" all year round. From these shooting galleries they make forays, hooking up with the local peddler, selling dope, burglarizing, robbing. Pushers barricade themselves in the ruins, stashing their stuff at the ends of elaborate tunnels and escape hatches to thwart the police. In a few buildings families, mostly women and children, hang on, struggling to maintain sanity and decency through work or welfare.

The Argus building had been abandoned, but we have reclaimed it. We are pulling children from the ruins as well. Inside Argus Community 150 adolescents are learning to throw off their numbness and their pain and to feel whole. They are learning to come to terms with their families, their society and their histories. Teachers are helping them to read and write, counselors are preparing them to go out and get jobs. Some are working already. And they are learning to paint pictures, make masks and puppets, put on plays and write poetry.

Our efforts are but a tiny stirring in the ashes. Mario Merola, district attorney of the Bronx, has said that on any given day there are 20,000 kids on the loose in the South Bronx. Many of them are "ghosts" on the Board of of Education rolls. Two hundred Arguses would make a dint. We are only one. We see some 300 of these adolescents a year, most of them black and hispanic—all, but for our efforts, shut off from education and access to jobs. Yet their television sets tell them that every American should have a nice house, good clothes and a new car. Television brings another ideal, that of equality and democracy and Horatio Alger success stories. They participate in the great materialistic feast vicariously. They compare what they see with what they have. Material possessions may not be our noblest culture ideal, but it is the one we tout the most. Ghetto residents know they are excluded because of what they are, by the good service their skin has done them in evolving a denser pigmentation against the rays of the sun.

Aubrey LaFrance, who has been with Argus since 1972 and

knows the South Bronx, puts it this way: "In working with the kids we start with what they know. For example, that businesses have left the area; factories that once provided jobs no longer exist. That shoe-shine boys can't operate on the streets because they get ripped off. They see that the number of minorities hanging out with beer cans and wine bottles has increased. There is plenty of money but none of it is flowing in their direction. They are not sitting back, festering and premeditating. They are working in their own way, from moment to moment. Whatever chance arises, they will take it. They would rather have jobs. But there aren't any. Parents are weary, discouraged. The kids pick it up; they feel they ought to go out and do something. Stealing is the obvious thing, the only thing they are qualified to do. Well, this is where we start. We work from those basics, the world they know."

We are contracted to work with 130 adolescents at any given time but usually have about 145 or more enrolled. Staff development groups are the heart of our process. We are people struggling to help ourselves, trying to get more out of our own lives and enough emotional freedom and understanding to persuade these kids to do the same. It's that simple—people being there for people, trying to turn them on to ways to help themselves and succeeding some of the time. To the extent that we do it for ourselves we are more likely to be able to do it for the Argus kids.

We try to act like an extended family for the kids and for each other, and that is important since many of us have lost our own kinship networks through one circumstance or another. But we do not pretend that the troubles our kids are caught up in stem only from the disorganization of their families. There are other factors as well, and powerful ones. Families are, after all, molding and supportive bodies which in turn are shaped by larger forces and supported or not supported. (In the South Bronx we tend not to support families.) Migration, poverty, joblessness, crime, bad schools, grudging welfare institutions are part of the picture. But it may be that the most walloping blows are the bad messages the kids incorporate from their environment.

This book is about rechanneling energies, releasing dammed-up energies and blowing life into dead energies. It is about fragmented people becoming whole. It will not focus heavily on causes, roots or etiologies, but on doing. It tells our approach to administering a multi-ethnic program, what we do to create a safe environment, to establish a value system and a structure, to heal wounds, change negative self-concepts to positive ones, promote positive mental attitude, provide successful experiences, reeducate emotions and behavior, develop competencies and mobilize resources for a few kids. It explains why we have no choice but to do the same for the staff who are their bridge to growth and change.

In these days a critical problem in our schools and on our streets is antisocial behavior. We must create a safe environment. The methods we use, both in our day center and in our residential program, work fairly well, even though our youngsters are hard-to-place black and hispanic adolescents who have been defined in terms of emotional and behavioral disturbances. Many have been passed from agency to agency in the system but with us rarely are disruptive. I describe how we handle violence when it does erupt, how we defuse it, and how we remove the support systems for disruptive, offensive and defensive behavior.

Creating a safe environment is closely related, of course, to building a value system and a structure. Many of our adolescents are so hungry for structure and boundaries that, failing to find them in the everyday world, they seek them in jails and prisons. How we build and maintain our structure and value system is discussed in some detail.

Safety, structure and values are tied to other aspects of the Argus program. One is the development of the positive peer group in both the day and residential programs. How we put together positive peer groups in both these settings and how we keep them going is described in Chapter 6.

Another aspect, which I go into at some length, is our use of touch and emotion as a language for getting through to these youngsters on a direct, deeply instinctual level, and why we find this necessary.

Improving self-esteem is another facet which is related to the preceding methods and, indeed, is dependent upon them. The self-concept group methods we employ—W. Clement Stone's approach to Positive Mental Attitude, modified to suit our special population—is presented in Chapters 11 and 12.

All of these methods are dependent upon one another. Each one has its own virtues and efficacy; taken together they make a program for the total person.

Underlying the methods and indeed basic to the whole program is the selection and development of the staff. In a sense, the staff *is* the program—people interacting with people as an extended family, as a community and a mini-society. How we screen and select staff members, fold them into our value system, get them to uphold our structure, make them aware of their own needs and aspirations, as well as those of the kids, inspire them to develop their own potential, teach them to deal constructively with their stress and rage and develop trust and bonding among themselves is the cornerstone of the Argus method. Nothing is more crucial to success with the kids. Indeed, without a highly developed staff, little can be accomplished. It is not Mary Taylor, C.S.W., Diane Moore, Ph.D., or David Freundlich, M.D., bringing enlightenment to some "paraprofessionals" who lack the benefits of formal education. Far from it. Staff members who have not been squeezed in the vise of professional training are generally more open emotionally, more capable of directness and assertion with the kids and each other. They bring warmth and understanding to the job. It is hats off in our groups: professionals are respected for their knowledge, not held in awe; staff members with street and welfare backgrounds have taught us a prodigious amount. In this book I try to convey the exchange, the flow of information, of insight and of feeling that goes on in our staff development groups and is carried over into interactions between staff and staff, between staff and kids and, eventually, between kid and kid.

Though this is primarily a book about how we do things at Argus, I include a discussion of some relevant matters, such as the labeling and mislabeling of children and some bureaucratic requirements which create turmoil and make it difficult to get good results in a program like ours.

Lastly, I put forward some thoughts about the implications of a program such as Argus—and possible ways of addressing the problem of children abandoned by society and growing up disruptive and violent. Some of these suggestions, such as mobilizing resources for our inner cities, removing Persons in Need of Supervision (PINS) from the Family Court jurisdiction and developing programs which would mediate and heal family conflicts rather than exacerbate them, are widely acknowledged as necessary steps toward alleviating the problems of antisocial youth. Others, I believe, are not as current, such as the suggestion for a special kind of training for child-care agencies. We are not proposing another training program confined to child-care workers and hands-on staff. By and large, those have not been productive. We are proposing the reorientation and retooling of entire agencies, beginning at the top, with board members and administrators, making the training available only to those agencies willing to devote substantial time to it, to participate in internships and immersion and to train a cadre of top people who could then "naturalize" the concepts and methods in their own programs. The press for more responsive child care in New York under the Child Welfare Reform Act is such that voluntary agencies might now be willing to consider a departure from the traditional social work approach—a model that does not produce results with today's hard-to-place adolescents.

When Michael Colon called me recently from Manufacturers Hanover Trust to tell me that he had received his third promotion since he went to work there, I asked him, "What was the single most useful bit of knowledge you got at Argus?" He chuckled. "Not to run my big mouth," he said. "To listen to other people and to realize that they know things that can be helpful. And oh, yes, I learned that even though I was a foster child for eleven years and don't know where my father is, that I'm still a valuable person. I feel like somebody instead of nobody."

Cisilyn Mais is in college, Debbie Williams types for the state and is studying to be a mental hygiene worker, Lorraine Ely is a nurse, Sheila Winston works in a bank and attends college at night. David Bastar and Danato Garcia are employed by Clearwater Publishing Company. Mike McCrae attended college, earns a good living in industry. Allan Ramsey, who put graffiti on more than a thousand subway cars, is attending the Fashion Institute of Technology. I cannot pretend that all our youngsters are successful, but a substantial number obtain the high school equivalency diploma (G.E.D.) each year and enter college or get jobs. We have been able to meet the tough New York City Department of Employment outcome requirements in terms of nonsubsidized employment, enrollment in advanced training or college or enlistment in the armed forces. We have met these criteria by the skin of our teeth in spite of disastrous unemployment rates, in spite of prejudice against high-risk minority youths, and only because we have an array of services in place in addition to what is provided by the U.S. Department of Labor youth employment and training programs.

Overall, this book is a plea for more opportunities, more programs, more jobs for high-risk youth and a reminder to the government and the public that deeply troubled youth need help of a kind they did not receive even under the $4 billion spent by the Carter administration on youth employment and training. Now these funds have been reduced by more than half, and youth centers and community programs all across the nation are losing the few resources they had to reach out and make even a gesture to high-risk youth.[1] It is unrealistic in the postindustrial society and in a time of high unemployment to imagine that the private sector can assume this task. The private sector can help, but only the federal government is capable of an undertaking of such magnitude. We must bite the bullet and assume the costs.

It has been our experience that delinquent behavior is often a misguided attempt by young persons who are not in control of themselves to gain mastery over their lives. The welfare mother syndrome represents the same phenomenon for adolescent girls. Argus offers these young persons a design for living and an enlarged vision of themselves and the world. This vision includes government agencies, institutions, businesses and individuals willing to reach out and help them along their path to self-realization.

Ceres was the first to break the earth with plough,
First to plant grain, and first of all to nourish
Natural things, she the creator of
All natural law—all things in debt to her:
Of her I sing, if I am fit to do so,
A goddess who deserves the best of songs.

Ovid, The Metamorphoses BOOK V

This book is based on my experiences at Argus. However, with the exception of certain staff members, the names, characteristics, and backgrounds of the people described in this book, and other details about them, have been changed.

1. TEACHING ALTON CROLY TO BE HUMAN

To start it off right, when I was a little guy, I used to
smoke joints like I smoke cigarettes. I had left Junior
High School, then had went to High School, and in high
school I was a big "Fuck up" (excuse the language). Now
that I'm in Argus things be changing with me. I stopped
smoking joints. I'm going to my classes, studying, trying to
get my G.E.D. diploma. The "teachers" help me a lot.
Especially Mr. Luna. My life now, it's not so bad.

COMPOSITION BY AN ARGUS ENROLLEE

It has been observed in various times and places that we are the
toad-eating animal, the political animal, the only laughing animal
(whoever said that never met Trotwood, our standard poodle, who
laughed not only with his face but with his whole body), the animal
of words and symbols, the bargaining animal, the praying animal, the
military animal, the only animal that blushes, eats when it is not
hungry, drinks when it is not thirsty and makes love in all seasons. We
are a "concert in discords," a dream, a breath, a groan, a curse, a
bubble that breaks, the most intelligent and noblest of animals and
the silliest and worst of animals, one of the few animals that preys
upon and kills its own kind.

Thomas Jefferson said, "I recollect no family but man, steadily
and systematically employed in the destruction of itself."

At Argus we knew how much lower than the angels we were
when Alton Croly drifted in our door at 170 Brown Place. Fourteen
years old, black, malnourished, sucking on a lollipop and smelling like
a charnel house, Alton had the scarred and "flakey-paint" skin which
may be the result of marasmus. His slight frame was bent under the
weight of a dirty cotton swag bag in which he carried the tools—and
sometimes the booty—of his various trades. Scavenging among abandoned or semiabandoned and burned-out buildings was his main
occupation, he told the Argus intake worker, Juan Vega. He spent the
better part of week nights crawling into foul, dank and pest-ridden
crevices, sawing out copper tubing when he could find it, but settling

1

for any saleable metal or material. He slithered in and out of spaces where normal people couldn't fit. In this one area his underdeveloped body was an asset.

After the interview, when certain formalities had been complied with and much paperwork had been done, Alton signed his name—and the intake worker signed his—to a contract committing Alton to develop his strengths and potential, to attend regularly and be on time and to abide by our cardinal rules; and committing Argus to help him define his goals and provide the resources which would enable him to achieve them.

An older Argus enrollee, a boy who had been with us three years and acted as a counselor's aide, took Alton on a brief tour of the building, introducing him to counselors, teachers and enrollees, explaining how boys and girls move from one phase to another as they become a part of the Argus family, learn the rules and make progress toward their goals.

We took Alton in, but we were by no means convinced that he could relate to our highly structured program of groups, academics, vocational counseling and work experience. His attendance was sporadic, and he almost never made it in before lunchtime because he was still pursuing his career as a scavenger and hanging out with his street buddies. From interviews with his mother, from his own accounts and those of his peers, we gathered that when metal in abandoned or semiabandoned buildings was to be had and the terms offered by scrap dealers were generous, Alton rode high. Pockets bulging with money (he loved to flash a bankroll at his "admirers"), lungs laden with smoke, skates on his feet, he zoomed through the night hours feeding on the honeydew of delusion. In less prosperous times he was obliged to ply his alternate vocation of armed robbery, for which he had been brought before Family Court on three occasions. Stealing pipes from buildings where people were still living deprived the tenants, mostly elderly or those who could not afford to pay rent elsewhere, of water and drove them into the streets.

Among ourselves we referred to Alton as our independent merchant. (If you don't find a way to laugh you will cry.) Asked what he did with the proceeds of his sales, his face blazed with greedy pleasure. "I git my friends and we git high, man. We git high. Then we go rollerskating till it be gittin light and time to go to school."

What substance did Alton use to produce his high? "I use pot, man, the way other people smoke cigarettes. To git real high, man, I sniff angel dust."

How many times had he used angel dust, or PCP (phencyclidine), the most destructive substance on the street today, and over what period of time? Alton didn't know precisely, or wouldn't say, but certainly for more than a year and as often as he could get it. He drank quite a lot of beer and at one time sniffed glue.

It was a familiar litany: seven children in the family, father's whereabouts unknown, mother on welfare, but working on the side, in this case as a barmaid in a popular discotheque, so that she too was out all night. Mrs. Croly is in her thirties, attractive and well-dressed. She insisted that there was "nothing the matter with Alton," that he had all the money he needed and a large wardrobe of clothing. The probation report stated that when he was "small," Alton was taken by Mrs. Croly, along with her other children, to the South and left with relatives who did not feed them properly. After "several years" she made a visit because of a death in the family, found the children emaciated and in poor health and took them to New York. Alton insists that when he was small he lived with his father and that he still sees his father "about once a year." His mother says that he never lived with his father and that there has been no contact with him. Of the seven children, five live at home. One brother is serving a prison term and another has just been paroled from an upstate institution and, according to Mrs. Croly, is giving her a hard time.

There are discrepancies and a certain lack of clarity in what Alton reported about himself and in what his mother told us. We learned of his truanting, his failing record in school and his arrests through probation reports and court records. Although Alton ran his mouth, he kept his real feelings and a lot of key information to himself. He did not trust the counselors, and several times he was caught in lies by his peers, who took a dim view of his fantasizing and let him know it.

The counselors did not dismiss the stories Alton told about himself as outright lies. His inventions as well as his acting out helped to shield him from a harsh reality. He had shown considerable ingenuity in adapting to his environment, being alternately a mole burrowing in the ruins and a bird flying and skimming through the dark night. As he did so the strife-ridden household where nobody paid attention to him, where he had no father and, as he saw it, no mother, faded. Erased from his awareness also were his smallness, his dependence, the sick feeling of fear in his stomach.

One weekend, after Alton had been with us about three months, the burglar alarm system was disconnected and the copper plumbing pipes were stolen from the work site of a building we were renovating as a second group home for girls. Alton boasted to the girls in the first group home (which abutted the renovation) that he was the author of the crime and asked if they had heard him and "his crew" in the building that night. The girls—and the staff—had indeed heard the thieves as they trampled the work site, sawed through metal, knocked down a heavily barricaded door at the rear and exited with the stolen pipes. The girls and the staff had huddled in their beds, afraid to move or call the police. You can be killed butting into the business of thieves.

Since Alton had been employed at the site as a carpenter's helper and knew the workings of the alarm system and the other security arrangements, we thought he might have been involved. Confronted by the senior staff he remained cool and aloof, maintaining that he had lied to impress the girls. We found no shred of anything but circumstantial evidence to implicate him in the theft, and enraged and frustrated as we were, we kept him at Argus and continued to work with him, though he was laughing in our faces and not a crack had appeared in his armor. He was still attending intermittently and coming in late after his long nights of salvaging, stealing, smoking and skating. We had small hopes of getting through to Alton, and yet he kept coming back to us—month after month. He knew how to exert himself, and small as he was, he was assigned, as part of our work experience program, to do odd jobs in building maintenance and to help out with the nonprofit moving company we ran at that time.

The following year he was given a paid job in the summer youth employment program and began to attend regularly and to be on time. By September his behavior and appearance were transformed. Tests showed a year-and-four-months gain in math (within a four-month period) and a more modest but significant gain in reading. Alton was placed in the most advanced segment of the program, Phase Three, and was extremely proud and pleased. (Advancement from one level to the next is on the basis of behavioral, personal and social growth; academics in each of the three phases are taught at whatever levels are appropriate to participants' achievements.) We noted that Alton was always present on those days when Jose Padilla held his class in mask making, paper sculpture, painting and puppetry. Alton seemed to derive a special satisfaction in letting another person smear his face and sometimes his hands, arms and feet with plaster of paris. He was fascinated with the molds of parts of his body made in this way. The masks he made of his own face oddly resembled the moldy gravelike muck that once covered his countenance as a result of crawling among the ruins and perhaps represented an outgrown aspect of himself which he playfully revived from time to time. He seemed to delight in showing himself in this frightful guise and then stripping off the mask and disclosing his real face—friendly and beaming.

Aubrey LaFrance and others had worked with Alton for a year before the breakthrough came. It happened in Sandra Eno's English literature class. Alton, who could not answer the questions that day, insisted that he had read the story under discussion ("The Rocking Horse" by D. H. Lawrence) but could not remember it.

His fellow students laid it on the line. "It's no wonder you can't remember anything with all the dust you smoke. Your brains are being eaten out with bad chemicals. It ought to be called angel death, not angel dust. You know all that and yet you go right on smokin it. When are you going to stop it, Alton?"

Tears welled up and rolled down Alton's face. "I can't stop gittin high, man."

"How come you can't stop, Alton? Don't give me that bullshit!"

"I can't stop. It's all I've got. I haven't got nobody. I'm all alone in this world."

No one made fun of Alton for crying. No one told him to stop. This is significant. In an ordinary classroom he would have been led from the room or allowed to sit there while his classmates scoffed at him for being a crybaby or turned away in embarrassment. Sandra Eno is a special education teacher, trained to work with emotionally disturbed children. More importantly, perhaps, she is an empathetic person and she cares about the kids. Assigned to Argus by the New York City Board of Education, she had become interested in our approach and works hand in glove with our counselors. Sandie knew that this was a moment of truth for Alton and that whatever happened next between him and his classmates and herself would be of vital importance. "The Rocking Horse" was laid aside.

The peers knew what to do. They gathered around Alton, put their arms around him, asked about his mother, his father, his friends. Sobbing, Alton told them how lonely it was at home. The kids he hung out with were not real friends, he confessed. They only came around when he provided them with smoke and skates.

The peers told Alton that he was no longer alone. "You've got us, Alton. We'll be your friends. And from now on we'll be your family, too."

Blanca Gonzalez said, "I'm four months pregnant. I'll be your mother, Alton. Everybody here will be your brothers and sisters. Who do you want for a father?"

Alton said, "I don't want nobody for a father, man," and sobbed uncontrollably.

They let him give free rein to his grief. He was still crying when the time came to move on to the next part of the schedule. Sandie and Blanca took Alton to Aubrey's office.

Aubrey put his arm around Alton. "You feel bad, man, I know. But one good thing: it takes real heart to cry. There's more manliness in crying and asking us to accept your real feelings than in hiding behind a jailbird image and stuffing it all inside you."

Aubrey sent out for some lunch for the two of them and they spent the afternoon together.

"If the roof fell in I had to be with Alton then. Not two hours later. Not tomorrow. Not next Friday at 3:30, but that moment. I might have patched him up and pushed him on into the next class but a very significant boiling up was taking place and it was desirable for me to stay with him so that he could feel free to let it happen."

Later in the afternoon, when Alton was calm and open as he had never been, they went into a special group of the peers who knew Alton best and liked him. Alton told them what was going on with him and asked for their help. They responded warmly. They committed themselves to helping him and to being his family provided that he got his act together. "We don't want to hear that you are still pulling any of that shit out there in the street, man."

Alton didn't turn into an open, honest, emotionally resonant young man in one day. He had been around Argus sucking up the atmosphere for almost a year. And he still had a long way to go. His method of handling unpleasant feelings had been to deny that anything was wrong and to escape first into drugs and then into fantasy. He still closed up at times and refused to let anyone in. At other times he walked around talking, laughing and cutting up, as though the new-found intimacy with his peers was the greatest "high" of his life. The trouble was that he wanted all of their attention all of the time. And when he couldn't get it. . . .

A watch was stolen. The counselors called a general meeting and asked for help in getting it back to the young girl whose pride and joy it had been. Quite often after an appeal like this the thief would come forward or the missing item would suddenly turn up. This time there was no response.

Later in the day Alton walked into the counselors' office, took off his jacket, turned out his pockets—all without being asked to do anything—and said, "See, I didn't take her watch."

Aubrey said, "Well, Alton, we didn't say you did."

Alton left the office and spread the story that the counselors had hustled him into the office, accused him, stripped him and searched his person.

The peers were indignant. They demanded a meeting with the counselors. A group was set up for that afternoon, as soon as the schedule permitted. The peers confronted the counselors. They let them have it. Who did they think they were treating Alton, a member of the family, like that? When they had upbraided the counselors sufficiently, the facts began to come out. Alton admitted that he had voluntarily removed his coat and turned out his pockets and that the counselors had in no way accused him.

The peers turned their wrath on him. "Why did you lie to us, Alton? Why?"

"I don't know," Alton mumbled, scrunching down and trying to hide in his chair.

The peers demanded an explanation. Alton burst out crying. The peers were not sympathetic.

"We're not gonna patch you up, Alton. You lied, now you feel bad. We trusted you and you lied to us. You deserve to cry."

"I know I do," Alton sobbed.

He apologized and agreed to stand up in the morning meeting and ask the "family" to help him not to tell lies. Then, with this assurance in hand, the peers patched him up. Alton and Aubrey had a long talk in the office. Aubrey did not let Alton walk out feeling low. (This is important.)

Next morning Alton was there bright and early for morning meeting. He sat alone in the last row but as the small auditorium filled up, Alton's row became the next to last and then the third and fourth and fifth from the last. He looked about uneasily and said nothing, nor did he participate in the singing, the philosophizing or the thumbs-up, thumbs-down voting on whether to accept the excuses of latecomers or send them home for the rest of the day. Clayton Willet came in thirty minutes late. The peers heard his excuse, that he had overslept, told him that this had happened before and that it was getting to be a habit. Someone suggested that Clayton be given one more chance. There were calls of "Make him go home. He's running a number on us!" "Hey, Clayton, you can get out of bed like everyone else. Don't give us that bullshit!"

Aubrey put it to the vote. "Let me see your thumbs. Which is it to be? Hold them high! Thumbs up or thumbs down?" It was thumbs up.

Aubrey said, "Okay, Clayton, you slid in under the wire. But if

I'm reading the sense of this meeting, this is the last time grace will be extended. If you're late again without a valid excuse, you'll be sent home."

Morning meeting is a key part of the day. The kids come in tired, droopy, wishing they were still in bed, or bright-eyed and bushy-tailed, thinking about the exciting things going on in the streets—and they get plugged in to our concept and our process. They loosen up, they sing and chant poems in chorus and some of the advanced ones get to their feet, go to the front and sing, recite or read in groups of two or three or even solo. Everybody takes part in some way—helps to plan a trip or party or suggests a way to make something better. In general the atmosphere is positive, it is the place where good feelings take over and people tell about their progress or some plea-surable experience they've had. Birthday people's names are called out and "Happy Birthday" is sung. Simple Simon, which previously would have been sneered at as a child's game, is played with avidity. Some teachers join in; one teacher who usually won't crack his image, proves to be adept at the game and makes a hit. The kids love his witty responses. There is a lot of fun and laughter, everybody gets in good spirits, and when it's time to go to class, the prospect is no longer intolerable. Occasionally, a serious matter or a crisis, such as violence or drug use on the premises, will be dealt with in morning meeting.

Before this particular meeting ends Aubrey reminds Alton of his commitment to the family. Alton goes to the front, whispers with Aubrey for a few minutes, then turns away. "I ain't got *nothin* to say to the meetin." Then he bursts into tears, returns to his chair and sits in solitude, sobbing.

"Alton, you better get your act together, man," one of the enrol-lees says. His tone is tough but not unkind.

"How bout that, Alton?" someone calls.

There is no response. Alton continues to cry. Someone passes him a tissue. He wipes his eyes, sobs again.

Aubrey observes, "You can say one thing for Alton: he lets it all hang out. There's a lot of heart in that. It takes more courage and manliness to come right out with your feelings. You know, feelings have a way of coming out anyhow, in different forms. This is the pure form, like raindrops or pearls that come from the wounds of an oys-ter."

"Alton, come sit near me!" It is Blanca. "You know I'm the mother of this group, bein that I'm pregnant. I be your mother too. Come on, Alton. I know how you feel."

Alton does not answer. He rises to his feet and stalks out of the meeting, defiant and forlorn. But Frances Foye is at the door. She puts her arm around his shoulder and steers him gently into the counselors' office.

Morning meeting breaks up. Classes get underway. Aubrey goes to the office and talks with Alton for perhaps fifteen minutes. Then Alton goes to class and participates. Later in the morning he is asked to help move furniture to the new group home, now completed and ready to be occupied. He is observed on one end of a bookcase. He waves and calls out some bit of banter. He is in high spirits, pleased at being asked to help, proud to be seen heaving and carrying with the best of them.

Next day Alton gets up and speaks to the afternoon meeting of Phase Three. He tells them that he does not want to lie any more and asks for their help. "I'm not gonna soup you up no more with big stories," he promises. "I know I be doin that to get you all to pay attention to me. But there's better things that I can do to get the family to like me than makin up fantastic stories about things that never happened."

His remarks draw applause from the peers and the staff. It is a sign of acceptance.

Alton has now become the mischievous child. There is no sign that he is using drugs or stealing, but we believe that he still smokes marijuana at times and at long intervals, dust. Like the others Alton has pledged to set aside eight hours a day free from any kind of crutch. Like the others he has promised that if he is using on the outside he will inform us of the fact so we can size up the situation if anything goes wrong and get the right kind of help quickly. This is to avoid the pandemonium and panic that befell one day when eight youths were brought into the conference room, vomiting and in convulsions. They were new to us and observing the street code of silence. Consequently, we were in the unhandy position of having to interrogate the most intact of them while waiting for the police emergency squad to respond and of dealing with convulsions and nausea. Two of the youths were barely rescued from death when we finally got them to a hospital.

From time to time, in morning meeting or in group, kids will cop to smoking pot and dust evenings and weekends. They say they do it at home when they feel uncomfortable with themselves or when they go out partying or dating and can't face the pressures. Gradually they become aware that a day on pot remains not as an experience to build on but as a blank, an empty hole in their lives.

If they come in high they are dealt with by the Argus family and are sent home until they return with a parent or guardian and a new contract is drawn up and agreed to. The year-round youth employment jobs are used as an incentive: you don't get one of these jobs, which run right on through the summer and pay the minimum wage, unless you are drug-free and making acceptable progress on all fronts, including behaving like a responsible member of the family.

"Alton is a pain in the neck but we love him," Aubrey says.

"At times I want to grab him and wring his neck!" exclaims Connie Phillips, a former Aid to Dependent Children (ADC) mother who trained with us and is now a full-fledged counselor. "If he were one of *my* kids—!" But the next moment she has her arm around Alton; they are walking, talking and laughing together.

"Alton is eager to show that he is a big man. And he's small and fourteen. That's the key to him," Aubrey adds. "Work with the peers keeps him steady and coming along."

Alton's mother, Mrs. Croly, reports that she finds her son greatly changed. Not understanding the process she sees Aubrey as a kind of warlock with magical powers.

"It's not me. It's what we *do,*" Aubrey says. "It's teaching people to be human, the way we see it. Developing the ability to feel with other people, that's all."

2. A SAFE PLACE: INTAKE PROCEDURES

The kids at my school called me Mad Dog, Black Dog and Maneater. One of 'em stabbed me with a pair of scissors. My aunt says the reason everybody hates me is that I'm so ugly.   ARGUS ENROLLEE

The day fourteen-year-old Marvin Manders was admitted to the Argus Learning for Living Center, he was accompanied from the Bronx Family Court by his probation officer. They walked from the subway along 138th Street, a thoroughfare in full summer bloom. Customers were shouldering their way in and out of the Brook Avenue Lunch Bar. LaRosa's Restaurant was doing a brisk business in cuchifritos, breaded steak, fried plantains and yellow rice and beans. People of all ages, as scantily dressed as the law allowed, were strolling along the pavement, licking ice cream cones, smoking, talking, laughing and gesturing with an animation that is typical of summer street life in the ghetto.

Marvin lived a little to the north and, like many ghetto dwellers, seldom ventured out of his own neighborhood. Without seeming to move his sharp eyes Marvin probed the scene, alert for signs of danger but eager also to discover which of the marginal businesses and hole-in-the-wall bodegas sold weapons, "joints," angel dust, cocaine and other illegal merchandise. As they neared Brown Place, a short street running from 138th to the service road of the Major Deegan Expressway, he noticed a housing project of a type he had not seen before —low, single- or two-family dwellings with small neat yards in front and back. The sidewalks and streets near these projects were carefully swept, and there were no drug addicts or bums lounging around the area—only neighbors sitting on their stoops or chatting over the fences.

On 136th between Brown Place and Brook Avenue, one building stands alone and intact on an entire square block of burned rubble and litter. The carcass of what had been an adjacent house clings to its southern flank like the incarnation of some black rot disease, threatening to penetrate and undermine the healthy structure that

11

remains. The intact building has a sign over its doorway: Argus Community, and the peacock emblem, painted by the kids in brilliant colors. Built early in the 1900s as an elementary school, the red-brick structure, one hundred feet long by fifty feet wide, is by no means ideal for our purposes. We are constantly running up and down its five flights of stairs, trying vainly to come face to face with one another in small chopped-up spaces. The old factory building that we previously occupied was better suited to the program but was cold and leaky and the water faucets ran red grime. We have our eye on a glorious building, which the Board of Education is threatening to abandon. If we can buy it, and somehow arrange to protect it from thieves and vandals during ULURP (a long bureaucratic land-use process), Argus will have its dream home. Meanwhile, we have 170 Brown Place, with its rundown narrow doorway into which Marvin Manders now entered with his probation officer.

The door was not locked, an unusual circumstance in an area where street gangs and assorted dangerous characters roam. Marvin and the probation officer walked up a few steps into the lobby and then into a main hall which runs the length of the building. There was no guard—another surprise. A young man a couple of years older than Marvin sat at a small desk near the door. He asked them to sign in and directed them to the intake office down the hall.

Inside, the building was cheerful. The walls were painted in light coordinated colors of yellow, ecru and white. Marvin found his eyes drawn to the brilliant tropical scenes and the black men, women and children depicted in a series of Haitian folk paintings hanging along the hallway. One wall was reserved for enrollee art work, big splashes of water color, magic markers and crayons. A switchboard operator and a secretary sat in an alcove, and Marvin saw a black man, tall and distinguished, step out of an office beyond to hand a sheaf of papers to the secretary. "Would you make three copies and put them together carefully, please?" This interchange, trifling as it was, struck Marvin as having a kind of mystery, like a vignette in a play, the plot of which he could not grasp. The quiet in the building was vaguely troubling, even eerie, moving Marvin to ask, "Is this a *school?*" and then to burst out anxiously, "I'm gettin outa here, man. I don't like this place."

Juan Vega, the intake worker, told him that the Argus program included a school, among other things.

"Man, this is too quiet for a school."

"Don't let it get to you. The kids enrolled here want it that way. They get more done when it's quiet."

"Shit! What kind of place is this?"

"Come on in my office, we'll rap about Argus and you can tell me something about yourself—how you got here and what you have in mind."

They crossed the threshold of a tropical forest. Almost everyone at Argus has one or two philodendrons and maybe a jade plant or a cactus. In Juan's office, leaves reached for you from all sides—leaves in star clusters with splashy markings, broad white leaves with green veins, wreathy, viney leaves, dark-banded, powdery gray, purple, silver, pink and mauve leaves. What caught Marvin's eye was an exuberant chlorophytum with clusters of its own tiny offspring sheltering under its spidery arms.

"Man, this place is like a florist's shop!" he exclaimed, backing into an elegant dizygotheca.

"Watch that thing. It has teeth. I may not keep it. I like plants that make me relaxed. Plants do that, you know. They breathe out something that calms the mind."

They sat in two chairs, facing each other. Juan never barricades himself behind a desk when he's talking to a kid. He doesn't think it's fair to protect his vitals with a big officious piece of furniture, while asking others to expose their guts. He and Marvin studied each other as they talked.

Juan grew up in the South Bronx, had used drugs, had been in prison and had found his way to Synanon, a self-help rehabilitation program. Coming from this background, he understood and sympathized with the small, very black adolescent who sat before him, masking his fear with cool superiority.

Marvin never cracked a smile or dropped his hard rock image. When Juan asked him what he was interested in, the reply was "The only thing I'm interested in, man, is getting the law off my tail."

"Anything else?"

"Yeah. I'm interested in not getting leaned on or iced. I don't want nobody walkin on my head."

"Chill out, man. You won't find that here. This is a serious place. Nobody at Argus is going to offer you any violence."

Marvin treated Juan to a gimlet stare. "I hear ya." But it sounded like "I don't believe you."

Juan is Afro-hispanic, lean, muscular and not overpoweringly tall. He sports a snuff-colored hairdo in the latest "natural" style (which means treated with chemicals so that the hair will curl, then washed and allowed to form tiny ringlets), and a mustache. Marvin in the flick of a street-wise eye had taken note of his strong face and jaw, the friendly quizzical eyes which looked through gold-rimmed spectacles. What impressed Marvin most, however, was Juan's attire, for clothes happened to be Marvin's passion. He himself wore nothing but superthreads; he had to look "fly," and he discovered to his surprise that the intake worker was as sharp as an ice pick: French Star jeans, Lil Abner construction boots, French cut shirt. Juan's jewelry also conveyed messages and raised speculations and fantasies: the hand-made silver ring on his left ring finger (might be married or living common-law), the Saint Joseph's medal (given to him by his mother probably), and last of all the tiny golden fist, a good luck omen. Marvin half expected to see a small golden spoon dangling on the intake worker's chest among the medals (a dude who dressed like that could afford cocaine and the Superfly utensil to dish it out). Meantime, Juan was contemplating Marvin.

Since Argus is a private, nonprofit agency, receiving funds from several public as well as private sources, and accountable to them all, a lot of paperwork must be done at intake. But we try not to come on like the welfare department or a free clinic. When he can the intake worker postpones filling out the documents until he has made friends with a kid. He takes the trouble to show each one that he is interested in him or her personally. If the kid or his mother is hispanic, the worker asks where the family came from. If it's Ponce, he may say, "Hey man, that's my home town!" If it's some other town or village, he tries to find a friend that they have in common or relates something positive he's heard about the place or people from there. Juan always tries to zero in on some special interest that a kid might have. Right away he and Marvin got into a discussion about clothes and how good it makes a dude feel to be well dressed; and this led quite naturally to some of the tactics they'd both employed to obtain their "mean vines." From there Juan was able to share a little of his life history, including why he turned square and how he came to be working at Argus. After that, with only a little prompting, Marvin's story came tumbling out.

He had lived in so many places he couldn't remember them all. He guessed that the family—his mother, his two older brothers, his older sister and a younger brother and sister—had moved at least ten times. When Marvin was eight they lived in a building known as "Dope Fiend Alley" because so many junkies hung out there. His father was hardly ever home, and when he was, he and his "wet cotton" friends (his cooker buddies) shot heroin in the boy's presence. In spite of this, Marvin said, he was close to his father and had grieved when he died in a car accident. Marvin said that no one could take his father's place. He was ten at the time and doing poorly in school, and increasingly unhappy as he passed from one grade to the next without comprehending the work.

When his mother took a common-law husband who drank heavily and disappeared without explanation for long periods of time, Marvin's bitterness increased. The family eked out an existence on Mrs. Mander's Supplementary Security Income (SSI) benefits.

When Marvin was thirteen he joined the Savage Skulls, a local street gang, in order to gain protection from rival gang members who made forays into the neighborhood. At the same time he became a runner for a dope seller who employed children because they were virtually immune from the penalties of the law. Guns were readily available to Marvin and his main man, Danny. Wearing a face mask, he and Danny robbed individuals and stores in their neighborhood. One night at a party, after he had defended Marvin in a fight, Danny was taken up to the roof of the building and hurled off. Marvin said he could not forget the sight of Danny, crumpled and broken on the pavement. He held himself responsible for Danny's death and said he would wake up screaming after nightmares in which he himself was hurled from the roof, while Danny looked on.

Disgusted with gangs, Marvin tried to resign, but the president and the war lord threatened to have him killed if he severed his connections. Desperate to get away from the gang, Marvin stepped up his drug dealing and stickups, deliberately risking arrest. Soon he was off the streets and, as he thought, out of danger. But in the training school where he eventually found himself, Marvin felt even less safe than on the street. Many boys inside were older and more street-wise than Marvin. They walked with a gladiator's swagger. Nearly everyone had a weapon—a knife or a piece of steel pipe—on his person, buried in the yard or hidden in a crack in the wall. A sizable number were preoccupied with "chasing behind other people's butts," as Marvin expressed it. Outside with most of them it would be women they were after; inside it had to be other males. His second day, Marvin, along with the other inmates and guards, witnessed a "wedding" in the yard. The "groom" was older, tougher and bigger. Marvin went into a cold sweat. His greatest fear, even worse than that of being killed, was that his manhood would be destroyed through the sexual invasion of his body by another male. If this happened, he told Juan he would never again be sexually potent with a member of the opposite sex.

When the Five Percenters, a Muslim splinter group, offered Marvin their protection on the condition that he espouse their beliefs and practices, he accepted gratefully. They were a power in the institution, and indeed they did protect him from the rapes and assaults which took place regularly in the showers, the empty classrooms, the walk-in refrigerators, the yard and even in the "rooms." Anyone who molested Marvin would have brought down the revenge of the Five Percenters on his head. Marvin thought at last that he was safe.

"The Five Percenters was cool, man. They treated me like a brother. And you will do anything for a brother—even die for him," Marvin said.

The Five Percenters taught Marvin to be punctual, to attend to hygiene, to look high in life and to glorify his blackness. But they also taught him that as a male he was a god, that females were "earths," slaves and childbearers to men. They taught him that the ecstasy brought on by cocaine and narcotics was okay because the drugs were natural substances created by Allah. They taught him that if a pregnant black woman was touched by a white, her seed would be contaminated and a monster would be born, that it was okay and desirable to stick up whites and to hurt them because this would bring joy to Allah. They taught him to transfix "white devils" with the sword blade eyes of hatred and revenge. He was enjoined, however, from robbing or harming black people because they were his brothers and sisters.

Marvin was released after a few months and returned home. Avoiding his old gang, he sought out the Five Percenters and followed a way of life which involved abstinence from alcohol and the use of heroin and robbery at gun point. Because his after-care officer was on his tail, he registered at Julia Richman High School and went there regularly. But he did not attend classes. The one day he did attend he was humiliated in front of his classmates because he could not read. He never went back. Instead, he roamed the halls, fighting and getting high. As far as he could tell, no one at the school cared whether he attended classes or not. "They didn't even know my name or if I was there," he said.

By this time Marvin's older brothers were serving long prison sentences for armed robbery. His mother was bitter and spoke about having Marvin "put away" again. Since he was ten years old, Marvin said, she had threatened to take him before the court and have him dealt with by a firmer hand than she possessed. Yet Marvin felt that she loved him. He also knew that he was a disappointment to her. Late hours, little or no food, drugs and a strenuous life were wearing Marvin down. He had been arrested four times for armed robbery and had been away twice. He had begun to accept crime as a career. Prison would be part of it. Since this was his fate, he was determined to "chill out" and prove that he could take it.

But his health was getting worse. He depended more and more on dope to ease the aching of his teeth and to push back a certain sense of futility. It was during this time of tension and conflict that Marvin once again came before the Family Court and was brought to Argus by his probation officer.

Without realizing it, Marvin had hungered for someone he could talk to, and finding himself in the presence of a sympathetic person with a street background, he had poured out his story. Not every newcomer to Argus speaks as freely—far from it.

Surmising that the kid regretted having been a fat mouth, Juan changed the subject and explained what Argus is about, how the enrollees help to run the place, how they're mostly dudes like Marvin who haven't found much "out there" for themselves, who've been leading more or less dangerous and unsatisfying lives and who want to come in out of the cold, *feel safe,* find out what their talents and interests are, and with the right kind of help, move ahead with their lives. Marvin said he wouldn't mind giving it a try; only then, after more than an hour of friendly and open interchange, in which Marvin agreed to abide by the Argus cardinal rules and to take on certain responsibilities, including helping to clean and maintain the premises as his contribution to the Argus family, did Juan begin with the paperwork. Sometimes the intake worker offers a kid the chance to think it over for an hour, or even a day or two, before making a final commitment. In Marvin's case Juan didn't feel it was necessary.

Three conditions were explained by Juan and agreed to by Marvin: taking off people, black or white, would have to stop, there would be no more cocaine or heroin, even though the Five Percenters considered these substances a gift of God, and he would not be allowed to proselytize for the Five Percenters among Argus enrollees.

Juan pointed out that Argus takes in people of any religious persuasion and while they are free to pursue their beliefs on the outside, they can't discuss religion or politics within the program because we focus on other ideas and pursuits that take up all of our thoughts and energies. After a certain amount of time in Argus, youngsters generally lose interest in groups such as the Five Percenters, and this usually occurs without confrontation or discussion, as they come to feel that they belong to the Argus family and as the old hard knots of anger and mistrust dissolve and wash away.

Since we came into existence, in 1968, we have been able to offer youngsters, staff and teachers a safe environment—which may be the strongest card in our deck. Over the years, time and time again, we have asked adolescents to turn in a variety of weapons—guns, knives, razors, chains—and they have generally done so more or less quietly. There has never been an act of violence connected with the surrender of weapons. We explain why we do not permit weapons on the premises and point out that there is no need to carry a gun or knife while in the Argus environment. We explain that no student or staff member has ever been assaulted or hurt in our halls, stairwells, lavatories, classrooms, lunchroom or on the grounds. We usually give the young person a choice between turning in his weapon and leaving the program.

Marvin maintained that he was not carrying a weapon and did not own a gun. His robberies had been committed with his brothers' guns (he knew where they were stashed and arranged his stickups during the hours when his brothers were sleeping). Juan decided to accept Marvin's word for it but made a note to himself to discuss the matter with the person in charge of Phase One, where Marvin would begin the program, and to have everyone keep a close watch on Marvin. Having disposed of this matter, Juan turned at last to the paperwork.

Usually, the initial contact with Argus is made by phone, although youngsters or their parents do walk in off the street, asking for help. In Marvin's case the probation officer had phoned. After a brief discussion of the problem, Juan had asked that Marvin himself telephone for an appointment, thus requiring from the outset that he take some initiative. A phone call may be a more or less casual matter for a middle-class adult, but for Marvin it had required effort and self-discipline. He had felt uneasy but had done it. (If an applicant cannot overcome this hurdle, the intake worker will make the appointment anyway, through a third party.)

About a third of Argus referrals are by word of mouth, from relatives and friends of enrollees. The rest come from the juvenile and criminal justice systems, school principals and guidance counselors, social welfare agencies and community groups. Most of those enrolled are from twelve to twenty-one years old and need our services because they have been involved in disruptive behavior, drugs and/or alcohol abuse, have been underachievers or dropouts, have been before the Family Court as neglected, abandoned or abused, as Persons in Need of Supervision (PINS) or juvenile delinquents, or before the criminal court on charges, such as car theft, shoplifting, assault, mugging and robbery. Those who do not have viable homes of their own will be placed in Argus Youth, our group home program, or will be assisted in finding placement in other settings.

Argus is not equipped to deal with psychotic, severely retarded or organically damaged persons. We do sometimes take in those who have been diagnosed as schizophrenic, if we conclude, after careful interviewing by the human development specialist and me, that the psychiatrist who made the diagnosis has defined the disease more broadly than we do or if we find that the psychosis is drug induced. Argus defines schizophrenia in the narrowest, biochemically related context. And although any theory or definition we might espouse would be disputed in some quarter, we do shy away from the notion that schizophrenia is rooted in intrapsychic dynamics or in the "double bind" situation within the family, or in the "schizophrenogenic" mother. Neither psychodynamic therapy nor family therapy has been effective in treating schizophrenia nor, in fact, has any method provided a cure. The temporary abatement of symptoms in many schizophrenics who are treated with the phenothiazines points to a biochemical basis for the disease.[1]

We turn away persons we perceive as suffering from bizarre, nihilistic thought patterns, who tell us that their thoughts are controlled by radar, for example, who believe that their stomachs are traveling throughout their bodies or who hear voices that must be obeyed or that speak to them from another planet or another age. When such hallucinations and delusions are experienced in a setting of clear consciousness and can be controlled by the phenothiazines or related antischizophrenic drugs, we reject the persons as being unsuitable for our program. Persons with these thought patterns would be out of place in our environment, and would find it disturbing. They might even be moved to harm themselves or others. On the other hand, we request that some young persons be removed from the phenothiazines so that we can speak with them and observe them in a drug-free state. Frequently we have found that they have been placed on the medication inappropriately, to control their behavior.

Juan had no question about the Marvin's sanity or his need for the program. And so Marvin was moved on to the next step: the Locator Test, a quick, nondetailed appraisal of his reading and math levels. Most of the young persons who come to us have a history of failure. They are nervous about taking tests, may become hostile or withdrawn and, instead of putting their best foot forward, put their worst. Juan explained that Marvin would not be rejected, whatever his score, and that the purpose of the test was to enable us to put together an academic and vocational program tailored to his individual requirements so that he could begin to make progress from the day he entered our doors. Thus reassured, Marvin took his Locator Test in a fairly stable frame of mind. We learned that he could scarcely read and was at about the third grade level in math.

After the test Juan gave Marvin a medical examination form and asked him to see a doctor and have it filled out. "When the medical form is ready, call me for another appointment, and ask your mother to come with you for the second interview."

Most parents of Argus enrollees don't want to be bothered. Their attitude is "I've got five other kids, no husband, no money, sickness in the family, and lots of other problems. You've got this kid. He's all yours. I don't wanna hear anything more about him." Their lives often have a frantic quality as they travel to and from welfare centers, schools, clinics, hospitals, courts, youth centers and prisons trying to keep one step ahead of disaster. Often they have chronic illnesses themselves—high blood pressure, diabetes, angina pectoris, kidney disease, arthritis, asthma, sickle cell anemia, depression. Some are groggy and unresponsive due to medication. Some relieve the aches and tensions of their lives by tippling or popping pills. From the beginning we have fought a battle to involve the parents, but it has been a losing one. Still, we insist upon seeing the parents or guardians of children under sixteen before admission, and we find it helpful to involve them at crucial points in the program. We can usually get most parents to come in before their children are enrolled. Only a few parents, those who have not been chewed up by adversity, are strong enough to keep coming in when we need them. We make contact by phone with those who have phones and with all of them by mail.

We need the parents at intake to help us assemble the many documents required to prove eligibility in the various government-funded programs run by Argus. Ours is a holistic approach. We believe it is more fruitful to address the needs of the whole adolescent rather than give "treatment" for separate problems such as drug addiction, alcoholism, "emotional disturbances," "social maladjustment," unemployment. But the government, and many foundations, make grants in discrete problem areas. In order to construct something like a coherent program, responding to the needs of our enrollees, we have put together funding from a number of public and private sources. At times this creation resembles a Frankenstein monster, out of control and with the crude stitches barely holding together at the seams. We have grants to operate a drug-free day treatment program, a child-care program, various employment programs, several training programs, and key bits and pieces financed by private foundations or corporations. In addition, the New York City Board of Education outstations fifteen teachers on our premises under an arrangement known as a cluster or institutional school. All of the government-funded programs and the Board of Education school have their separate eligibility requirements. Numerous documents must be collected, not because they make our interactions with the adolescents more effective but simply in order to prove eligibility in terms of the statutes, rules and regulations. The hours spent at these tasks may seem reasonable, on the surface, as a way of accounting for the tax-payers' money, but in actuality the process is counterproductive and wasteful, as it cuts deeply into the time we could spend in effective work with the kids. We produced better results in the years before 1978, when the paper collar was put around our necks and tightened to the point of strangulation. We do not object to being held account-able, but we believe that a method can be devised to assure that funds are not wasted and that programs do what they say they are going to do, without eating into the productive hours and paralyzing effective-ness.

Unaccustomed and inept as our enrollees often are at dealing with papers and documents (one of the prime reasons they are shut out of our paper oriented society), they are required at intake to assemble: (1) a birth certificate or a baptism certificate or statement by a priest or minister; (2) proof of income, such as a welfare budget, a letter from an employer or a pay stub; (3) a Social Security card; (4) working papers for those under sixteen; and (5) a statement from the last school attended, showing the most recent date of attendance. Collecting these documents can be a formidable task. A functioning adult might be appalled. (I would.)

Marvin's mother seemed glad to be able to do something for her son. "I've been so worried about him. I'm afraid he'll end up in prison like his brothers. Or that he'll O.D. or get shot by a police."

Mrs. Manders had been a school aide ("para" is the term used by the Board of Education). Her job had been abolished in the finan-cial crunch, but she had had some experience with paperwork. She helped Marvin collect the documents and signed the array of consent forms giving us permission to send for records from the schools, hospitals, clinics and State Division for Youth facilities that had figured in Marvin's history. We do not need these additional docu-ments to facilitate our work with the enrollees. It is better not to burden the staff with a lot of past history; instead we encourage them to make their plans for the enrollee on the basis of what they observe, what they learn from day to day and what the enrollees themselves begin to develop in terms of goals and plans. Counselors are human; confronted with the dismal records of some of our kids, they may throw up their hands. But because the atmosphere in our building is generally peaceful and orderly, monitors have argued that Argus has no "disturbed" clients, and have recommended that the funding be cut back. To keep the financing and the staffing patterns at a reasonable working level, we must present proof, again and again, that we are indeed dealing with "disturbed" adolescents.

With the intake forms filled out, the consent forms signed and the documents assembled, it was time to turn to the contract that Argus makes with each individual who enters the program. Juan read the contract aloud (since Marvin was virtually a nonreader) and they discussed each of the terms in detail. Marvin agreed that if he did not live up to his side of the bargain, he could be terminated by consensus at the case conference, with the right to appeal to the phase leader, the director of operations, the senior staff and, ultimately, to the director of Argus. Juan, signing on behalf of Argus, agreed that we would help Marvin with court and legal problems, social services and whatever difficulties he might have, that we would lend assistance in obtaining educational, vocational, employment and other resources and do everything within our power to help him attain the goals he set for himself and move toward a happy and rewarding life.

With the signing of the contract, Marvin was ready to be escorted upstairs by an older enrollee and introduced to the counselors, teachers and peers in Phase One.

3. A DIFFERENT KIND OF VALOR
The First Phase

My mother plays the numbers and sells them too. She can't say too much bout me smoking chiba cause I know too much about her.

I went up to a woman, I was going to rape her. But she said, "Good God Almighty, son, I've got nine children and some of 'em is as old as you." That turnt me off.

ARGUS ENROLLEES

At the time Marvin Manders came to Argus, Aubrey LaFrance was the senior counselor and Aldo Reyes was in charge of the "clinical" program, as our funding agencies call the interaction of our staff and our environment with the enrollees. Because I involve myself in cases where there is a history of violence or where some harm might befall the Argus family, I asked these two experienced counselors about Marvin. Gang members, heroin users, armed robbers and even those who have killed are no strangers to our premises: we have worked with them since 1968. Yet I was uneasy about Marvin.

The court had turned him over to us. No formula, no prescription. Just a small, black, half-starved body, a face that never smiled (perhaps because he was ashamed of his teeth, which were rotten and black) and a brain which might or might not be damaged (we had no idea why he hadn't learned how to read and, if past experience was a guide, the experts wouldn't be likely to provide us with much more than the surmises which we ourselves had already made). Society was saying, Have a go at this kid, nobody else wants to. So we said, Okay, we'll give it a try.

All of us become inured to degradation, brutality and horror. If we cannot distance ourselves we go mad. Like the surgeon whose fingers plumb the tidal caves of the heart, I had come to know the inner landscapes of boys like Marvin Manders. Aubrey LaFrance, Aldo Reyes and others before and since have guided me over the terrain.

Aldo had come to Argus in 1974. An old honcho from his street days was on our staff, and Aldo, between jobs, was curious to see the program. He asked my permission to look around for a day or two, which I granted, hoping that I could lure him away from the job he was considering and get him to sign on with us.

After inspecting the program, Aldo reported to me that he found too much laxness. "You need someone to play Mr. Bad around here," he said, with a comical grin.

I hired him for the job. He was splendid, a toughie who required the staff to take a full load on their shoulders and made them love it. I depended on Aldo to pull me back from middle-class sentimentality.

Aubrey had been transformed in the Argus program from an impenitent street addict and dealer into a staff member who supports his family, sees that they become the carriers of positive values and pursues his avocations of painting, music, hang gliding and building model airplanes. Half the kids in his neighborhood wait for him in the park on Saturdays and Sundays, helping him launch his model planes and keep them flying. What emerged when the eye-killing, Hook Alley trappings of the underworld were stripped away was a man of dignity and a wise philosopher. Of working with the kids Aubrey says, "It's okay at times to act as if you've lost your temper. Anger can be a therapeutic tool. But never let them push your button. If you *re*act instead of acting, *you* need help." He also says, "When I'm sizing up people I let my intuition have full sway. I trust it more than any case history. No scientist has solved the mystery of the universe. Human beings are the heart of the heart of the mystery."

My office at 170 Brown Place has the feel of a living room. The big desk, piled with papers, occupies only a small portion of the space under wide high windows. The rest of the room is furnished with sofas and arm chairs, a cocktail table and end tables of somewhat gaudy marble (a gift) which I happen to love. All of our offices are furnished more or less in this fashion, and we all go in for prints, paintings and plants. It makes for a homelike atmosphere that kids and staff respond to. Over one large comfortable sofa (also a gift) hangs the Argus coat of arms, a framed batik of three African peacocks, handsome and high-crested, purchased from a young artist in Kenya, along with other batiks that ornament the conference room.

Aubrey and Aldo seated themselves, one on either sofa. I sat in my usual chair of dark green pseudo-leather, placed catty-cornered to the desk, near the phones which are silenced during sessions such as this.

"How do you see this kid, Aldo?" I asked. "Based on what you know of him so far."

"Marvin? He's a wheeler-dealer." Aldo's broad face crinkled in a wry laugh. "You know the kind. We've had hundreds of them here. He tells the kids on the corner, 'Hey, I'm bigger and badder. I really came off last night. Look at my stash. Hey, this is it, man.' And he shows them the rings, money, jewelry, whatever, that he's lifted off of somebody. But Flaco is waiting for him. Whatever Marvin takes off someone else Flaco will take off him. Flaco is the skinny man who stands on the corner. 'Hey, go see Flaco,' the kids say. 'He's the best. He's got a good supply of skag, hardly cut at all.' So that's where Marvin's money goes. To the local skinny dope dealer—and to put clothes on his back."

"Yeah, always the clothes," Aubrey agreed. "That's where it goes—into their arm or onto their backs."

"He's not a hard-core heroin user?"

"No. Not yet. But he goes for the smoke like there's nothing else to breathe," Aubrey said. "Oh, he might buy an ounce of chiba—about forty cigarettes—and run through it in two or three days. That would include turning on his friends."

"Where do they get all that marijuana? Don't the cops do *any*-thing? Doesn't anyone give a damn?" I demanded indignantly and somewhat rhetorically.

Aubrey answered anyway, hashing over the outrageous facts. "This town, from Mount Vernon to the tip of Brooklyn and on out into Long Island until you hit the potato fields has got at least one candy store on every block that doesn't sell candy even to the police. They operate in the open. Almost no area is free of it."

"The kids smoke on the way to school," Aldo said. "You can see them on the subway, standing between the cars, rolling and smoking joints as big as cigars. It's everywhere. Down in the Wall Street section they call out to people passing by, 'Good smokes! Good smokes!' They've got decks of heroin in their shopping bags. They hawk it by brand names: Black Power, Dynamite, Foolish Pleasure, True Blue, Death Wish, Black Out, Could-Be-Total, Black Love. You name it, they've got it. The attitude of kids like Marvin is: 'Hey, I gotta get me a piece of this.' That's where their heads are at."

"And where are their dreams?"

Aubrey flashed me a smile. "I knew you'd ask that. The dream with them—the only one they're in touch with—is to be sponsored by someone at the top of the line. Someone who handles pure stuff, who can put them in the way of earning some real money."

"Do they have any feeling for the people they hurt? Does Marvin suffer any pangs of conscience?" I have asked this question before, always hoping for a different answer.

"Not really. No more than a lion when it falls on its supper," Aldo replied. "At least that's the image these kids put up. They call people they mug 'meat for the lions.' They stalk them like lions. They can pick out the easy victims, people who won't give them a hassle—the weak, the infirm, the old, those who have vague looks on the faces, who shuffle or walk off-beat, who look like they don't know who they are or where they're going."

"Do these kids ever look inside themselves?"

"They have to maintain their stature with their peers," Aubrey said. "That image doesn't allow anyone to see the real humanity inside. And once you commit a really ugly act, it's easier to gloss over your feelings and do it again."

"The way they see it," Aldo said, "they're shut out of getting theirs by any licit means. Not only that, they look *down* on the proper thing. You're a patsy, a punk, if you're straight, if you work for it. *'I'll get mine.'* That's their attitude. They think that everybody is criminal but that only a few get caught."

"Do they see any options?"

"Nah, not usually. And if they do, they feel they couldn't make it, that they're not good enough, and then they'll cover that over because it's too uncomfortable. They'll say the option is no good, it's for punks. See, I'm very familiar with that because that's how I thought for years."

"Do they have a conscience?"

"Some don't," Aldo replied. "I happen to believe that most of them have something under that facade."

"I agree," Aubrey said. "They block it out but with many of them there's deep down conflict. Especially if they've had any concern at all from their parents or if somebody, anybody at all, has cared about them. If they came up where the parents fostered caring about other people, it's in them somewhere. With Marvin I think values were instilled at an early age and then he hardened the opposite way."

"So there may be something under there to work with. Even though he's killed people? Why did he do that, why, for heaven's sake?"

"It's a type of vainglorious behavior," Aubrey said. "To impress, to be feared by the crimies—your crime mates. They take an unsuspecting person who hands them money and jewelry and who can't strike back, and they shoot him—or her. Shoot or stab. They boast about it in the bull pen when they get locked up or speak about it with the peers. They establish a rep. The peers say, 'Hey, you know what Marvin did?' And they strut and embroider on the facts. But they never share the lonely pangs of conscience."

"Marvin thought he would be Mr. Superfly and make it big," Aldo said. "He never thought 'I'm fourteen. I can't read. I'll end up doing twenty-five years to life.' Or if thoughts like that came up he ran for smoke—or skag."

"You know why I think we can get at Marvin?" Aubrey said, with a flash of inspiration. "Even if he doesn't have a single pang of remorse or any guilty feelings (which I think he does), we can work with him. As long as there is *life*, as long as there is a *personality* to be worked with, remorse can be developed. Even when the person has been deprived and brutalized. It happens to kids all the time. They find someone to reflect themselves in. A teacher, an uncle, someone along the line. We're here for Marvin. He already sees himself in Aldo. I can tell."

"Marvin said he loved his father, even though he was a heroin addict," I offered.

"I don't buy that," Aldo said. "Marvin romanticizes his father. He *wishes* his father had cared."

"That's right," Aubrey said. "His mother is the key. She impresses me as being a decent woman. If we scratch the surface, we'll find that Marvin cares about her."

Aldo nodded. "She's a fine lady. It's really not her fault that Marvin is in trouble and that his brothers are serving long terms upstate."

"Okay. We've got a spark in there somewhere, underneath that cool. How are we going to get at it and blow it into a fire? What are we going to do?" I asked, trying to pin it down. "He's in Argus eight hours a day when he attends. Among the peers in here there's still a lot of acting out. And out in the streets where he spends the other sixteen hours, he'll get a full blast of negativity. How can we combat that?"

They both thought deeply. Then Aubrey said, "You don't accept the surface. You let him know that we are going to deal only with the inner part that he's trying to hide. We let him know that we're looking straight into his insides, that we see that remorse. We massage that remorse. We water it. We make it grow. We let him know that the area is real. We'll relate to the real Marvin in ways that he will find very attractive. And he'll respond."

"It'll take time," Aldo said. "But I think we can do it."

"How do we know he won't go out and kill somebody else?" I asked.

"We don't. There's no guarantee. But if he weren't with us, if he were on the streets, we could be certain he'd be ripping people off. If he were in prison he'd be learning fancier ways to do it," Aldo said.

"If there is a spark there and we blow on it, he'll respond," Aubrey said. "Through human input we can give him the strength to stand up and cope with the world in a positive way."

"Okay," I said. "We'll try."

"Yep. Well, let us get upstairs and get to it," Aldo said. "We'll keep you informed."

I felt more confident, but I resolved that I would monitor Marvin's progress, or lack of it, as he went through orientation and the rest of the program—if he got that far.

Marvin told us later that everything about Argus puzzled him. He was amazed that Errol Inwood, another kid, was assigned to take him on a tour of the building. He kept stealing glances at Errol, thinking that he must be a fink or crazy. More than anything else, it was the quiet, industrious atmosphere in the classes and group rooms and the lack of rowdiness in the halls that stunned him. He had never heard kids speak to each other in such polite terms. They said, "Excuse me" and "Please" and "Thank you." No one was screaming or cursing. The kids looked up briefly, waved at Errol and the new boy, then bent over their books or went on with their groups, as Errol escorted him through the program.

Like most of our kids, Marvin was extremely sensitive to the signals given out in any environment, quick to pick up the cues. His survival depended on it. He wasn't good at books, but when it came to body language and human interactions he was sharp. He realized immediately that some of the elements that he had assumed to be as pervasive as air were missing in this environment.

He heard a boy (also new) call Aldo a big faggot. Instead of flattening him, or at least yelling at this affront to his masculinity, Aldo drawled, "Yeah, and you're my boyfriend." The bystanders laughed, and even the kid who was trying to provoke a fight joined in.

Marvin realized that Aldo was respected. His appearance on the floor in the middle of a clash was enough to make the contestants subside. Marvin sensed that they were not afraid of Aldo; rather they liked and enjoyed him.

"What kind of a cat is that?" Marvin asked Errol.

"Aldo? He is cool people, man, like most of the counselors around here," Errol replied.

"How about the teachers?"

"You'll see. Some of em is very nice and helpful."

"Oh man, you must be on their payroll."

"I am for a fact. But I'm not a punk, if that's what you're thinkin."

One of our first tasks was to bring Marvin to a point where he would look upon academic work and vocational training as acceptable or even relevant. We assigned him to four classes, remedial reading, English composition, social studies and math, but arranged his lessons so that the work was slightly below his level. This way he could experience immediate success and develop a taste for it. Given a choice between woodworking and art as an elective, Marvin could not decide. He was allowed to sample each course and at the end of two weeks opted for art, a decision that showed that he was ready to say goodbye to some of his old prejudices. "I thought art was sissy," he said. "But this looks like a death little workshop to me, run by Mr. Jose Padilla who is cool people." ("Death" is a term of high praise in the South Bronx.)

We usually put off giving the California Achievement Test (the CAT) for two or three weeks or until the new enrollee has had time to simmer down and finds the ordeal less threatening. The CAT is a long test. We sometimes give it in two sessions.

Eddie Dickerson, who gave the test to Marvin, is the school administrator, a substantially built black man with threads of gray in his hair. His full face, large eyes and generous features express a good-humored shrewdness. He has what some psychologists call "groundedness"—down to earth, solid, predictable and kind. Eddie explained the CAT to Marvin, assuring him that it is not something you can "fail" at.

"Nobody here is going to judge you or call you stupid or compare you to anyone else. I'm the only one who will see the results and I'll put together a plan that will be tailor made just for you."

Marvin's CAT confirmed what the Locator Test had indicated earlier—that he was virtually a nonreader and was a little better, though still very low, in math. He was placed in a small class of five or six slow readers under the Title One reading teacher, who immediately assigned him to a task that he easily mastered and praised him for his success.

Marvin stayed behind as the class ended to ask the teacher, "Do you think I can learn to read?"

"I *know* you can," the teacher replied. "You're already doing it. Just come every day and apply yourself and you'll learn."

Like the other enrollees in Phase One, Marvin was assigned to two one-and-a-half-hour groups a week; and in one way or another spent an additional seven hours a week with the counselors—in life skills and vocational counseling sessions, in one-to-one raps, playing chess, checkers or other games, in sports, and going on trips.

Marvin had been in Argus a month when Aldo approached him in the activities room.

"Hey, Marvin. I see you sitting up here in this window a lot. What's the attraction?"

"I'm interested in what's going on in the street, man. And I've got my book here. I'm reading."

"You really keep right on top of that reading, don't you?"

"I was low in my reading when I came here. But I'm getting better now. I have to practice a lot."

"What's the book about? Can I see it?"

Marvin showed Aldo a tract on white devils put out by the Five Percenters. "That's one of the few books that don't lie, man."

Aldo thumbed through the tract, pausing to read a paragraph here and there. Then he gave it back. "How bout a game of chess?"

"Naw."

"Checkers?"

"I'm too much into this."

"Some other time then."

A boy named John Whitley was beating and kicking on the door to a closet where athletic equipment was stored. Several other boys and girls were milling around, trying to stop him, kidding or giving advice. Aldo strolled over and joined them, conscious as he did so that Marvin was watching to see how he handled the incident.

"Hey, John," he said in a calm tone. "There's a note pinned to the door. If you stop kicking we can see what it says. Might be important."

"That's right, John."

"Listen to de man."

"That's what I been talkin, John. Look at the note."

"Come on, John. Let's have a look."

The kicking stopped. Aldo removed the note and opened it.

"It's from Fernando, your counselor. He says, 'I promised to take you to Saint Mary's Park to play ball today but I've been called away on important business. I'm sorry to disappoint you, guys and girls. We'll go tomorrow. P.S. John, I hope you'll believe me when I say I'm sorry.' "

This last brought roars of laughter from the kids, including John.

"How come that mother-fucker single me out for criticism?" John demanded when the laughter died down.

"Fernando's not criticizing you. He sounds concerned to me. I guess he knows you get impatient and impulsive at times. Like the other day when you broke down the door and took the equipment out to the ball field when you weren't sposed to. You had a terrific game with your friends, but then you walked off and left the balls and bats on the ground." Aldo's voice was tough but good-humored.

"Yeah, John, you never thought about what was we going to play ball with the next day," said one of the peers.

"Yeah, John. How bout that?"

"Shit, man, that mother-fucker, he always git in my path," mumbled John.

"Why don't you give some thought to us, John. Huh?"

"Hey, John. The peers are right. You should show more concern."

"I did! I showed concern!" protested John.

"Yeah. After you were caught and confronted, you showed concern, but only to save your own hide. We're asking you to be concerned for other people because they like you and you like them."

"Shit! Oh, all right. I'll think about it." John said with a crestfallen look.

Not once during this interchange did Marvin's eyes stray to the scene outside the window where some kids from the housing project were breaking bottles on the pavement.

Nevertheless, Marvin sat in Aldo's group for more than a month without opening his mouth. One day Errol Inwood, who acted as Aldo's assistant, or catalyst, in the group, confronted him.

"Why you come into this group about every other day drowsed out? Are you doing some dumb shit out in the street and expectin to get over on us?"

"I ain't usin nothin," Marvin replied with a cool smile. Then suddenly, uncontrollably, a wave of intense anger burst from him. "You called me a duck!" he yelled. "You called me a fuckin duck!" (A duck is a wimp or an inferior or incompetent person. The term has sexual overtones.)

"I ain't called you a duck," Errol replied.

"You're a liar! You called me a duck! I ain't no fuckin duck!" Marvin got up from his chair and advanced on Errol, his fists raised.

"Sit down, Marvin! Go back to your chair!" The cry rose from all sides, impellingly.

Marvin sat down but continued to glare at Errol.

"I ain't called you a duck," Errol said.

"You're a liar! You did!"

"What I said was, there's some duck dudes round here."

"Yeah and you must be one of them!"

"You wouldn't a threw that in the street, Marvin," Aldo said. "Tit for tat is where it's at. That's where it's at in the street. You ain't in the street. This abuse of people in here is getting ridiculous. I guess we're going to have to put muzzles on people's mouths until they stop it. We can't have people running around smacking one another on the floor. Ain't no physical violence in here, Marvin. Don't give Errol that Murder One look, either."

"Errol called me a duck. I ain't no fuckin duck!"

"I was trying to relate to you, man. Trying to get close," Errol said. "An you come at me with that little skippy shit about a duck. You were so spaced out you didn't know what I was talkin about. You didn't even know that I was tryin to relate to you. You don't even know what it is to relate to someone."

Marvin's anger collapsed. Big, handsome Errol was asking him to be a buddy. He couldn't quite believe it. He sat there with his mouth open.

"Where are you at, man? Where's the progress that you are showing?" Aldo asked quietly. "Here is Errol, trying to get close and you're playin shit games. What are you doin playin games in here? We don't do that in here. This is a serious place."

Marvin said nothing.

"Hey, Marvin, how does it make you feel, Errol wanting to be your main man?"

Marvin said, "I'm thinkin about it, man."

"You'd better think about it," Aldo said. "It's written all over you that we've jolted you out of that jailhouse image. You are hurting, man, because Errol offered you something worth having and you were too full of street shit to reach out and take it."

"Yeah, you blocked me out, Marvin," Errol said. "You blocked me out. But I'm not gettin off your case because if you smoke any more dust you'll be locked up in Bellevue."

"That's the real deal, Marvin," Aldo said. "That's the real deal. This is no time to come out of a bag, Marvin. Errol was sittin and rappin with you an you were comin out of a bag. I hope you get the message because this is the make-me or break-me test for you, Marvin."

"I get the message," Marvin mumbled. "I been doin dumb shit."

"What are you goin to do bout it?"

"I'm gonna do my thing. I'm gonna do what I have to do."

"That's not good enough, Marvin. You're fuckin gonna have to stop your shit and reach out to Errol and the others here too. They need your help just like you need theirs. You're gonna have to follow up on everybody else. You're gonna have to pull people in. We're all gonna have to do that—unless this group wants to G.I. [scrub] this building forever."

"I don't want to," Errol said. "No one does. But I'll do it if I have to. Because this place is falling apart. We had visitors from the U.N., visitors from Africa and Holland an all them places, and I was ashamed of the way the stairwells look."

"We really have to take a whole day off, no classes, no recreation, nothin but clean the fuckin place. Then maybe we would have a building worth showin to visitors," Aldo said. "What about it?"

There was a go-round. Each group member promised to get his shit together and take a serious interest in his job. Some said things like "I was flaggin, I wasn't relatin." "I was being selfish." Marvin was amazed at these tough dudes and chicks falling into line and seeming to relish it.

From time to time Aldo asked someone who was slouching, mumbling or slumping over defensively to sit up straight, uncross his or her legs, look at the group and speak up. They obeyed without hesitation.

"You got that?" Aldo said. "We're gonna take care of responsibilities around here. And we're gonna follow up on everybody else. Okay, that's it for today. Marvin, come down to the office. Let's rap, okay?"

As they got to their feet and started out of the room, good feelings spread like a contagion. There was a lot of laughter and animated talk. Group members who had been at each other's throats verbally walked off with their arms around one another's shoulders. Errol put his arm around Marvin. "Hey, come on, I'll walk you down to Aldo's office. He wants to see you."

Aldo asked Marvin, in the course of their one-to-one rap, whether there was anything he liked about being at Argus.

"One thing I like," Marvin said. "Everybody knows my name."

He explained that in Julia Richman and the schools he attended before the teachers didn't know his name. "I was gone once for three months. My mother carried me down South for a funeral. When I got back they gave me my report card and it said I passed in everything. How could I pass all them subjects when I wasn't even there? *They didn't even know I had been gone.*"

"Whoo! They didn't know your name and they didn't know you weren't there! How did that make you feel?"

"I felt bad, man."

"But you told yourself it didn't matter."

"Yeah. I did. Those mother-fuckers."

"I had the same thing happen to me when I went to school. It made me feel like Mr. Prize Ass Hole. Kind of like a nobody. It's a feeling that can linger with you for a long time—until you finally learn, once and for all, that no matter what they do or say you *are* somebody. Hey, when you've been around here for a while and get to be a member of the Argus family you'll *know* you're somebody. I came in off the streets myself, you know, and got my shit together. The stuff you're doin, I used to do it too."

"How long was you out there?"

"Eight years."

"You was in the joint?"

"Yeah. In and out. Sing Sing, the whole number."

"What made you turn?"

"I caught a dirty needle. Hepatitis. I went home to my mother's house to get well. While I was there she got a terrible pain in her heart and she died." There was a tremor in Aldo's voice. "You know what, it still hurts me to think about it. She had that pain on and off for years. I always thought it was the aggravation I caused her. Worryin cause her son was on drugs, knowing that he would end up in the morgue or in the joint, not doin a thing to make her proud. She was a pretty nice lady, all in all. She had a hard life. I made it worse. When she died I blamed myself. I began to get those pains like she had, in my heart and my left arm. I knew I couldn't make it in the street at that time, so I went into a place called Daytop Village, thinking I would just stay there long enough to get my shit together. I didn't have any place else to go."

"How was it?"

"I hated it. They were strict. Asking you questions. How do you feel about being hispanic? How do you feel about being black?"

"Sounds like Argus."

"Nah. They cut my hair. Made me wear a sign saying 'I'm a baby.'"

"You stood for that?"

"Yeah. But I was smoking mad. After a while, I began to hear what they were saying to me. I had planned to rip them off and run away but I didn't. You know what? Some of my best buddies I found in that place."

"You was in the Panthers, wasn't you? Is that true?"

"Yeah, I was. Daytop went through a civil war after I'd been there a year and a half."

"A year and a half!"

"Sounds like a hundred years? Well, in a way it was. But it was worth it because I've never been back to the joint again. And I've never used dope. But I did get mixed up with the Panthers. There was two clicks at Daytop. One wanted to hit the streets and make a revolution; put an end to racial discrimination and social injustice. The other click said we should get our shit together first and then do whatever we wanted to about politics. The revolutionary click split off and some of us joined the Panthers."

"How come you ain't with em now?"

"The Panthers did some good things. We kept drug pushers out of neighborhoods. We put out word that we would shoot any pusher that tried to operate in the area and they left."

"What happened?"

"A lot of stuff. I found out that the other click had been right. I should have stayed at Daytop. Some of the Panthers turned out to be police agents. They provoked us to break the law and then they arranged to have the cops there. They tortured their own people and killed them because they suspected them of betraying the Panthers. But the point was they didn't really know. They killed people they suspected without any real evidence. It was like my old street gang all over again. I broke with the Panthers. Got me a job as a truck driver. After that I came to work here. Why? This work has more meaning to me. It gives me a chance to know people, to be honest and open. And I'm in college at night. I'll be getting my degree next spring."

"I won't ever git to college."

"Do you want to?"

"Naw. I never thought about it."

"Well, think about it. And if the idea seems good to you, and you really want to do it, you can. And you won't have to wait till you've got gray hair like me. You can do it in like three or four years. You're lucky, Marvin, to have bumped into Argus while you're still young."

Aldo sent Marvin to a dentist who took care of his teeth. All of the uppers had to come out; they had been neglected too long. After Marvin got his plate he began to talk more and to smile. There was a change in the way he carried himself—less of the self-inflated swagger (really a kind of desperation) and more of genuine pride.

I asked Marvin to drop by my office for a chat about this time, told him how handsome he looked and complimented him on the way he was speaking up in groups.

"I don't know whether you've really grown but you're standing a lot taller. You look like you've added a few inches," I said. "Maybe it's because you're learning to assert yourself instead of sitting in that window."

Marvin laughed. There was a new-found freedom, an actual joy in his face. "I was really watching what was going on inside *Argus,*" he said. "I liketed what people were doin but I couldn't admit it. I wanted to join in but I didn't think they would accept me. My teeth was all rotten, and I thought I was too short and too black and too dumb. At home they always made fun of me for those things."

"Not your mother?"

"No, she didn't say those things."

"Your mother really loves you. I can tell."

"Why did she always be saying she wanted to put me away?"

"I don't know. But my guess is because she was desperate and didn't know what else to do. Hey, you know, I'm really glad you're doing so well in the groups."

"At first I thought I would bring in my steel and ice some of these smart asses," he said. "But after a while, I saw that they was sayin them things because they cared. They really liketed me."

"Why don't you take a chill pill?" Marvin said to some new kids who were acting up in Phase One. "Don't you hear the teacher talkin? We're here to learn. If you got somethin else in mind, why don't you just leave?"

New enrollees would come into the group, go round chatting up the girls and holding out their open palms to the fellows, calling out, "Gimme five! Gimme five! ooh! ooh! ooh!" "Can I sit on your lap? Well now, I'm hittin on the wrong one! Frankly, the girl doesn't wear Valenti's, so I ain't got nothin to say to her!"

Marvin found himself, somewhat to his astonishment, telling them to take off their hats and sit down. "We don't allow hats in here."

One young girl called, "Hey, Mr. Group Leader, can I get my cough drops?" and went into an elaborate fit of coughing.

Marvin said, "Listen up, girl! This is a group. There's nothin wrong with your throat."

"Oh, you're cute. Let's do some of them filly-willies!" she retorted, giggling and wiggling.

Marvin treated her to a cool stare. "You know, Cynthia, you're not so bad."

"That's what my mama says."

"All right, baby. Then set yourself the goal of sitting through one group without talking out of turn."

"I hope you choke!" She flashed him venomous leers for the rest of the session, but kept quiet.

In Phase One groups the Argus cardinal rules are discussed and explained again and again until everyone understands the parameters. No violence or threats of violence. No weapons. No verbal abuse. No four-letter words on the floor although they are permitted in groups. One five-letter word, "bitch," is totally prohibited because it has shown itself to be the most incendiary of all epithets. When someone finally proposed that we ban the word completely, it was a relief to everybody, including those enrollees who felt most tempted to hurl abuse at someone's girl friend, mother or sister.

Violating a person's social space (moving in closer than ordinary amicable relationships dictate, unless for a supportive touch or hug) is taboo. The group leaders touch and hug the kids in a fatherly, motherly or brotherly and sisterly way and set the example for the others to follow.

In groups and in meetings it is constantly repeated that all of us —kids and staff—are part of one extended family. This gives everybody a lot of extra resources—we have brothers and sisters, fathers, mothers, aunts, uncles and cousins by extension, who can give us the attention and affection that we need, who can follow up and see that we are doing the best we possibly can for ourselves. As the director of Argus, I mean it when I tell the kids that I want them to help me, that I need them. If I step on somebody's toes, or if they just plain don't like what's going on, I want them to march into my office and speak up. And they do. I then call in the people involved and we probe the matter until we come to a resolution. I seldom know in advance what that resolution will be. The kid or kids may be manipulating, in which case they will hear all of the data and will be told in no uncertain terms to pull their noses back inside the fence, that they can't slide out of doing what is right and what is best for us all. But if I am wrong —or the staff is—we will modify our behavior or back down. The kids don't always get their way but they do walk in and speak their piece, and this is an important lesson for them. The fact that somebody will listen, and that a grievance can be carried to the top, is of enormous consequence in breaking free of the feeling of powerlessness.

Another theme that they hear in groups is: be honest, be open, be responsible. Don't hide. Let other people get to know the real you. Share the experiences you're having. Help other people. It's the better part of manliness and womanliness to show your feelings. Fear is an instinctual feeling that helps us to survive. It's nothing to be ashamed of. Your tears are beautiful. Let them flow. Your needs are human; show them and people will love you. You are unique, the only one printed by nature just like you. You are valuable. You are lovable. You are terrific. We *all* need each other. Don't be afraid to reach out.

The counselors, working closely with the human development specialist (we avoid the term "psychologist" because our enrollees mistrust it), write up a treatment plan for every new enrollee. For Marvin the plan was to get him to attend Argus, to learn to trust Aldo and the staff and to relate to them and to his peers. At the end of three months, when the plan was to be updated, it was the consensus at the case conference that these primary goals had been partially achieved, but there was some doubt as to whether solid progress toward the long-range goals of weaning Marvin from drugs and crime and setting him on the road to positive achievement had been made.

At this time (three months seems to represent a special danger point) Marvin was arrested again and charged with possession of a dangerous weapon. Aldo went to see him at the Spofford Juvenile Detention Center. After a grueling session, Marvin admitted that he had borrowed his brother's pistol to do a heist. Aldo made two visits, gave Marvin a strong blast, and left him to stew in his own juices. Marvin swore never to use the gun again and to give up drugs for good. Aldo made him repeat these promises forcefully many times. Finally, he said, "I guess I have to believe that you're telling the truth because you know that you would be letting me and the whole Argus family down if you were lying. I don't believe you would do that because you know we care about you, and I think you care about us."

Marvin broke down and cried.

Aldo wrote a letter outlining Marvin's progress in the program and stating that Argus was willing to take him back, should the court see its way clear to permit this. "I'd be very surprised if they do," he said. The Family Court judge gave Marvin the maximum probation time on condition that he return to Argus, attend regularly and show steady progress on all fronts.

Spofford had shaken him up badly this time around. He told the group that he could never go back to the old life. It was a cesspool, full of degenerates who would kill you for a roach (the shank end of a marijuana cigarette). "They kept tellin us, 'Make a good adjustment to the place.' Shit man, the day I make a good adjustment to that place they can bury me. You can't rely on anybody there—counselors, officials, nobody. People say one thing and turn around an do somethin else. I never felt safe for a single day while I was there."

He came back with new literature excoriating the white devils and their reign on earth and exhorting the elite 5 percent of blacks who were aware of this fiendish situation to rise up and bring white ascendancy to an end. Argus had enrolled another Five Percenter, a sixteen-year-old named Keith Hornsby. Keith's mother had taken him before the Family Court when he was seven (the earliest possible age) and signed a petition stating that he was an "incorrigible child" and was in need of "guidance, supervision and control." The court ordered an investigation which revealed that Mrs. Hornsby was a fanatically religious woman who punished her son for his "wickedness" by withholding food, locking him in a dark closet, tying him to the bed and beating him with ironing cords. She had, on occasion, held a hot iron against his arms, legs and chest, burning and scarring him for life. Keith never wore short-sleeved shirts or shorts and would not go swimming. He had been taken to a shelter, pending placement in a foster home. In the shelter he flew into rages "at the least provocation" (he violently resisted rip-offs and homosexual threats and rapes) and was so "ferocious" that the staff resorted to a leather strap and then to tranquillizers to subdue him. The voluntary child-care agencies had rejected him, and after more than a year of waiting, he was "placed" in a training school upstate where the doses of medication continued, as by then he was considered dangerous.

Although he had never been accused of any crime except by his mother, Keith remained in custody for nine years. When the move toward deinstitutionalization came and the State Division for Youth (DFY) was no longer allowed to commingle PINS with delinquent children, Keith was returned to the community to live in a group home for boys, which in turn asked Argus to undertake his schooling and socialization. We did the best we could for Keith, but we were unable to find a way through his pervasive suspicion and mistrust of people. Nor were we able to touch a responsive chord of friendship or tenderness. I never let the staff see the reports which accompanied him from DFY, describing him as cold, unemotional and withdrawn, though capable of uncontrollable rages in response to any perceived threat. The institution and the group home had maintained him on high doses of Thorazine, but we had refused to take him in until the tranquillizer had been discontinued. Only once did he indulge in a violent outburst with us (see Chapter 5). He was completely wrapped up in the Five Percenters and regarded any attempt to get close to him, except in terms of their ideology, as an intrusion, if not an attack. He searched continuously for confirmation of his view that the world is unjust and that blacks are exploited and shut out by whites. Of course, he found plenty of it. Even Aldo could not make him smile.

We knew that Keith used cocaine and other stimulants condoned by the Five Percenters. Therefore, we were distressed that Marvin and several other young persons were drawn to Keith and his preachings. Marvin in fact became almost a co-leader at the meetings they began to hold at Argus.

One day Leslie Ross, our administrative associate, discovered that Keith had run off a number of copies of a Five Percenter tract on our IBM copier. She called for a meeting of the senior staff and demanded to know how long this would be tolerated.

"I know that Keith has had a terrible history and we all feel compassion for him," she said. "But no other group is allowed to hold parliamentary sessions or religious revivals in Argus. Why are we tolerating this from Keith? We have other things to do here." Leslie was an extraordinary beauty of a deep, rich Slavic stamp, voluptuous, yet unaffected as rain. High color had mounted to her cheeks and her dark eyes flashed. "I never expected to see the day when I would advocate that we get rid of a child. I'm surprised to hear myself talking like this. Honestly. You know I haven't done it before, ever. But I really think that unless we get Keith Hornsby out of here, we may not have a program. He is pulling others down. We could lose Marvin Manders. That would be a tragedy after all the work Aldo and others have done. I saw some of Marvin's art work the other day. He really has talent. And furthermore, I think we can do something with him. Maybe it's a question of sacrificing one to save the other."

"There's something to be said for that," Aldo replied. "Especially when it looks like we're not getting anywhere with Keith."

"Maybe it won't be a question of sacrificing one or the other," I said. "Maybe we could find something else for Keith.

"Keith is very bitter because we won't give him one of our YEP [youth employment program] lines," Aubrey said. "But we can't give a line to someone who is on dope. That would destroy our standards. He wants a job in the worst way. That may be the key."

A few days later, Marty Wishnoff, the school guidance counselor, found Keith a job at Kentucky Fried Chicken. He left the program willingly and the Five Percenters fizzled out at Argus. Marvin's heart wasn't really in it anymore. He turned his attention to the art class and to his friendship with Errol and others among the peers.

Marvin studied this group assiduously. They were the leaders in Phase One at the time. They confronted kids about their behavior without getting into a fight. They told group members to get to work, stop bad rapping, drop their image, stop acting one way in front of counselors and another way behind their backs. They went into detail about who was hanging out with whom, who was smoking pot, using cocaine or dust. All of this was spoken about openly, as people confronted, yelled, attacked one another verbally and fifteen minutes later walked out talking and laughing as though nothing had happened. On the streets if you confronted people, you got hurt. Like others before and after him Marvin was mesmerized by this process and began to make it a part of himself.

Gradually Marvin began to see that Argus was a safe place. He found himself talking more in group and to his surprise people listened. They didn't make fun of him. He was troubled about having stuck up black people. It was after his friend Champ bled to death from knife wounds received during a holdup that Marvin had begun to sniff heroin and sell drugs. "That's the onliest thing that made me want to stop from sticking up was Champ's bleeding to death like that. I had another friend that was pushed off a roof. I had got busted burglarizing houses. That's how I went to jail. . . ."

Marvin started talking to a white counselor named Jerry Blaine and grew to like and trust him. "That's when I stopped bringing my Five Percenter shit inside the program. I could see what it really was: I was studying the Five Percenters more than I was into my own work. I mean the things that could give me some tools to be somebody. Jerry made me see what I was doing. That began to clear my head up."

At first he hadn't wanted to talk to Jerry. He didn't want an attachment to anyone who was white. But Jerry wouldn't let Marvin alone. He put demands on him to speak out, to show his strength, to take responsibility. Marvin found out that Jerry had come up the hard way. That was a revelation: he had not thought that white people were deprived.

Marvin began to realize that one of his big drives was to help his mother. "I want to stay next to my family," he told us "Close to my mother. Cause I know sooner or later she going *really* to need me, and I want to be there to help her."

He would not hear his mother criticized. "She did a good job in bringing me up. All those little devious things I did out there, she ain't had no part of that. She really nice. She don't be hitting on us and stuff like that. Anytime we really got beated, we had to do something devious, something that was really *irrelevant*. What I did get into, it was so I could hand her somethin, and could dress good and hang out with the crowd."

After a time we were able to get Marvin a stipend for the tasks he performed in Phase One. This permitted him to contribute small but regular sums to the household. Aubrey managed to get Mrs.

Manders taken back as a school aide and so the money tensions eased.

Of his street life, Marvin told the group, "I had to do the things the crowd would do. It's like being in the gang—only it's different because you don't wear dirty clothes. You be *clean.* Your body don't stink. You don't have dirty shoes. Oh, I hurt people. I have cut people up. I have shot people and stuff like that. But the reason I would hurt people would be if they would do something. They would do something wrong about money. It would be mostly about money. All I got is hostility in my mind, anger and hate for this person, so when I see him I just going to tee off on him with no questions asked, and that would be my money and also it would be my revenge."

The future shaped itself differently in his mind. He told the group, "I want to have my own corporation, dealing with various things. I know it's going to take a great deal of study, a great deal of time and aggravation. And I just can't drive all of this into my mind, because that would cause me to collapse and fall back, get out of place, misplace things."

Marvin was able to move into positions of increasing trust and responsibility within Phase One as his behavior and attitudes changed. His progress was measured by a number of objective yardsticks and a few impressionistic ones. Attendance, punctuality, level of drug abuse, involvement, if any, with the juvenile or criminal justice system, participation in groups, obeying the rules of the program, assuming responsibility for his own behavior and that of his peers, reasonable progress toward academic and vocational goals are the principal objective measures. The impressions of counselors, teachers, peers and family of before-and-after attitudes and behavior constitute a less formal measure. Progress in all of these areas taken from attendance, classroom and other records and from discussions at case conferences and groups and individual sessions were noted down in Marvin's folder under the supervision of the Phase One Coordinator, and formed the basic documentation of Marvin's standing in the program.

When he advanced from pushing a broom to coordinator of the clean-up crew, that was a big step up. It was his first promotion, announced in the general meeting. He received many congratulations. But there were mutterings also ("Fink," "Copout,") from unreconstructed rebels among the peers. And there was the jealousy and the envy engendered when any advance is made. These new problems, fear of his peers' rejection, and his own shaky and ambivalent response to success, had to be confronted. The counselors were trained to be on the lookout for these reactions and to help Marvin interpret and deal with them before he had time to translate them into the "acting out" which was his habitual mode of coping with stress.

By confronting his feelings, talking about them and letting out the bad feelings, Marvin was able to clear the atmosphere so that good feelings could come up and be enjoyed. At each stage of his progress in Phase One, from cleaning crew coordinator to messenger to group catalyst to peer counselor aide and finally to expeditor, this process of becoming aware of the hazards and dumping the bad feelings and the appreciation and enjoyment of the good feelings had to be repeated. If these reactions are not dealt with openly, the danger of falling back is greatly aggravated. It happens sometimes even when these steps are taken, and then a demotion and retrenchment become necessary, usually precipitating an outburst (or repeated outbursts) of abusive anger and bitterness, in which the blame is shifted to the counselor, the administration, a peer who "ratted" or any convenient object. Sometimes there are threats.

We deal with this kind of crisis in groups and in one-to-one sessions with the counselors. It is crucial that the counselors not abdicate at this time and that the value system be maintained. We all must keep firmly in our minds, however threatened we may feel, however fed up and impatient and full of a wish to strike back or to make concessions in order to get the kid off our backs, that under all the bluster and hectoring, the true desire of the adolescent is that we hold firm, so that his (or her) need for structure, long starved and scarcely recognized as such, can at last be satisfied. If we give in, it is tantamount to saying "We don't care about you." By insisting that kids live and work within the structure we are sending the message "We consider you valuable enough to prevent you from harming or degrading yourself. We are convinced that you can make it." Innumerable times the youngster who one day rages and storms, threatens to hurt people, to leave, to go back to the streets, to commit suicide, to burn down the place, the next day acknowledges, in a calm and reasonable manner, the necessity for following the rules. "I know you had to take my job. I was doin shit. I'm gonna do what I have to do and move up again." And often they have done so.

The cardinal rules cannot be negotiated. The structure of Argus is not up for grabs. This is the most expressive, dependable and believable code for conveying the message that we value our enrollees as human beings. It is a tough pill to swallow, but it brings relief and a sense of security. It gives them—and us—dignity and establishes a matrix, a mold in which to cast future transactions. Adolescents—and others—who act out are essentially people who have not learned (because no one ever taught them) to become aware of their feelings and to express them in another mode, including, but not limited to, putting them into words. (Direct, nonverbal expression, in groups, of pain, anger, fear and the need for bonding—touching, hugging, giving and taking support and affection—is another vital mode, rooted in survival needs, and very possibly a necessary basis for the attainment of the highest emotional and social growth.)

After a year Marvin was ready to move into Phase Two. His reading remained low, but he had a talent for art. He could lose himself for hours in Jose Padilla's class, painting, making masks, modeling in clay and working in the silk screen process. His ability was outstanding and he developed a feeling of trust and admiration for Jose. The well-deserved praise and recognition that he got in this class offset his frustration at his snail's progress in reading. As he developed his talent as an artist Marvin began to experience a new form of enjoyment—a reward beyond clothes, money, prestige or praise: the feeling of being one with his creative power. He found that he could immerse himself for hours in drawing and painting and feel that only a minute had gone by.

Marvin emerged from long hours of painting and drawing, when it went well, fresh-faced and full of energy. When it did not go well, Jose helped him to tolerate the frustration. In groups he learned to give himself positive, not negative, feedback at those low ebbs, to tell himself, "I can do it. This is a slack time but it won't last. I'm restocking, reenergizing. Soon I'll be riding high again."

Fortunately, it is not only artists or gifted youngsters like Marvin Manders who learn the pleasure of burning brightly. The feeling can come while performing well in any task or sport. You don't have to have a high calling, you don't have to be better than someone else, you don't have to win.

In Phase One Marvin became part of the Argus family. He was reconditioned by men and women of his own kind, whom he trusted, to believe in himself and to realize that there were alternatives. He learned to feel safe for eight hours of the day, and gradually he came to trust the Argus structure—after testing it repeatedly to see if it would crumble. He saw that people cared about him, and he felt remorse if he let them down. Bit by bit, he incorporated their sense of responsibility, their honesty and openness, their way of viewing the world. He co-opted their language, their tools.

4. PHASE TWO
Jobs and the Youth Crime Connection

Our opportunities in the city just leads us into trouble.
Because all we can do is hang out. When you have time
on your hands, there's nothin for you to do but get in
trouble.   ARGUS ENROLLEE

Phase Two is where everyone wants to go. There are paid youth employment lines there and also the sense of pride in forging ahead. The decision to move a kid to Phase Two is taken in a case conference where counselors, teachers and the human development specialist discuss the young person and proffer their opinions. If anyone seriously opposes the move to Phase Two and presents evidence that a youngster is not yet ready, the decision will be deferred.

Marvin was moving ahead steadily in math but his reading lagged, and at the fifth grade level ground to a halt. The Columbia Center for Child Study, where we sent him for a diagnostic workup, could find no apparent cause. Marvin was expressing himself fluently in the spoken language but after a certain point could not connect with words on paper. We speculated that some neurological damage had been done and had been compensated for, so that it did not show up in the tests. This was a time of despair for Marvin, but he gradually learned to express himself in other areas.

The move to the higher phase of the Argus program is not pegged to academic progress, but to behavioral, attitudinal and emotional growth. For those who are not academically talented we provide other avenues to knowledge and self-esteem. Kids can shine as counselors' aides, tutors or catalysts in groups. We try to discover the talent or bent that each of them has and involve them in training, work experience and, eventually, nonsubsidized jobs best suited to their potential.

In Phase Two Marvin would prepare to move out into the world; he had to be placed in a job and hold it. But getting a job today is tougher than it once was for those who have no educational skills, no training, no work history and no recommendations. Phase Two takes these factors into account and finds ways to satisfy them.

45

The overall rate of successful outcomes for Argus enrollees in 1980 was 67 percent. This includes all those in Phase One who never made it to Phase Two (and some who barely made it past the front door). In our Office Skills Training Program that year we placed 80 percent of the enrollees in nonsubsidized employment or college; and in the final cycle of that year, before the program was discontinued for lack of funds, 100 percent found jobs as secretaries, typists, receptionists, clerks, finance assistants, medical secretaries, et cetera. The graduates of this program were mostly young women, sixteen to twenty-one years old, who had never thought that they would be able to support themselves or their children (some had one or more children when they enrolled) or aspired to a career beyond "getting their own budgets" and living out their lives on welfare. Now, instead of being a burden to the taxpayers, they are taxpayers themselves.[1]

It is the task of Phase Two to consolidate the gains made in Phase One and find a way to make the models we hold up, of honest and independent living, a reality. The CETA youth employment and training programs played a crucial role in this. Marvin's experience and that of several others illustrate how this works.

Success Story One

NAME: **Marvin Manders**
AGE: **21**
OCCUPATION: **Printer, silk screening company**

The move into Phase Two, with the prospect of a paid job in Project Foothold (our CETA youth employment program) or in another of our CETA-funded programs filled Marvin with tension. Aubrey LaFrance probed Marvin's interests, job preferences and career goals. He explained that Project Foothold is made up of five work experience components: peer counseling and tutoring, in which Foothold aides, supervised by the Argus staff, help enrollees with their academic and group work and act as monitors in the halls, lunchrooms and on the grounds; maintenance, where enrollees interested in the building trades learn under a skilled journeyman to plaster and paint, lay floors, make plumbing and carpentry repairs, et cetera in the buildings and storefronts owned by Argus; neighborhood recreation, in which Project Foothold aides supervise the games and sports of younger children in the area; the art workshop, where Foothold aides help the instructor teach paper sculpture, mask making, puppetry, silk screening and painting to Argus enrollees and neighborhood children; and lastly, outside jobs, where Foothold enrollees work in public and nonprofit agencies for three hours a day. All Project Foothold enrollees are involved in classroom work (academics) during the morning hours.

Marvin thought it over for a week, while wielding a broom, then chose the art workshop. The clincher was a talk with Martin Wishnoff, the Argus guidance counselor, who told Marvin about the Parsons School of Design and the Fashion Institute of Technology, where scholarships might be available.

The art workshop can lead to a career in the field, but we view it primarily as a setting where young persons learn that they can create objects of beauty and value. As Jose Padilla, the instructor, sees it, art can be a way of tying yourself in with the world.

"When you make a mask of your face, you can't do it alone," Jose says. "You need someone to help you and you have to trust that person to come close, to touch your face. We usually reserve our faces for intimate kinds of experiences. To let someone cover your face with sticky stuff is an act of trust. Taking someone's face under your hands is an act of responsibility. It may not seem like much, but for these kids it's a big step. Somehow, in making a mask you get into the person. The kids comment on the masks, share their feelings and impressions."

While making the mask they are nervous.

Mask making serves another important purpose. Just as when people are photographed, there is the instant feeling that notice has been taken, recognition accorded. A representation of oneself gives validation and importance. The message is, "I must be valuable."

Jose brings in masks or pictures of masks from other cultures. The members of the workshop brush up against the mystery and the message of Africa, consummate mask-maker of the world. Enthralled, they experiment with fantastic elaborations upon their own face masks, adding cascades of "hair," brilliant swatches of color, representations of plants and animals, to the stark plaster of paris. Some change and distort the features, working them into expressions of rage or mirth. Marvin gave no outward sign of whatever it was that mask making aroused in him; but we observed that like so many others he was magnetized by the process.

As an art workshop aide Marvin took the attendance, distributed art materials, kept checklists so that new supplies could be ordered when necessary, assisted in teaching and helped to prepare for an art exhibit which would be shown first at Argus, then at a nearby elementary school and eventually at Taller Boriqua, the Puerto Rican art workshop. He was placed in charge of a traveling workshop which

*showed people in other agencies how to make masks and paper
sculptures and how to do silk screening.*

*For Marvin Manders, the art program became a central focus.
The daily ritual of creation (reaching into teeming chaos to snake out
beauty and orderliness, tearing off pieces of dreams and remolding
them in clay, wet newspaper and flour or plaster, running amok with
red, purple, yellow and green paints, making objects to show off and
be proud of) was for him a healing and synthesizing process. As an
aide to the art instructor, he earned $48.75 a week. He was proud of
his position in the art class, and in addition, he assumed part-time
role of catalyst and peer counselor, for he was determined to master
the fine points of group work which had attracted and challenged him
from the first.*

*Marvin stayed at Argus three and a half years. At the end of that
time he was ready to pass the G.E.D. exam in all areas except
reading, where he remained at the fifth grade level. Even without
having his G.E.D. Marvin applied for and was accepted at a leading
design institute, with tuition paid by a government grant. After
earning twenty-four credits at the institute, he was automatically
granted a high school diploma. He remained there two years, creating
beautiful designs, some of which he brought to my office, turning my
workaday lair into a wonderland of riotous color and design. His work
has been exhibited on Park Avenue, and he is now employed in the
design industry, earning $13,400 a year.*

Success Story Two

NAME: **Chessie Washington**
AGE: **22**
OCCUPATION: **Typist, State of New York**

*Chessie came to Argus at sixteen, with a history of having been
shunted from one institutional setting to another. She did not know
her father, had been rejected by her mother, had been in Children's
Center, Spofford, two training schools, three group homes, two
residences, and a live-in drug program. The staff in nine placement
situations had found her behavior disruptive and violent and had
requested the courts to send her elsewhere. Her specialty was
instigating rebellions and riots, spurring other inmates to break the
rules and defy and attack staff.*

*She was not a lesbian but her manner was "butch." Bopping
(dipping) as she walked, dressed in sneakers, jeans and scarves, her
face and arms greased so that she could slip out of the clutches of*

attackers, she specialized in provoking male counselors and had been beaten by several before coming to Argus. When we first saw Chessie her considerable attractions were negated by a loud, brassy, bossy, abusive voice and manner (every other word was a curse), a case of acne and too much fat. She was stunned that no one at Argus tried to attack or rape her, and she was with us six months before she was convinced that ours is actually a safe environment. DJ street rappers (disc jockeys who talk and rhyme to music) and dancing were her only interests, aside from drugs (reefers and cocaine) and gang activities. She was an expert in the hustle and spent her days at "jams" in the park instead of attending school.

After being exposed to the Argus process for about a year and throwing up as many impediments as there are broken bottles on 156th Street, Chessie began to change. She made spectacular progress in her studies and at seventeen passed her G.E.D. examination. A loss of weight brought to view an elegant figure. Her acne improved and she began to walk in a feminine, high-spirited way. As the hard rock image crumbled, a sensitive core emerged. She could still be strident at times, but she became interested in the new residents and helped them in groups. It was partly because of her cooperation that we were able to put a positive peer group together in the group home.

Accepted by two colleges, Chessie enrolled in the one of her choice but flunked out because play was still her main focus. At this point Mary Taylor took her by the ear and insisted that she learn to type before enrolling in a school of beauty culture that she was clamoring to attend because a friend was there. She was not genuinely interested in a career in cosmetology, but to win the point she took us before the Family Court. Like many who have been in the child-care system, Chessie knew how to milk it. The law guardians chose to believe that Argus was stifling Chessie's career aspirations, and we were ordered to place her in the beauty culture school of her choice (even though the school in question was a ripoff institution). Luckily the order did not become final until Chessie had learned to type fifty words a minute without error. Three weeks after she enrolled and paid her money, having taken out a government loan, Chessie's career in beauty culture came to an abrupt end. She dropped out to involve herself with a dude in "the life"—a handsome, foxy hustler who dealt in whatever was around, including female flesh. She moved into his apartment and, as she told me at the time, "Whatever he feeds me, I eat." Along with his sweet talk he beat her up, which she said she enjoyed because "he's the only person I've ever known who can control me."

"You won't like it for very long," I said. "Eventually you're going to have to learn to control yourself."

Chessie broke with her foxy friend a short time afterward and hid out with acquaintances in Washington Heights. In a few weeks she found a job as a typist. This skill enabled her to break from the life, and she has been earning her living as a typist ever since.

She got a provisional job with the state, starting at $9,300 and benefits, gets along with her co-workers and bosses and has had several raises. She has been there three years, has taken maternity leave and will be back at work shortly. Chessie said in an article she wrote for the Argus Peacock *that our group home was different from any other placement she'd been in because it's a safe environment and "the staff care enough to make you do what you're supposed to do." She gave the youth employment program credit for her success. Chessie is studying at night for a degree in human services and counseling.*

Success Story Three

NAME: **Frank Darrow**
AGE: **22**
OCCUPATION: **Sanitation worker**

"That judge had no business sendin me away. I was only fifteen. They sposed to let a kid mess up till he turns sixteen. He should have remanded me to the custody of my mother. That was how I saw it. And I was pissed."

Frank had been paroled any number of times and when the judge finally did send him away he was outraged. The system wasn't supposed to behave that way.

Big and broad—nearly six feet tall, with heavy muscles sheathed almost to the point of rotundity in dark flesh—Frank was one of 4,449 children under the age of sixteen who were arrested in New York for robbery in 1973.[2]

"There was more crimes inside those places than out on the streets," Frank recalled. "I was born and brought up in hell. But man, the joint is double hell. All the negative dudes are locked up together and they run the place. Nothing is sacred in the joint. They'll stab you for a quarter. I had to make believe I was totally crazy, that I didn't care whether I lived or died, so they wouldn't steal my manhood. Course, I'm big. And I can act like the baddest. They

*didn't mess with me. But the smaller, weaker fellows are ripped off
everyway. I saw it all—theft, assault, rape, extortion, homicide, every
kind of brutality and exploitation. I did some of it. But I'm not bone
mean like some of those entrenched criminals. I was hurting, we all
were hurting, but we never let anyone see it. We cried alone, never
together. And when we came out we were twice as hard, twice as
tough, and twice as cunning as when we went in. And pissed off.
Ready to turn on any mother-fucker that got in the way. Feelings
running over into violent deeds. Taking action before you have time
to think or even to feel your feelings."*

Frank's mother died when he was born, and his father was killed
seven years later in a knife fight "over a woman's love," as Frank
expressed it. His mother's sister, who raised him, treated him like one
of her own, and his memories of life in Tupelo, Mississippi, were
those of struggle and hard work, but basically warm and decent. The
family sent him to New York City when he was eleven years old, to
live with an uncle and have access to better schooling and
opportunities. But the uncle wasn't doing as well as the family
thought. He was out of work a good part of the time, harassed and
overburdened, and though he did what he could for Frank, the boy
began to run with a gang, to steal and to get into trouble with the
police and the Family Court.

*"I knew that I was doing wrong but it just didn't hit me that
way, I guess because it seemed like everybody was doing it. We even
robbed people's Christmas presents that they had scrimped and saved
to give their children some joy at that season. We would follow them
as they came out of the stores and snatch their shopping bags. I
remember one woman cried her eyes out. I don't know how I could
have done it. But I did. I don't even think the things meant that much
to me. Not like they did to some of my crime buddies. For me it was
more the adventure of it and the fun we had together. But I really
shrivel up inside when I think of how many children and their parents
too were disappointed and hurt because of us. I found out I could
scare people half to death because of my size and my being black and
I guess I liked that."* At sixteen he finally made it into the adult
system, sentenced to a four-year term for having killed the brother of
his common-law wife in a knife fight. Frank was indignant that he had
been sent away for so trifling an offense. *"That mother had a yellow
sheet two yards long,"* he said. (A "yellow sheet" is a criminal
record.) *"He attacked me. I took his knife away from him and stabbed
him with it."* The police seemed to think that Frank had a knife of his
own and had used it. *"But my wife's brother, he was a bad man."*

Frank, like Judge Roy Bean of frontier fame, thought that the first duty of the court in a murder case was to determine "whether the deceased ought to have departed."

Frank was paroled to Argus when he was twenty years old. We were amazed that he was not more deeply scarred by the life he had led. Perhaps his size and his well-advertised dexterity with weapons eased his way. This allowed him an option, too, as to the lengths he would go in victimizing others. He seemed at bottom a rather kindly person who had adapted as best he could to the city environment. True, he was twenty years old when we got him. But we see any number of twenty-year-olds who are acting out of pure rage. The "maturing out" phenomenon, when people get out of crime or commit less of it, moving into the work force or resigning themselves to welfare and the bottle, generally occurs in the early thirties.[3] If Argus hadn't come into the picture, Frank's pattern of robbing, with some incidental assaults, probably would have peaked when he was in his twenties; that is, if he hadn't been caught and sent away for a longer term. In either case his criminal career would have cost society a pretty penny before he "aged out."

Frank had found himself in a subculture of crime, he had made the best he could of it, and then, cast up on our doorstep, availed himself of what we had to offer. He was the type of older enrollee who was useful to the counseling staff. He became so effective with the kids that for some time we resisted putting him to work in an outside agency. Nor did Frank want to go. And he would have made an excellent counselor, but he needed more money than counseling jobs pay. He was not really interested in classroom work though he did become literate. In Phase Two of the program, he was assigned first to the Victim Services Agency, where he performed quite well; but his strength and energy demanded movement and the out-of-doors. We shifted him to a work experience job with the Department of Parks. Then, through one of the counselors, he found a full-time paid job with a private sanitation company and now earns between $300 and $500 a week. He has not been arrested again, and said recently when he dropped by for a visit, "I could never go back to the old way again. When I think back to how it was and the things we did, man, garbage is clean by comparison. I've got a job for life with the DiFalco brothers. They really like me. I'm strong and I give them everything I've got."

His wife stuck with him through the years, in spite of the fight in which he killed her brother. "When two mens fight with knives somebody's liable to get killed" was the way she summed it up. "We

*have a good life an I don't have to worry all the time bout the police
an will Frank be killed or kill somebody an go away again. My
childrens is real proud of their daddy. An Lord, you ought to see him
if one of them misses a day of school. He tell them, 'Don't be a
nobody. Don't be a know-nothin pretendin to be a know-it-all. Learn
somethin and be somebody.' "*

Success Story Four

NAME: **Vincent Scoffo**
AGE: **29**
OCCUPATION: **Manager, food store**

*Vince grew up in Belmont, a community of about 30,000
persons, known as the Little Sicily of the South Bronx. This was the
original Italian settlement in New York City, predating the Little Italy
of lower Manhattan.*

"*Arthur Avenue in Belmont looks like Palermo," Vince says.
"Fifteen square blocks of pushcarts, including a lot of things to eat. I
used to walk around there on Saturdays with my mother. She would
buy fresh baked bread, salami, black olives, cheeses, veal, pork,
chicken, clams, mussels, peppers, onions, eggplants, zucchini. The big
thing was to choose the macaroni for the Sunday, the only day in the
week I got to see my father. We would go to mass at Our Lady of
Mount Carmel—I was confirmed and made my first communion there
—and when we got home my dad would be there. He sneered at
people who went to church; my mother was a devout Catholic, born
to suffer. No matter how much money we had she was on her hands
scrubbing. Shopping, cooking, cleaning, that was her life. And the
family. She loved me. In her mind I'm a good person. She knows I'm
good.*

"*I used to think about my father during the week and wonder
where he was. As I grew up I learned that he had an apartment on
the Upper East Side in Manhattan, that he had other women, that he
drank a lot and spent money like crazy. He had a very successful wine
business and was the big shot and patriarch of the family. When the
house was full of people he was very outgoing, very generous, very
charming. But the minute they were gone he turned on us.*

"*Nothing we did was good enough. I tried so hard to please
him. Jesus, I remember a time when it was everything in the world if
he just smiled at me. I was an honor roll student, I helped my
mother, I was quiet and respectful, and all I ever got from him was
criticism. He made all the decisions about us children, and he was*

always wrong. He didn't know us. We never sat down to have a talk."

Vince was a rugged kid, on the stocky side, about five feet ten inches tall, with intense dark eyes. He did a lot of moping and brooding when he was alone but with people he lit up and was friendly and adaptable. "A chameleon," he called himself. "I could disappear into the woodwork or come out and get with it, depending on the circumstances. I was very athletic. Played stickball and baseball. Never was in any trouble. But sometimes I felt bad, especially as I began to grow up. Really anxious and desperate. Almost like a panic. I didn't know what it was. I used to wander up to the Fordham campus and stroll around under those big trees and look at the old Manor House and the chapel and I would think, 'My father hates the Irish. He hates Jesuits.' He hated blacks and hispanics too. And dope addicts and criminals. Everyone in Belmont hated all of those categories of people. I asked myself, Why? Why did they hate them? As soon as they got close to one individual Irishman or black or hispanic they liked him. They would say, 'Old Sam, he's different. He's not like the rest of them.'

"I would walk down to 183rd Street, to the southwest tip of Belmont and look over at the burned-out buildings and the garbage and the despair that hung over everything, and I thought how strange it was that it stopped right there. Like somebody had drawn a line, a magic circle around Belmont. Inside the circle the buildings were intact, families were together, crime—except for very tightly organized crime—was almost unheard of. There was no arson, no prostitution, no theft, no dope. Jesus, we left our doors unlocked! People walked the streets at night. If a crook strayed into our neighborhood, people nabbed him and held onto him till the police came. I learned later that blacks and Puerto Ricans thought the Mafia guarded our turf and that if they attempted a mugging in Belmont they wouldn't live to tell about it.

"So why was my father so ashamed of being Italian? He used to say, 'Italians are ignorant, uneducated, low people.' The kids had called him guinea and greaseball when he was in school. I used to think, 'Jesus, we got enemies on all sides—the micks to the north, the jigs and spics to the south. And we're just a bunch of greaseballs ourselves.' It looked to me like the rubble that was just over the line in the South Bronx would open its mouth and gobble us up in one bite.

"I was sixteen, getting ready to go to college. My mother was proud of me. Even my father doled out a little grudging praise, said I might make it after all. What they didn't know was that for two years

*I had been sniffing heroin. I never smoked reefers. I liked the feeling
heroin gave me. I had no idea of the consequences. I did it every
weekend. My allowance covered the cost and my friends had money
and knew where to buy it. We never stuck a needle into our arms.
Just sniffed. I might have gone on like that, through high school,
college, and into a job, but one weekend, in New Jersey, my two
friends and I drove through a stop light without realizing it. A police
car drove up beside us. We panicked and threw the heroin out of the
window. The police saw us do it, picked up the bags, took us in and
charged us with possession of dangerous drugs. My parents got me a
lawyer, tried to get me off. But the prosecutors went all out. Three
Italian hoods caught with heroin. Came over the state line to sell to
their clean suburban kids. We were unlucky enough to come before a
hanging judge. My lawyer introduced evidence showing that I was an
honor roll student, never in a day's trouble, that my family had solid
roots in the community. I offered to enlist in the Marines. Nothing
washed. The judge threw the book at us. We were sent away to a
state reformatory for five to seven years. I still get a sick feeling in my
stomach when I think of it. It changed my whole life. I had never
heard of rehabilitation then. But that's what we needed. We weren't
vicious, just mixed up kids."*

Vince made no waves at the reform school and by a combination
of diplomacy, friendliness and toughness (his rep as a big city hood
helped) he evaded the predators. The worst was the disgrace and
being pulled away from his family. *"I swore I would come through
this and make it up to my mother. That kept me alive for the three
and a half years I served in that place."*

Vince came out confused, having learned nothing except how to
be a criminal. *"My mother stuck by me. But in Belmont I was totally
stigmatized, shunned by everyone. As far as they were concerned I
was a dope fiend and a criminal. When my community wouldn't
accept me, the humiliation was unbearable. Even today this is painful
to me. Especially since we hadn't hurt anyone. We didn't sell dope.
We needed someone to straighten us out. We needed help and we
didn't get it from strangers or from our own people. If someone had
reached out for me. If my own people had understood. If someone
had given me a chance."* But they didn't.

Vince crossed over the line, drifting down into the South Bronx
to Fox and Kelly streets, a major dope fiend area. For the first time
he put a needle in his arm, and for the first time willfully committed
crimes. In three and a half years in the joint he had absorbed the fine
points of stealing. Now he became a specialist in stealing typewriters,

office machines and supplies, forging checks. When the monkey on his back got too bad, he would check himself into the hospital and detox. At one point after cleaning up he amassed enough money to start a legitimate business, supplying specialty foods to restaurants.

"But when I cleaned up I was never committed to it. I needed large, quick sums of money to feed my habit, and that meant that I couldn't make the right decisions to keep a business going. I married twice. I was a fast talker, full of charm. I lost the women, too. I sacrificed them to dope. After four years on the streets it felt like a rat race. I wasn't happy with dope, yet I couldn't live without it. Or so I thought. I'm just beginning now to get a glimmer of what I was doing with dope, of the statement I was making and why I began to sniff when I was fifteen. It has to do with a big emptiness inside and I know now that it was a hunger for my father's love.

When Vince was arrested for theft, the judge adjourned his case on condition that he enroll in Argus and accept treatment for his drug addiction. The procedure is known as ACD, "adjournment in contemplation of dismissal." An Argus representative returned to court with Vince at intervals over the next year to report on his progress.

Vince was one of many addicts who kicked cold turkey with the help of peers at Argus. It was tough but it helped him to see that he had guts and that he could control his life.

"The first thing they taught me at Argus was to be honest," Vince said. "It was uphill work. In reform school, on the streets, in the joint my whole life had been lies. I knew that. What I hadn't known was that it went way back to when I was a kid at home, trying to survive in that scarey atmosphere where my father downgraded me and wouldn't talk to me. After waiting for years for him to show some love and understanding, I rejected all of his values. I couldn't accept my mother's way either—to suffer and be a martyr. So, not aware of what I was doing, I built a life on everything my father despised and ranted against. But at the same time I arranged to have myself crucified, so in a way I acted out my mother's pattern too."

Argus had an evening program at that time—1974—for adult criminals and drug users who were hanging on to jobs. Aubrey and Juan Vega, who ran the evening program, insisted that Vince get a job after the first four or five months. He was on welfare. They pressed him to get off. "I was glad because the welfare system is demeaning. My first job was for the Argus Moving Company. Argus needed someone with business expertise. It was good for my morale. After that I took over the kitchen at Argus and did a really good job with training the kids to shop, prepare and serve food and do the cleanup."

Vince stayed clean for nine months, left Argus, went to work in a classy restaurant on the Upper East Side, branched out into a business of his own and then relapsed. "I got in my Mercedes, put on my $400 suit and went to see my father. He said, 'Yeah, that's nice. I'm glad you're doing okay, Vince. You may have a little of my talent after all.' The bad feelings came up again: no matter what I achieved I would never be good enough in his eyes."

One evening at a party the butler brought around a tray with white stuff and a silver spoon. Vince said, "What the hell. I'll snort just once to prove I can do it without getting a habit." And bang, he was back on. "I couldn't do what the rest of my Upper East Side 'friends' did—get high on the weekend and forget about it the rest of the week. I had to do it every day. When I fall I crash; I go all the way, straight to the bottom. Pretty soon I was speedballing and stealing—the full catastrophe."

Aubrey took Vince back into the program when he hit rock bottom. He dealt with his belly this time, let himself feel the emptiness he had tried to fill with money, flashy cars, women, winning people's admiration and approval. All the stuff he had held back came pouring out. He sought out his father, laid his feelings on the table.

"We finally had some real talks. I had to confront him hard to make him relate to me as one human being to another. He still tried to play God with me. Jesus, it scares me silly when I look at him. He's lost everything but the house he lives in. Pissed everything away on women and booze and cutting a bella figura. He's a half-assed alcoholic. He's unhappy. And I know now that somewhere along the line he didn't get it. His father didn't recognize him. He was cold and distant. No emotional connection. I think he sees me a little more as a human being. We've got something like the beginning of a bond. But I'm not going to get it from him. He just doesn't have it to give, not the way I need it. That's why the male staff at Argus were good for me. We made a very warm bond. I got in touch with how much I need and want a warm, loving male relationship and how angry and hurt I am that I didn't have that when I was coming up."

Vince went back into the food business. But this time he continued to come to groups at Argus. He took it more slowly. The compulsion to make a lot of money fast had lost some of its grip. Courses in accounting and food management gave him a more solid grasp of business.

He had learned that if you need chemicals or lots of money or *approval to turn you on, there's something wrong. The warmth and spontaneity that are your birthright have been dammed up. He could get in touch with good feelings without sniffing or shooting up. Heroin had blocked out the pain and filled his emptiness for a little while. But in the long run, the only thing that was really satisfying was to break through that wall that kept him from feeling and enjoying and sharing that warmth and spontaneity. "I find I really don't have to have the $400 suits and the Mercedes Benz. If they happen to come along, well, this time around maybe I can enjoy them and not get angry and bitter and self-destructive because they don't give me the human warmth that I need. I think I'm finally growing up. I feel entirely confident in terms of drugs. It's been four years. I have no drive to hurt myself anymore. I don't want to hurt my mother. And I have no need now to hurt my father. I've done enough of that.*

With these enrollees, we concentrated in Phase Two on preparing them to get jobs in the outside world and to hold on to them; a job readiness program was tailored to the needs and talents of each individual. We then made a major effort to persuade outside employers to take a chance and open their doors. We follow this approach with all our kids, whether they are college bound, working toward the G.E.D. and a job or toward basic literacy and jobs without the diploma.

It is difficult in today's world to place people without high school diplomas, but we have been able to find placements. Those with nine years of schooling or who are reading at the eleventh grade level, *and* who do not have juvenile or criminal justice involvement, are eligible for the armed forces, and a small number who can meet the criteria sign up, with the thought of getting further education and training in the army. (The armed forces will accept juveniles and adults with one misdemeanor offense only if they have a high school diploma and can prove that they have taken steps toward a positive lifestyle.) Enrollees who do not have the G.E.D. have been placed in training programs or jobs as nurses' aides, dental hygiene or mental retardation aides, medical clerks, cosmetologists, warehouse persons, telephone company linemen, assistants at Con Edison, groomers of pets, veterinary assistants, stockpersons, cleaners of clothing, draperies and upholstery, layers of linoleum and tiles, air conditioning and refrigeration repair people, hotel clerks and bellhops, dressmakers, orderlies in hospitals, chauffeurs for the owners of car fleets, museum guides, private sanitation workers, and so on. Knowing how to behave, armed with resumes, references and work experience gained under the

CETA programs, and with their employability enhanced with training in specific fields, some of these young persons are able to find jobs and to stay in them in spite of their low educational level. Argus's role in teaching them to behave themselves and to approach work with a positive attitude is crucial. But the value of the work experience, the resume and the references they are able to gain under a CETA type work experience program cannot be overstated.

For those who obtain the diploma and do not go on to college (we send fifteen to twenty to various campuses each year), we are in touch with a broader range of apprenticeship and training situations, among them butcher's apprentice, bank teller and cashier, food preparation and management, upholstery and park maintenance training. We try to match the young person to the training and to the supervisor on the job, and we monitor them to see that neither party takes unfair advantage and to mediate any disputes that arise. Trainees are usually paid a little more than the minimum wage with a raise when the apprenticeship or training period is completed satisfactorily. These are modest beginning situations, but the kids are delighted to have them, once they are convinced that they have a stake in the work world. It is hard for those with poor self-esteem to cross over and take the chance.

One of our girls had been severely disassociated when she came to us. Denying and blocking out her painful realities, she had been misdiagnosed as schizophrenic. After some time at Argus, she spent $80 on a multiple-braid-and-bead hairdo before going for a job interview. She was turned down, and hearing later that the boss hadn't cared for her hairdo, she called back and asked if she could have the job if she changed her hairdo. "I'm very flexible," she said. She got the job. Because she felt better about herself, the boss's criticism didn't seem all that devastating. She was free to make accommodations to get a job.

Chemical Bank sends one of their employees to Argus twice a week to train our enrollees. With mock teller cages in a "banking" room prepared by the youngsters, they learn the teller's trade. Several are working in that capacity. We train older, more responsible adolescents in the specific requirements of a number of businesses, brokerage houses, and organizations such as Trinity Church and the New York Port Authority. A couple of our kids are modeling the new lines in the garment center. Two have jobs with the Port Authority at $18,000 a year. Others are acting as salespersons, receptionists, typists and clerks. One who graduated from college is an accountant with a leading auditing firm.

For Argus youngsters the now nearly defunct year-round work experience program (YEP) worked well. Our kids were in demand in public agencies that provided work-experience sites. Two Argus enrollees went to work in the methadone clinic at Bellevue, a large municipal hospital with a perennial problem of understaffing. They did so well that the pediatrics clinic asked for them, then the dental clinic, then the hospital print shop. Lincoln Hospital, in the South Bronx, requested seventeen of our kids. Although we had a hard time making the first placement, after that the performance spoke for itself and letters and endorsements from enthusiastic employers, along with the references they write for the kids, made the job developer's task easier.

Patricia Huntington, in her 1982 report *Youth at Risk and Work,* put unemployment among youths fourteen to nineteen years old at 50 percent. Ms. Huntington estimates that 20 percent of youths who are jobless are ready to hold jobs if they could get them. Forty percent are almost ready to work, and 40 percent are not capable of offering anything of value to employers even if jobs were available to them. It is from this latter 40 percent of jobless youths that Argus draws its clientele. These are the youths who present the greatest problem and the gravest threat. Although the CETA programs claimed to address this group, they never actually did so, either in their concept of what was needed or in the provision of resources adequate to do the job.[4]

In the Argus model the CETA programs became components in a comprehensive array of services designed to meet the overall needs of young persons who have scorned legitimate employment (often because they believed that only menial, low-paying jobs were open to them) and are experimenting with, or are fully involved in, negative identities. Without the complementing components, including intensive socialization and remedial academics tailored to their needs, for youths not ready for jobs the CETA youth employment programs tended to operate as "income transfer" situations: Much-needed funds were handed out not because the work produced justified such payments but *because the youths needed money.* They were in effect a glorified welfare handout, a kind of ultimate condescension that smacked of payoff, confirmed the kids in their belief that they had nothing of value to contribute and encouraged a false sense of entitlement and a rip-off mentality.

A well-planned work-experience program for high-risk kids should make provisions to meet their special needs. Well-administered and with the necessary support services, such programs can work and they are badly needed. But the agencies that run them must see that the kids report to work regularly and on time, that they are given actual work to do, that they produce something of real value and that they refrain from disruptive or criminal behavior. This is an enormous task and it cannot be accomplished solely with the means put at an agency's disposal by the old work experience programs. The basic idea of the YEP was a good one for kids who are ready or almost ready, and it can work for high-risk kids *providing* that other program elements are in place to bolster and make it actually happen. For the young people Argus works with, that is, those who are the present focus of attention because their activities are a threat to the quality of life in our society, other components *must* be provided. Argus has been fortunate enough to put together the supplementary services which make it feasible for us to prepare these young people for change: to interact intensively with them, sometimes for months, before they go out to work sites, to develop productive work experience situations, to monitor the performance of both the kids on the job and their employers and to take an active role in sponsorship of these kids for jobs in nonsubsidized employment at the end of the process. In addition, Argus staff has to be there for those who may leave their nonsubsidized jobs for whatever reason, to reprocess them and help to find them new situations, where, it is hoped, they will be able to stick it out.

Paring down administratively, tightening the ship, making agencies accountable—these are good measures. New York City has shown that sound fiscal and administrative control can be achieved in CETA programs.[5] But beyond that, if we are looking to make high-risk kids employable over the long haul, two things have to happen: we've got to acknowledge the problem in its full complexity and go at it from various angles, not depending solely upon CETA (or some similar employment program), and we must be sure that business and the private sector are willing to make a sincere effort to promote equal opportunities for high-risk youth. These two facets are interdependent. The kids are not going to be turned on to the business world unless there are jobs with at least some eventual upward mobility out there for them; and business, rightfully enough, will resist incorporating high-risk kids unless they go in with acceptable behavior and attitudes.

In the long run full employment would make significant inroads on crime. But even then, because of the heavy damage already inflicted by long-standing deprivation and exclusion from the job market, the hard-core poor are going to need help, even if, as I believe, the main cause of family instability, alcoholism, drug addiction and crime lies in unemployment and underemployment, problems which full employment would gradually diminish.[6]

Certainly, until full employment has somehow been made a fact of life, we are going to have to struggle with large numbers of fourteen- to twenty-four-year-olds who are jobless and are committing crimes in disproportionately great numbers.[7] Since occupational deprivations underlie so much of juvenile delinquency and since the young contribute heavily to the crime rate, and specifically to those crimes of violence that we all abhor and that are undermining the quality of our lives, it is imprudent to abolish youth employment programs which have the potential, if properly conceived and managed, of alleviating crime.

5. SOME INCIDENTS OF VIOLENCE
What We Do and Don't Do

*Fighting begins when the conversation ends. You've got a
lot to say, but you don't know how to say it, except with
your hands.*   ARGUS ENROLLEE

One Monday morning in late spring, Riggy (short for Rigoberto) Vidal walked into the reading laboratory presided over by
Calvin McBee, a former shop instructor who had been grandfathered
in as a special education teacher. For eighteen years McBee had
taught boys and girls, largely black and hispanic, the art of burning
their names and those of their relatives and friends into pieces of
wood to be hung on walls or stood on tables as ornaments. Losing
interest in this line of work, he had the previous year persuaded the
school administrator at Argus to give him a chance to run the reading
lab, which he thought would be more varied and stimulating. McBee
was taking in-service courses after school at a Board of Education site
in order to be granted the license necessary to retain his position as
a teacher of "emotionally disturbed" children and to satisfy minimum
eligibility requirements established by the city and state.

On this particular day Riggy came about five minutes late to the
reading lab. McBee had already given out the workbooks and had
assigned the pupils to their Junior Control Readers. He was seated
behind his desk sipping coffee, smoking a cigarette and thumbing
through the *New York Daily News*—activities forbidden to teachers and
pupils in our classrooms. McBee was none too pleased to see Rigoberto Vidal advancing toward him, especially as the young man was
late and had his "box" suspended from his shoulder by a leather strap
—a fifty-five-pound radio in flashing silver tones, with as many dials
and buttons as a computer and with eighteen speakers which could be
heard four to five blocks away. Riggy had purchased this piece of
equipment the previous Saturday on Forty-second Street, paying $40
down and signing an agreement to pay the remaining $210 from his
weekly YEP checks. The students in the reading lab left their carrels
and crowded around to examine the new acquisition.

Riggy played it cool. He was intent on delivering a message to

63

the teacher. Turning the radio down slightly he approached the desk and began, "Mr. McBee, I—"

McBee held up an imperious hand. "I will not exchange one word with you." He was a thin, nervous man with a red complexion and scanty rust-colored hair. His neck was bright pink, crisscrossed with white lines where the sun had not got into the creases. He wore glasses which he wiped frequently, batting his eyes and shaking his head as though he were endeavoring to drive away a swarm of gnats. He often spoke to his students in a withering tone of voice (he rather prided himself on his sarcasm), and it was this tone which he now employed. "Not one word! Not one word!" he cried. "You may not speak to me!"

"But Mr. McBee, I've got to—"

"Hell, no! Not until you have taken that blasting, squealing, earshattering box out of here. Then come back and speak to me, if you must, boy!"

Among the courses McBee was taking was one in transactional analysis, in which he had learned to identify the levels of the personality as child, parent and adult. Perhaps that was why he chose the word "boy" in addressing Riggy. Or perhaps he had forgotten that any adolescent is likely to consider the term an insult and that most blacks find it especially unwelcome.

Riggy found McBee's reference to his beloved "box" churlish and unappreciative. However, he knew that he was breaking the rules by bringing a radio onto the Argus premises, especially into the classroom. He had been prepared to let that insult pass. But when McBee called him "boy," Riggy felt that he had been "disrespected." He was righteously angry at McBee's remark and the bottled-up rage of his life came uncorked and spurted out, not in words, for he found himself entirely speechless, but in action. He retained just enough of his sanity to realize that he should not hit a teacher. However, he had to do something quick and satisfying with his hands. McBee's desk was piled with papers. Riggy lunged toward these, picked them up and threw them up into the air and at the teacher.

McBee came out from behind his desk, fists raised. "Are you looking for a fight, boy?"

Riggy turned his back on McBee, bolted from the lab, ran down the stairs to the lounge, put his box on a chair, crashed his fist through a window and proceeded to hurl chairs about the room, kicking and smashing them.

The two counselors on duty were aware that Riggy was having grave difficulties at home and was unsettled, but they were stunned by this outburst of violence. "Hey, Riggy, chill out, man! We don't bust up the furniture around here! Stop it right now!"

"*All right!* I'll go back upstairs and bust up Mr. McBee's face! That's what I want to do anyway!"

Like a flash he was gone. The counselors ran after him, but he was sixteen, in a fury and full of adrenalin, and he outstripped them easily.

Fortunately, Aubrey LaFrance happened to be coming down the stairs. Riggy ran straight into his arms.

"Hey, you're all steamed up, Riggy. What's going on? What are you angry about?"

"Mr. McBee an I'm gonna bust his face. I'm gonna take him off the count."

"Well, come in my office and tell me about it. What happened? We'll talk first and after that you can see what you want to do."

Aubrey is tall and strong. He could have overpowered Riggy if it came to that, but he preferred to leave him with a choice and a way out. Riggy chose to go with him back down the stairs. Once in the office, he was still stomping, swearing and trying to hit at things. Aubrey suggested that they go down in the street and run until Riggy calmed down.

An hour later they came back and went over the incident. Aubrey and the counselors made Riggy promise that he would hold his anger and dump it in group. They praised him for attacking the papers on the desk instead of Mr. McBee. They agreed that McBee's use of the word "boy" was insensitive and insulting and assured Riggy that they would probe the matter, take statements from those present, write up the incident and pass it on, with a strongly worded protest, to the principal of the cluster school, who was not on the premises that day (he usually visited Argus only once or twice during the week, for our environment was generally under control).

In addition, McBee was invited to a meeting, along with other school personnel and the Argus staff, to discuss the matter and search for ways to prevent incidents in the future. Unfortunately, those teachers most in need of such a meeting, including McBee, refused to attend. For the rest of us it was useful to remind ourselves that though we have precious few incidents of violence, this is not because our kids are not volatile (as most teenagers in our culture are) and capable, under certain circumstances, of violence (as all humans seem to be). We live in a violent society, and the way of life in many poor ghetto homes, in the streets and in our so-called correctional institutions is the distillation of that societal violence.

At Argus, our efforts to counteract this, to defuse violence, to provide alternative ways of interacting and to substitute another kind of rule and a safe environment have paid off so handsomely that teachers pull strings to get on the faculty of our school. Once on the staff, they resist any attempt to transfer them elsewhere. Generally our teachers are competent; five or six are superb; and about three are really not suited to our environment. From time to time, teachers and Argus staff forget that this safe and positive atmosphere did not fall on us from the laps of the gods. We had to invent it, we have to keep reinventing it every day and we need the help of the teachers in order to do that. The moment we lapse into complacency the system will come unhinged. Among the efforts we must keep up, lest the whole community be endangered, are the staff development groups and case conferences where Argus staff and teachers learn what the youngsters are going through and formulate short- and long-term goals for their growth.

If McBee had been attending case conferences—which he had refused to do—he would have had some vital information about Rigoberto Vidal. He would have known that Riggy's mother had borne children by another man and had run away with this man when Riggy was seven, leaving him and his older brother with his father. Riggy has never seen his mother since. Furthermore, McBee would have known that Riggy's father had placed him in institutional care, a decision that Riggy never understood and that hurts and rankles still. McBee would have been aware, too, that only three months before, Riggy's father had finally given in to eight years of the boy's pleas and had taken him back into his home on a "trial basis." It was an arrangement set up by the Department of Social Services and, as Riggy had been experiencing it, one in imminent peril of collapsing. His father is a highly nervous man, very critical of his son, and he and the older boy were disturbed by the sudden reappearance in their midst of a sixteen-year-old whom they scarcely knew. The brother was jealous and, according to Riggy, set him up for trouble, then would complain to the father, who threatened to return the boy to placement.

Riggy does not know, and we do not know either, why he was "put away" in the first place. He suspects that it may have been his uncontrollable temper. He is moody and impulsive and before coming to Argus had hit the principal of his school. He blames himself for his troubles and has made a sincere effort to control his outbursts. In fact, this was the first such episode since he came to Argus a year and a half before. The staff of the senior citizens center where Riggy works have given him their wholehearted endorsement. They say that he is mannerly and respectful, works hard and shows a particular sympathy and kindness for older people.

He had never before had a row with any counselor or teacher at Argus. But this is because, in part at least, the staff was aware of the changes he was going through. On the morning of the episode in the reading lab there had been a blowup at home. The counselors had called a special group to try and help Riggy deal with his feelings. He had come to the lab that morning expressly to tell McBee that he could not be present because he had to attend the group. In other words, he was behaving as responsibly as he knew how. Had McBee been attuned to Riggy's situation, he might have behaved more compassionately; or, barring that, more forbearingly, if only to forestall an explosion and a possible threat to himself.

Our counselors, and the best of our teachers, attend the case conferences and groups and make a point of finding out all they can about our enrollees. Even so, we sometimes unwittingly provoke violence or take actions that escalate instead of defusing it.

For example, a quarrel over the use of a basketball court broke out among two groups of young men in Phase One. Both wanted to play and neither side would yield. One of the contestants spied a two-by-four lying in the street, armed himself with it and plunged back into the battle. One of the enemy laid hold of the two-by-four. Then everybody tried to grab it and, failing this, fought with fists and feet. The only counselor on duty was a trainee, a former street person who had been with Argus less than a month. He waded into the melee, trying to stop it, and was instantly slammed in the head with the two-by-four and knocked unconscious. He had to be rushed to Lincoln Hospital.

What did the counselor trainee do wrong? Why did violence escalate on this occasion? Could anything have been done to prevent or stop it?

First a bit of background. This was 1978–79, the year our painstakingly constructed program was all but destroyed by one city and one state agency, when they peremptorily ordered us to more than double our enrollment or lose staff, teachers and funds. Their rationale was that we could easily handle more numbers since our youngsters were well behaved and attended fairly regularly. Officials from these funding agencies refused to look at case records, interview youngsters or be present at intakes or groups. They claimed that since our participants were orderly and studious we had to be "creaming," that is, taking in those without serious problems. We protested that among truants and dropouts in the South Bronx even the cream is none too creamy, and we were being penalized for our success. Throughout the year we fought the ruling, got the numbers partially reduced, and eventually cut back to a manageable level; but in the meantime the fabric of the program was torn. For the first time in our ten-year history, incidents of violence occurred.

Under normal circumstances a counselor would not have been assigned to supervise youngsters without a fellow counselor to back him up. A trainee would have been paired with an experienced counselor and would have been under his supervision. When the disturbance occurred the trainee would have been sent to fetch strong male staff and advanced peers to handle the emergency. We would not have permitted any counselor to wade into the melee. Counselors would have asked the kids to stop fighting, put down their weapons and negotiate. If they refused, we would have called the police. If they complied, counselors would have taken the angriest and most vocal into separate rooms and allowed them to blow off steam with no kids for an audience. Later the counselors would have brought the antagonists together for a verbal battle, letting them yell and eventually getting them to talk. Meanwhile, the balance of the two factions would have been dispersed to different parts of the building and dealt with in groups. Later we would have called a general meeting where everybody could learn the outcome for the young man who brought in the two-by-four (we would have put him on two weeks' "research," that is, banned him from Argus to ruminate on his actions and his situation; or, if his attitude was negative and he still had strong street connections, we might have extended the research period).

We have been confronted with many situations of this type and, when fully staffed, have handled them fairly well. But since this situation had been allowed to escalate and a counselor had been struck and knocked unconscious, we had no choice but to bar the leaders from Argus for the remainder of the year, with the possibility of returning next year if they could demonstrate a changed attitude. A general meeting was called so that everyone could speak his or her piece about the incident, learn the fate of the leaders and hear a report on the counselor's condition from Aubrey LaFrance and others who had returned from the hospital.

The incident got out of hand because we had too few staff members for the number of youngsters enrolled. For the same reason counselor training was not carried out as thoroughly as it should have been and a relatively new recruit was given a task beyond his capability at that point. He was not lacking in bravery but he was foolhardy— and no wiser person was there to restrain and guide him.

In general Argus achieves a deescalation of violence by giving enrollees new options, by exposing them to alternative ways of expressing their feelings and reaching their goals. But we cannot accomplish this if we have too many youngsters together at one time. A ratio of ten youngsters to one counselor is possible; six or eight to one is safer in the early stages. Now, with the budget cuts, we must manage with one counselor to every thirty-five enrollees. Our counselor trainee program, which provided the extra help, has been wiped out. This means that we cannot take in as many volatile and angry kids as before—and that is unfortunate, considering the chaos these kids are causing.

The best way to cope with violence is to create an atmosphere in which it is unlikely to develop. I described in Chapters 2 and 3 how we take away the support systems for offense and defense; in Chapter 6 I explain how we build positive peer groups, probably the most dependable deterrent to violence a program can have. And, of course, the more closeness there is, the more powerful the bonding that grows up among participants and staff, the less motivation there will be for angry, acting-out behavior.

In our residential program we hold marathons, minithons, or "love-ins," at least once or twice a year, so that pent-up feelings can find an outlet and bonding can take place. It is astonishing how much better everybody feels after a love-in. People tend to be elated and to act like angels for days. A big bank of affectionate, good feeling is stored up and can last quite a long time. When we perceive that this store is running out, the time has come to do it again.

Sometimes we don't read the signs. We're overburdened, swollen with our own feelings and tuned out to the kids. We need someone to arrange a minithon and a love-in for *us* or we begin to flag, as we were doing when the girls in both group homes ran amok. A staff member was let go when repeated efforts to pull him into the counseling process failed. Walter was a decent person but rigid, and he belonged in a different kind of job. The girls had complained about him steadily, and I guess we took it for granted (foolishly) that they really wanted him to go. However, our decision to terminate him had nothing to do with their complaints. They did not know this, of course. And we stupidly did not let them know what we planned to do.

There were so many other events taking place in the two homes that we lost sight of the fact that any coming or going by staff or residents is a potential bombshell and must be handled as such. Glenny Beers was on a ban for bad behavior and had put up signs all over Argus Two reading "Children Have Rights Too!" The girls in both houses were full of piss and vinegar. They demanded a house meeting at 6:00 P.M.

Mary Fritz, the director of the group home program, and Patricia

Ivy, the housemanager, who normally went home at 5:00 P.M., decided to stay for the meeting.

The group, consisting of girls and staff from both houses, convened in the dining room area of Argus Two. Someone asked where Glenny was. No one had seen her for about an hour. Chessie was dispatched to Glenny's room on the fourth floor to bring her to the meeting. Chessie came back and reported that Glenny was nowhere to be found.

Full of anxiety, Mary Fritz said, "Maybe she broke the rules and slipped over to Argus One."

It was decided that one of the girls should search in Argus One and that in the meanwhile the meeting should get under way. At this point the girls realized that Walter was not present and demanded that someone fetch him because they had "a lot of stuff for him." When informed that Walter would not be coming to the house meeting, the girls demanded to know whether he had been fired.

"Walter has left Argus to go into work that is more suited to his talents," Mary said. "I should have told you before but I didn't know we were going to have this meeting and—" Mary's voice was drowned out by howling and wailing.

"You fired Walter!"

"He was my daddy!"

"What if he can't find a job no place else?"

Mary and Patricia looked at each other in despair.

At this moment the door opened and Glenny staggered into the room. She had drunk a can of Colt 45, a strong beer favored by the kids of the South Bronx, and she was both drunk and acting the part of a drunk.

"I heard! Walter's been fired! I refuse to live here any longer!" she announced and lunged toward the window.

Everybody thought she was going to throw herself into the courtyard. One of the girls jumped up and hurled a chair at Glenny, not intending to hurt her but to prevent her from hurting herself. Glenny let out an agonized scream. Several girls rushed over and pinned her under the chair, pressing it down over her body so that she could not escape. Two girls struck at her face—again, not to hurt but to snap her back to reality.

"Oh, what are you doing!" Glenny screamed. "My beautiful face! You're ruining my beautiful face!"

Mary Fritz cast her body between Glenny and the girls and was battered in the process. Her watch was broken, her dress was torn and her arms and hands were scratched and bruised as she fended off blows intended for Glenny.

Coralia Rivera had remained in her chair, huddled in a damp ball, sobbing. She now rose, uttered a piercing scream and ran out of the door. Fearing that she might do herself harm, Patricia Ivy, who was trying to be everywhere at once in an effort to comfort and calm the girls, ran after Coralia, grabbing her just as the girl threw herself down the stairs. The housemanager was able to break the fall but could not stop it altogether and in the process lost her balance and rolled all the way to the bottom with Coralia. Both were battered and bruised.

Meanwhile, Adela Danaso smashed her fist through a window, shattered a pane of glass and cut an artery. Blood poured out all over her and the counselor who was trying to restrain her. He tore off his shirt and made an impromptu tourniquet, got Adela into his car and rushed her to Bronx Lebanon Hospital.

With two counselors out of commission, Mary Fritz, Patricia Ivy and the counselors from Argus One strove vainly for the next four hours to calm the girls, who ran up and down, wringing their hands, flinging their bodies about, beating on themselves and others, threatening to jump out of windows, put their heads into the oven and throw themselves down the stairs.

Finally at 11 P.M., when the staff was desperate and absolutely exhausted, the girls calmed down. They all gathered in the wreckage of the living room and tried to talk about what happened.

The girls accused Mary of not loving them.

Mary said, "What am I doing here right now and for the last four hours if I don't love you?"

The girls without exception said that they understood that Walter was not cut out to be a counselor and that he had to go. The only problem was that they hadn't been able to stand it when it actually happened.

Coralia said it reminded her of the time her father left home for good. "I always thought I was the cause of him leaving."

Several other girls related a similar loss to their reaction to Walter's dismissal.

Adela returned from the hospital. She came in smiling, well pleased with herself. The doctor had taken fourteen stitches in her arm and put it into a sling. The girls wept and embraced her. They thought she had died, there had been so much blood. Adela said she had not meant to smash her hand through the window. She said that her hand acted independently of her will. It just went through the glass all by itself. She promised never to do such a thing again.

Everyone was too drained to talk much, but they agreed to meet the next day and make an effort to understand what had happened and the girls finally dragged themselves off to bed.

At their meeting the following day, the girls were contrite. They apologized for their behavior. And for a couple of weeks they were calm and composed, going about their business and expressing appreciation of one another and the staff.

Mary, Patricia and I held an inquest a few days later. We tried to reconstruct the incident, pulling out what we thought were the key elements. We agreed that the girls should have been informed earlier and prepared for Walter's going. But staff members come and go; only the strongest and most qualified persons can stand up to the pressures of helping twelve girls come of age. And even these must sometimes leave for personal and professional reasons, because they need more money than we can pay, because of illness or family problems or to further their education. The girls "broke" (went on the rampage) because they were overburdened with feelings, ready to burst, and we hadn't provided them with a means of ventilating in a safe setting and of then taking in love.

We must watch it and keep the minithons and love-ins going.

"Tell Aldo Reyes for me that as soon as he steps out of the building I'm gonna bash his head in. I'm gonna off that mother-fucker if I have to go to jail for it."

Keith Hornsby, an angry sixteen-year-old, had posted himself outside the building. In his hand was a chunk of concrete, and he looked as if he meant business. There were several thorns in Keith's side, placed there, he believed, by those who hated him and conspired against him, among them Aldo Reyes, director of the Learning for Living program. Aldo had broken up a Five Percenter meeting Keith had tried to hold in one of our group rooms, explaining that we don't allow any sect to preach or proselytize on our premises. Keith was also upset because his mother, a bossy, abusive woman, had put him out of the house a few nights before when he refused to eat some pork she had cooked.

Aldo was told of Keith's threat. He could have called the precinct and had Keith jailed. But there was always the hope that we might get through to Keith. It is our practice to call the police only in extreme emergencies. When someone threatens with a weapon, however, we need help and usually we call.

Aldo went out at once and asked Keith to put down his rock and come inside for a talk. Keith refused.

"I'll talk but I won't put my rock down," he said.

Aldo said, "Okay, wait here. I'll be right back." He went upstairs to the closet where the recreation equipment was kept and got out a baseball bat. Thus armed he went out again to the sidewalk; Keith saw the bat in Aldo's hand.

Aldo said, "I've got my bat, you've got your rock. Now let's talk."

He led the way upstairs to his office. Keith followed. "I won't hurt you, Keith, but I definitely am not going to be hurt. Now why don't you put your rock down?"

Keith put his rock down. There were no peers there to see. He might not have been able to retreat from his macho stance if they had been there watching. Aldo put his bat aside. They talked. "You have a right to your beliefs," Aldo said, "but you can't preach them in here. We do other things at Argus. You can't demand that kids follow along with your cult if they don't want to."

They discussed the ins and outs of this and Keith's other difficulties. He was trying to force his attentions on a girl who didn't want him. Girls had rights, Aldo told him. You can't threaten or force them.

"What are you going to do now that your mother has put you out?" Aldo asked.

Keith said he would like to get a job, try to make it on his own.

Aldo promised to help him. The next day the two of them went to see Marty Wishnoff, the guidance counselor, who sent him over to Kentucky Fried Chicken, where he got a job as a counterman—fast food joints provide an interim job for some kids; they earn the minimum wage and get a taste of reality. It was a relief when Keith left our community.

I sometimes picture the two of them, Keith with his hunk of concrete, looking like one of those mythical lizards that could kill a person by breathing poisonous fire on him, and Aldo with his bat and his tough unruffled gaze; and I have to laugh. Aldo has plenty of brain cells, but he seldom deals in abstractions. He has a genius for acting out the core of any situation in terms that kids can grasp. What he was essentially saying to Keith was: "Look, I learned through experience that force doesn't work too well. No matter who wins in a violent fight, both sides lose. My bat is as good as your rock. We could fight it out but it won't take us where we want to go."

It is significant that Marvin Manders, who had committed more antisocial acts than Keith Hornsby and who was quite capable of committing robberies, nevertheless carried within him a germ of decency and prosocial feeling. His robberies cannot be condoned in any way, yet the truth is that, however misguided, even these violent acts were an attempt to wrest a living from an unyielding environment, to provide for his mother. His concern for other people did not extend beyond the immediate family circle and one or two buddies. But the basis of a broader concern was there and it flowered as he encountered people who were trustworthy and helpful. For Keith the shut-out had been complete. Or so it appeared. What we know is that we did not find a way to reach him. We learned that he became increasingly alcohol and drug dependent and when he was on cocaine or amphetamines, more violent, although he drifted away from the Five Percenters.

When a boy stole a classroom folder containing another student's work, erased the rightful owner's name, substituted his own and claimed credit for the work there was a near fight.

When two girls make eye contact and one makes a gesture of disgust, or is thought to, the other lashes out verbally or physically. It's called "You rolled your eyes at me." The offended party may have heard that the other girl didn't like her or made a critical remark; she might wish that they could be friends but fears the other girl would reject her. Whatever the precipitating incident, when two kids get into it, the counselors immediately separate them from each other and from the onlookers—who take sides, are eager to see a circus and would only cheer them on. The counselors make a quick judgment on the basis of what they know about the kids and their relationship with them, as to which one is most likely to go quietly into an office. The second kid is then taken into another room, away from the peers, to cool off. Then the kids are brought together in one room and each is required to listen while the other talks. Abuse usually subsides and an interchange becomes possible. The counselors keep in mind that the incident that touched off the quarrel is almost invariably a superficial one. Maybe a kid is a role model, close to the counselors, doing well. A girl may be jealous. One may be a scapegoat—no clothes, no status, the typical victim. The counselor will be alert for such situations and for ways to create alternatives.

It is unusual, after kids talk, for them to go at each other again. Just listening to another person is often a new experience for them. They pick up signals they hadn't noticed before. Sometimes they become friends. Almost always the session ends with both of them agreeing that the trouble was really about something besides the trifling incident that set it off. At the least they feel good because they were listened to. There is a kind of respect in that.

We have a rigorous rule against violence. That rule isn't just for kids. It's for the staff as well. But in our staff development sessions, we learn that almost every new staff member or trainee believes that "kicking ass" is a better method of dealing with kids than the ones Argus puts forward. We learn that almost without exception the trainees themselves had undergone severe physical punishment in their own homes or in institutions and that they are bringing up their own children by the same methods. Most have trouble controlling them. As kids grow bigger they become defiant, rebellious, run away. They act out in every conceivable way, sometimes violently. From this parents draw the conclusion that they didn't beat their children often enough or hard enough. But it is not impossible to get them to realize that persuading kids to *want* to behave works better. Staff members and parents see this demonstrated before their eyes as the Argus kids make seemingly miraculous turnabouts in the program. Talking about child-care methods is much less persuasive than seeing the methods carried out and changes taking place.

We have to be doubly careful in screening job applicants who have spent time behind the walls, either as prisoners or as guards. After a while you get a kind of sixth sense about how a potential staff member really feels, deep down, about staff violence. One woman I interviewed had served as a guard for eight years in a women's prison. She had told me on the phone that she wanted to work in a more enlightened and humane environment. She knew all the "right" jargon. I observed her as she entered the building and as she sat in the waiting area; she was a tall, handsome, light-skinned woman, well dressed and impressive. However, an emergency came up and I was twenty minutes late in getting to her. I came out and apologized but observed that a certain steeliness had formed about her jaw. I put out my hand. She took it in hers and crushed it with such force that I involuntarily cried out, "That hurt." She looked at me and laughed. I knew at that moment that whatever patter she might put forth, our kids would probably not fare well at her hands. In the interview, as she began to "race her motor," she revealed that the institution where she had been employed used physical force, punishment and the threat and actuality of staff and peer violence to control the population. Yes, she herself had slapped people and locked them in the hole. "Some people don't respond to any other form of treatment," she said. It is possible that she was making an honest attempt to escape from this tragic cycle, but she showed little awareness, and, in my judgment—and that of senior staff who also interviewed her—she basically looked upon people in prison and youngsters in placement as inferior and herself as entitled under provocation to kick them around because they "deserved" it and "asked" for it. We didn't hire her.

Only three times in our history have staff members struck enrollees. In one case the counselor was sorely provoked. Nevertheless, keeping him would have encouraged the notion that physical violence is a possible—and acceptable—way to deal with Argus enrollees. Besides, it was part of our bargain, when he took the job, that he would not strike the children and that whatever the provocation he would find another way to respond and that we would help him to develop other approaches. But he considered the staff development groups unnecessary, and found an excuse to stay away. Without a safe way to let his own feelings come to the surface and deal with them, he exploded at one of the enrollees and punched her in the jaw. In truth, we should have replaced him as soon as it was evident that he was not going to attend staff development. But he had talent and potential; it is hard to find good people; and we hoped he might come around. He taught us something. Since then, not attending staff development groups is tantamount to walking off the job. And any staff member who hits an enrollee is asked to seek more suitable employment.

Our classrooms are generally free of disorder and violence. The good teachers, those who care, create an atmosphere that is warm and productive. The counselors are available in case an incident does arise. Teachers who are indifferent, bitter and burnt out (we have about three out of fifteen in that state at present) have more incidents, and the counselors pull their chestnuts out of the fire on a fairly regular basis. Since the teachers are paid by the Board of Education and are outstationed on our premises, it is of paramount importance that Argus be allowed to screen them and that they share our philosophy and values. By and large, since 1972, this collaboration has worked well during periods when the principal and the on-site administrator have provided forceful leadership and were backed by the central Board. Our teachers never have to act as disciplinarians or policemen. The classroom never becomes a circus or gladitorial arena. There is practically no abusive language in the classroom. Our enrollees are not angels but once they are past the orientation stage they tend to be serious and to comport themselves properly. The counselors—and the peers—step in to take care of any problem, leaving the teacher free to continue the lesson for those who want to learn.

Recently we moved to a more spacious building, ideally suited to our needs. The Board of Education has asked us to continue collaborating with them and wants to provide more teachers and greater resources. If all goes well there will be a joint staff development program where teachers, as well as Argus staff, can iron out problems, unburden their feelings, refresh themselves, broaden their comprehension of the children and the program and develop bonding. The teachers need this kind of dynamic experience as much as the Argus staff. They get burned out, too.

A teacher who was undergoing a great deal of stress became

snappish and irascible with everybody. One day in class he lost control of himself and struck an enrollee who was in the process of doing the teacher's bidding but was doing it too slowly. Another teacher, also under a lot of pressure from outside forces, "playfully" hit a young man across the buttocks with a ruler.

Both of the incidents could have caused a conflagration but for the self-control and judgment each of the young men displayed. They both flared up. But they didn't act on it. They expressed it another way. In effect, they both said very nearly the same thing: "I'm angry. I'm teed off. I would like to hit you back. I have every reason to hit you back. Three months ago I would have. But now I know what my goals are and how to get there. Hitting a teacher would hurt me a lot worse than it would hurt you. So even though I could mop up the floor with you I'm not going to do it." They had learned well one kind of lesson that Argus has to teach.

Another factor in the ability of these young men to keep cool was that their peers, instead of egging them on to the attack, urged them to "chill out" and keep their eyes on their goals. They said things like "He hit you because he doesn't know any other way to handle himself. You do, because you have learned it here at Argus where you've got a family to tell you how to act. Leave him alone. He's worse off than you are."

We were enormously proud of the forbearance of these young men. We took it as the living proof that our methods work. One of them had been with us a year and a half and was doing well on all fronts, but the other was fairly new to our process. His gang offered to come in and "ice" the teacher, but he told them he had the situation in hand.

They got tons of praise from us. The principal wrote them each a letter of commendation. They remained in the program and achieved their goals. The two teachers got over their stresses and have not laid hands on anyone else. We believe that a joint staff development program would ease many of these stresses and reduce the danger of violence all around.

Basically, we achieve de-escalation of violence (1) by the careful screening out of sadistic or unstable job applicants; (2) by removing the support systems for offensive, defensive and scapegoating behavior; (3) by putting our young people in touch with the very considerable strengths which nearly all of them possess in one form or another and at the same time freeing them from their sense of powerlessness and the rage which is its twin; (4) by providing them with new options and alternatives; (5) by inculcating and modeling nonviolent approaches in human relations.

We have no security guards per se in Argus. No staff is hired for the express purpose of physically controlling, repressing or expressing violence toward the enrollees. The Board of Education recently provided us with two guards but they act more like receptionists and counselors and try to protect our cars from street vandals and thieves. All staff are responsible for maintaining a safe environment *and* attending to the human growth needs of the enrollees. This is a decision of the utmost importance for a program such as ours that asks participants to set aside violence. Responsibility for security *and* growth is lodged in every staff member and, by extension, in every enrollee; in short, in every member of the community.

By this arrangement we avoid schisms among the staff, conflicts of interest between a counseling and a security faction and also the likelihood that the participants would play one side off against the other. In traditional settings the security staff tend to sacrifice the interests of the program for their special and singular goal. Since in these places the program staff does not know how to create a climate of safety and must depend entirely upon security officers to protect them and since security personnel in consequence build up a mystique about their powers and their knowledge, program staff can easily be beaten down in terms of their interests and priorities.

At Argus we confront violence—as we confront every other problem—as a group. Raw recruits from the streets or from institutions find themselves face to face with a wall of strength that does not depend upon counterviolence or the threat of counterviolence but upon purpose, philosophy and consensus; in other words, upon program and bonding or community. Very few persons, no matter what their backgrounds, can remain impervious to the pressure and the attractiveness of these forces.

This is the kind of force that we must bring to bear in a continuum of services for youth and families, in both the child-care "network" (which at present is not a network in any creative sense of the word) and in the juvenile justice "system" (which again is not a system as presently constituted nor very just, often). The gaps, the incongruities, the self-serving aims of these "systems" and their tragic consequences for children and families have been well documented. It is not within the scope of this book to delineate them further. My purpose, rather, is to lay out some counterstrategies that could, were they put into place in a real network of services, conceivably reduce the everyday reality of violence in our schools and in our streets and the time bomb of violence that lies hidden in locked institutions which only temporarily take out of circulation certain of our uncared-for and uncaring youth.

6. THE EYES OF THE PEACOCK
Putting a Positive Peer Group Together

You think you'd be snitchin on somebody, man. You'd be
savin somebody's life.   ARGUS PEER LEADER

"The senior staff had better get together and talk about what's going on in the group home. We've come to the point where we have to take drastic action." It was Mary Taylor who made the suggestion, voicing what was in all of our minds.

Earlier that day Mary, Don Cole and I had talked to three of the younger, less street-wise girls from the home. What they told us, if it proved to be true, was serious indeed.

It was the winter of 1974, cold and gloomy. When we gathered for our meeting at 2:00 P.M. we didn't mind being sequestered in that soundproof room without windows. We had a long session ahead of us, and there was no sense in looking out at yesterday's snowfall already sludged with grime and garbage. The room was dead quiet except for the purling of fresh air through ducts in the ceiling. There were six of us sitting in a circle: Mary Taylor, Donald Cole, Aldo Reyes, Aubrey LaFrance, Kate Woodbridge, then director of the group home program, and myself.

"I'm sure we are all aware that no one is present from the on-site group home staff," I began. "Kate has been meeting with them on a regular basis and, as you know, the senior staff has had quite a few sessions in the last three months with Milagros, the social worker. These meetings have not been productive. The housemanager, Reina, has been out for days. Does anyone know where she is?"

"Milagros says that Reina is sick. But when I call her home there is no answer. There is no record in the log of her having called in," Kate said. She looked as though she had been transported from Camelot—reddish gold hair, milky skin sprinkled with freckles and blue eyes. Nothing dashed the warmth of her smile. But we knew that Kate was concerned. A professor's daughter and a product of the best schools, Kate was a diplomat and mediator, a valued link with officialdom and the world outside the South Bronx. She understood Argus

79

and was a part of us. She had helped us to be born and to shape ourselves.

"We must all be thinking the same thing," Mary said. "We've put so much of our lifeblood into this group home, and after six months and one crisis after another we have reached a point where it's going down the drain."

Mary is about five feet five inches, in her early forties, light-skinned, with a lamb's wool Afro sculpted over a wide face, a generous mouth, and warm, lively eyes. The copper and silver jewelry which ornamented her neck and her shapely, flexible hands had been bought on a recent trip to Nigeria. She loves to venture into exotic places, and everywhere she visits programs for young people and gets a sense of family life and institutions. Aside from getting a master's degree in social work, she has immersed herself, along with me, in Dr. Casriel's New Identity Therapy. Her combination of background, credentials and street savvy makes Mary uniquely valuable to Argus.

Don Cole laid out the situation. His dark force and velvet softness reminded me of a sable antelope—but watch out: a sable is more than a match for a lion. "None of us will ever forget the sheer unmitigated hell that we went through to get this first group home open last August," he said. "Three years of agonizing preparation, acquiring the building. That was a saga. Being told by the city for a whole year that they owned it and discovering at the last moment that it still belonged to the bank. Elizabeth, you and I had to hit the foundation trail and beg for the money to pay off the liens and back taxes. Whoo! I'll never forget it. There were other nightmares. Like getting those masses of papers together. Kate, I know you're aware of that part of it. We had to devise a program—our grand experiment. We had to get everything into the pipeline at once: raise funds for the renovation, keep the money flowing, assemble a crew of honest journeymen, guard the work site round the clock for two years. Then, struggling with contractors. Some merely *tried* to rip us off, and some succeeded, I regret to say. And the supposedly simple act of getting our hands on the city code governing the construction of group homes. That required a full year of negotiating, dogging officials, pleading, beseeching, baring our throats one minute, throwing temper tantrums the next, pulling strings, threatening to go to the governor, the president and God himself. The Building Department insisted that there was no legal category called group home, and therefore they had no code for it. They were right. There *was* no provision in the code for group homes, and the city council was in no hurry to create one. But we were being asked by Special Services for Children, a city agency, to develop a group home program."

"Sheer lunacy as usual," I remarked.

"Absolutely," Kate said. "However, we went ahead and re-habbed the building as a multiple dwelling, following the state guide-lines on space, safety and fire regulations. We took a big chance."

"Sho. We were lucky," Don said. "If we had waited for them to settle their squabbles. . . . But we stuck our necks on the block. How come it's people like us, on the front lines, under fire and not exactly overflowing with money, who have to take the risks?"

We sat for a moment recalling the antiquated, creaking process of getting the building approved once the rehab job was complete. Inspectors had their hands out and dragged their heels when we refused to ante up. We had sworn never to pay a bribe, and we never have on any of our building projects before or since. But it was by the skin of our teeth. Tony Bouza, then police chief of the Bronx, sent a captain in full regalia, plastered with medals, to sit in our meetings with the inspectors to let them know that the chief was keen on getting the group home open for the children of the South Bronx. They finally caved in and got the approvals to us.

When at last the house was ready and beautiful beyond our expectations, we invited those who had helped us, regaled them with soul food, beans and rice, pasteles and wine punch. There were speeches, tears and elation.

"We thought the hard traveling was behind us," Aubrey said, with a wry laugh. "Now look where we are."

"The group home is just a mini-snake pit, like so many others," Don said.

"That's right. We've got a staff that is into negative contracts or has totally abdicated and a negative peer group running the place," I said. "We've become a prime example of all the problems we set out to overcome. What we need to talk about is how we got that way and what we can do about it."

"We haven't got a counselor there who is worth hot shit," Aldo remarked. "We've got a boozed-up housemanager who is never there and a social worker who is full of revolutionary grandstanding. She thinks if you give the girls everything they never had and love them enough and never make demands they'll settle down and become angels. I haven't seen any signs of it yet. They're getting worse. We've got a bunch of young ladies who come in to pick up their allowance and complain about the food and how we keep them in rags. They smoke chiba, snort cocaine when they can afford it and bully and harass the staff. They never sit down to a meal together. I say, let's make a clean sweep of everything over there, staff and girls, and start over again." Aldo made a large gesture with his arms. "And when we do it again, let's do it our way."

"Aldo is right," Aubrey said. His tone was fervent but he relinquished none of his composure. Shifting the weight of his long body, he leaned forward, an intense, questioning expression in his slightly protruding eyes. "We've lost control. It is not possible to say whether we could have done any better with our plan, which entailed building a positive peer group, slowly and painfully, brick by brick. But I am reasonably certain that if we had been allowed to do it our way, things would be better over there."

Mary proposed that we send Aldo to observe and gather facts for a week. Although Aldo was up to his ears in work, he agreed to do it. The remainder of the discussion centered on the alternatives that were open to us: (1) admit that the odds against us were too great and close the group home; (2) get rid of the present staff and try another round with a new staff of the type permitted by the regulatory agencies; (3) take a chance, put in the kind of staff we believed could do the job and hope that by the time the monitors got around to reviewing us again, we'd have such a positive atmosphere in the house that they would not be able to resist it.

If Aldo's findings confirmed our misgivings, we would have no choice but to replace the staff. The discussion heated up around the issue of what the new staff should be. None of us believed that changing one group of middle-class, traditionally educated people for another would make a crucial difference. We might get individuals who were stronger, more integrated. But would they have the stamina and the street smarts to stand up to the manipulations, wrong-headedness and abuse of the girls—or the magnetism and warmth to pull them into our orbit?

"We know what we have to do and how to go about it," Mary said. "It's a question of whether we will be allowed to do it. I say we should try it our way, and if they do close us down, at least we will have shown *somebody,* even if it's only ourselves, that it's possible to run a group home that's more than a warehouse and a crash pad for a bunch of tough, acting-out adolescents."

What to do with the acting-out girls who now ruled the roost at 402 East 156th Street? Don, Kate and I thought it would not be fair to kick them out, though it would mean a lot of hard work to bring them into line. Aldo, Mary and Aubrey were afraid that if the strong negative leaders remained, they would jeopardize our chances of setting up positive peer control.

"Since they're already *there* and in control and used to kickin the staff's ass, they'll die rather than give up."

The discussion went on, with occasional confrontations and fireworks, but got nowhere.

"Let's defer the decision until Aldo investigates and gets back to us," I suggested. "Maybe then we'll reach a consensus."

After two days Aldo reported that affairs in the group home were worse than we had thought. One girl was prostituting herself on 125th Street and Lexington Avenue, absent from the group home from 11:00 P.M. to 7:00 A.M., using her earnings to keep herself in chiba round the clock and her blind father, who was on SSI, in Night Train, the cheap fortified wine in which he soaked himself.

"Lord, the taxpayers are spending roughly $16,000 a year on this fourteen-year-old girl, believing she is receiving intensive care," Don moaned. (By 1983 the cost of keeping a child in intensive care had risen to $19,879.)

Aldo had discovered that our social worker already had another job and that took care of that. We decided on a compromise: we would introduce some of our methods and one or two of our type of staff. Don Cole would take charge. The present housemanager and the child-care workers would be replaced with people we thought could learn our methods, whether they had formal credentials or not. The only way we would get the negative peer leaders out would be to bring them before the Family Court on juvenile delinquency charges. None of the staff was willing to do this.

Training sessions for the new staff were stepped up. By sheer force of his personality Don emboldened them to stand up to the girls, to insist that the rules be obeyed.

John Dixon and Gary Stovall, two hefty males, who were full-time employees at the Learning for Living Center, were given rent-free living quarters in the group home in exchange for maintaining the premises, acting as weekend and backup staff and helping out in emergencies. In addition to being a skilled journeyman, John was a philosopher and a burning ray of intellect in an irrational world. He had the English language by the tail.

During the first three weeks of the new regime angry girls kicked or knocked out eleven windows. After replacing the eleventh broken pane, John called the girls and the staff together.

"I appreciate the fact that you are in a state of frustration," he said. "Any alteration in the environment arouses resentment. The human organism seeks homeostasis—psychologically as well as biologically, if you can speak of those two separately, which I doubt. I am not infrequently frustrated myself. I understand your in-dwelling urge to overthrow the regime in this group home. I am reasonably certain that you will not succeed for the simple reason that you are up against a new kind of power. Be that as it may, I feel obligated to pass along one piece of information. It concerns my own state of equilibrium and Gary's. We are fed to the gills with replacing window panes. As of this moment, we are on strike. If any more windows are broken we will not repair them. And, dear young ladies, let me remind you: it is twelve degrees outside. You will freeze your charming little rear ends off in here."

The girls listened, but they were getting another kind of message. As soon as John stopped talking they burst out.

"I don't know what you're talking bout, honey, but I love your charisma!"

"He's cute!"

"Don't he look death!"

"Your contours are fabulous, sweetheart!"

"Yeah, you're on the money!"

For whatever reason, John made an overwhelming impression. No more windows were broken.

The girls fell under Don Cole's spell also. He was an irresistible father figure. Even the tough peer leaders, though they didn't immediately change *what* they were doing, went about it in a different spirit. They seemed to enjoy being caught, lectured and disciplined by Don. He ran the place like an old-fashioned patriarch, strict but kindly and loving. He lectured and scolded them, spent hours reasoning with them, persuading them to do what was in their own best interest. He told them, "Look, I will never give up on you. Under that hard image, you are sweet lovely young girls. That's the part of you that I'm addressing myself to. I know you're going to hear me."

Wherever Don was, at the group home or at the Learning for Living Center, the girls gathered around him. He gave them little treats, took them to lunches and movies and sometimes theaters and concerts. They called him their daddy. Day and night (Don kept a hot line open for them) they poured their grievances, their frustrations, their fury and their love for him into his ears.

Three girls absconded during the next six months. Others left for one reason or another. (Three of the "worst" girls turned out well: one graduated from college, one is working in a bank, one is a nurse.) The girls who replaced them came into a stricter and more loving atmosphere and, however tough and rough they were, never dared—and perhaps never quite wanted—to act in the same way.

Heroically, and almost single-handedly, by his determination, his compassion and the benevolent regard he had for the girls, Don brought the group home under control and blew the breath of decency and goodwill into it. It was an incredible feat, but it wasn't right or workable over the long haul because the job is too hard for any one person. Without the active cooperation and participation of at least a core group of the residents in a live-in setting, the staff will either melt like snowflakes on a sizzling stove or if they are tougher and more enduring burn themselves to a frazzle.

We had all been mesmerized by the energy with which Don had thrown himself into the task of putting the group home to rights. He seemed to be performing miracles. And he was. But the cost was too great. His health broke down. When he went into the hospital with high blood pressure, we were anxious both for him and for the group home. Girls and staff fell apart, for he had been a powerful father figure to all of them. We realized at last that we had no choice but to put our full plan into effect: to bring on board a staff who could put a positive peer group together, "brick by brick," as Aubrey had said, and use the positive peers to help us run the place.

Kate Woodbridge got married that year and moved to Colorado. Lorraine Mayfield, a young black sociologist working toward her doctorate, tall and queenly and a diplomat, joined our staff. Lorraine kept the paper trails open and backed up the staff. She won the respect of the girls without ever having to get tough.

Mary Taylor took over as director of the group home program. Her main task was the creation of the positive peer group, which would insure support for the staff. She also concentrated on building knowledge, competence, self-reliance and peer support and bonding *among the staff*—another source of refreshment (and energy) which would make their labors more fruitful. To understand what Mary did, and how it was done, it is necessary to review some of the things we know about peer groups.

Argus subscribes to the view of many social scientists and primatologists that the group is of major importance to human development, survival, and inventiveness.[1] The survival group among early hominids (humanlike ancestors of people) may not have differed greatly from today's adolescent peer groups who seek relatedness, a life of action and a means of exploiting the environment. For various reasons the group is more pervasive and more powerful among blue-collar workers and the poor, whereas the individual functions fully only in the peer group.[2] Peer groups may or may not be negative but often they hold members in bondage, forcing them to choose between expulsion from the group and developing an intellectual or artistic talent or entering a profession that is seen as "square" or effeminate. Schools and programs have generally encouraged young people to cut their ties with the peer group, setting them perhaps on the road to a career but leaving them empty and unsatisfied emotionally.

Argus works against street peer groups, which are negative. From 1974 to 1976 we were in an area, around 161st Street and St. Ann's Avenue, where seven gangs operated. At one point the Black Spades kidnapped four Argus teenagers who they thought were wearing the colors of rival gangs and took them to a vacant building. Two were discovered to be unaffiliated and were released. They ran back to Argus, told us what happened and, with police, guided us to the two remaining prisoners. But not before gang members had stuck needles into their ears and under their nails and had burned and beaten them. The youngsters who defied a threat of death to lead us to the gang headquarters had to leave town for an extended period. The two victims might have died had it not been for the heroism of their peers who had been weaned away from their former gangs and had identified with Argus peer groups.

Some agencies work with street gangs as entities, in the hope that they can be turned around. This tactic, widely used during the explosion of gang activity in the mid-seventies, strengthens the identity of the gang and accomplishes very little that is positive, despite glorified stories in the media. We were told of whole gangs diverted to positive activities, but when we looked into such reports, we found that a prosocial jargon was thrown up for accommodation and manipulation and that behind it the same negative forces were operating. We would not dream of admitting a whole gang or any sizable portion of it into Argus at one time. It would be dangerous and not effective. Our environment could not gulp down and digest such a large wad. Our strategy, instead, has been to identify kingpin gang members, lure them into Argus and enfold them. These were often presidents or warlords who came to Argus to hide out or because they imagined we were another rip-off program or a bunch of sentimental weaklings. But when they found themselves up against formidable ex-street people *plus* the strength and charisma of the program itself, they were outwitted and outmaneuvered at every turn and became fascinated with power used in a new way to different ends. The old bonds can be cast off if there are new and satisfying ones to take their place. Once the gang leaders were inside many of the foot soldiers followed. The old street gangs were weakened or fell apart from lack of leaders and followers.

Using these methods we made substantial inroads into the gang activity of that time and place, and the police gave us credit for it. But like fireweeds that spring up on burned and tortured ground, street gangs will flourish, die down and flourish again until we change the conditions that give rise to them.

When Mary went over to the group home she concentrated on developing peer leaders from among the girls. Some counselors act like superparents. That may be helpful in a way, but it has its limitations and its risks. The young people may transfer their dependency to this new focal point, snuggle in and stay put; the superparent herself (or himself) will expend an inhuman amount of energy and burn out.

Mary picked out the most sincere residents and gave them responsible jobs. One was made house captain; another was put in charge of supplies (shampoos, soap, cosmetics, etc.); a third was assigned to keep on hand and give out snacks; a fourth prepared the breakfast. These were positions of importance carrying power and prestige and an augmentation of the weekly allowance. In order to keep their jobs, the girls were told, they had to maintain a high level of deportment and take responsibility for themselves and other residents. Besides, Mary explained, she could not run the house without their help.

Each girl in the house was assigned to a certain level, depending on her behavior, attitude and willingness to set goals and work toward them. (These levels are described in Chapter 7).

Two group meetings were set up. The first, on Monday from 6:00 P.M. to 8:00 P.M., dealt with peer issues and behavior. Girls and staff brought up their gripes and problems. Things that had gone wrong were discussed. Confrontation was encouraged and girls got a lot of anger out but were pushed into a recognition of how their behavior affects other people. An attempt was made to deal with and reconcile feelings and issues and to get the parties to make commitments that could carry their interactions to a more satisfactory level. The second group meeting, on Thursday, at the same hour, resolved unfinished business from Monday night. Also, some girls needed to be prepared for the weekend—for visits to relatives, dates with boyfriends. The main purpose of the Thursday group was to help the girls get in touch with here-and-now feelings on a deeper level. Personal and family matters were brought up; these were sensitive issues and needed a lot of time. Because of this, the group was divided into two sections of six girls each.

In these groups girls learned to be the bearers of values, structures and techniques. They became as fearless as the group leaders in being honest, sharing themselves and accepting other people's feelings. At first they dumped on each other indiscriminately and used the groups solely to get their anger out, to punish those who had offended them or to try and get people they didn't like in trouble. Counselors had to be in touch with themselves and with what was going on so that nobody got "rat packed." At the same time they let the kids know that it's okay to express whatever feelings they have. They may be angry for the wrong reasons, but the *feeling* is valid. Often it is unfinished childhood business invested irrelevantly in the here-and-now. On the other hand, there may be a real grievance, and though the reaction may be overcharged, it is important to recognize the reality. Just plain dumping is necessary at times, particularly for these kids who have many residual feelings, but they need to learn the difference between coming off on someone and confronting a person constructively and finding a way to help that person. Usually, the kids learn this as it is modeled for them by skilled counselors. A counselor knows how—and teaches the kids how—to convey the message, "You are a good and worthwhile person. It's some of the things you're *doing* that we're criticizing."

Often pain lies behind the anger, as well as a fear of expressing it in any form but action. Once this bottle has been uncapped, and the feelings pour out—the pain, the fear and the need—bonding can take place. The overwhelming need then is to be held, cuddled and loved.[3]

All of this is very scary—and very attractive. The kids grumbled and complained about groups when Mary first went to the group home. But before long they began to use them and to depend on them to let out bad feelings and to get good feelings. Soon the tension level in the house was lower. The girls expressed more loving feelings in everyday life. Their quarrels and fights were less desperate because the parties could hope to settle their disputes in group. As they developed their own powers and resources competition for staff attention —and the demands on staff to settle quarrels—became less acute.

In putting the positive peer group together Mary was assisted by Learning for Living Center staff who came over evenings and weekends to act as supplementary staff and as co-leaders in groups.

One of the toughest barriers to break through in getting kids to be honest and to confront one another is the street code of silence. At first they see it as "ratting," "snitching" or "dropping a dime," and they don't want any part of it. Another reason for ex-street people in leadership positions. They deal with this reluctance in vivid ways, by showing what can happen if you don't speak up.

In the early days of Argus a young girl took an "overdose" of heroin and died. Her close friend came to group devastated by guilt, crying and feeling utterly miserable: he had known about her habit but had kept it to himself. Now she was dead and the counselors and peers who might have helped could do nothing.

Alton Croly was getting high and riding the trains in the railroad yards. His friends knew but refused to "snitch." They didn't confront him about it in group. One night Alton and his pals climbed on top of a moving car. Alton fell off, the wheels rolled over his arm and severed it. His "friends" realized that they could have helped him by speaking up and that by remaining silent they had contributed to the accident that crippled him for life.

You have to paint a vivid picture of the harm that may come from not assuming responsibility for another person. The contracts have to be uncovered and dealt with. "I won't rat on you, don't you rat on me." It is important to let everyone know when someone is slipping and sliding so that people can reach out and do something. In the South Bronx tragedy strikes quickly.

A trainee was hanging out with a dangerous hoodlum. His friends knew it but said nothing. A few weeks later his body was found. He had been stabbed forty-seven times.

A framework for the creation of a positive peer group is one thing; putting these ideas into practice is another. Sometimes the child-care workers don't understand why they are being asked to do certain things. They have been told the reasons but they haven't sunk in. They will learn from experience, but there is a lag. During that time they often feel scared, abandoned, resentful. In the early days we didn't have a smooth running, orderly house to point to. Today we can say to new staff, "See, it works," and it's fairly convincing. But during our start-up period we had nothing to show but kids running wild. It seemed as if the rebellion would never end. In the group home girls went AWOL whenever they pleased and snapped their fingers at the staff. If we tried to interfere there was bedlam.

Mary Taylor recalls that early period. "I was *scared*. The girls were used to having their own way. They had gotten a lot by intimidation, and they weren't about to give it up. They rebelled violently against the on-site staff. When that staff began to make demands on them, the girls would scream, holler and curse. I didn't know if they were going to hit me. If you don't think that's scary, try it sometime."

Both Mary Taylor and Mary Fritz remember general melees— someone in the bathroom cutting herself; someone else drinking a bottle of Florida water cologne, another girl running out in the street screaming. And it would go on hour after hour. Even after a positive peer group was established and the atmosphere was generally calm, there were occasional outbreaks.

Mary Taylor recalls an incident which underlines the choices a child-care worker has to make and how easy it is to abdicate, to wash your hands of any real responsibility and act the part of a custodian. The incident involved fifteen-year-old Darlene Brian, a very pretty waif who had made serious suicide attempts in between bouts with the bottle and various men who wore her in their buttonholes like a badge of machismo. Darlene came in drunk one night. Mary told her she was not permitted to drink. Darlene broke a mirror, picked up a shard of glass and came at Mary. Frightened, Mary ran for John Dixon, who was on call. Together Mary and John talked Darlene into dropping the broken glass, got her into her room and to bed. But they were drained in the process. The following Saturday night Mary was again on duty. She found Darlene in front of the record player, snapping her fingers, dancing and singing, which she loved to do. The only problem was that once again she was drinking. Mary smelled it on her and hesitated, remembering last week's scene. She was tempted to ignore the situation this time and go about her business. No one would have known.

"Darlene did not know that I knew that she was drinking. But everything hung in the balance, not just with Darlene, but with the whole house. If I let her off, if I swept her wrongdoing under the carpet, everything we were trying to build could go down the drain because *I* would feel differently. It would mean that I was acting off a different principle. So, weary as I was, I turned off the record player and confronted her. It was quite a scene. But you know what? Darlene gave up and went to her room. I knew then that we had begun a new phase with her."

At the time Mary Taylor, who had become director, was taking a shift in the group home to cover a staff shortage but also to experience firsthand what the child-care workers go through. Any administrator interested in building a positive atmosphere and a growth experience in a child-care setting should be on the scene enough to participate in problems in person. Mary Fritz, the present director of the Argus group home program, and Charlotte Bowman, the assistant director, fill in on shifts from time to time for the same reasons.

Mary Taylor: "It's important to understand the terror that child-care workers face. That's a very real thing. The child-care workers in some programs actually get hurt."

Only rarely has an Argus Youth staff member been hit by a group home girl and only in the process of stopping a child from hurting herself. One might suppose that this is because we restrict ourselves to girls, but some of our girls have hit staff in previous placements. In fact, some of them were famous for it. Almost anyone in the field will tell you that girls are harder to handle in house than boys, perhaps because girls let out their frustrations at home while boys use street crime as an outlet. One reason we have so little violence at Argus is that our staff is trained to show concern even while delivering a reprimand.

Mary Taylor: "Staff in a lot of group homes don't know how to give love *while* giving a pull up. They don't know how to express angry concern which the kids experience as love. The staff in those places have not been taught how to give angry concern to another person nor have they experienced it themselves."

This is a part of the Argus experiential staff training that takes place in formal sessions each week, and through on-the-job training as well.

The first big breakthrough with the girls came when they expressed anger at Flavia Jackson for staying out, reverting to her old street ways and coming in drunk and dirty, like a stray cat. The girls made Flavia admit that she *needed* the group home, that she had nowhere else to go, and that she wanted to come back.

"When the girls did that," Mary Taylor says, "we knew we were on our way. When Flavia broke down, the girls comforted her, took her into their bosom. That was the moment when the positive peer group took hold."

"Another milestone was when Chessie shared in group that she was really scared and lonely," Mary Fritz recalls. "You remember how angry Chessie was, how belligerent and abusive? Well, she told the girls she needed them and she confessed she needed the group too. It was a big turning point because Chessie had been a negative peer leader of the tough charismatic type. Frankly, I doubted whether we would ever get through to her. But we did and once she came around, other girls followed her lead. Part of it is they need to feel safe."

Once the kids are convinced that the staff is not going to hurt them and that they really care and are capable of providing a safe environment, then an alliance can be formed and the value system and the behavior of the staff become acceptable and even desirable models. Our staff generally have warm, attractive personalities and the method itself is exciting. There is relief in allowing yourself to become a part of something. And there are security and pleasure too. Once some of the kids get involved and say, "Okay, this thing is *mine;* I'm doing it because I like it," then the other kids follow. It is easier to accept it from one of their own. When this happens, the street code is broken. Confrontations among girls begin to show concern and caring instead of an "I'm out to hang you" attitude. Each time they take a step outside the old code they are less scared, more sure. A feeling of sisterhood grows up. They make pets of the younger girls, begin to bring them along, insisting that they behave themselves.

All of the links in the chain are vital, but none more so than the part played by administration. If the top people do not grasp the concept, if they do not foster the process all the way, it cannot get off the ground.

Mary Taylor: "When child-care workers are out there, facing hostility and abuse, they need to know that they are working within a structure where they are valued and appreciated. They need to feel that they are marching in step with the whole staff. When the administration doesn't know what is going on, when they aren't in touch with what the child-care workers are up against, when they don't know how to provide a structure or methods or the right training, when they don't know how to develop a positive peer group, then everybody's in trouble."

Child-care workers in other settings, Mary Taylor has found, would generally like to help the children but they don't know how. Their main concern is for their own safety. One child-care worker or counselor is no match for a bunch of wrongheaded, negative, hostile kids. The kids know their power. And they know when the institution is weak. They are clever at sizing up an environment. They recognize that the staff in some places are on their own. The administration is far removed and doesn't know the problems. There is no consistent set of values, no common philosophy or methods. One staff member does it one way, another has a different idea. The kids encounter one approach on the night shift, another in the morning. One person is permissive, another is strict. Still another may be tippling on duty and hardly aware of what is going on. The kids play off staff members against one another. And they manipulate the administration.

Mary Taylor: "Administration is not *with* the child-care workers in any useful way. The workers are out there by themselves in a little piece of space. When the residents and the child-care workers clash, the workers don't know which side the administration will take. Administration has no idea what the staff has to do to get children out of bed, to get them to school on time, to get them to do their chores. The kids compete with the child-care workers. They go over their heads. If they topple them and get the administration's approval, they say, 'You ain't got no juice no way.' The administrators stand on the mountain top and say, 'What is the staff doing? They can't get the kids to behave themselves.' But child-care workers have needs too. Just like the kids need, they need. They need to feel that same kind of supportive concern that the kids get. They need to be *taught* and strengthened and supported. Administration has to do this."

In her evaluation of a staff training project funded by DFY and Huntington Associates, Dr. Michelle Fine found that child-care workers feel helpless and can't do their jobs when they do not have the proper training and the support of the entire agency. They blame themselves and also quite often blame the children they should be helping for their failures.[4] In order to provide the staff with knowledge and support, administrators themselves must have a thorough knowledge and appreciation of the problems and the process. They must have ongoing training and be willing to get into the fray when necessary. Without this we will continue to pour money into a child-care system which at best is merely custodial and at worst subjects children and staff to indignities, dangers and tragedies more destructive than the environment from which the children have been "rescued."

By training, supporting and backing up the child-care workers and counselors, by undergoing training themselves and by staying close to the situation, administration can turn this negative situation around. And child-care workers can realize how important their role is and can get the backup they need.

An agency must be unified, in close touch from top to bottom and know what its values are before it can develop a positive peer group among the adolescents in its charge. Putting a positive peer group together depends on every other positive thing being in place. You can't have a positive peer group in the midst of conflict or moral wishywashiness.

The messages Argus sends out are (1) we as a staff accept and find rewarding certain ways of behaving and certain values, which include obeying the rules, refraining from harming ourselves or anyone else and being honest and open with ourselves and other people; (2) we accept and like you as persons, and we believe in your potential and want you to change so that you can realize that potential; (3) we are strong, and we are gathering power around us; (4) the old negative ways are dangerous and unsatisfying and lead to a dead end; (5) we are offering safe and creative alternatives and real choices; and (6) our way is attractive, it's terrific; you'll find it's fun to be a part of us.

For the group home we took a ball of starter dough from the

Learning for Living Center—a little yeast, as it were, and made a new batch of bread. But what about the Learning for Living Center? How did we manage to get that going? In pretty much the same way, except that it took longer because we had to generate the starter dough ourselves. After about three years we got it fermenting. Then we had to keep it alive and provide the kneading, the rising and a baking oven of the right temperature.

The Greek myth has it that Argus, giant of many eyes, was lulled to sleep by music and murdered. A compassionate goddess, not wishing this marvel to pass from the world, gathered up the eyes of the giant and placed them in the tail of the peacock, a bird of transcendent beauty that for our community symbolizes insight, awareness and concern—and also the pride and vigilance of our extended family and peer-supported environment. At Argus we try to restore sight to the "dead" eyes of the peers.

7. GROUP HOME STRUCTURE
A Total Environment

I am like an ocean
my mind flows
like the waves of blue
and sometimes like the waves
of darkness most of the
time   I am hid away in my
Closet of Secrets. Secrets
that I hold inside
of me for many years
and the only person
or thing that knows my
Secrets is my Closet where
I sit every night.

Poem by ARGUS GIRL,
age 12

Working with children eight hours a day is one kind of scenario; being responsible for them around the clock until they reach their majority is another. Important as structure is in the Learning for Living Center, it is even more so in the group home program. For this reason, I will describe it in some detail, along with the routines and the process which accompany it.

REFERRAL

Most of our girls are abused, neglected, abandoned or PINS, twelve through seventeen years of age. We can continue to provide live-in care for girls eighteen to twenty-one if they are in college, advanced training or some other productive situation. We can take girls into group home placement at eighteen if they are transferred from another child-care agency funded by Special Services for Children (SSC), which is part of the New York City Human Resources Administration (HRA).

When a girl is referred to us we ask ourselves the following questions:

95

1. Has she been rejected by other agencies? If she were not accepted by Argus, would she be relegated to a public shelter or training school?

2. Is she functioning below grade level as a result of little support at home, chronic truancy, a learning disability, mild retardation or brain damage or some other condition? Would she be helped by having the Argus Learning for Living facility available to her?

3. Does she have physical problems, such as partial loss of sight, impaired speech, asthma, epilepsy, diabetes, blood, heart, skin or endocrinological disorders that we are equipped to deal with but that might make placement elsewhere difficult?

4. Does she defy authority, run away, engage in sexual promiscuity, use drugs?

5. Has she attempted suicide, been assaultive or set fires?

If the answer to one or more of the above questions is yes, Argus will accept the girl. In fact, our residential program, funded by SSC, was started with the express purpose of providing a home for girls who were not acceptable to traditional child-care agencies. These agencies developed their methods in an era when fewer adolescents were in care and when the children who needed homes were nothing like the disruptive and sometimes desperate children of today. Public agencies, such as Special Services for Children and the State Division for Youth, are required by law to provide care for any child who cannot be placed elsewhere. The voluntary agencies reject children with severe behaviorial problems, so the public agencies become dumping grounds. Some severely acting-out youngsters get "stuck" in city diagnostic centers which, though run by knowledgeable and compassionate people, are not able to offer the long-term solution so sorely needed. In other institutions youngsters are controlled with heavy tranquilizers and lock-ups. This is inhumane and costly in the long run. Society needs a broader capability for working constructively with troublesome young persons.

Argus is not set up to handle severely retarded, brain-damaged or psychotic persons. By psychotic we mean either manic depressive or the seriously disturbed thought patterns and hallucinations not resulting from drug use, controlled only by those drugs that act specifically to compensate schizophrenic symptoms. It has been our experience that such persons cannot respond productively in our environment and, in fact, are agitated by it. We are not equipped to care for and do not accept into our group homes those who are dysfunctional from such disorders as cystic fibrosis, muscular and neurological disorders and cerebral palsy.

We do accept those with a range of behavioral and emotional problems at times misdiagnosed as schizophrenia and have found, when medication has been discontinued, that they respond to our environment.

We take into consideration the fact that our youngsters and their families have been buffeted by migration, unemployment, ethnic and economic discrimination and the disintegration of their kinship and social networks. Many parents and family members have been caught up in drugs, alcohol and ill health. With little to lean upon, these children become overly self-reliant and are apt to mistrust adults. This requires patience and special handling. They can become enraged, depressed, dissociated or depersonalized, which frightens the staff and makes them think the kids are crazy. They act out also in the form of marijuana and alcohol abuse, promiscuity, destruction of property, theft, fire setting, assaultiveness and running away. In Argus, as these children become bonded to others in trust and affection, they experience remorse and welcome the opportunity to expiate their guilt in a group setting. Their maladaptive coping mechanisms generally are discarded in response to our process and the warm environment we try to maintain. I say "try to" because, given the obstacles in our path, including red tape, excessive paperwork, the perils of the job and the low salaries of people on the firing line, our effectiveness is constantly undermined, and we are forced to spend almost as much energy keeping a staff together as we do on the children. We recognize our obligation to protect and support the staff as well as the children.

Referral materials are sent to us from Special Services for Children, the Family Court and the voluntary child-care agencies. If there are no vacancies and none are anticipated, the materials are returned with a letter of explanation. If there are vacancies we fill them, accepting the youngster sight unseen. Our practice is that once we ask a girl to visit the program, she is free to accept or reject us, but we do not turn her away, for to do so would add another layer of pain and rejection to the burden she already carries.

At the beginning we chose girls because we liked working with them and because there were a greater number of girls than boys for whom proper placement was unavailable. Girls tend to be more difficult in residence than boys. They have been subjected to a double dose of discrimination—as females and as members of minority groups—and they tend to express their turmoil and rebelliousness by in-house acting out, whereas boys are likely to express theirs in street crime and antisocial acts in the community. Argus will shortly open a facility for twenty-four hard-to-place boys and we will have a better basis of comparison.

PRE-PLACEMENT VISIT

Whenever possible, a prospective resident is given a tour of the group home, is introduced to the girls and the staff and is given time to decide whether she wants to accept placement, thus getting a sense of control over her destiny. Occasionally a girl who has been in a group home where there is no curfew and where she could come and go at will rejects Argus as being too strict. And we have been rejected by girls who refuse to live in the South Bronx. But most girls decide to accept placement. Although they grumble about the structure, they really like it because it makes them feel safe. Many of them have been in situations where verbal and physical abuse, sexual molestation and even rape were commonplace.

SETTING

When we opened the doors of our first group home in 1974, the neighborhood at Melrose Avenue and 156th Street, an area about twenty blocks from the Learning for Living Center, was relatively intact. People in the area were sympathetic and kept a watchful eye on our building sites. Melrose Avenue, with its busline, intersects seven blocks to the south with other busy thoroughfares—149th Street and Third, Willis and Westchester avenues—to form the Hub, the traditional business and entertainment center of the South Bronx. The group homes are within easy reach of the Hub and yet sufficiently removed from its hectic milieu, where black and hispanic mores meet and sometimes clash. Within a stone's throw of our two group homes are a post office, a Pentecostal church, Saint Albanese's Roman Catholic Church, and an elementary school with a community center where our girls attend dances. At 161st Street and Melrose Avenue is Pyramid House, a State Division for Youth facility with a swimming pool and gymasium to which we have access. The plague of fire setting has left only two apartment buildings intact and fully occupied on our block, and the blackened rubble which dominates the scene is dispiriting. However, the South Bronx Local Initiative Support Corporation, the Community Board, the School District and Father Louis Gigante's housing rehab efforts are making their influence felt and the neighborhood is slated for redevelopment. We look forward to better times.

THE BUILDING AND LIVING QUARTERS

Argus One, the first group home, was rehabbed and began to operate in 1974. Argus Two, rehabbed in 1978, abuts Argus One. The two houses are connected by a door at the kitchen and dining level. The evening meal for both houses is prepared in Argus One by a cook; girls share in the preparation of breakfast, lunch and snacks. The two houses function as separate entities but they join together for parties, dances, discos and talent shows. The connecting door allows the staff to pass from house to house without going into the street, which can be dangerous. Since the girls in the two houses are on different levels of growth and since our process demands that they interact primarily with peers and staff in their separate houses, we do not allow them to intermingle on a daily basis. Each house has a large, comfortably furnished living room, a dining room, a kitchen, a pantry, a laundry room, and bedrooms where twelve girls sleep, two and sometimes three in a room. Each girl has her own bed, chest, desk, chair, bookcase, lamp and closet space. There are ample bathroom facilities for the girls and staff in each house.

STAFF LIVING QUARTERS AND ARRANGEMENTS

The overall staff includes a program director, a social worker, a caseworker and an administrative assistant. In addition, a housemanager, a licensed practical nurse (LPN), counselors and on-call relief staff are provided for each house. The cook and the maintenance man are shared by the two houses.

Although most staff live out, there are two staff apartments in each building, created to provide stability and security. They are occupied by persons who hold full-time jobs in Argus or elsewhere or attend college. They are on sleep-in duty every other week and contract to deliver services in lieu of paying rent. The arrangement works well, providing that the occupants of the apartments are carefully screened and keep their lives in harmony with the value system in the group homes.

INTAKE

On the day a girl is admitted, the caseworker follows a number of procedures. An entry is made in the group home log with the pertinent background information (name, date of birth, Social Security number, family background, previous placement, etc.) and a city bill number is assigned. Child Welfare Information Service (CWIS), a consulting firm engaged by the city to keep records on all children in care, requires ongoing reporting for its files. These forms are time consuming but necessary, because all the information is gathered together in one master file, of which we have a copy. Girls come to us from diagnostic centers, both private and city run, from other voluntary child-care agencies, from the SSC allocations department and from the Family Court. Family Court judges can remand a child directly to Argus or place the child with the Commissioner of Social Services. The referral package which usually accompanies each girl includes a psychosocial history, a recent psychiatric report, a psychological evaluation, previous placement history, current status report, and school and medical reports.

Before a girl is brought into the house the staff inform the other residents that she is coming and ask how they feel about it. Not surprisingly, the arrival of a new girl is generally experienced as an intrusion and can set off anxiety when girls feel down, have lost a favorite counselor or are in a chaotic growth period. The counselors try to bring these feelings into the open, reassure the girls in residence that the coming of a new girl does not mean less love and attention for them and ask their help in making the newcomer feel at home.

HOUSE RULES

New girls and new staff members are given a copy of the house rules.

1. No physical violence or threats of physical violence by residents or staff.

Residents are permitted to express feelings of hostility toward each other and toward staff members in weekly groups, specially called groups or in arranged sessions in the office. In instances where fighting occurs between two residents, both are penalized. The penalty should reflect the residents' degree and kind of involvement in the incident. If a resident strikes a staff member and the issue cannot be resolved, placement will be sought elsewhere.* A staff member who threatens or strikes a resident will be terminated.†

2. No possession or use of drugs or alcohol, on or off the premises. (Staff may indulge in moderate drinking off the premises and off duty but may not return to work showing signs of drinking.)

Residents in violation will be restricted and scheduled for special counseling. If more than one girl is involved, a special house meeting will be called. Staff members in violation will be terminated.

3. No stealing.

If articles or monies are stolen, a house meeting or group is called promptly after the theft is reported. The staff extends a general plea for honesty and asks the culprit to return anonymously the stolen property. If the property is returned, as it often is, the staff will encourage the culprit to confess in private in hope of persuading her to confess to the rest of the house. The other residents are generally concerned about the motive and may encourage the person to ask for articles rather than take them.

4. No sexual acting out.

The residents are not to engage in heterosexual or homosexual activities in the house. Younger girls are encouraged to postpone sexual activity to a more appropriate age. Older girls are counseled as to the consequences of sexual activity. Residents who engage in intercourse are given family planning and birth control information and guidance.

5. No weapons.

Residents may not possess weapons at any time. Random room searches are made. All new residents are searched for weapons such as knives, razors and chains. If weapons are found, they are confiscated. Residents who violate this rule are placed on restric-

---

*This rule discourages attacks on staff. We have sent away only one girl over eight years; she was hallucinating and violent. A second girl ran away after striking a staff member, and we could not get her to come back, although the staff member was willing to work it out.

†This rule is adhered to under all circumstances, even though provocations can be severe. Staff members know that their role is to model nonviolent, alternative ways of dealing with feelings. Weekly staff development groups allow full ventilation of feelings and help staff to understand that the children's anger is not meant for them and to distance themselves from it. They see that other methods work and are generally receptive to tools which enable them to diffuse violence instead of escalating it. In eight years, only a very few staff members have struck a girl; they were dismissed.

tion unless they are newcomers, in which case the staff will reread and reexplain the rules and place the violator under contract.

6. No cursing on the floor.

Confrontation sessions in the office and in group are the only places where cursing is allowed. When a conflict arises that does not require a special group, it may be handled in the office. Residents or staff are otherwise forbidden to use profanity. It is to the advantage of the girls, in their growth and careers, to establish the habit of conversing and feeling at home in a language not dominated by profanity.

7. Cigarette smoking only in designated areas of the house.

Although all bedrooms are equipped with a sprinkler system and/or fire escapes, the New York Fire Department forbids smoking in the bedrooms. We do not allow smoking in the kitchen and dining room to prevent contamination of the food. Smoking is not permitted in any areas of the house where there is carpeting. Smoking is not permitted by staff or residents during groups, house meetings or counseling sessions, because smoking, like doodling or fidgeting, may be used as a distraction or a means of "stuffing" feelings.

8. All chores must be done and rooms must be cleaned before residents are allowed to go out on visits and weekend excursions and before visitors are allowed entry.

9. All residents must make a written request to go on dates and weekend visits.

The residents submit written requests on the evening before case conference. The request should state the person they wish to visit, the address and telephone number and the date of the requested visit. The staff member on duty then verifies the information and screens the persons to be visited if they are not known to the agency. The time of the visit and the time of return are stated and confirmed with the person they wish to visit. Overnight weekend requests and curfews are based on the level the particular resident occupies. The escort system must be honored. If a parent or responsible relative wishes to pick up a younger resident and bring her back, no escort is needed.

10. All visitors must sign in and out of the house.

A sign-in book for visitors is maintained in the staff office. Visitors must sign their names, addresses, the name of the person they wish to visit and their arrival and departure time.

11. No visitors are permitted in the residents' sleeping quarters.

Visiting occurs in either the living room or the dining room. Visiting or lingering is not permitted on the stairs or in the vestibules. If parents wish to see a resident's sleeping quarters, they are escorted by the staff person on duty.

12. Male staff or service men must alert residents when approaching their sleeping quarters.

A loud alert of "Male on the floor" is sufficient. Residents may be undressed. The alert will allow time for them to cover themselves.

13. Clothing.

An inventory of clothing and other personal articles is taken when a girl enters the group home. From the inventory a clothing needs list is developed and presented to the housemanager for approval by the director. Clothing should be well maintained and periodically inspected by the child-care staff.

14. Residents are encouraged to lock up valuables for safekeeping in the staff office.

The residents must sign in for their property and sign out when it is returned. Sums of money in excess of $50 must be forwarded to Argus Community to be locked in the safe. Failure to adhere to this policy entails accepting responsibility for loss or theft.

15. Use of property.

No resident is permitted in another resident's room unless she is accompanied by an occupant. No resident is permitted to use anyone's property without the permission of the owner. If clothing or other articles are loaned, the owner is responsible for it.

16. Groups—House Meetings.

Residents are asked not to discuss the issues addressed in groups or house meetings outside of these meetings.

17. All residents must report promptly to school, work or appointments.

If a resident refuses to attend any of these required functions, she is automatically restricted and not permitted to take part in the social activities in the house. If a resident refuses because of illness, she is placed on bedrest for the entire day or escorted to receive medical attention.

18. If a resident is late for required functions because she did not prepare clothing, she is restricted.

Clothing must be prepared prior to bedtime. No washing or ironing is permitted in the morning before school or other appointments.

19. If a resident is sent home from school because of poor behavior, she is automatically restricted to her room.

She is not permitted to mingle with her peers until the issue has been settled with the school.

20. Telephone Calls.

Each resident is permitted to make one outgoing call per day and may speak for ten minutes. She may receive all incoming calls with a twenty-minute interval between calls and speak for twenty minutes.

21. Residents are assigned a laundry day and may do laundry only on that day.

Only staff members are permitted to operate machines and dispense detergents.

22. Residents may look out of the windows providing they exhibit proper behavior.

Loud talking, provocation and throwing things from the windows is forbidden.

23. Residents who are employed are permitted to spend $50 per month from their earnings. All other monies must be placed in a savings bank and their use deferred until the resident is ready to live on her own.

24. Supplies are issued by the 7:30 A.M.–3:00 P.M. person on duty.

Residents will be notified in advance of the day and time when supplies are to be issued.

Some of these rules may seem arbitrary or redundant. I have suggested that the list is too long and have asked if preserving the negatives on paper might not invest them with a kind of attraction and inevitability. Aren't we suggesting ways of acting out which the girls might never have thought of? The staff assures me, however, that there is no form of acting out that the girls will not have thought of and that the older girls themselves not only participated in formulating the rules but would have preferred them to be even more severe.

But why are only staff members permitted to use the washing machines? Experience has shown that when the girls were allowed to operate the machines, they repeatedly overloaded them with clothing and detergent, burned out the motors and stripped the dials. They seem not to have developed a respect for machinery or an understanding of it. We can't afford to repair and replace machines while waiting for this level of understanding to develop.

Restricting the way a girl looks out of the window may seem arbitrary, but outside those windows is a jungle of predators whose eyes are attuned to every signal we emit. Consider the response when girls sit in the windows in provocative postures and stages of undress (which some have done), when they call out, flirt and make assignations, arrange to purchase beer or drugs from below and haul up their booty with a string.

As we learn to care about the people who care for us, internal controls develop. We watch for signs of "conscience," "superego," "ego," or whatever one is disposed to call the inner regulator. A few of the girls have it already. Most struggle toward it with our help. Meanwhile, rules and enforcement are necessary to set up a model of what self-protection and consideration for others is all about.

In addition there are some seemingly small matters that may be more or less easy to manage under an ordinary roof but which can cause pandemonium if not controlled in a group home setting.

For example, the doorbell. In both houses, the doors open electronically when the buzzer upstairs is pressed. Experience has taught us that it is unwise to allow any but the most responsible girls to open the door, and only after they have learned the identity of the caller on the intercom. Only girls on Levels One and Two are permitted to admit visitors. Girls on lower levels may answer the bell only with the permission of a staff member on duty. Visitors are screened during a brief interview with staff. No one under the influence of alcohol or drugs is allowed in. We learned the hard way that these precautions are necessary. Twenty-four young girls can act as magnets for the good-time Charleys and other elements in the neighborhood. For pushers, pimps and assorted predators it is open season in the South Bronx. One of our young residents, fifteen years old, absconded to a brothel run by police for police; we got her back but not before she had cut an artery and almost bled to death. She was our little clown, making everyone laugh, going into wild "uppers," then crashing in serious suicide attempts.

Girls are allowed visitors two evenings a week and on Saturday and Sunday afternoons and evenings. Visitors are expected to treat girls and staff with respect. No visitors are permitted to stay overnight.

Another item is mail. The postman arrives at midday. The nurse on duty takes in the post and distributes it in each house. Private letters addressed to the girls are given to them directly, but official mail (from the Department of Social Services, for example) presents a problem. Such communications may be difficult to decipher even for the staff because of official jargon or complicated instructions. Girls may ignore, forget about or lose such communications, which sometimes require a response. A staff member, therefore, hands an official letter to a girl and asks her to read its contents and share it. The girls are usually willing to do so in order to get help with a bureaucratic matter.

THE DAILY ROUTINE

The LPNs work Monday through Friday from 7:00 A.M. to 3:00 P.M. They wake the girls as soon as they arrive, see that they get out of bed, dress and groom themselves, attend to hygiene, take whatever medicines may have been prescribed, get a nourishing breakfast (prepared by one of the girls) and set out for their various daily activities. The wake-up staff must get all youngsters not physically ill up and going. This is one of the hardest tasks for staff, requiring toughness, persistence, ingenuity and diplomacy. A whole chapter could be written on any one of the daily tasks, but the strategies and vicissitudes of the wake-up could fill a book. Girls who arrive in the dining room after 8:15 are not allowed the full breakfast but are given juice, toast and beverage. Most girls attend the Argus Learning for Living Center, traveling the 20 or so blocks by bus or on foot. Older residents leave for college, training programs or jobs. The two LPNs look after those girls who remain at home because of illness, arrange appointments with internists, gynecologists, family planning experts, ophthalmologists, dentists, neurologists, dermatologists and other specialists and escort them to their appointments. The LPNs are responsible also for maintaining health records and for keeping medications under lock and key and dispensing them according to prescription. As these tasks require tact and firmness (including getting the girls out of bed), we choose LPNs of good habits and character to whom the girls can readily respond. In effect, the LPNs serve as counselors, as well as health and hygiene specialists.

Lunches are mostly eaten out, although a light lunch is prepared for those who remain at home. Snacks are available after school and in the evening. The cook works Tuesday through Saturday from noon to 8:00 P.M., preparing the evening meal for both houses and leaving prepared dishes or ingredients for the Sunday and Monday main meals. We cater to the girls' food preferences as fully as sound nutrition and budget allow.

Unless they have advanced beyond it, girls in Argus One and Argus Two attend the Learning for Living Center, where they are tested and tracked according to their achievement levels and take part in all programs for which they qualify.

Group trips allow residents to experience other environments and channel their energies in healthy, pleasurable ways. They like roller skating, volley ball and other sports, and go to African, modern and Latino dance recitals. Our funds allow us to pay for trips to museums, beaches, parks, movies, et cetera.

Parties, talent shows and disco dances are held in the group homes on special occasions. The girls plan these affairs, do the shopping, invite two guests each, make all the preparations. They love it.

Many of our girls never had a birthday party until they came to Argus, where they are embarrassed by such attention and feel that they don't deserve it. But their peers encourage them to relax and enjoy to the fullest the celebration of the day they came into the world. They are bombarded with reassurances on these days, are reminded that they are unique, that no one quite like them was ever born before or ever will be again.

CHORES

Many of our girls have not known what it is to live in a clean and attractive environment. They are assigned chores on a rotating basis so that no one gets too bored or irritated and everybody learns how to perform each task. Each week a girl is given an area to clean—the living room, dining room, kitchen, hallways, stairwells, linen closet, pantry, laundry room or bathrooms. A staff member or an older, responsible girl shows her how to clean, supervises her work and inspects it when she has finished.

In addition to special chores, each girl cleans her own room once a week. She also does her own personal laundry and her bed linen and towels when her turn comes to have access to the laundry room.

This is valuable experience for girls who will one day set up homes of their own. Meanwhile, the group homes are kept in good order and everybody gets to live in a pleasant environment. The girls grumble but not bitterly; they perform their chores and are pleased with the result. The learning process, and whatever conflicts arise on the job, are grist for house meetings and groups. If, as sometimes happens, a girl refuses to do her chore, a special house meeting is called where she hears from the other girls as well as staff how they feel about her unwillingness to help care for their home and hers. Peer pressure is more effective than anything the staff might say or do.

Chores must be completed, inspected and approved before leisure time, visitors, evenings out, weekend trips can be enjoyed.

LEVELS

Each girl is assigned to a level, from Housewarming to Level One.

Housewarming. All new girls spend one week on this level in order to become acquainted with the other girls, the staff, the schedules, the rules and the general climate of the house. In one week they experience the basic routines except groups. They receive a great deal of attention from girls and staff, and an effort is made to draw them in and help them learn the ways of the group home. The group process is explained, and they are told what to expect. They are assigned to school, to a room, a carefully matched roommate and a one-to-one counselor; and they are given a laundry day and a chore. During this period staff members become acquainted with the new girls and bring their impressions to the case conference. After Housewarming, a girl is assigned to Level Three A.

Three A. The girls on Level Three A, those who have advanced to it, as well as those who have slipped back from a higher level, are required to work at changing their negative behavior and attitudes to positive ones. They are expected to involve themselves in the encounter and sensitivity groups, both of which are held every week, and the house meetings. Importance is placed on getting out of bed, bathing, dressing, getting off to school, attending classes, relating to counselors, teachers and classmates, arriving home at a good hour, doing homework and chores, going to bed in a reasonable manner. Level Three A girls get an allowance of $3 a week.

Three. From Level Three A girls move to Level Three. Here they are expected to behave themselves, do their assigned chores, keep their rooms and themselves clean and neat, and work seriously toward the goals they have set for themselves with the help of their counselors. They must show an interest in the affairs of the house and in the well-being of other persons in their environment. They are expected to address all of their scheduled appointments and activities in a positive way. Level Three girls receive $4 a week, are granted all request days allowed and may have one day a week unescorted.

Three Plus. Designed for younger girls, aged thirteen to fifteen, Level Three Plus carries all of the obligations and privileges of Level Three except that girls of this age are not permitted to go out unescorted for a full day. To compensate, they are given one day a month for a group activity, such as skating or going to a movie, concert or play, for which Argus pays.

Two. On Level Two girls maintain and refine the attitudes and behavior acquired on Level Three. They must be helpmates to the girls on Housewarming, on Level Three A, Level Three and Level Three B (the ban level). They receive a weekly allowance of $5, have the right to go out alone, receive visitors and make phone calls at appropriate times. They are entitled to two free weekends a month.

One. Girls on Level One have made significant academic and/or vocational progress. They are enrolled in college or advanced training or are focusing on the steps leading to these avenues. Level One girls act as role models for those on lower levels, take leadership positions, act as catalysts in groups or give support to and take responsibility for girls who are still struggling with negative behavior and who are still afraid to open up emotionally. Level One can receive visitors and make phone calls at appropriate times. They receive $7 allowance and have four free weekends a month.

Three B. Level Three B is the ban level, the lowest and most restricted status in the group home. On Level Three B girls lose all privileges because of serious misbehavior or continued disregard for the rules. Their allowance is put into a fund which will not be available until they are at a higher level of behavior. Phone calls and visits are not permitted. Outings are allowed only in the company of a staff member. Ban-level girls receive additional counseling in a one-to-one or group setting. As they begin to work through their problems, girls on the ban level are considered for advancement to Level Three A.

In order to progress from one level to another, a girl must decide for herself whether she meets the criteria for the next level and write a letter to the treatment team requesting the move, stating the reasons for the request and why she believes she is eligible. Her request is presented at a case conference the same week that it is received, and the team decides by consensus whether or not to grant the request.

STAFF RECRUITMENT, SCREENING AND TRAINING

Recruitment and Screening. Many of our staff are recruited from the local community, are black or hispanic (or both), have overcome the kinds of trials and stresses that the girls are experiencing.

However, we find it broadening and reassuring for the girls to interact with some staff of caucasion or other backgrounds. We screen out fragile persons, bullies, sadists, those with problems, such as drug and alcohol use, and persons of shaky values. We look for warm, nurturing males and females with enough strength to stand up to tough situations. Special skills, such as dancing, sewing, acting, athletics, can help create a pleasant, stimulating atmosphere. All staff must be willing to undergo training and development.

Staff Training and Development. Apart from training in the Argus philosophy, structure and routines, the entire group home staff takes part in weekly sessions devoted to self-awareness and self-expression. Through these groups they learn to listen to girls, understand them, and interact with them in productive ways. Awareness of their own feelings, attitudes and behavior is essential to their development as effective counselors and staff members.

These sessions are facilitated by outside consultants with specialized training and experience in residential settings. Staff are encouraged to give free rein to the feelings of anger and weariness that beleaguer those who work with adolescents. Ignoring or disguising anger, sweeping it under the carpet or telling people to stuff it and go about their business won't work. Exercises in self-expression and self-awareness lead to an appreciation of why the girls are so full of pain and anger, and to the bonding that heals old wounds and makes everyone less vulnerable.

The staff group also provides a protected arena in which to resolve any differences staff members may have with one another. At one of these groups the nurse was indignant because she had needed help with a special situation before 8:00 A.M., but the live-in staff, who should have been available to help her, had already left the house. She confronted the parties and they made a commitment to stay at their posts in the future. Small matters must be dealt with. Someone may turn over the petty cash box without the proper slips having been filled out or a key may be carried off in a moment of carelessness or someone may be perceived as hiding out in the office and letting others carry the weight. All of this has to be sorted out. And even if the facts remain obscure, as they do on occasion, everyone has a say. Feelings are aired, and there is less of a tendency for pockets of resentment to form. On occasion a type of behavior which is forbidden becomes an issue, as one staff member accuses another of coming to work smelling of alcohol or forming a negative contract with another staff member or with one of the girls.

A negative contract is an agreement between staff members,

between girls or between a staff member and a girl to condone and keep silent about behavior which would normally be brought out and discussed in groups. A whole nest of negativity can grow up behind these contracts and do great harm. Sooner or later someone gets an attack of conscience—or gets caught in the act—and blows the whistle on the others. (For more on staff development see chapter 19.)

CASE CONFERENCES

The staff in each of the group homes—comprising a social worker, case worker, housemanager, senior counselor, counselors, a licensed practical nurse and a cook—functions as an interdisciplinary team. The kitchen and the preparation of food, as well as the personality of the cook, play a central role in our therapeutic process. Once a week the team meets for a case conference where members bring their expertise to bear on specific problems encountered by each girl and on the design and implementation of individual goals. In case conference, the team assigns a caseload of four girls to each counselor. They attempt to match the girl and her special needs to the most appropriate counselor. If a girl is interested in dance, poetry or drama and we have a counselor or a housemanager with these talents, the girl will be assigned to that person. She may be able to express much of what is bothering her through art.

Jenine was rejected by her father when her mother abandoned them both. He prefers his children by a new wife, showing his favoritism by taking their side in quarrels, buying them clothing and gifts, holding them up as examples to their older half sister and finally, when she began to make trouble, by putting her in placement. The father continues to wound the girl by promising repeatedly to visit her and then not appearing. The staff hoped by pairing Jenine with a warm, dependable male counselor to offset some of this hurt. One girl, taken from a psychiatric ward and removed from the heavy tranquilizer Thorazine, could not tolerate female staff anywhere near her but gradually developed a trusting relationship with Donald Cole, then director of the group home program, who spoon-fed her with pablum and milk and his own blend of warmth, security and love, which ought to be bottled and sold. For a street girl who was brassy and abusive, used cocaine, instigated fights and was flirting with prostitution, we chose a counselor with a similar background who talked turkey, outwitted and outmaneuvered her and, in the end, convinced her that "our side" was where the most power and gratification were lodged.

Where a family is available, the counselor makes contact, pays home visits, holds interviews and if there is a germ of a productive relationship with a parent or other relatives, nurtures it. The director of the group home program is present at the case conference in each house, supervises and assists with the work done by the team and is available for consultation throughout the week.

Angela and Camilla Starks are half sisters who were placed at Argus. The whereabouts of their parents were unknown. They had resided with their grandmother until her drinking problem drove first Angela, and a year later Camilla, to seek help from the Bureau of Child Welfare, an agency within SSC that investigates child abuse. Angela was a wild and self-destructive fifteen-year-old, while Camilla, at seventeen, appeared stable and well organized. The sisters were often the subject of discussion at case conferences, and since Angela was in Argus One and Camilla was in Argus Two, they were at times the focus of interhouse meetings and consultations. A sampling of the subjects discussed in connection with these sisters will convey some idea of the issues counselors must face and solve at the conferences.

Angela had been placed in Argus One because at the time of her arrival there was an opening in that particular house and in general Argus Two is reserved for older, more advanced girls who may be working or attending college. When the grandmother locked Camilla out of the house and threw her clothes out of the window, she came to the group home and was assigned to Argus Two. Angela immediately demanded that she be transferred to the house where her sister lived. Angela's counselor brought up her request at the case conference, and it was discussed at length. The consensus was that Camilla's growth level made her an appropriate candidate for Argus Two but that Angela was not yet ready. The decision enraged Angela and set off an unremitting campaign on her part to be transferred. She was very bright and as she was reading two years above grade level (our girls are generally below grade level), she began a campaign also to be transferred from the Learning for Living Center to a public school. The staff were divided on this latter issue. Some favored it while others feared that she would be lost in a large public school and would succumb to negative peer pressure. Angela persisted. Eventually she wore everybody down on the school issue and for a time I was the only obstacle. I refused to let her go until she was strong enough to stand up to the world. When she did go she had many ups and downs. I was never too pleased with the decision.

Eventually Angela was transferred to Argus Two. But the rivalry between the two sisters became acute. Angela felt that she was constantly compared—unfavorably—to her older sister. She sought and got attention by stirring up trouble and was the despair of her counselor and of the members of the case conference. Camilla did her chores, progressed in school, made many friends and all the while asked herself how it was that her half sister got all the attention while nobody noticed her. Just before Christmas Camilla stole a check from her roommate's purse, forged the girl's signature and deposited the money in her own account. The theft was discovered and readily traced to Camilla. Staff and peers asked one another why Camilla had done it. She was working and had saved to buy Christmas presents and new clothes. She really didn't need her roommate's money. The case conference restricted her to the house and cancelled her part in the Christmas show, the big event of the year. Why had she let herself in for all of that unpleasantness?

Both Camilla and Angela were talented singers. It was particularly hard for Camilla to sit silent while the other residents, including her sister, Angela, presented their songs and skits to round after round of applause. Knowing that Camilla was forbidden to take part, Angela took her by the hand, led her to the front and looking into her eyes, sang "I Believe in You." Camilla and the entire audience were deeply moved. Some of us shed tears. It was the beginning of a more loving bond between the sisters.

By this time everybody realized that Camilla's theft of the check had been a desperate bid for attention and that under that calm and well-organized exterior, her need was as great as Angela's or any other girl's. We set ourselves the goal of paying particular attention to the quiet "good" girls and not letting ourselves be totally subsumed by responding to crises and acting out.

Mary Fritz, director of the group home, and Mary Taylor, the staff trainer, who lead the case conferences, encourage staff to make comments and suggestions and to bring in whatever information they have. Besides handling routine matters, such as requests for weekend passes, level changes and clothes, and imposing disciplinary measures, the staff probes various incidents and situations, devises strategies for treatment and sets short- and long-term goals to be achieved with clients.

RECORD KEEPING

In planning and in resolving issues, the team refers to the Argus case records and to the CWIS files. The CWIS files, developed for SSC by a private consulting firm, contain computerized histories of the children in care in New York City, including the twenty-four girls who live in our group homes. Our staff adds material to the CWIS computer on an ongoing basis.

A completed fact sheet and a photograph are included in each girl's folder developed by Argus caseworkers. The entire staff has access to the records, a fact carefully discussed with the girls. Though the CWIS service is convenient, I have many reservations about feeding computers highly personal information and whether confidentiality ultimately can be observed. This is one way in which we label and possibly stigmatize human beings.

Within thirty days of admission the social worker completes an intake study and develops a treatment plan. A strategy for working with the girl's family—if the family can be reached—is a part of the treatment plan. It also includes long-term (discharge) plans, short-term goals and a strategy for achieving these goals. The treatment plan is reviewed and updated every three months. It is reviewed with the girl and, if possible, with the family. The plan is utilized by the treatment team in working with the girl.

The social worker and the caseworker are responsible for supervising the records. They must submit a report requesting a change of status, information update, or request for services in conjunction with the appropriate uniform case record. These reports are sent to SSC for approval, and copies are placed in the group home files. Requests for status change, notification of a change in treatment plan, documentation of accidents, illness, injuries—must be submitted to SSC, with copies to CWIS.

The counselors in each house are responsible for maintaining an up-to-date record of significant incidents which occur with each girl.

A monthly medical report for each resident is prepared by the LPN, documenting treatment by physicians, dentists, psychiatrists, medications prescribed and taken, illness or accidents which may have occurred, special regimes followed, et cetera. The medical report is placed in the file as part of the girl's treatment and progress at Argus.

All written accounts—psychosocial histories, counseling sessions, group and case conference notes, medical records, CWIS reports—are kept in locked filing cabinets in offices locked when not occupied by staff. Staff have access to the records with the understanding that the personal affairs of the residents are not to become the subject of gossip or private conversation. When case records are shared with outside agencies, as they sometimes must be, the resident's written consent is secured and placed in the file.

ACCOUNTABILITY, COMPLAINTS AND INVESTIGATIONS

In addition to the Office of Placement and Accountability (a department within SSC that monitors our residential program on an ongoing basis), a special assessment team, also from SSC, each year evaluates our record keeping, our program and reporting procedures, and our achievements in terms of the goals and standards of the Child Welfare Reform Act. Argus has had few problems with these assessments: we have been meeting the standards of this new law from the early years of our program's existence. Also, we are inspected annually by the City Departments of Health and Environmental Services, the City Fire Department, and the State Department of Social Services.

The Children's Rights Unit (CRU), an arm of SSC's Office of Advocacy, handles complaints brought by youngsters against agencies where they are in care. Children may accuse the agency of not allowing them to visit their parents, for example, or of not permitting them to enter the career of their choice. They may complain that the agency is not moving them toward desired goals, such as the return to their parental home or into independent living. The CRU will investigate these sorts of complaints and will advise the agency of their decision. All youngsters in placement are given a brochure describing the CRU and encouraging them to call in their complaints or questions. If youngsters accuse the agency of mistreatment—of being deprived of food or clothing, locked in their rooms, shut out of the house, or sexually abused or injured—the CRU will pass the complaints along to the Confidential Investigations Unit (CIU), which reports directly to the head of SSC, and an investigation will be carried out by that body.

Argus is required to report all serious injuries, accidents and illnesses requiring hospitalization, suicide attempts, serious fights or incidents of violence, and deaths of children in our care to the CIU, which conducts an investigation of each incident and determines whether the agency followed proper procedures and responded adequately. In addition, the CIU looks into the medical aspects of pregnancy and alcohol and drug abuse, again to determine whether proper services are being provided.

Children's complaints involving health violations are passed on by the CRU to the Institutional Inspection Unit (IIU), which inspects the agency for roaches, mice, lack of proper sanitation, broken windows, inadequate heat and hot water, leaking showers, defective equipment, and so forth.

Being accountable to and cooperating with the inspections and investigations conducted by these sundry groups takes a large bite out of our time and energies, and it digs deeply into our store of patience, which could better be expended on the youngsters in our care. Of course, we could do with a jog now and then, and we don't mind the Assessment Team casting an outside, objective eye over our program and our premises on an annual basis. Our regular year-round accountability team is generally helpful and creative, making suggestions that we follow.

We have cooperated fully with the CRU and the CIU, even when we know that children's complaints are not valid. We try to keep firmly in our minds that these units were set up to protect children from mistreatment. However, it is unfortunate that, as presently constituted, this mechanism can be used by angry youngsters in their struggle against supervision and structure and in their testing of our value system—in short, to undermine the very aspects of Argus that have enabled us to create a safe and growth-promoting environment. It is counterproductive for youngsters to be in a position to bring an investigation on us and to get the staff over a barrel any time they get angry. In our experience, unjustified complaints are invariably brought to CRU by youngsters with long histories of disruptive behavior and deep-seated anger at authority. Argus has from its inception willingly taken in such children and has worked with them, often successfully. But in the last year, since CRU has given them access to the complaint mechanism, new youngsters who are especially disruptive have used it as a weapon against staff, against our group process, against the rules and regulations. The investigators have little or no understanding of our methods and have ordered us to cease and desist from procedures that have worked well over the years—indeed so well that one psychiatrist who spent four months evaluating our youngsters reported that we had performed "psychiatric miracles" with some very seriously disturbed youngsters.

We understand that there must be an investigative procedure. We believe in children's rights. But we also see a firm structure and an understanding of limits as necessary to growth and to internalizing values. Argus is willing to be held accountable. But what is happening here is something else. Out of idealism, no doubt, or perhaps misguided liberalism, mechanisms have been put in place which encourage manipulations and adversarial relationships between youngsters and agency staff. The majority of our youngsters have progressed to a point that they are not interested in such tactics. But angry, vengeful new residents now have access to a means of striking at us, and can cast a cloud of suspicion and doubt over the staff. They take an exquisite delight in it, not diminished in the least by the fact that their charges of mistreatment, upon investigation, have not been upheld. They have, however, been able to create a misunderstanding about our methods, and these are now being contested. We cannot give up our tools and we do not intend to. We sincerely hope that CRU will reevaluate their criteria for deciding when an investigation is justified and that a substantial portion of these complaints will be weeded out without leaving their office. We hope that they will get a sense of us as a responsible agency that constantly monitors itself, is dedicated to the aims of the Child Welfare Reform Act, and was setting goals for adolescents and moving them toward self-realization and successful outcomes years before the act was written. All but a little over 4 percent of our ex-residents are in college, in training, or holding jobs and paying taxes. We believe that when the CRU gets to know us better they will realize that our methods deserve recognition, support and backing.

If this does not happen, Argus may be forced to reevaluate its policy of taking in the highly troublesome, hard-to-please youngsters —these defined in terms of serious behavioral and emotional disorders. We would not want this to happen. Few agencies are in a position to take a chance on these kids. We would like to continue to do so.[1]

TREATMENT

The voluntary child-care agencies have been accused of taking children into placement and keeping them there when they could be cared for in their own homes. This happens in some cases, no doubt, and we deplore it. Some families can surely be helped to become functional, and resources should be devoted to this. But many families do not lend themselves to rehabilitation. Argus specializes in providing long-term care for children twelve to twenty-one years old whose families are broken up and unavailable or incapable of providing a viable home. We also take in children whose behavior is so disruptive that families cannot manage them. In addition, we take in a few girls whose parents, caught up in the clash of cultures, put their daughters away for sexual offenses—getting pregnant out of wedlock or for dating and staying out late at night. Argus further provided a variety of treatment modalities:

Individual Counseling. Counselors talk many times a day with the girls. Unscheduled encounters and interchanges are as important as more formalized sessions, probably more so. For since adolescents deny and hide even more than the rest of us, we depend on their actions and interactions as they go about the business of the day to tell us what they feel and need.

For me the counselors are heroic figures. They are on the firing line, they keep the wheels turning and their antennae alert them to the pain that shelters itself like a tender bird within the storm of threats and abuse that not infrequently pours out of the girls. Counselors make a difference in the girls' lives, and the awareness of this and the certainty of their ability to get results reduces powerlessness and burnout.

Each counselor meets privately once a week with each of the four girls in his/her caseload, focusing on areas that are key to the girls' development or may be cause for concern. The counselor reviews the girl's requests, encourages her to work toward her goals and helps her to see the advantages of self-regulation as opposed to exterior controls. The counselor writes a weekly progress report, and each girl reads and signs her report. These sessions address concrete goals. If a girl is overeating, using marijuana, quarreling, stealing, the sessions and the short-term goals agreed upon will focus on these. The girl's strengths are always emphasized.

House Meetings. There are two weekly house meetings in each group home—additional house meetings are called when problems arise that need the immediate attention of the entire house (when something is stolen, someone is using drugs, when a conflict can't be otherwise resolved). House meetings are for discussion, information-sharing and conflict resolution. Their tone is formal (no cursing allowed); however, when the conflict is severe and feelings run high, we announce that the house meeting is at an end and declare an encounter in session, with all of the seating and space rules for the protection of group members in force, allowing them to ventilate without threatening anyone or being threatened in turn. No one is allowed to get out of her seat or violate another person's space except for a hug or a reach out. No touching is permitted unless in affection.

Behavior Improvement or Encounter Groups. These take place once a week on Monday evenings. Girls confront staff and each other; staff confront girls. In Argus One, where more girls are on a beginning level, this group often is used for ventilating hostile feelings. It is the first time in these girls' lives that they can let their anger out in a safe environment. This clears their bellies so that good feelings can get in. It also keeps everyday hostilities from festering and erupting and makes it possible to develop a loving atmosphere in the house. In Argus Two, where there are more advanced girls, encounters have a different tone. Here the girls have already resolved a great deal of anger at their parents and at society, as well as a lot of self-hate. Feelings of caring and sharing have developed. They approach each other with more kindness and empathy. They have little need to hurt, and they confront people to show concern, to be helpful and to resolve conflicts and bad feelings. For the most part, these are resolved. The staff and higher level girls in both houses model more advanced ways of showing angry and loving concern and of resolving disputes.

Sensitivity Groups. These take place in each house with as few as six girls to a group. This ensures that each girl will have time to go into her feelings without shutting anyone else out. These groups are not confrontational, not harsh, and if conflict resolution takes place it tends to center around problems with family, girlfriends or boyfriends, teachers and employers. Group members are supportive and pass along helpful information. The emphasis is on understanding oneself and others. For example, if a girl was confronted on Monday for stealing from a peer, she would be encouraged in the sensitivity session to get in touch with her motives and her needs and with the fact that she didn't feel entitled to ask for what she needed.

Seminars. These are held extemporaneously or as needed. Staff members, older girls or lecturers from the outside are invited to lead seminars on drug use, family planning, dating, hygiene, college, career possibilities, crime, youth employment, Black History Week, ethnic holidays, how to spend holidays, et cetera.

FOSTERING SELF-ACCEPTION

Girls are encouraged to resolve situations inside and outside of the house without staff intervention in line with our policy of fostering independent thinking and decision making. If we see that a girl is being taken advantage of, we will try to get her to stand up for herself, both in and out of house meetings and groups. If a girl lends clothes or personal property and doesn't get it back, for example, she may come to the staff and ask for help, which she will get at first. She will also be reminded of the house rule which says that anyone who lends things is responsible for them, and she will be encouraged to take on this responsibility for herself in the future.

When a girl demands that her counselor intervene in her disputes at school, the counselor will assess the situation and decide if intervention is necessary. If it proves to be a run-of-the-mill kids' dispute, the counselor will ask her to resolve it, give her some pointers on how to do it and will explain that it is better for her growth that she learn to take charge of such issues herself. Assuming this responsibility makes a girl more careful about how she embroils herself. Self-assertion is also fostered as girls share a room and divide the chores. Only when someone violates an agreement or when a girl is being taken advantage of or scapegoated by a stronger girl will the counselors get involved, and then with a view to teaching a girl how to stand up for herself in a nonhostile, straightforward manner. In the kitchen, a strong girl will sometimes push the less palatable chores onto a more compliant co-worker. Both girls will be encouraged to confront their behavior and to ask themselves what purpose it serves and whether some alternative might not be found.

WORKING WITH FAMILIES

Argus's clients are "throwaway" children—the children nobody wants. Even with these children we continually scan them and their families (when a family or a shred of a family remains) to determine whether discharge to the natural home or to a relative or to some appropriate person in the community is possible. We seek viable family or community alternatives, if for no other reason than to ease the wound that homelessness and rejection inflicts. Some children can be socialized and strengthened to the point of rejoining their blood relatives. When appropriate, we bend a great deal of effort to this end, and goals are developed accordingly.

If the aim is to facilitate a child's re-entry into the home, the parents must be helped to grow with their child. The parents' ability to be emotionally and physically available to their child is crucial for such an outcome. An individualized treatment plan is devised for each adolescent and her family to utilize strengths within the family and mobilize community resources.

Once an alliance with the family is established, treatment can begin. There is an emphasis on the total family since work with all family members can prevent scapegoating the adolescent. Often parents are angry at children because they see them acting out parts of their own personalities which they have driven underground. Children, sensitive instruments, receive and act on messages which parents are unaware of transmitting. The message may be "It's no use trying. You can't make it no matter what you do." Or it may be "I am trapped and half dead; don't be like me; strike out; do anything, be anything but what I am." The child's struggles may be an attempt to clutch at life. The mother may act as a sister and a rival to her daughter. She may want the older children out of the house so that she can be sexually free. The daughter may be catching the eye of her stepfather; she may be pursuing him.

The counselor must judge the degree of intervention a family can tolerate. Interventions poorly timed can be destructive. The counselor must be sensitive to the level of tension, to prevent the parents from becoming so frustrated that they drop out or from receiving so much support that no change is effected.

The adolescent and her family work to examine unresolved feelings. Parents learn to explore the meaning of adolescent struggle, to be firmer in setting limits and more supportive and nurturing. The teenager is encouraged to express feelings directly, rather than act them out. We try to teach families to resolve their own conflicts in a constructive manner.

As positive growth and change occur, the child should spend more time in the home, remaining overnight and on some weekends and vacations. Gradually, all parties will come to an agreement that the child is ready to return to the family.

Argus prepares the child and the family for her return home, as well as preparing the other residents for the loss of a friend. (We try to be sensitive to the feelings that separation arouses in all residents.) It may be desirable to purchase furniture or equipment to facilitate the girl's return home.

Argus is responsible for continuing involvement with the family for ninety days following the date of trial discharge. The counselor is available to the family and is ready to intervene should a crisis arise. If the family adjustment remains positive during the three-month period, the counselor sends a report to SSC requesting a final discharge for the girl and her family from the child-care system.

TOWARD INDEPENDENT LIVING

For girls with no viable family we concentrate upon the long-range goals of independent living. These girls stay with us until that goal has been accomplished, up to age twenty-one. Some parents are hospitalized or in prison or have problems which make good parenting impossible; others have been separated from their children for years and feel their presence in the home as an intrusion. With children who are to all intents and purposes parentless, we discuss adoption as an alternative to continued group home living and may list their photographs with an adoption agency.

Much of the discussion at case conference centers around plans for independent living. By the term "independent living" Argus does not mean, as many agencies do, helping a girl get her own apartment and her own budget on welfare. The Human Resources Administration views moving onto welfare as an acceptable outcome for a child who has been in care because it is a great deal cheaper than residential care. To us this is selling the children short—and the taxpayers, too, in the long run. With proper growth the vast majority of girls in care can hold down jobs and pay taxes. That is what Argus means by independent living.

Long-range strategies are developed early and are stepped up as the girl matures. Preparations take place on two levels: the emotional and the concrete. The treatment plan must maximize strengths and make the most of community resources. Always the emphasis is upon getting the girl to develop satisfying and effective ways of relating personally and vocationally. Since most of our girls are below grade level, they obtain their high school equivalency diplomas or attain basic literacy at the Argus Learning for Living Center, which also reinforces the growth patterns and the treatment plans developed in the group home. The next step is college or vocational training and, finally, nonsubsidized employment.

With the help of the staff a young woman who is ready seeks an apartment in a decent neighborhood. Sometimes two or three girls take a place together. A list is put together by the girl with our help, and with her own savings and a $500 grant from SSC, furnishings are purchased, and the month's rent and a month's security are paid. No resident may remain in care after age twenty-one.

We try to accomplish separation with dignity and respect, but the anxiety and ambivalence can be intense. Immense feelings of loss crop up and must be dealt with. There is the need to go and the wish to stay, the desire for independence and the longing for eternal childhood. We must be sensitive to these themes, bring them into awareness and interpret them.

Having a job, a place to stay and friends eases the passage to the outside world. The staff remains available for at least three months after the separation takes place, and many girls come back to Argus Youth for years, to visit, to tell us with pride of their accomplishments, to ask for advice or just to get a hug and a kiss from the members of their "extended family."

8. THE HUNGRY COW SYNDROME

I used to say, maybe I should have a baby to help solve the problem at home. Maybe if I had a baby my mother and father wouldn't act so crazy.

I'll spank my baby to go to sleep, not real hard. Other mothers punch their babies. They punch their babies right in the eye, beat them up, break their arms. I have seen a lot of little kids with black eyes, broken heads, broken wrist, broken legs.

It's such a long time ago. I'm trying to bring my mind back to why I wanted a baby. I just started saying that I wanted a baby as soon as I turned sixteen.

I said, I'm seventeen. It's time for me to have a baby. My mother done had hers. It's time for me to have mine.

Maybe I might find the right dude, one that won't leave me, that's right for me. How could I tell? I don't know. I'm just lucky. I'm a lucky child. So I'm just playing and praying that I will find the right dude to have the baby, who will support me and take off all the pressure I got.

All the guys here are girl crazy. When you find someone with a big image, he got to have two or three girls at one time. Everybody got his image as a lover. They try to have at least two. At least two.

ARGUS ENROLLEES

The calf of a hungry cow will low in vain, the proverb tells us. Ramona Ruiz was no exception.

It was hard to believe that Ramona had committed the offenses she was charged with: assaulting a police officer and possessing a glassine bag filled with heroin. She was thirteen, apathetic, tiny (barely five feet tall), with medium brown skin and pigtails, eyes that seemed to look everywhere and see nothing and a limp, caved-in quality, like a doll that had lost part of its stuffing. She had only one previous arrest but owing to the serious nature of the charges (both felonies) her case had not been diverted at the precinct level and a juvenile delinquency petition had been filed.

The foster family with whom Ramona had been living refused to have her in the house and she had been sent to Spofford to await a finding in Family Court.

When we interviewed her in the visitor's area she hardly looked at us, did not once make eye contact, never smiled and seemed scarcely aware of our presence. We were told that she slept most of the time, made no friends, was not interested in her peers, refused to enter into games or sports, would not attend school and was eating next to nothing. She was not experiencing withdrawal symptoms and had none of the gray pallor characteristic of the heavy user; so we concluded, though she would not answer questions, that the involvement with heroin was probably not extensive. A psychiatric examination had been made but the report was not available. The psychiatrist was expected to appear in court.

The law guardian assigned to her case told us that a PINS petition had been brought by her foster family (a cousin and her husband), that Ramona had ignored a summons to appear in court, had run away and after a few weeks had been apprehended by the police. In the course of the arrest on the PINS charge, according to the officer, Ramona had struck and bitten him. Ramona alleged that the officer had knocked her to the pavement, held his nightstick to her throat and put his foot in her face, almost choking her to death and producing bruises on her neck and one side of her face. She also said that he had called her a "black bitch" and a "whore." Ramona denied having attacked the officer, and he in turn claimed to have done nothing beyond subduing the girl in order to apprehend her.

The law guardian and the social worker asked if Argus would be willing to take Ramona into our group home program if the judge agreed. We replied that we would be happy to consider taking her in but that our contract with Special Services for Children, City of New York, under which the group home program operates, does not permit us to take in children for whom a juvenile delinquency finding has been made. The law guardian said that the charge of assault on the officer could probably be "adjusted" if Ramona would confess that she had committed the offense and apologize, but that Ramona had refused to admit her guilt and had stated that she would go upstate rather than apologize, maintaining that the officer owed her an apology.

So the girl was not altogether apathetic. Prompted by this cue, we again approached Ramona and asked her if she would be willing to answer a question. "If you could be right now with one person of your choosing, who would that person be?"

She answered without hesitation and with a suddenly radiant face, "I'd be with my mother."

We asked her if she had lived with her mother at one time. She said that she had stayed with her mother about a year ago for a few months.

"You are not living with her now."

"No. She was hard up for money and she had to sell me."

"She *sold* you?"

"Yes. She couldn't keep me because she didn't have enough money. She all the time giving money to Aida and to the police. They was always after her for money an if she didn't give it to them they beat her up."

"Did you mind that she sold you?"

"No. I miss my mother. But I know she had to do it. She didn't have no money."

After this her story came out in bits and pieces. She lapsed occasionally into her purblind and wordless state, but flamed into life whenever her mother was mentioned.

Ramona told us that she did not remember having seen her mother until she was twelve years old. Up to that point she had lived in a distant city with her paternal grandmother, Rosario, a devout convert to the Pentecostal religion who did not spare the rod and who forced the child to pass the whole of every Saturday on her knees in church, "tarrying" (praying for forgiveness and waiting for the Holy Spirit to visit her).

The grandmother told Ramona that her mother, Celeste, was "evil" and "worthless" and a "dope fiend" who would burn in hell for her sins. These were lies concocted for the purpose of keeping her from her mother, Ramona said. When she asked relatives where her mother was, no one would reveal her whereabouts. When the grandmother died, none of her aunts or uncles would take Ramona; she was put on a plane for New York with the understanding that her mother would meet her at the airport. Celeste did not meet the plane. Ramona was taken to the Traveler's Aid Society and then to a shelter where she stayed for several weeks. When the mother was finally located she said that she had never received word that her mother-in-law had died or that her daughter was expected to live with her. However, she took the child to her house and kept her for about a year.

Ramona spoke of this time with her mother with a kind of rapture. It seemed not to matter that men visited the apartment afternoon and night or that her mother's friend, Aida Rivera, behaved like a bully. The child thought the gaudy surroundings were beautiful and that her mother dressed like a queen. One morning Celeste and Aida shot cocaine and engaged in a lesbian sexual relationship in the presence of the girl. When Ramona screamed and begged them to stop Aida laughed and promised to show the child how much fun it could be. Not long afterward Aida, Ramona and Celeste engaged in sex together. After she turned thirteen Ramona was taken into the bedroom by her mother and told to remove her clothes. Two men were there. Celeste said, "Do everything exactly as I do." After that Ramona accepted male and sometimes female clients. Then her mother sold her to a forty-five-year-old man who kept her a prisoner in his home until he was arrested for drug dealing.

Ramona was taken into custody and was remanded to a juvenile detention center. Her mother had moved from her house and could not be found. Finally a married cousin who lived in Queens agreed to take the child. And so she was transplanted once again. Her new foster parents were factory workers without children of their own. Ramona found their way of life drab and alien. They found hers disturbing. She thought nothing of trading her body for a modest supply of chiba, getting stoned and lying on her bed day and night, listening to her tapes—the flailing guitars, the whining, smacking and bashing sounds that send the devotee straight into outer space.

Ramona says that during this time her cousin's husband abused her sexually whenever the opportunity presented itself and then took a high-and-mighty tone about her pot smoking and her morals. The family forbade her to smoke in their house but she ignored them. She refused to go to school, saying that she hated teachers and that academic subjects bored her. Her story of being sexually abused, blurted out in anger, was not believed by the cousin, and the husband and wife decided to take Ramona to court and have her put away. Ramona refused to accompany them to Family Court. The husband then tried to have Ramona arrested, but the police declared they were not permitted to make an arrest under the circumstances they described. The husband then went into Family Court, obtained a PINS petition, and the court served Ramona with a notice to appear. She ignored the notice and the court, after much prodding, issued a warrant for her arrest. Ramona got wind of the warrant, ran away from her cousin's home and took up residence in an abandoned building.

One day she returned to the cousin's neighborhood to cop (purchase drugs), and was spotted by a neighbor who knew about the warrant, tried to reach the cousin and then called the police.

Ramona admitted that she had bitten and hit the police officer as he tried to arrest her but claimed that he struck her first, "disrespected" her and then, when she lashed out at him, used that as an excuse to cut off her wind, force her to the pavement and kick her in the face.

"They would let me out of here if I would ask his pardon," she said. "But I won't."

"Why not? If it would get you out?"

"My mother wouldn't like it. And besides, I haven't got a place to go. They can't find out where my mother is living."

"Would she want you?"

"Sure. If she had enough money to keep me."

In court the law guardian argued that the heroin charge should be dismissed because the police officer had not obtained a warrant to search the girl's pockets. The judge agreed. He said that although the officer was within his rights when he subdued Ramona and frisked her for a possible concealed weapon, no warrant had been issued which permitted him to search her person. "I am not allowing the glassine bag to be introduced in evidence," he said. "The heroin charge is dismissed."

The assault charge and the PINS petition remained to be disposed of. There is a limit, under the Family Court Act, to the time a child can be held in detention—no longer than seventeen days on a Class A, B, or C felony. Ramona had been in detention three months, and all parties seemed eager to get on with the fact finding and move her out—to somewhere. She had been referred to a number of agencies for placement but none would accept her. Asked whether they would take Ramona back, the cousin and her husband burst out in a tirade: the girl was a vicious liar and an "ingrate"; she had eaten their bread and tried to destroy their good name. The cousin said that Ramona had taken after her mother, who was a "puta," a drug addict and a lesbian.

A psychiatrist had examined her said that Ramona had undergone a psychotic seizure and in his opinion was probably in that state when she resisted arrest. She had refused to talk to him, and he described her as an "elective mute" who had good comprehension but would communicate only with gestures, if at all. She displayed compulsive traits and negativistic, oppositional behavior, particularly in the home and in detention. She had been uncooperative and there were no test scores available so that he was unable to say whether she was mentally retarded. Because of her self-imposed silence, he was unable to make a differential diagnosis of her "eating disorder" or of the "phobias" and anxieties from which she seemed to be suffering.

It appeared from her history that she was undersocialized, egocentric and manipulative and did not experience appropriate feelings of remorse for her acts. He was inclined toward a diagnosis of Atypical Psychosis, with Schizophreniform features, but on second thought, he had decided upon "diagnosis deferred" as being the more prudent designation until further material became available. He recommended placement in a highly structured environment, with psychiatric consultation available around the clock.

The judge asked the psychiatrist if he meant the Bronx State Hospital. "That is far from ideal."

"Well, yes, Your Honor, but I don't know that any other setting would be available."

The judge scanned the various reports dealing with the case, seeming to ponder for some three minutes—a vast amount of time in a court where the calendars are crowded and many matters are handled with very little semblance of wisdom, let alone law and order. He seemed to be genuinely concerned about Ramona. Finally, turning to the caseworker he asked, "Have you anything to say in this matter?"

"Your Honor, if I may say so, this case seems complicated by several factors. In view of the psychiatrist's report, it doesn't appear that Ramona was in her right mind when she and the police officer had their encounter."

"The officer was not hurt, and although striking an officer is a serious charge, I am not inclined to make a finding of delinquency in this case. Beyond that, even though the girl used drugs and comported herself in a rebellious manner, making a PINS petition appropriate, still this smacks more of neglect than anything else."

"That is true, Your Honor. But neglect is difficult to prove. The case could drag on for months, while my client sits in Spofford. . . ."

"Do you have a recommendation, Miss Jellinek?"

"Well, sir, since there is a PINS petition on file it seems to me that it would work to everybody's advantage to place this girl in Argus Community."

"Do they have twenty-four-hour psychiatric care available?"

"No, Your Honor, they do not."

"Is Argus willing to take her?"

"Yes, their representative is present."

"In that event, I am going to dismiss the felony petition and remand the girl to Argus for thirty days, at which time we will review her progress and decide upon further remand or placement."

The judge in Ramona's case made a wise decision. He chose to focus upon and respond to the needs of the child, rather than to

legally defined categories. Family Court judges have large discretionary powers: the judge in Ramona's case could have introduced a
neglect petition, but it would have been up to the Commissioner of
Social Services to pursue it, which might have taken many months,
would in all likelihood have been fought by the foster parents and the
other adults in her life and would have been extremely difficult to
prove. Meanwhile, Ramona would have continued to languish in detention or a public shelter where the odds of getting her needs met
would not have been great. The judge saw that the course most
beneficial to the child was to utilize the power of the PINS petition to
place her with a reliable community agency. He realized from the
reports before him that Argus was more aware of Ramona's history
than the psychiatrist, who had not gained the child's confidence. This
consideration, coupled with the hard fact that psychiatric placement
for children is difficult, if not impossible, to effect and that even if such
placement can be obtained, the "treatment" often consists of custodial care and the prescription of one kind of tranquilizer or another,
influenced the judge's decision.

The Argus group home program is allowed under its contract to
take in PINS, neglect, abuse and voluntary placement cases from
Family Court, but not cases where the finding is juvenile delinquency.
In our view the distinction between these categories is somewhat
artificial and, indeed, in Family Court practice they are fungible. Actually, we should be scrutinizing the histories of individual children and
placing them where their needs can be met effectively, regardless of
the specific offense they are charged with or the type of petition that
has been filed, with the exception, of course, of those who have
repeatedly committed felonies involving violence against others.

As Jody Adams Weisbrod and her colleagues point out in their
study of Family Court dispositions, neglect and PINS cases are very
similar. The statutes themselves contain much of the same language.
"Again and again we found the circumstances to be alike in these two
categories. In effect, it is a matter of who becomes the focus of the
prosecution," Ms. Weisbrod, an attorney and researcher at the Vera
Institute, told me. "In a PINS case the kid is considered 'bad.' In a
neglect case the parent is 'bad.' Parents are bigger and have more
rights so more PINS petitions get into the system."[1]

Here again, our observations have paralleled those of the Family
Court Disposition Study. PINS kids commit violent assaults, destruction of property, thefts and robberies in their homes or elsewhere and
the cases do not get into the court as juvenile delinquency cases. Furthermore, we have found that though fewer PINS cases have been be-

fore the courts on prior delinquency charges, this does not mean that many of these youngsters have not actually committed delinquent acts —and that they may not continue to do so. Social agencies expend prodigious thought and resources in categorizing children's offenses and pathologies when in fact they would obtain better results by focusing upon and providing truly adequate nurturing and socialization.

Before Ramona was remanded to Argus, a staff member had talked with her about the group home program, being as explicit as possible about what she could expect from us and what the girls and the staff in turn would expect from her. The girl had expressed a willingness to be admitted to Argus. We now talked with her again, explaining what a court remand was and that there was to be a thirty-day trial period to determine whether the program was right for her. We again explained our program structure to Ramona, emphasizing the no drugs, no alcohol, no violence rule and the reason for it.

In Ramona's case a pre-entry visit was not possible. Because of the remand she had to take the group home sight unseen. She would have a chance theoretically to reject us at the end of the thirty-day remand period when she would return to court, but the reality was that the other child-care agencies had already turned her down.

She was assigned to Patricia Ivy, at that time the senior counselor in Argus One, where, with few exceptions, newcomers are placed.

For several weeks, deprived of marijuana and in a strange environment, Ramona refused to speak or to participate in any of the activities of the house. She lay on her bed and refused to eat, except when Patricia fed her from a spoon. When anyone else approached her, she screamed or whimpered and after a week or two went into tantrums. At such times Patricia put her on a pallet on the floor and lay beside her, warming, soothing and rocking her as she flailed, screamed and sobbed. As soon as she felt the child could tolerate it, Patricia asked a second counselor to lie on the other side so that Ramona was surrounded by body warmth and learned that she could derive comfort from more than one source. It was the death and rebirth of a thirteen-year-old girl.

At the end of three weeks Ramona was eating and taking an interest in her surroundings. Patricia took her into a group. The girls had been prepared for her. There was quite a bit of jealousy, which was natural since Ramona was monopolizing most of Patricia's time and attention. The housemanager, the social worker and the director of the group home program devoted extra time to the other girls in Argus during this period and tried to help them sort out their feelings. Because of this, when Ramona came into the group they were able to be supportive. Two girls told her about more or less similar experiences they had been through. She listened but pushed them away when they tried to hug her. "You'll get over that. You just don't believe that we really care about you. But you will," the girls told her.

After this Ramona was encouraged to take part in the regular routines of the group home. She entered the Housewarming Phase, where all new residents are placed for roughly seven days while they become familiar with the staff and girls, learn the rules and get their bearings. During this period Ramona was registered in the Learning for Living Center. The staff there had been briefed and assigned her to a female counselor who would keep in close touch with Patricia. Ramona kicked up quite a fuss about going to school and, indeed, the first day regressed to her most helpless and angry level. She had formed an attachment to Patricia and now any separation, even for a day, was seen as a permanent loss. We learned that one day in her past life she had gone to school and had returned home to find that her grandmother was dead. She had both loved and hated her grandmother and on an unconscious level thought that she had killed her with her "wickedness" and bad thoughts. Patricia explained that her grandmother was old and had had a heart attack, and that wishing her dead—a child's natural response to punishment and repression—had nothing to do with bringing about her death. Ramona was not convinced. Still, she consented to go to school if Patricia would take her. Patricia made a bargain: "I'll take you today, and tomorrow you will go with Chessie and the other girls."

This worked out, though not without some tears and resistance. Everyone encouraged her to go ahead and get through the scary part so that she could come out of Housewarming, collect the allowance that had been accruing to her account on that level and move into Level Three A, where she could go out in the company of higher level girls and collect $3 a week allowance.

Ramona had not been concerned that Patricia had other girls on her caseload until, as she grew stronger, the counselor began to devote time to them. Having always been the only child in the homes where she had lived, it was a shock to realize that she had to share Patricia's affections. This came at a time when Ramona was at liberty to collect her allowance and was permitted to make phone calls (she had no one to phone), to receive visitors (she had none) and to make limited trips to the neighborhood store. She went on a more extensive expedition and managed to purchase some chiba, returning a few hours later in a wretched state. The marijuana had been laced with another substance, probably PCP. She was rushed to the hospital and treated and returned to the group home the next day. This incident, dangerous though it was, had the effect of frightening her off marijuana for the time being.

It was pointed out that she would be returning to court soon and that Argus had to tell the judge how she was behaving. "If we have to report that you are buying smokes the judge will probably not let you stay with us. He'll think you can't control yourself and he'll send you to some place where the doors will be locked," Patricia told her. "I wouldn't want that to happen because I care about you. But I can't be with you every minute of the day. So it's up to you. You have to decide. If you want to stay with us, you have to follow our rules."

After repeated protests that she did not care one way or the other, Ramona finally said that she wanted to stay. When the court date came round, Patricia went with her. Again she was remanded, this time for a sixty-day period. This was actually a help in that it gave us another tool. Our plan for Ramona included keeping her in contact with reality, getting her to work through her conflicts and bad feelings, ventilate and dissipate them, while at the same time filling the "vacuum" with as many satisfactions as we could devise. The nurturing provided mainly by Patricia but also by the rest of the staff and some of the older girls was the first big step. The more bonded she became in trust and affection, the more relief and comfort she derived, the less she needed chiba to wipe out her bad feelings or produce good ones. It was a long time though before Ramona was able actively to work in groups, to share her pain, anger and fear with the other girls and to reach out and take her fill of affection from them. She remained in a baby and little girl phase for a long time, which had been expected, given her chronological age and the little she had had to grow on.

Ramona relied heavily on marijuana before and after going into detention (the substance was available at the institution). As she pulled the smoke into her lungs bad feelings were wiped out and a euphoria, depersonalized but peaceful and sensuous, took their place as if by magic.

We all like to have good feelings and get rid of bad ones. Many people believe that marijuana is harmless, perhaps because they wish to believe it, but certain evidence points to damaging effects, particularly when the brain and nervous system are not fully developed. With more and more young teenagers and pre-teenagers abusing the substance, some psychiatrists believe that we may find ourselves with a generation of damaged and more or less dependent persons on our hands.[2] For this and other reasons marijuana is forbidden in our group homes. The other reasons are well illustrated in Ramona's case. There is little doubt that with the drug Ramona was suckling herself, bestowing upon her starved being what no one else had provided for her: the sensation of being fully nourished, cherished and blissfully at one with her mother and with nature.

Is there anything wrong with this? Yes, because the substance going into her was not mother's milk. It gave the illusion of providing nourishment but left her hungrier than ever and wasted. Ramona needed true nourishment. Because marijuana spun a cocoon around her, she was prevented from recognizing, trusting and reaching out for bona fide nourishment even when it was there for her, as it now began to be.

And there were other reasons. In order to learn and grow she had to be in touch with her inner and outer realities. Getting high precluded this. She cut herself off from what was happening inside and outside herself. She had severe doubts and conflicts revolving around her feelings for her mother, the different value systems to which she had been exposed, her own self-worth, the transition from childhood to adolescence, her femaleness, incest, punishment, the trustworthiness of her fellow beings and whether life was actually worth living.

In order gradually to bite down on the bitter reality that her biological mother did not want her, that she had not provided the care she craved and needed, in order to chew up, swallow and incorporate this and other hard truths, Ramona had to experience for herself the presence of other nurturing persons, to open herself to what they were offering, to take in good feelings and begin to grow strong from them. Any drug would have insulated her from her surroundings and prevented this process from taking place. Nor could she have made progress in the classroom while under the influence of drugs.

Within a year after entering Argus One, Ramona had come to terms, more or less, with her mother's shortcomings, realized that her needs would probably not be met in that quarter but that bonding and affection and people who cared were hers for the taking. She was learning how to take, and to give, too, to some degree. Meanwhile, she was attending school regularly and was doing well. She was flirting with boys, concerned about wearing the right jeans, the appropriate shoes, having her hair braided in the latest style and doing everything her girl friends did. She was sad, giggly, silly, stubborn, hot tempered and impulsive at times and had a good sense, at least in part, of moving somewhere with her life. She is still working on herself, a creation which will never be completely finished.

She is now a prodigious talker. Eloquent, though not always willing to share the floor. The girls have to shut her up sometimes to make themselves heard.

9. USING THE LANGUAGE OF TOUCH AND EMOTION

*I didn't jump out the window because while I was
sitting on the ledge I looked down an saw all of that
garbage in the courtyard. I remembered how Mary Taylor
held me in her arms and kissed me. I said to myself, I
ain't jumping into all that garbage. I'm better than that.
If I jump at least it'll be out the front window where
everybody can see me an say, "Poor girl! Ain't she
beautiful! What a shame she had to die so young!"*

ARGUS ENROLLEE

Sabine, at eighteen years old, was strict with herself and everyone else. In 1982, after four years in Argus, she passed the regents'
examination, overcoming a language barrier, and planned to enter
college with the aim of obtaining a master's degree in social work.
Sabine had no close friend in the group home or at school. She
burned the midnight oil and let people know that she was a cut above
the other girls. They resented her superior attitude, but they respected her, as did the staff. They also commiserated with her, for
they knew that she was a girl with a tragic flaw.

In her time off Sabine was seeing Soul Jack, a man of thirty with
ex-common-law wives and children scattered over several states. Soul
Jack recently completed three years at Green Haven Prison, and
though he had no ostensible means of earning a living, he sported
mean vines, drove a Cadillac and spent freely at the local disco-
theques. Soul Jack believed in keeping women in their place. He took
pleasure in rejecting and humiliating Sabine. Now and then he beat
her. Sabine believed that if she could get pregnant, Soul Jack would
marry her and they would be happy. She persisted in this fairy tale in
the face of everything that was said to her and what she in moments
of lucidity told herself.

The house did not regard Sabine as a victim except in the larger
sense. After all, she had selected Soul Jack. He was the third man of
this general type she had been involved with since coming to live in
the group home. She became pregnant by two of them and insisted

134

that she wanted to have the babies. Peer pressure persuaded her to do otherwise. But no amount of reasoning could convince Sabine that she deserved a man who would treat her with tenderness, offer her a partnership in life and encourage her to develop as a human being. Indeed, such a man was available to her in the person of Christobar Elfinstone, a Jamaican of thirty-two who was very much in love with Sabine. Elfinstone was a widower with two children. He owned a thriving green grocery in the area. The staff thought that Elfinstone was too old for Sabine, but they saw him as trustworthy, decent and genuinely devoted—a good provider and a faithful family man. And anyway, Sabine never looked at a boy her own age. Elfinstone offered to marry Sabine. He would give her a stable home and would not interfere with her career plans. But Sabine's interest in Elfinstone was to tease and make fun of him.

The girls did not know Sabine's history, except in vague outline, for she never brought herself to the point of sharing it with them. They were amazed and exasperated that a girl of her beauty and talent went from one self-destructive and agonizing relationship to another.

"It seems like you're not satisfied unless some rotten man is beating you half to death," Chessie said to her one day in group.

"That's not true. I don't like to be beaten any more than anyone else," Sabine replied.

"Bullshit! Then how come you stand for it? He must be some lover."

The truth was that Soul Jack was not an especially good lover. In fact, he was hardly adequate, and although Sabine could experience some pleasure in sex if she were beaten, she never achieved an orgasm with any lover. Her counselor was aware of this and of the complex history behind it.

When she was thirteen an older brother had raped her, and thereafter, for one year, had beaten and attacked her sexually. She had tried to defend herself, but her brother slapped her around and terrorized her completely. When these attacks began Sabine had not seen her brother for three years and felt in awe of him. Furthermore, he told Sabine that his attacks were a punishment for her previous sexual promiscuity which had disgraced the family.

Sabine *had* been sexually promiscuous and blamed herself for it. It began when her parents died and her married brother took three of her siblings to New York with his own children, leaving Sabine in the care of an uncle she did not know near Port-au-Prince. Feeling deserted, scared and lonely, she became unnaturally meek and compliant, and when her uncle led her into an abandoned shed and molested her sexually Sabine made no protest. She said afterward that she had permitted him to have sex with her in order not to offend him and also because she enjoyed being held in his arms. It felt good to be close to somebody. He gave her candy and little presents. Her uncle brought other men to her. She accepted them because he told her to and again because the warmth of their bodies and their attention met a need which she felt but did not understand.

People in the village talked. Sabine's aunt informed her brother. Finally, when she was thirteen and confused, her brother, Jean Christophe, had her her brought to the Bronx to live with his family. It was then that her brother began to beat and attack her sexually as a "punishment."

The brother's wife, Chantal, worked as a nurse's aid. She left the house early and came home late. The brother was employed intermittently, unloading vegetables in the Bronx Terminal Market. The other children were in day care. At first Sabine endured her brother's attacks because she felt that she deserved to be punished. And again, she enjoyed the warmth and the "reconciliation." When she began to experience sexual pleasure in these encounters, she was filled with dread and loathing. She attacked her brother several times with a kitchen knife, wounding him twice in the hands. Jean Christophe told Chantal that these attacks were unprovoked and were evidence of his sister's vicious disposition. Chantal said that she was crazy. The adults threatened to have Sabine "put away."

Depressed and desperate, believing they would put her in prison, Sabine blurted out the story to a school counselor, who urged her to tell the police. This idea was strange to Sabine. She had assumed that adults were all powerful and that children had no rights or redress. But in the company of the counselor she went to the police precinct and, trembling and sobbing, begged for their help. The police called the Bureau of Child Welfare. The girl was placed in a shelter and then in temporary care while an investigation was made. The brother was summoned to appear before the Family Court. Sabine's story was believed by the court and she was forbidden to live in her brother's home. Nor did she wish to live there. But because she had attacked her brother with a knife and had actually shed blood, Sabine was turned down by one agency after another. She felt exceedingly bitter, not only because no one wanted her and she was languishing in a city diagnostic center, but because her sister-in-law, who had become a mother figure to her, refused to believe her, stating publicly that her husband would never have been guilty of such repugnant behavior. Chantal put in twelve to fourteen hours a day caring for her patients. Though her earnings kept the wolf from the door while her husband worked only intermittently, she cherished the hope that one day he would support the family. She did whatever she could to keep him in the clear.

The case workers at the diagnostic center were convinced that Sabine's lapse into violence was circumstantial, but they were unable to find her a foster home until, in 1978, at fourteen, she was admitted to Argus. After probing into the matter, our staff concluded that Jean Christophe was guilty. Sabine insisted on taking her brother before the criminal court. She was advised by the district attorney's office that the criminal charges would not stand up because she had not kept a record of the dates and times of the assaults and had no other proof to put forward, but Sabine pursued the case in spite of his advice. She was consumed with hatred of her brother and a desire to see him punished. The case was pending at the time of her admission to the Argus group home, and we stood by her while she pursued it, although we tried to turn her from it. The case was dismissed for lack of evidence, and she emerged from the experience angrier and more embittered.

The family shut her out entirely for the next four years, except for her sister Naomi, who had been brought up from Haiti, and who believed Sabine and sympathized with her. It was touching to see the two sisters together. Naomi was the only relative who ever visited Sabine while she lived in the group home. Our plan for Sabine was to expose her to responsible adults, male and female, to persuade her to express her pain, anger and fear and, by showering her with body and emotional warmth, rebuild her shattered confidence.

Sabine's story is not unusual. Many of our girls have been the victims of rape or incest or both. A number have been promiscuous and have selected sexual partners who humiliated and beat them. Not uncommonly children who are sexually abused blame themselves and contrive in one way or another to punish themselves while replicating whatever comfort and pleasure they had derived from the encounters and perpetuating the feelings, attributions and misinterpretations which attended their victimization. Often these children, like Sabine, have not been fondled, cuddled or loved and in fact suffer from a kind of affect and tactile starvation that makes them easy prey for irresponsible, abusive and exploitative relatives or strangers.

In our experience, the tendency to sexual promiscuity, depression and suicide (attempted or actual)—widespread among adolescents in general and particularly high among homeless girls—is intertwined with an intense and chronic hunger for emotional relatedness, affection and cuddling. And often, this affect and tactile starvation co-exists with a generalized feeling of worthlessness, powerlessness and rage. Their attempts to find warmth or to get their needs met have so consistently come to nothing and they have been scared and lonely over such expanses of time (time stretches out endlessly for children) that they no longer are in touch with the object of their quest. They live it out, sometimes in ways as antipodal as water and fire, milk and poison.

On a spring evening Glenny Beers, a resident in a sectarian home for children, took a box of matches from the kitchen and set her mattress on fire. The child-care workers on duty put out the fire, took away Glenny's clothing and placed her forcibly in the lockup room, a space six by fourteen feet, with barred windows, and bare of furniture or any object a child might use to hurt herself or anyone else. In this cage that resembled a jail cell, Glenny ran up and down, sobbing and screaming, "I want to talk to Miss McDade!" When no one heeded her, Glenny beat her head against the wall, warning her captors that if Miss McDade was not brought to her she would batter her brains out. A child-care worker called Miss McDade and the social worker, who had heard of a girl who had actually dashed out her brains against a wall, decided that she had better see what it was that Glenny wanted. The girl had tried to see her on three separate occasions that day, but Miss McDade had refused.

Actually Miss McDade wouldn't have minded talking with Glenny. She liked the girl and thought that she had potential. But the rules of the institution did not permit her to talk to anyone not on her own caseload. Because of her assaults on staff members, her suicidal tendencies, and her fire-setting "compulsion," Glenny was considered to be one of their more serious cases and had been placed on the caseload of Dr. Jeremy Fitzpatrick, consulting psychiatrist to the home. The social worker had been reprimanded once before for getting between Dr. Fitzpatrick and his patient. She dared not stick her neck out again.

As soon as she heard that Glenny was beating her head against the wall, Miss McDade left her office and went to the lockup room.

"It's Miss McDade, Glenny. I'm here. What do you want?" she called through the door.

"Come in and talk to me."

"All right, if you stop behaving that way."

"I promise."

The social worker opened the door and stepped across the threshold. "You've got your way as usual, Glenny. Now what is it?"

"I was wondering if you heard anything about my foster mother?"

Previously, Glenny had been in placement at another institution and had become attached to one Muriel Rayburn, a child-care worker. For reasons unknown to Glenny, Mrs. Rayburn had left the institution and the child had felt baffled, angry and, on a deeper level, grieved. A few days later Glenny developed the notion, no one knew quite why or how, that Muriel Rayburn had quit her job in order to become eligible to take foster children into her own home. Glenny believed that she was to be Mrs. Rayburn's first foster child.

For several weeks, Glenny waited expectantly. Any day now, she told the staff and residents, she would be leaving the institution and would move in with her favorite child-care worker, who loved her and was going to be her mother.

"She might even *be* my mother. Maybe she became a child-care worker so she could be near me."

A month passed and no word came from Mrs. Rayburn. The meaning of this struck Glenny all of a heap one afternoon when the building was almost empty. She swallowed a bottle of aspirin tablets, had her stomach pumped out and was placed in the psychiatric ward of a city hospital until "more suitable" placement could be found. In an attempt to reduce the shuffling of difficult children from one setting to another, the State Department of Social Services had made a ruling that the institution where a child is placed is itself responsible for finding future placement for that child and may not be relieved of its responsibility until such placement is found. In Glenny's case the previous home had not been able to get any outside institution to accept her, though the materials sent out described her as a "black fourteen-year-old, bright and charming, with the potential to develop into a lovable young woman." Agencies are skeptical of such descriptions. They write the same kind of thing about children they are trying to pass on. They refused to take Glenny. The decision to transfer the girl to a sister institution, under the same voluntary sectarian control, was taken in response to pressure put on central management. Miss McDade and Dr. Fitzpatrick, who knew something of Glenny's history, through the grapevine, had protested the decision, saying that the girl was incorrigible, had actually committed crimes and should be treated as a juvenile delinquent. They did not believe she would benefit from placement in their home and thought in fact that her behavior would be so disruptive that the other children in their care would suffer.

So, although on one level she could not help liking Glenny and felt sorry for her, Miss McDade's tone was quite acerbic as she confronted the girl in the lockup room.

"You've got to get this idea out of your head, Glenny. I have inquired into the matter, as I told you I would, and I found out that Mrs.—What's her name?"

"Mrs. Rayburn."

"Mrs. Rayburn has no intention of becoming your foster mother. They would never have transferred you here if there'd been the faintest possibility of getting you into a private foster setting. I've explained on several occasions the procedure we use to transfer children into private homes and community care. I have the impression that you don't listen to me at all. We don't expect you to be a perfect angel, but we do want you to control yourself. Why did you set that fire?"

"A girl told me when she set her mattress on fire she was transferred out of here."

"Where do you think she was transferred to?"

"I don't know. Back home, I guess."

"I have no information about this particular incident, but I can tell you that if she set a fire she was not sent home. Most likely she was sent to a psychiatric hospital or to jail. Setting a fire is a serious business and in no way does it show that a child is ready for community placement. In setting your mattress on fire you have endangered the lives of the staff and all of the other children in this institution. That will not help you to go home, I can tell you. Now don't go getting upset again. Crying and whining won't get you out of here either. These are manipulations like your fire setting and your temper tantrums. You will have to get that all under control. Then perhaps you can have a mature conversation with Dr. Fitzpatrick."

"I don't need no psychiatrist. There's nothing wrong with my head. I just want to go home."

"The only home you had was with Mrs. Brand, the woman you thought was your aunt. Now we know that she's not your real aunt, even though you are the half sister of the other nieces and nephews who live with her. Mrs. Brand won't consider taking you back until you learn to control your temper tantrums and your fire setting and all the rest of it. You're going around in circles, Glenny, getting nowhere."

In spite of this advice, two days later, out of the lockup, Glenny swallowed a bottle of Johnson's baby oil and dangled herself from a third-story window.

It was back to the psychiatric ward and another round of interviews, tests, evaluations and heavy tranquilizers. Since the hospital would not keep her and no placement had been found, the agency filed a petition of juvenile delinquency on grounds of assault and fire setting. Glenny was removed from the agency's care and was placed in detention, from whence she came to Argus, after the juvenile delinquent petition was vacated and she had been restored to dependent status.

Glenny did not assault anyone in Argus, though she at first threatened to. She smashed her fist through panes of glass, swallowed a bottle of Florida water, drank beer and dangled out of a third-story window. Within three months Glenny left off threatening to kill herself and began to torment the staff by registering a series of complaints with BCW. (This was before the Children's Rights Unit and the Confidential Investigations Unit were formed in SSC.) Glenny stated that Argus refused to give her clothes or to feed her. Two investigators came from BCW, interviewed the staff and residents at Argus One, went through the records and found the complaint to be without foundation. Later, Glenny complained that Argus was treating her cruelly and that, whenever she protested, locked her up in a psychiatric hospital. A full investigation was made and again Argus was exonerated. Glenny's next complaint was that Argus had taken away her clothes and that she was living in the group home entirely naked in a room bare of any furniture or amenities. Another time she reported that she had been physically abused. It was an exasperating business, being investigated and exonerated, but it had to be gone through. Glenny demanded to be placed elsewhere.

Actually, our process had begun to take hold. She had developed a bond with Mary Fritz and she really didn't want to leave Argus. Even though Mary was responsible for two group homes and had a lot on her head, since Glenny had singled her out, she made the time to establish a relationship with the girl and to see that she got a lot of attention, and in addition, specifically, a great deal of cuddling and hugging. The rest of the staff did the same. Rhoda Keller, our human development specialist, reported that Glenny was always looking for an excuse to nuzzle up against staff members. One afternoon at a play Glenny got up and walked across the theater in the middle of the second act. Rhoda feared she was about to create a disturbance, but instead the girl threw herself into the housemanager's lap and remained there for the rest of the performance, taking in body warmth and a feeling of security, and perhaps healing old wounds.

It seems never to have occurred to members of the healing professions who were asked to evaluate, treat or devise treatment plans for Glenny to ask themselves whether fundamentally she might not be suffering from touch and affect starvation.

If such a diagnosis had occurred to them they probably would not themselves have considered touching and hugging her or laying hands on her except in restraint. Although the laying on of hands is an ancient and respected tradition in healing, prevalent in all times and places, both among doctors and priests, it fell into disrepute, particularly in America, when our Puritanical fear of touching was reinforced by the Freudian notion (which the master himself seems not to have adhered to strictly) that the psychotherapist should neither stimulate the patient, reveal himself socially or interject himself in any personal or human way into the therapeutic relationship; and when parental fears of stimulating children sexually deepened.

Our experience with children such as Glenny and Sabine has taught us that traditional therapeutic methods are not relevant to their needs and can in fact be counterproductive and harmful. Talking about caring and relating can be satisfying under some circumstances, but for these children with their deep tactile and affect starvation, verbal contact alone exacerbates their hunger. Verbalizations in and of themselves cannot convey love, any more than the distilled spirit of the grain can substitute for bread. Trying to meet their need with words is like asking them to read a menu instead of sitting down and eating their fill.

The language of touch and emotion has been around longer than words. Touch reverberates in all facets and phases of our being, sending its message ontogenetically through the encoded patterns of behavior, flashing along nerve circuits, flowering through veins and arteries, echoing in the chambers of the heart, stirring the centers of pleasure, emotion, thought and verbalization. Touch reaches deep into the individual experience, revising and rearranging; and into the history of the species (and perhaps of all life), verifying and validating.

Friends of mine have spent twenty-five years on the couch without learning that they are lovable, without experiencing pleasure, let alone ecstasy. It is frustrating and mystifying to be told what an orgasm is; only direct experience will convey the acute and exquisite concert of sensations. Keats's phrase "a wilderness of sweets" conjures up a very real place to those who have been there but remains only metaphor to those who have not.

Blows, abuse and afflictions have been heaped upon children like Sabine and Glenny in very concrete and corporal forms. That the body can speak the language of pleasure and love is a lesson they need to learn. Gentling, touching, cuddling and fond handling enhance development, promote trust and secure feelings, enrich the neurotransmitters and the limbic center, improve the immune system and promote good health, as many experiments and studies have shown. Anyone who doubts this should read Ashley Montagu's excellent book *Touching: The Human Significance of the Skin.* [1]

It is most telling that although we have experienced many ups and downs with Glenny since she came to us, she has never assaulted any staff member. Nor has she set a fire. She put us through some troubled times. As our message, conveyed in many ways, but most directly and fundamentally by means of touching, hugging and cuddling, came across to her, these behaviors and her suicidal tendencies fell away or evolved to a "higher" level of expression.

These days Glenny writes letters and memos. I got one the other day.

TO: Elizabeth L. Sturz
FROM: Glenny Beers
RE: Conditions in the Group Homes
Dear Elizabeth:

I am requesting an interview with you to discuss the following issues in the group homes:

(1) We have too many rules. Argus One where I am is worse than Argus Two. Only babies have to have rules and regulations. Every time we turn around someone is telling us we can't do this or that and yet they are doing the same things themselves. The rules should be abolished.

(2) We never will grow up as long as you deny us the chance to find out what the world is really like. We already know more about life than you think because of our histories. The curfew is harming and not helping us.

(3) The counselors don't bother to find out what is going on with us girls because they are thinking about themselves. No wonder some of us act out the way we do. They are not our parents but they are paid to watch over us and should be confronted if they don't.

Thanking you in advance for your cooperation.

Respectfully,
Glenny Beers

I answered Glenny's letter at once. I told her that I was very happy that she felt enough confidence to share her thoughts with me. I asked her to call or drop by and make an appointment so that we could talk. She popped her head in my door on a Monday morning. I left my meeting, came out, gave her a hug and a kiss, and set up the appointment for that same afternoon at two o'clock. At the appointed hour we kissed and embraced again and then talked at our leisure.

"Have you ever told Mary Fritz or the counselors how you feel about the things you mentioned in your letter?" I asked.

Glenny said she hadn't. "I'm funny. I get hurt easily. I get hurt and mad. But I can't go directly to the people that hurt me and tell them what they did. I always take it out on someone else."

"Why do you spose you don't want to tell them directly?"

"I don't know. Well, maybe because it's too scary, I don't have enough confidence."

"In them?"

"In them or myself."

I told her that I thought she was being very honest about her feelings. *"That* takes a lot of bravery."

Glenny said that when someone she likes a lot—a counselor or a friend—does something she doesn't like she goes off and broods about it. She is so hurt and angry that she feels like the world is coming to an end, that she doesn't want to live. "Something like that brings up all the bad things that have happened to me in my life. I don't think I'll ever get over them. When thoughts like that come to me I go and take it out on someone completely different. I dump everything on them and they had nothing to do with it."

I told her to use the groups to let the bad feelings out. "If you do that and keep doing it those bad feelings from the past will go away. They really will. Of course, you'll have disappointments. Not everyone will treat you right. But some people will. You'll learn to pick out those you can trust and let the others go by."

Glenny asked me what I was going to do about the things she brought up in her letter. I said that the rules must stand but I would talk to Mary Fritz and Mary Taylor about the other matters and maybe call for a meeting. Glenny said that would be okay.

"Counselors are not perfect. They have a hard job and they're human like you and me. They have their feelings and sometimes they make mistakes too. That's why we have our staff training sessions and our own groups. Because we get feelings too and we need a safe place to put them out. If bad feelings build up we get confused and do the wrong things. It's hard to tell from where I sit exactly what's going on over there. But I do know that you can help the counselors by talking to them directly about what you feel. They may or may not agree with your ideas, but they can accept your feelings."

Glenny set herself the goal of speaking directly to the next person who hurt her and made her mad. She said she would try to bring it up to their face in the group.

I said that would probably be a very important step for her. I also told Glenny there was a danger that the youth employment programs might lose their funding. Would she sit down and write a letter to her congressman?

Glenny not only wrote to her congressman; she wrote her senator and the Bronx borough president as well, telling them what her CETA job meant to her and the other young people. Later she went to a hearing sponsored by the statewide organization at which several of our staff and members of the Argus Youth Council made statements, along with people from other agencies. Without any prompting, without our knowing what she was up to, Glenny arranged with the chairperson to make a statement. She stood up in the big auditorium full of politicians, officials, experts and community people. She adjusted the microphone like an old pro, waved and smiled. Without a tremor she read the statement that she had jotted down while sitting in the audience:

> Mr. Chairperson, ladies and gentlemen, and friends: My name is Glenny Beers. I'm fifteen years old and I work three hours a day in the Argus Youth Employment Program, which we call Project Foothold. This is the first job I've had and it means a lot to me. I speak for all the youth in Argus and in other CETA programs across the country when I ask you people in government please not to cut these programs. You will be making a big mistake if you do. These programs are the only hope we blacks and hispanics have of getting into the job market. If we're left standing on the street corners, we'll turn to crime for the simple reason that there won't be anything else for us to do. So please, think twice before you make a move. Give the youth of this country half a chance. We'll make it the rest of the way ourselves. Thank you.

Glenny was the only person delivering a statement who got a standing ovation. That so young a girl spoke with such poise and conviction stunned the audience and caused them to burst into wild applause.

The following week Glenny went with two busloads of Argus enrollees and staff members to Washington where she spoke for one of the delegations who visited congressmen and senators. The kids behaved beautifully, singing and chanting as they marched along broad avenues between the citadels of government. They were well received and listened to, and afterwards they visited the Washington and Lincoln memorials and got a glimpse of the White House, the Supreme Court, and the Smithsonian Museum. They arrived back in the South Bronx at 9 that night, having been on the road since 5 A.M. Their mood of adventure, accomplishment and exultation remained

with them for days, and was strongly expressed at the meetings we
held to tell the stay-at-homes about the trip and to repeat the chants
and cheers.

The kids felt certain that Congress would not dismantle the
youth employment and training programs and that their efforts would
influence this decision.

Glenny has made many changes since coming to live in the group
home. But her adjustment is still fragile. When things go wrong in her
life, as when she broke up with her boyfriend or when a certain staff
member left (even though she had railed bitterly and loudly against
him or more probably *because* she had done so, blaming herself when
he lost his job), she tends to go to pieces and revert to some of her
old ways. At these times she may threaten to harm herself, "in order
to keep from hurting the person I'm angry at," as she says; or she may
demand to be transferred out, declaring that she hates Argus and will
not stay another day.

We do not always handle these outbreaks well. They can come
on suddenly and catch the staff unawares. Then, too, the counselors
and the housemanager are only human; they are not always feeling
and acting their best.

What we work for, during these crises and at other times too,
is to communicate to Glenny primarily through touch and feeling
that she counts, that we care about her. The periods when she is
cheerful, cooperative, contented and productive are growing longer.
We believe that the decisive factor, the thing we do which makes the
difference, is speaking to her directly in the language of touch and
emotion. Through this language, as through no other, she may
eventually come to feel that she is good enough, that she is lovable,
that she is valuable, that she is entitled, that she is, in short, a wonderful human being.

With Sabine, we are less sure. The scars of incest are deep and
pervasive. She may carry them always. Even so, it may make a difference if she can come to realize that she is not to blame, that she is now
loved for herself, that not all adults are irresponsible and crazy and
that not all males are driven and sadistic. Here again, we believe that
a storehouse of confidence can be built up through affection, by
hugging and cuddling. By continuing good and responsible treatment
a new matrix of response may be formed, displacing the old. We hope
that Sabine will come to feel and understand that her sexual compliance was for the most part the blind attempt of a child to satisfy its
desperate hunger for cuddling and affection. When she learns how to

satisfy these needs in everyday ways she can perhaps turn to sex as a pleasure to be enjoyed for itself.

It seems fairly certain that these two girls will become successful manipulators of their world. They are bright, talented and well organized. But having been denied adequate caretaking and nurturance and, perhaps even more importantly, tactile affection and love, are they not likely to become, as so many Americans are, success oriented, achieving as required, adapting like chameleons to whatever coloration they find, in touch with whatever of themselves is marketable, but pushing back and denying trust, emotionality, love and friendship? Our efforts, coming late and at best a substitute for what should have been their birthright, may or may not enable them to reach out for happiness.

The stories of our girls are still unfinished. We do a lot of waiting and wondering. And hoping. No one knows whether the language of the skin can be learned in adolescence or whether the chasms created by affect deprivation can be crossed. But we do a lot of touching and cuddling and rocking and cooing and cradling, just in case.

10. UNDERSTANDING THE PROCESS

Give me the exact names of things
I want the word to be the thing itself
Created by my soul a second time.

From a poem by ARGUS ENROLLEE

Argus uses the power of community and simple truth to restore persons to themselves and others. We provide an atmosphere where young persons—and the adults who act as their guides—can slough off the shell of isolation or acting out and become comfortable with their own responsive skins and their need for other human beings.

To accomplish this we use an eclectic bag of tools. What works for some people may not work for others. We make use of any method that is conducive to our end.

We do not view the mind as separate from the body; we work with the total human organism. Neither do we conceptualize emotions, attitudes and behavior as entirely discrete areas or even as parts of a whole but rather as ways of experiencing, thinking and acting which are knit together in our sensitive and potentially effective organic and social beings. Our process must take into account what we are biochemically and what culture and society have schooled us to be. This includes what we feel, how we think, what we do and how we interact with ourselves and society. At Argus we try to confront all of these levels, stimulating (1) more resonant expression of the emotions; (2) new ways of thinking about the self and others and about the world; and (3) changed modes of behavior, proself and prosocial actions, leading to competence and success. These areas feed into each other like the jets of a fountain, creating the energy and upsurge that characterize human beings at their highest level of development.

Argus provides an eight-hour environment for those attending the Learning for Living Center and, for those in residence, round-the-clock care. The structure—the rules and the daily routines—are the bedrock under our feet and the roof over our heads. Within this structure, a nurturing environment is the oxygen we breathe.

148

Usually, counseling or therapy denotes a sit down, face-to-face interaction, mostly talk, which takes place at stated times in an office. At Argus every interaction—in the classrooms, on the job, in hallways and offices, at meals, in meetings and groups, at the switchboard, in sports, recreation, disco dancing, at play and on trips—is restorative, generative—therapeutic, if you will. At least that is the ideal; we carry it out to the extent that the staff is properly developed. We like to think these interactions are structured so that they promote trust, pleasure and a flow of satisfying experiences that add up to enhanced self-esteem, respect for others, a more optimistic view of the world and of one's place in it and better performance in school and on the job. For example, although he is now the administrative director of Argus, Aubrey makes time to talk to enrollees—about themselves, their goals, what his own life was like, growing up in the ghetto, about his job. Counselors take enrollees out to lunch to mark achievements or to give them a feeling of being "special." Frances Foye's door is always open to program enrollees, even though her job as director of operations is very demanding. Rhoda keeps treats and lots of sympathy in her office. Frank Valenti used the rock lyrics written by one of his students to teach reading, chalking the words on the blackboard and asking the class to sing them. And when a new enrollee angrily refused to sweep the floor, Fernando Quiñones picked up the broom, saying, "Here's how you do it." A few minutes later the kid took the broom and performed his chore. Fernando is now director of intake, but he stays on top of the kids in the program, helping them through the bad patches, praising them when they do well.

When they first arrive at Argus—and sometimes for months afterwards—the kids test us to see if we are "for real." When they find that we do as we say we do, that we "walk the walk" as well as "talk the talk," they begin to trust. If they find that a staff member is "getting over," they are confirmed in their suspicion that everybody lies, cheats and rips off. Being in the "people business" is a little like being a priest or doctor. If you can't adhere to the ethics of the profession, you had better find another way to earn a living. Many of our youngsters feel that the significant adults in their lives have let them down. We should not add to that disappointment and betrayal. How we conduct ourselves is crucial in getting through to the young people we work with; living up to our own rules is a part of our method.

To create and sustain a therapeutic environment every Argus employee—from the switchboard operator, the cook and the maintenance men to the director and the board members—must be conversant with our rules, values and methods and must be committed to seeing that they are carried out. By adopting and living by certain principles and rules, the staff tries to show what it means to treat others with respect and to demand respect from others, to express anger without causing harm, to forgo verbal abuse and violence, to employ a professional manner of speaking and acting, to behave responsibly, including arriving on time, attending to business, taking care of ourselves and others.

Knowing what the rules are, learning to abide by them, coming to see that the structure cannot be knocked down, that the staff will not abdicate no matter how hard the kids kick and threaten, no matter how they lie or manipulate—these are important lessons for the enrollees. Much as they appear to hate the rules, deep down they are glad when they cannot get around them. They realize that they are in the hands of adults who don't want them to hurt themselves. This lesson may take a while to sink in; they may continue to rebel; and the counselors have to put up with a lot.

From every quarter enrollees receive the message: you count, you are valuable, you are entitled to grow, to get your needs met, to find decent lives for yourselves. But they also hear that what they are and what they do with their lives depends on the actions they take. Yes, they have had it tough; yes, we sympathize. But we will not condone their using the past as a cop-out. We expect them to take responsibility for themselves. The world is rough but we are here to help. Step by step they can put themselves together—by attending classes and groups, by being on time, by making use of the resources at their disposal, by leaving off drugs, booze, violence and verbal abuse, by putting anger and bad feelings into a holding pattern and dumping them freely in groups or in the counselors' offices.

We send out another message to a kid when we think he or she is able to trust it: you are a beautiful person. You are unique—the only one in the history of the world with your imprint. Nature didn't make any other just like you. You may be *doing* some things that are not so great and we want you to stop; but you're a good person. You're lovable. You're valuable. You're entitled. You can do it. In short, you're terrific.

Can psychotherapy help our clients?

Except for one or two who have snuggled into cozy identities as psychiatric patients before they come to us, our young clientele will go once or maybe twice to a psychiatrist or psychotherapist for an evaluation. After that they put their foot down flat. We tried having a psychotherapist on the premises, but the children did not keep their appointments or were uncooperative, made up stories or sat silent during the sessions. The traditionally trained psychologists and psychiatric social workers we have had on staff had little background in behavior disorders and often were manipulated by the youngsters. They tended to indulge the self-destructive propensities of the youngsters and did not take a firm stand with them. The children laughed at them behind their backs and sometimes to their faces. Diane Moore, in contrast, related to the kids in a firm, realistic manner. She cared for them, and her brand of therapy was tailored to their needs.

Our enrollees will take part in exercises from encounter, Gestalt, New Identity Therapy ("scream") or other humanistic psychology repertories, and from these they can sometimes get in touch with levels of pain, fear and need which are ordinarily not available to them —provided these exercises are led by people they know and trust. They make "transferences" to staff members and develop deep and special affection for certain of their peers—thus preparing the way for the emergence of conscience. This generally has to happen with "their kind of people," at least at first. Later, when a certain amount of growth has taken place, they can take a chance and open themselves to persons who before might have struck them as alien or untrustworthy. Our most talented teachers, such as Eddie Dickerson, Roy Fields, Ruth Green, Sandra Eno, John Cardile, Mike Feldman, Tyde Carbone, Frank Valenti, and John McGuire, regardless of color or ethnicity, set up two-way relationships with the young persons in their classrooms by "being there" and by pouring out warmth and relatedness. Xenophobia can seldom thrive when people, of whatever ethnicity or economic background, share their emotionality. This too is therapy.

Researchers seem to agree on two points: (1) that the type of treatment—psychoanalytical, behavioral, client-centered, humanistic or eclectic—matters less than the experience, warmth, skill and dedication of the person administering it; and (2) patients who are emotionally healthier when they begin therapy do better than those who are less so.[1]

Psychotherapists themselves speak of specific attributes that "good" patients, that is, patients considered good prognostic risks, should have. Hans H. Strupp writes that patients should be

> young, attractive, well-educated, members of the upper middle class, possessing a high degree of ego strength, some anxiety which impels them to seek treatment, no seriously disabling neurotic symptoms, relative absence of deep characterological distortions

and strong secondary gains (gratification from their symptoms), a willingness to talk about their difficulties, an ability to communicate well, some skill in the social-vocational area, and a value system relatively congruent with that of the therapist. Such patients tend to remain in therapy, profit from it, and evoke the therapist's best efforts.[2]

The qualities that make a good patient are also associated with improvement in the absence of treatment. Dorothy Tennov summarizes the attitudes of psychotherapists she surveyed: "Psychoanalytic treatment and most of its derivatives depend on patients who are bright and cooperative, who realize their need for treatment and come regularly, who verbalize freely, tell the truth, and are able and willing to pay. . . . "[3]

Clearly, this is not a combination of qualities found in the youngsters who enter our program. Our kids are not "cooperative"; do not always achieve a rating of "bright" on the intelligence tests; will not go voluntarily for treatment sessions or will not go at all; do not recognize that they "need treatment"; may not tell the truth or verbalize freely (least of all to a middle-class professional); do not share the values of most professionals; and above all are not "willing and able to pay." Even so, the profession has opened its doors to this "untreatable" and "unqualified" clientele since government funds became available for treating the "psychological" ills of the poor. But our clientele do not relate in a sincere manner to sessions in an office with these middle-class professionals, whatever their color or ethnicity, nor do they get much from most university-educated and formally trained psychotherapists. This raises questions about the investment of public funds for the purchase of traditional psychodynamic therapy for clients such as ours.

New Identity Therapy, invented by Dan Casriel, provides us with one of our most effective psychotherapeutic tools. Dr. Casriel, a psychiatrist who practiced traditional psychoanalysis for years, finds that there has been a change in the type of patient coming into treatment. Freud thought that 80 percent of patients were neurotic and 20 percent were "character disordered." Since then the ratio has reversed itself, Casriel finds, with 80 percent showing behavioral or personality problems.[4] Casriel began to use screaming as a tool to help patients express long-buried emotions before Arthur Janov began to practice. I have met psychiatrists, psychologists and other professionals from every part of the United States and from many countries in Europe, South America and Australia in his training workshops. From his institute in New York City, Dan has traveled all over the world to train practitioners, and institutes have opened in London, Paris, Geneva, Berlin, Oslo, Copenhagen, Caracas and other cities.

Dan believes that his method can help people to stay healthy emotionally and physically in a culture which has sought to turn off the deep, survival-based feelings. "Ours is . . . a dynamic which draws people into a circle of love," Dan writes. "Arms flung round each other, eyes peacefully shut, contented sighs and hums rising up like some forgotten campfire song which everyone somehow knows. It is a very human dynamic, and it is far older than civilization."[5] Underneath the great variety of symptoms which people display in the dynamics of scream exercises, there is an astonishing similarity in human feelings and needs, Dan has found. Insights often rise or even swarm into the mind after screaming; experiences long buried emerge clear and vivid and can be understood and reconciled or incorporated in a more realistic, less compulsive way. It is a greatly accelerated process, made possible by emotional, physical and cognitive openness and supported by the caring of the group.

"In emotionally honest interaction," Dan says, "each individual feels sufficiently secure not only to feel and show genuine emotions but also to experience the emotions of other people. The result is mutual vulnerability and meaningful emotional contact." Dan sees symptoms as an acted-out camouflage, designed to protect the hurt inside.[6] This approach works for both "neurotics" and "behaviorally disturbed" persons. We use it whenever we can in the Argus program. Adolescents are more open to it, in our experience, in a live-in situation. Aubrey LaFrance, Mary Taylor, Elsie López, Patricia Ivy, Mary Fritz, and I have experienced Dan's process ourselves, have attended his workshops and lectures. Since Dan's illness, our staff is being trained by David Freundlich, M.D., of the Center for the Whole Person. By helping us to relive our childhood and adolescence, by teaching us to be "good parents" to ourselves, to overcome our fear of success and good feelings, Freundlich is giving us powerful tools for our work at Argus.

Since World War II many types and modes of group therapy have proliferated, partly because there were not enough therapists to provide individual treatment to all those traumatized by the war and the postindustrial society but also because psychoanalysis, even when practiced within a group setting, did not fill the bill. In less traditional groups reactions are intense and emotional. Participants get feedback from group members. Even though it may be painful, group members are relieved and exhilarated when their intellectualizations and verbal controls are attacked and broken down by their peers. They find that the secrets they have guarded do not drive people away but are understood and sympathized with. They let out their feelings of anger, pain and fear, and the group supports and encourages them. They are confronted about their behavior and attitudes and are told to give up destructive ways of trying to cope. If they withdraw or ramble, the group brings them back to the here-and-now and to their true feelings. If they are honest, they are praised; if not, they are scolded. Group members feel free to express their thoughts and feelings, to touch and offer love to one another.

Casriel, who practiced classical psychoanalysis for ten years before experimenting with groups, reports in his book *A Scream Away from Happiness* that "group members . . . reached more intense anger than they ever had with me . . .," and, "clearly, without the impediments of the psychiatric education I had experienced, my catalysts—and my patients—were freer to get involved and interact with others."[7]

Encounter from the beginning has been a broad umbrella under which many kinds of intensive experiences take place. Encounter groups can be structured, task oriented, have strong leaders or no leaders. Some are so loose that it may take weeks for the members to discover what it is they want to accomplish. But in all encounters there is the requirement that the group members search for ways to relate to themselves and one another and that they be honest.

Carl Rogers, in his book *On Encounter Groups,* tells us that "a facilitator can develop, in a group which meets intensively, a psychological climate of safety in which freedom of expression and reduction of defensiveness gradually occur." Rogers goes on to say that with the freedom to express real feelings, positive and negative, a feeling of trust develops. "Each member moves toward greater acceptance of his total being—emotional, intellectual, and physical—as it *is,* including its potential."[8]

There are several "don'ts" in encounter. Don't try to make people feel "better." Accord them the dignity and the strength to feel their bad feelings. They don't need to be coddled or "red-crossed." Don't rush to the rescue. Don't play nurse. Don't interfere with the "leveling" process. Don't tell anyone not to cry, not to feel their feelings. Don't condemn the person. (I don't like what you're *doing,* but you are a beautiful person.) Don't show off or exercise your wit at another person's expense.

And there are several "dos." Do allow room for people to overcome their shyness and show their feelings. Do help people to see how they are relating to other group members as mothers, fathers, broth-

ers or sisters. Point out ways that group members are hurting themselves. Tell them to stop. Reinforce new learning (with praise, with
rewards). Let participants stand on their own two feet.

In our groups at Argus we use a range of techniques from the
repertory of humanistic psychology—encounter, Gestalt-type sensitivity and Positive Mental Attitude exercises.[9] In encounter groups we
do not employ the battering-ram techniques often used with hard-
core addicts, as in the Synanon "game" groups, where angry attack
is used as a therapeutic tool. When not used unfairly or irresponsibly,
such confrontations can be effective in changing behavior, especially
when the addict or character-disordered person is encapsulated in a
shell of psychopathy and acting out, for there is no other known way
to penetrate the shell and get at the feeling, needing person behind
it.[10] But with dysfunctional teenagers who use marijuana and alcohol
to excess but who are not hard-core addicts and who still have access
to their feelings (at least in part), it is more productive to use moder-
ate encounter techniques. They may be put on the hot seat at times,
for behavior must be dealt with. But whenever possible it is better to
draw adolescents out, to interpret what they are doing and going
through and to steer them into prosocial attitudes and behavior. It is
important to realize that our youngsters feel bad about themselves
most of the time. They are unsure of who and what they are and doubt
that they can make a place in life for themselves. They need to hear
that we understand, that we have been through it, that behaving
responsibly and thinking positively will make them feel better, that
setting and achieving goals can lead to more satisfactions.

We have several kinds of groups at Argus. In Project Outlook
groups, Positive Mental Attitude is taught through a series of exercises and games, first to establish trust and develop caring and sharing
and then moving to goal setting and goal attainment. The emphasis
is on overcoming adversity, on sharing experiences and on building
positive thought and action patterns. The goal is to improve self-
image and outcomes. (Our use of Positive Mental Attitude is described in Chapters 11 and 12.)

We also have guilt sessions where everybody, including staff, can
cop to antisocial behavior and clean the slate for a fresh start. Marathons (group sessions lasting all day or half a day and the whole of
the following day) are held periodically, especially in the group
homes. At present eight groups of ten to twelve youngsters and a
leader and co-leader meet two times a week for one and a half hours.
All the groups use encounter, sensitivity and/or emotive approaches,
and all are permeated with Positive Mental Attitude.

One-to-one counseling, or counseling in dyads or other small groupings, is available at any time in response to problems or crisis situations.

Parents and relatives are counseled, both privately and face-to-face with the youngsters. We are in touch with families on an ongoing basis, although most of the parents of our young people are so over-burdened that they cannot become involved in Argus in a consistent way.

General meetings and special groups for enrollees and staff are called when unusual problems arise, such as a crisis in the home or drug sales, drug abuse, theft or violence on the premises.

Any approach to treatment that focuses primarily on the individual will, I believe, further alienate today's young people. Conventional one-to-one psychotherapy only serves to heighten their sense of being cut off from the community and, in consequence, of not really existing. The existential point of view is unique in proposing pure awareness as the end-all and be-all of the therapeutic intent. But this kind of awareness—that we are naked and alone in a desolate place —is an "illness" in itself and cries out for a cure. That cure is human bonding because (in my opinion) human bonding is all we have. It is as life sustaining as good bread, and it has to be brought to the table every day.

Example: The girl in the Argus Youth Council who comes to my office to show me her newly acquired certificate from Cornell University, where for the past four Saturdays she has been studying parliamentary procedures, said, "Look at this! I'm ready to sit on MERB [the Argus Management Employee Relations Board, made up of enrollees and staff] and nobody can stop me. I'll be the chairman before long!" She is an impressive girl, intelligent, dignified and hard working. But the expression in her eyes, a vulnerability about the mouth, her posture, and a mantle of sadness that hangs over her tell me that what she probably means is, "In spite of this piece of paper, I don't really think I'm good enough." I tell her, "It's going to be exciting sitting on MERB. You'll know more about how to run a meeting than anyone here." Then I put my arms around her and give her a hug and a kiss. It is essential that she be acknowledged as a lovable human being. So much physical pain has been inflicted on most of the young persons at Argus that they have developed a fear of the contact they crave and attempt to express it, chiefly, through sex. By a homeopathic rule, they can best be cured of their fear of touch by touch itself. That is why we do as much hugging and touching as we can.

The structure and the incentive system have led to a mislabeling of our program as behavior modification by some of our monitors who know us only superficially. What we offer is closer to reality therapy than to behavior modification, but it has the crucial elements of allowing for the expression of deep feelings and experiences and of touching, hugging and bonding, which would not exist in either of these approaches, or only incidentally. The warm extended family is an essential component. Programs based on a token economy or other behavior-shaping techniques have been successful only when the staff generate warm human interactions and have failed in settings where they do not.[11]

The behaviorists believe that what you *do* serves as the basis for your self-concept and that self-assertion is important to building self-esteem. We go along with that and try to reinforce positive acts and self-assertiveness in our kids and staff. However, it may take time and effort to get them to see the difference between being self-assertive and being manipulative and/or aggressive. If the staff do not know the difference or are not fully supported in confronting it, the kids will not progress to that point.

But we also teach young people (and counselors) that cognition influences feelings and behavior. In building healthy self-concept it is necessary to become aware of the blueprint or picture of yourself that you carry around, to eliminate the self-denigrative content and substitute realistic upbeat auto-suggestions. We have found that Positive Mental Attitude, although it is not psychotherapy, is an excellent method for changing the way people think and feel about themselves, for spurring them to new goals and changing the course of their lives. The Positive Mental Attitude learning level of the materials that work so well in the business and middle-class world presuppose a development which our enrollees have not reached. We have therefore experimented with new exercises and have developed a training package appropriate to our population. I believe that people are purposeful and goal-oriented by nature and that they have been and are being "programmed" by their environments and their "minds," that is, by what they have incorporated from their culture and the interpretations they make of their interactions with it and with the environment. Therefore, it seems appropriate to put people in touch with the creative ways in which they can use and *direct* their own brains and nervous systems to build positive and realistic self-concepts, to set goals and to lead their lives more successfully.

We are committed to working with *behavior, attitudes and feelings* in a setting oriented to the here-and-now and to achievement of future goals; and, although progress can be made by focusing on one of these to the exclusion of the others, why leave out any vital area?

With our young clientele in such extremities of need, I am convinced that we must use whatever tools are effective in developing all of these areas: attitudes, self-concept, and cognition; feelings, including affection and living in groups successfully; and behavior which is prosocial in its overall effect.

Our method, in essence, is to fuse and create a new state of being, believing, belonging and relating out of shards that had been broken and scattered or had not been available heretofore. Dreams, fragmented and wandering, are knit into a cloth of everyday existence. Those who have few words find a language, a code, and a meaning.

And if we want to save our skins, we had better think about how to achieve something like this on a societal and world scale. I have great faith in the human creative mechanism—our marvelous brain and nervous system—and our ability to work out varied solutions in the postindustrial world.

11. THE SLEEPING GIANT
Positive Mental Attitude

Basically what I learned from Positive Mental Attitude
was to feel good about myself. If I don't feel good about
myself, there isn't anyone else that's going to.

ARGUS ENROLLEE

W. Clement Stone introduced the concept at Argus. Some of
the staff were skeptical. A Positive Mental Attitude? They had heard
of it in a vague sort of way. At worst, they saw Positive Mental Attitude
as a gimmicky, marketplace technique used by salesmen in drumming
up trade; at best, they thought it was psychology watered down and
made palatable to those who were prejudiced against its more rigorous forms. I was convinced that the concept was sound and that it
could affect staff and enrollee attitudes for the better but wondered
how psychologists and social scientists would respond if we asked for
their advice on putting together an experiment at Argus. We wanted
to create a package of materials suitable for instilling Positive Mental
Attitude in our population and, in the process, to learn more about
how our young people's self-concepts and world views are formed.

We had some big surprises in store.

Judge Mary Conway Kohler, chairman of the National Commission on Resources for Youth, and a member of the Argus Board, first
brought Mr. and Mrs. Stone and their daughter, Donna, to the Learning for Living Center for a morning's visit in the spring of 1980.
Michael Shimkin, publisher and friend of Argus, was present. The
Stones are fond of Judge Kohler and trust her in a special way. Stone
calls her his "saint." I had invited Michael because he had immersed
himself in Argus and was interested in anything that might enhance
our process and because a flash of intuition told me that he and the
Stones would be compatible.

W. Clement Stone is the founder and chairman of the Combined
Insurance Company of America, a multimillionaire and a supporter of
conservative causes. But the idea that means more to him than any
other is Positive Mental Attitude.

159

There is a touch of Merlin the Magician about W. Clement Stone. He looks the part for one thing: the optimistically up-curving hairline mustache (almost a trademark), the bold eyebrows, the polka-dot bow tie with breast pocket handkerchief to match, the arrowhead of black hair shooting down the middle of the high polished forehead and the concentrated gaze set the stage for conjuring or ultraplanetary events.

Clement Stone has an uncommon focus. He has thrown out the extraneous, has centered, strengthened and activated his being with one purpose. He *is* what he believes. Positive Mental Attitude is the essence and the extension of himself. He has power beyond that of money. He aspires to lead a noble life and to share what he has and what he knows with other people. Personally, he is a caring man, devoted to his family; and he has extended this family feeling throughout his company, having figured out, like the Japanese, that it is good business as well as good ethics to give people a secure base and to protect and remain loyal to them. This concern came across when he stood before two separate groups of Argus enrollees, told them his history and explained how Positive Mental Attitude had helped him and many others to succeed. It was his mission and his pleasure to share the formula with those of us at Argus who would be willing to make use of it in our own lives.

"I have a magnificent obsession," Stone said. "To change the world through Positive Mental Attitude."

As he laid out his idea that morning I thought, if anyone *can* change the world, he probably can.

He spoke first to a group of nine young girls in our small conference room on the first floor. They had finished a six-month office skills training program and were excited by the Stones' visit, curious to know what Mr. Stone would say to them and hopeful that it would somehow help them in the ordeal they faced—of calling up prospective employers, making appointments and going downtown for job interviews. Not one among them had ever held a job before or gone for an interview and some had never been out of the Bronx. They were scared.

The Stones shook hands all around, said pleasant things and made little jokes, putting the girls at ease. Stone asked what their goals were. They told him what they were up against in the coming weeks.

Stone confided that he had once been a young man without a job, without connections or prospects. By selling newspapers he managed to save $100 and with this small sum and the help of Positive

Mental Attitude had launched his own business and had become a millionaire. Positive Mental Attitude, he said, had helped him not only to make money but to help other people by giving them a unique and effective way of helping themselves. He said that if the girls would take the trouble to learn a few Positive Mental Attitude principles and practice them until the time came for their interviews, they would be able to approach employers with more confidence, feeling good about themselves and their abilities. This would mean that at the very least they would put their best foot forward in the interview. They might get the job. "But even if you don't get the first job you go for, Positive Mental Attitude will enable you to turn that disappointment into a positive experience."

"How can not getting a job be a positive experience?" the girls asked.

"It can be a very positive experience because you will have been through a job interview. The next time you will know what to expect. You will be less nervous. If you do make mistakes, you can learn from them. And next time or the time after that you will do your best and *your best will be good enough.* You will know that if one employer doesn't hire you another one will."

He got them to shout, "I can do it!" "Do it now!" and "I'm healthy!" "I'm happy!" "I'm terrific!"

All nine of the young ladies in that group got jobs with reliable companies as secretaries, receptionists or clerks, though not always on the first try. However, even their brief exposure to Positive Mental Attitude, they said, showed them how to give themselves positive feedback and to face the interview situations with more poise and confidence.

After talking to the girls, Stone got up to speak before a packed auditorium. The counselors were edgy. I was not at all certain how the young persons from Phase One, new to our process, would view this self-made millionaire when they themselves were poor and their houses, many of them, were sinking into the sewers of the South Bronx. I remembered that the French minister of justice, on a visit to Argus, was amazed when he saw our kids clamber aboard buses sent by the Exxon Corporation and speed away to a state park. In France, the minister said, those buses would be torn to pieces, and no wealthy person would set foot in a poor part of Paris.

But the teenagers and young adults in the two phases gave Stone their attention. In spite of their perception that they were shut out of the job market, they still believed that some people would be helpful and would reach out to them. Stone shared his enthusiasm for a concept that more than any other, he believed, would help these young persons if they would reach out and grasp it. They didn't quite know what to make of him or of what he was telling them, but they shouted along with him, "I can do it!" "I'll do it now!" and "I'm healthy!" "I'm happy!" "I'm terrific!" and they very nearly blew us away with their energy and their vociferation. They were so turned on and in such high spirits (we all were) that we decided then and there to experiment with a formal program of Positive Mental Attitude at Argus. Both Clement Stone and Mary Kohler were enthusiastic about the idea. Mary and I thought that Positive Mental Attitude could provide a road map to a better future for our kids if we presented it in such a way that it would take on substance for them. Positive Mental Attitude could rid their minds of the self-denigrating thinking which acts as an undertow and substitute the positive self-suggestions and self-motivators that can build confidence and self-esteem. It could show them how to set goals that are, in the words of Napolean Hill, "conceivable, believable, and achievable."

Most of us undergo sufferings and misfortunes in our lives, the proponents of Positive Mental Attitude remind us. One has only to glance at the daily papers to realize that human misery is spread widely across class lines. Painful experiences can be damaging, *but the way people view their experiences* may cripple them even more severely.

In Shakespeare's *As You Like It,* the rightful duke is driven from his throne by his brother and takes refuge in the forest of Arden. Instead of moaning and blaming himself and others, the duke tells his co-mates and brothers-in-exile that he finds life in the forest sweeter and less perilous than the painted pomp of the "envious Court." He prefers the cold breath and bite of winter to flattery. He says of the wind and frost:

> . . . these are counsellors
> That feelingly persuade me what I am.
> Sweet are the uses of adversity,
> Which, like the toad ugly and venomous,
> Wears yet a precious jewel in his head;
> And this our life, exempt from public haunt,
> Finds tongues in trees, books in the running brooks,
> Sermons in stones, and good in every thing.
> [act 2, scene 1]

This noble passage has been dear to me from childhood, for my mother knew it by heart and used to encourage my sister and brother and me by quoting it when we were caught up in whining and self-pity.

In the introduction to *Success Through Positive Mental Attitude,* Stone says, "When you read this book, read it as if the authors were your personal friends and were writing to you—and you alone. Underscore sentences, quotations and words that are meaningful to you. Memorize self-motivators. Keep in mind that this is a book to motivate you to desirable action."[1]

My copy is underscored in many places and studded with paper clips. Incidentally, Diane Moore, director of the Argus Positive Mental Attitude project, Anthony Duverese, director of Project Foothold, Mary Fritz, director of the group home program, Aubrey LaFrance, administrative director, and other staff members, all feel that we have gained a great deal personally from our practice of Positive Mental Attitude. The following are some of the passages which I underlined in Stone and Hill's book. These little nuggets, though taken out of context, summarize the main points:

> Effort and work can become fun when you establish specific desirable goals.

> Our attitudes shape our future. This is a universal law . . . this law works whether our attitudes are destructive or constructive. The law states that we translate into physical reality the thoughts and attitudes which we hold in our minds, no matter what they are.

> The most important living person is *you,* as far as you and your life are concerned.

> What is the *right* mental attitude? It is most often comprised of the "plus" characteristics symbolized by such words as faith, integrity, hope, optimism, courage, initiative, generosity, tolerance, tact, kindliness and good common sense.

> Accept the priceless gift—the joy of work. Apply the greatest value in life: love people and serve them.

> Fixing your goals may not be easy. It may even involve you in some painful self-examination. But it will be worth whatever it costs, because as soon as you can name your goal, you can expect to enjoy many advantages. These advantages come almost automatically.

> . . . conscious autosuggestion is the agency of control through which an individual may voluntarily feed his subconscious mind thoughts of a creative nature, or, by neglect, permit thoughts of a destructive nature to find their way into the rich garden of his mind.

> So you've got a problem? That's good! Why? Because repeated victories over your problems are the rungs on your ladder of success. With each victory you grow in wisdom, stature, and experi-

ence. You become a better, bigger, more successful person each time you meet a problem and tackle and conquer it with Positive Mental Attitude.

Do you tend to "blame the world"? If you do, memorize the self-motivator: *If the man is right, his world will be right.* Is your immediate world right?[2]

Most young persons when they come to Argus have poor self-esteem and self-defeating attitudes. We have not been able to find self-esteem measures which have been validated on a population similar to ours; consequently we have no widely accepted "pencil and paper," or self-report, scales which would "prove" our observation.

Although I have stressed the importance of touching and bonding in helping our young clients to grow, we see our task also in terms of making them aware how they are misinterpreting the many negative messages they are getting from the outside world and internalizing the negative. Once they become aware of these negative messages and the damage they do, they can be taught to replace them with positive thought sequences.

In a study of nearly a million public school students Coleman found that *attitudes* toward achievement were a better predictor of academic success than IQ or a number of demographic and attitudinal variables. Most of us at Argus are convinced that this is true of our enrollees.[3]

How do ethnicity and race enter the picture? It is generally agreed that black and other minority students do not perform as well as whites on standardized tests of cognitive skills (IQ tests) and on scholastic achievement tests. Furthermore blacks tend to terminate their schooling at an earlier age than whites.[4] Stodolsky and Lesser found that Puerto Ricans had relatively low scores on IQ tests administered to a number of ethnic groups in New York and Boston.[5] Sexton reported that there is a tendency for IQ test scores of Puerto Rican children to fall as they move into higher grades.[6] And according to New York City Board of Education figures, Puerto Ricans show lower IQ scores than Anglo-Americans whether they were born in Puerto Rico or on the mainland.[7] Low scholastic performance and low IQ test results have been found among other minorities in the United States, including Mexican-Americans and American Indians. Coleman's study provides partial comparison of these groups.[8]

There is widespread disagreement, however, as to the reasons for these disparities. Most explanations have centered around (1) biogenetic theory, (2) family inadequacies, (3) "cultural" deprivations and (4) institutional deficiencies (schools not rising to the task).[9] Without going into these claims, I will only say that I have seen no convincing evidence to support the first three arguments. Nor am I able to follow the circular reasoning of well-meaning liberals who argue that economic inequality would be wiped out if blacks could be brought to perform better in school. To the contrary, I believe that if economic disparities were abated, levels of academic achievement would equalize themselves over time.

Genetic differences do exist, of course, and will continue to exist unless we go in for some fancy engineering of the DNA, but those differences spread themselves more or less equally across those mythical frontiers that we are pleased to call the various "races" of mankind. With no scientific evidence to support the idea that blacks and other minorities are less intelligent, the question is, what causes minorities to perform less well in school and how does this relatively poor performance affect the developing self-images of the children in these groups?

As Ogbu sees it, "one of the main reasons why blacks do not perform as well as whites under the present system is that the schools have traditionally made less serious efforts to prepare them for the desirable adult roles for which they prepared white students." Ogbu finds that the reason for this differential treatment is that schools are agents of a caste society that assigns blacks and whites different positions in adult life requiring different levels of education and skills. "So long as the schools remain agents of the caste system," Ogbu says, "there is no guarantee that they will do better in educating black children under a reorganized, alternative educational system."[10]

According to Ogbu an important determinant of school performance is what children and their parents expect to gain from education in adult life, which he calls "incentive motivation." For nearly a century, Ogbu points out, "blacks have attended schools with inferior resources and this background may have had a cumulative effect on their performance today; and for nearly a century education has not provided blacks and whites with equal access to jobs, wages, and other benefits, which according to Americans, depend on education."[11]

After a meticulous review of the various studies purporting to prove or disprove the "Pygmalion in the classroom" thesis, Persell concluded that teachers are more likely to entertain "negative expectations for lower-class and minority children than for middle-class and white children." She also finds that "teacher expectations are affected by testing and tracking, procedures that are themselves biased against lower-class and minority children." She finds, as do other researchers, that negative expectations might have more potent effects on student cognitive change than positive expectations. "Teacher expectations," Persell says, "influence the learning of many pupils under specifiable conditions. Moreover, their consequences for students low in the societal structure of dominance are intensified by interrelated and cumulative processes. Thus, the educational experiences of lower-class and minority children work to depress their academic achievement, while the educational encounters of white middle-class students help them to achieve."[12]

Unlike Europeans who felt more or less locked into their traditional stations in life, Americans have always assumed that through hard work, energy and talent they could move to any level. The War on Poverty, with its many compensatory educational and job programs, was designed to help minorities and other poor people who had been shunted aside to achieve equality of opportunity with other groups. Head Start and other preschool interventions were a part of this design. The theory was that early education, parental involvement and enriched services would provide poor children with the impetus and the tools to break out of poverty and enter the middle classes. Did these early interventions have significant, long-lasting impact on low-income children? For years, critics have been reporting that these programs had little or no impact, that effects on IQ scores faded out after a year or two of formal schooling.[13] The elitist position (emanating largely from Harvard University) is that intelligence is mainly genetic (Herrnstein); that any intervention after age three is an exercise in futility and that the only effective intervention for a child up to that age must be done at home by a sort of Supermom (White); that children will outgrow their early traumas without public monies being spent (Kagan); and that when poor kids succeed it is largely a matter of luck anyway (Jencks).

My experience of Head Start and other early intervention programs had been positive. The little ones seemed to flourish and the parents were delighted with the advances made by their children. In Trenton the IQ scores of our Head Starters had risen remarkably after a year in the program. Therefore, I was baffled by the negative reports appearing over the years and wondered whether they were based on sound research. Finally, in 1977, a long-term follow-up study of fourteen infant and preschool experiments was published by the Office of Human Development of the U.S. Department of Health, Education and Welfare. The longitudinal study was carried out by a consortium of scholars from leading universities under the direction of the Community Service Laboratory, Cornell University at Ithaca, New York. Its findings leave no doubt that investments in early education have long-term benefits for low-income children that are both humane and cognitive. The study was conducted with great care. The follow-up data included a parent interview, a youth interview, school record and achievement test forms and the Wechsler Intelligence Test appropriate to the age of the youths. The evidence strongly supports the notion that early education improves the academic performance of poor children. Children who had taken part in Head Start and related programs (who at the time of the study were from nine to eighteen years old) were not assigned to special education classes as often as those in the comparison groups nor were they held back in school as often. Furthermore, the Stanford Binet IQ data collected earlier reveal that children in the program surpassed the controls for at least three years after the program ended.[14]

I have dwelt on this because, from the Positive Mental Attitude point of view, it is worth considering whether the children in these early intervention experiments may have incorporated, along with the cognitive materials offered, the basic message that "all this attention and consideration means that I am a valuable and worthwhile person." This is only speculation, of course. No measures of self-esteem were taken, to my knowledge, and I am not sure that they would have been feasible. Nevertheless, many of these children *performed* as though they set high goals for themselves and had good self-concepts. After all, the Head Start experience is pretty much the opposite of what we usually provide for children of the poor. Furthermore, the fact that these children had been in Head Start projects and carried themselves with more self-confidence and showed that they knew more may very well have influenced the view that their teachers in elementary schools took of them.

It is of utmost importance for us as parents, educators, therapists or what-have-you to understand how upward—or downward—spirals can be initiated in which one action, attitude or experience can lead to another and relationships all along the line can change. Behaviorists would argue that action would be the key link in the chain; emotive therapists would say, change the feelings and behavioral change will follow; while those concerned with cognition would hold that feeling and behavioral changes follow upon a change of attitude. It may be that we can start at any one of these "points," and that if our intervention is effective, we will have a tripartite effect. I believe that we must work on all three fronts at once and that the particular starting point is not as crucial as the necessity to recognize that all three areas are key and must be addressed. I have no problem with the "three Rs" of operant behavior, that is, that reinforced responses recur. But feelings and thoughts also are reinforceable and contagious and must be dealt with as such. It is one thing to get kids to tell themselves, "I am good enough, I am lovable, I am valuable, I can do it, I'm terrific." But thinking this way can be a more effective tool if they follow it up with action that proves it and if they learn to open the door to the good feelings that follow and feel fully entitled to them.

The theoretical underpinnings of Positive Mental Attitude go back to the 1920s when the teachings of French psychotherapist Emile Coué were in vogue in Britain and the United States. Coué at one time had practiced hypnosis but abandoned it in favor of conscious autosuggestion. He observed that what a doctor says to his patient (external suggestion) is not nearly as effective as *what the patient tells himself.* The therapist can best help the patient by offering him suggestions which he can apply to himself. "Day by day, in every way, I am getting better and better" was Coué's formula for optimistic autosuggestion, and following reports of its effectiveness in curing and preventing illness, this formula became a household slogan in several countries.[15]

Alfred Adler, Karen Horney, Harry Stack Sullivan and Erich Fromm—sometimes called the Neo-Freudians—rejected Freud's libido or instinctual theory, focusing instead upon the importance of culture and interpersonal relations in the formation of the human personality. Horney was one of the earliest to talk in terms of "striving toward self-realization." Though they differed in some respects, these analysts all saw security needs, pride and its feeling counterpart, self-esteem, as displacing sexual drives in a hierarchy of motivating factors. They saw evil differently also. Sullivan held that malevolent attitudes developed in persons who had certain types of experiences and that those who did not undergo these experiences did not turn to malevolence. When parents and others discharge their social responsibilities, Sullivan believed, the product was a well-behaved, well-socialized person. Adler, in his therapeutic method, emphasized here-and-now conflicts and dilemmas and the daily strivings and goal-oriented behavior of his clients. He was concerned that they develop strategies for living and for self-evaluation which were realistic and nonpunitive. Although the "Neo-Freudians," with the exception of Jung, tended to merge the unconscious into consciousness, Adler moved further away from Freud in this respect, discounting the unconscious and fertilizing the therapeutic ground in which many of today's goal-oriented approaches have taken root.[16] Abraham Maslow, Carl Rogers, Erik Erikson, Daniel Casriel and David Freundlich, among others, have also done significant therapeutic work utilizing the "attitudinal" approach.

Among present-day practitioners and researchers who have focused on attitudes and attributions, probably the most relevant for our work with troubled adolescents are Martin E. Seligman, with his theory of "learned helplessness," and Aaron T. Beck, who has developed Cognitive Therapy as a treatment for emotional disorders.

Seligman's model of "learned helplessness" is consistent with clinical descriptions of depression—helplessness, hopelessness, reduced activity, passivity, retarded ability to learn adaptive responses, discouragement, sadness. This description fits many of the young people, both black and hispanic, male and female, who are enrolled in Argus. Seligman believes that "a person is helpless with respect to some outcome when the outcome occurs independently of all voluntary responses." In other words, no matter what you do, you cannot influence or change the outcome. Nothing that you do matters. Learned helplessness, along with poor self-concept and self-blame, has been reported to precipitate psychological depression. Freud defined depression as the transmogrification of hostile feelings which have been turned inward on the self. But present-day theory sees depression as a sadness and hopelessness, often accompanied by open, other-directed hostility, arising from a feeling of powerlessness and a loss of self-esteem.[17]

The National Institute of Mental Health (NIMH) recently supported a five-year study of the causes of depression and came up with yet another approach. People feel depressed because they *think* the wrong way. They misinterpret the situation, blaming themselves and their own inadequacies when things go wrong. The NIMH research concluded that these *faulty thought processes, these misinterpretations, rather than the events per se,* cause people to be depressed. Most of us, if we lose a parent or someone close to us, will mourn for a period of time, maybe as long as two years, according to some reports. But a young man who is still depressed about the loss of his father after five or ten years may be thinking, "I caused his death." Or, "If I hadn't been so bad or unworthy he wouldn't have left me." Such misinterpretations can keep the wound from healing and can bring more pain and loss in their wake.

These findings are compatible with Beck's cognitive model of depression. In his book, *Cognitive Therapy and the Emotional Disorders,* Beck, whose approach has received well-deserved recognition in recent years, emphasizes the role of the *thought sequences* that intervene between an event in a person's life and the unpleasant emotional consequences. Beck believes it is often *the thoughts about the event, rather than the actual event itself,* which evoke the feelings of anxiety or depression. It is of utmost importance to tap these "internal communications," Beck believes, to make persons aware that they are continually processing, decoding and interpreting messages from the outside and that this self-regulatory system puts out messages of its own, approving, praising or reproaching and blaming.[18]

Psychologists and others have long warned us against a policy of letting our feelings—our wishes and our fears—govern our thinking and influence our standards of judgment. In a way, we have been armed against this distortion. But few of us, before Beck and others pointed it out, realized that thoughts—misinterpretations, faulty attributions, self-condemnations—can actually give rise to feelings which are extremely painful, counterproductive and destructive.

One of the heartening features of Beck's approach is that it is often possible on the day of the patient's first visit to start with techniques that make a real difference in lifting the depression. He gives them some task, however small, which they can perform successfully, and then praises them for it—precisely as we at Argus have been doing for thirteen years! We are proud to be in Dr. Beck's company, though we merely stumbled upon the technique. Many therapists—psychoanalysts as well as behaviorists—have been impressed with the results of cognitive therapy and, without deviating from their basic allegiances and values, have incorporated these approaches into their treatment process.

I am happy to report that we had no trouble whatsoever in putting together an interdisciplinary team, composed of social and clinical psychologists and educators, as well as counselors out of the same background as the participants, to assist in introducing a new climate at Argus—one of Positive Mental Attitude. Diane Moore, a clinical psychologist who specializes in self-esteem and depression, returned to Argus (she had been our human development specialist previously) to become director of the project. Dr. Michele Berdy, clinical psychologist and psychotherapist, and Mary Taylor, C.S.W. and psychotherapist, acted as staff trainers and as advisors on the package of materials we are developing. Dr. Michelle Fine, social psychologist and assistant professor at the University of Pennsylvania, was evaluation director.

As we have put together the research design for Project Outlook and have gone about the business of instilling Positive Mental Attitude at Argus, in an exciting collaboration, our team has engaged in many theoretical discussions. Dr. Fine's particular sphere of interest —how victims perceive themselves and under what conditions "helpers" (professional and grass roots) derogate these victims—overlaps with the Positive Mental Attitude project.

I am delighted that Positive Mental Attitude has so many respectable and scientifically sound antecedents and first cousins in the psychological and psychiatric community, as well as great possibilities for future development. The method has done so much for me personally and for the staff and enrollees that simply on the empirical evidence we now consider it one of our most valuable tools. The results of our experiment at Argus showed that the group which received Positive Mental Attitude training performed significantly better than the comparison group which was not exposed to Positive Mental Attitude, even though the comparison group were more advanced at the start of the program since they worked in outside agencies and had to be generally more responsible than those who remained at Argus and benefitted from Positive Mental Attitude training. Those in the experimental group had almost a 10-point higher attendance rate, received more G.E.D. diplomas, and went into nonsubsidized employment and other favorable situations more frequently. We have plans to incorporate Positive Mental Attitude into our entire employment and job development program. We find it effective in dealing with employers, too.[19]

A wise person once said that adversity is a good school if you don't enter too early or continue in it too long. All our kids matriculated too early, and most are in danger of staying too long unless we can give them some exceptionally effective tools and open the job market to them.

Positive Mental Attitude provides another way, and a very effective way, of getting people to take responsibility for their lives, which means recognizing their strengths, developing whatever talents they have, converting their psychic and physical energies into creative action. It's what we've always tried to do at Argus, but Positive Mental Attitude provides us with a crystallized and focused way to go about it.

12. MARK CHALEFONT AND POSITIVE MENTAL ATTITUDE

Positive Mental Attitude means thinking good about yourself . . . of your accomplishments, and how many good things you can get out of your life.

ARGUS ENROLLEE

Although Mark Chalefont had been in Argus almost two years and had told us next to nothing about himself, he had made significant progress. What we did with Mark illustrates the way we work with people when we don't know their histories and when they can't or won't tell us what is going on in so many words.

Mark's mother, Carmen Tapia, came for an interview when Mark was admitted. She told us that he was behind in his school work and that he had been absent a great deal. Apart from this, she said, there were no pressing problems except that she was on welfare and money was scarce. This was painful for her and Mark, as well as for his young stepsister, who lived in a tiny apartment on St. Ann's Avenue. Neither Mark's father nor the stepfather contributed to the support of the family. The stepfather had lost his business after becoming involved with drugs and was now living in Puerto Rico.

Mrs. Tapia was a vigorous woman, still handsome, and seemed concerned for the future for herself and her children. She and Mark have the same amber skin and moss-green eyes. She would not tell us anything more, and Mark sat through the interview like a zombie. However, his sad face, his slumping posture, and his avoidance of counselors, teachers and peers told us that he was depressed. He skipped breakfast and lunch, entered his classes and groups at the last minute, slouched into a chair near the back, or cut out altogether to envelop himself in a cloud of chiba. In the spring of 1979, when he enrolled in Argus, his pretests showed a reading level of 6.9 and a math level of 6.5 —between four and five years below the eleventh grade level where he belonged at sixteen years of age. Yet he seemed intelligent.

"Mark, you've been smoking pot again," Fernando, the counselor in Phase One, would say.

"Nah. Nah. Nah."

"We know you are."

"How do you know? You didn't see me do nothing."

"I don't have to. I just look at you and I know. How do you feel right now?"

"I feel all right."

"Yeah? Well, you look wasted. Your nose is runny. You shiver at the least little breeze. So don't lay that on me. I know what you're up to. Hey, Mark, what do you really want for yourself?"

"To get my education and get out of the South Bronx. I want to help my mother." Mark replied.

"Okay. But if you go on smoking and cutting out and whatever else you do in the street there's no way you'll achieve that. If you go to group, pay attention in class, get your stuff together, keep your head clear, work hard, you'll get what you want. It's as simple as that. You have a choice. It's up to you."

Mark wouldn't rap. And he wouldn't change. His inner weather continued to be dismal.

Fernando lived in Mark's neighborhood and knew what was going on. The word was that Mark and a buddy would play basketball, then drink beer and smoke reefers. They were quiet. Never got in an altercation. Didn't really take part in anything much.

"Did you see Mark's eyes this morning?" Tyde Carbone, one of the teachers, asked Aubrey LaFrance.

"Yeah, he looked jaded again. He's high. What happens in the classroom, Tyde, when he's like that?"

"His performance falls off. He's disconnected. It's like he's only half there."

"Yeah, it's the same in group or at his work experience assignment. But we can't seem to get through to him."

Fernando had nothing to work with.

Mark talked a little to Constance Phillips, head of Phase Three. He talked to Sandie Eno, his English teacher. He seemed more comfortable with women. If a male counselor came on the scene, he clammed up. "You're not my father," he seemed to be saying.

For seven months in Sandra Eno's class Mark would slump into his seat, heave a deep sigh, put his head down on his folded arms and drift off into a half sleep.

On rare days Mark was alert, but seemed immobilized by a lack of confidence in his ability. "Everybody in here knows more than I do. I just can't make it, Sandie."

"You can learn just as they do, Mark. You're just as smart. You can do it," Sandie said.

He looked at her mournfully, "I can't. I really can't."

Once he told Sandie, "I'll never amount to anything. I never learn anything so how could I? I'll be stuck in the South Bronx for the rest of my life."

On his alert days Sandie insisted that he make the effort. She kept at him until he accomplished one or two real pieces of learning. Then she gave him warm praise.

Fernando learned that Mark's father was Ruben Rios Chalefont, a professional basketball player who played guard for the Milwaukee Bucks and had been famous in his day. He was still a celebrity in the Bronx. Mark did not share this information; Fernando found it out. Ruben Chalefont had seen very little of his son over the years. Mark showed no promise of becoming a basketball player, the father said, and in recent years appeared to be going down the tubes on drugs. Ruben's other son, by another woman, was talented at basketball and the father spent time coaching him and taking him to games. We guessed that his father's neglect and the attention shown his half brother were another sign to Mark that he wasn't good enough.

We surmised also that Mark blamed himself for not being able to get a job, that he did not see himself as a sixteen-year-old who needed support and help himself. He had been cast or had cast himself in the role of the man of his house. Perhaps his refusal to talk stemmed from a fixed idea that we would reject him if we knew what he was really like. On the basis of this fragmentary information, the human development specialist and the counselors formulated a treatment plan, consisting of a concerted campaign by everyone to make him aware of his strong points. Aubrey in Phase Two, Fernando as his counselor, and Sandie as his teacher began to bombard him with encouragement and, when he deserved it, with praise. It was difficult to convince Mark that he was smart and talented because he was well insulated by his derogatory self-concept. "He never once looked back to the six years when his marks were excellent," Sandie said. "He sat there telling me that he was incapable of learning."

Whenever Mark had a drug-free day Sandie pressed him, insisting that he work, not only in her class but in math, social studies and science as well. His other teachers, Tyde Carbone, Mike Feldman and Roy Fields, paid particular attention to him on these days also, saw to it that he learned something, made him aware that he had made progress and praised him.

Meanwhile, Aubrey and Fernando were challenging Mark by giving him more responsible chores and insisting that he perform them well. After seven months in Argus he cut back considerably on marijuana. He was still absent a lot but the days when he was present had become drug-free days. He was demonstrating to himself that he could learn and that he was capable of acting in a responsible manner. Aubrey made Mark one of the leaders of the morning meeting and insisted that he sit in the front row. But Mark was still absent too often.

Eighteen other boys and girls also were taking care of business when at Argus but were skipping school and messing up on the outside.

In September of 1980 the counselors decided that the time had come to get tough with this bunch, which included some of our most talented kids. The eighteen were called to a meeting where the counselors were present.

"This is a different kind of meeting," the counselors told them. "We've called all the fuck-ups together because we are fed up with the way you're acting."

They tried to defend themselves, but the counselors silenced them.

"We've talked to you by the hour. We've listened to what you have to say. You have a wonderful program here, counselors who are knocking themselves out to help you, small classes where you can learn, teachers who care, an administration that is behind you 100 percent and responds to you in every way they can. And what do *you* do? Cut classes, get stoned, refuse to apply yourselves or take advantage of the opportunities a lot of kids would give their eyeteeth for. Hey, a lot of people are on a waiting list to get into Argus and you act like you don't give a fuck about it."

The counselors drew up a separate contract for each of the seventeen, detailing what would be required in the way of changed behavior and attitudes. In the succeeding months fourteen of them shaped up dramatically.

Mark's attendance improved, and he cut back still more on his use of marijuana. He continued to be reticent in the classroom, but he was learning. The California Achievement Test that fall showed that since entering Argus he had gained almost four years in math and more than two years in reading. Mark took the G.E.D. examination and came within eleven points of making it. He was not happy, particularly when forty of his peers passed and went on to college or outside jobs. But teachers and counselors, instead of commiserating with him for failing, heaped approbation on him.

"You're almost there, Mark," Sandie told him. "Don't take the attitude that the glass is half empty. Think of it as half full. Think about how much you learned just by taking the test. Now you know exactly what to study and how to prepare for next time."

Mark was enrolled in Project Outlook and assigned to Anthony Daverese's Positive Mental Attitude group.

"On one level I was glad that Mark didn't pass the G.E.D.," Anthony said. "He still had a long way to go. If he had passed he would have been out of the door, looking for work, when he really needed a lot of what we hadn't yet been able to give him. When he came into my group he was very reluctant to take part. You could tell he was still equating himself with all of the things that hadn't gone right for him. His self-esteem was low. Oh, it had improved a lot, but he hung back, and I'm sure he was sending himself very negative messages. He still didn't have enough confidence to reach out for things for himself. And he was still denying that anything was the matter."

Mark sat in Positive Mental Attitude groups, which we considered crucial to his development, and refused to participate in the simple self-awareness and trust exercises which were a part of the reeducation process.

"That's not for me," he said. "I don't need to do that."

After the third group Anthony sat down with Mark in his office. "You know, Mark, we can't force you to take part, and we wouldn't if we could, but I do want to tell you why you should get involved."

Mark listened. He likes to be acknowledged and is appreciative whenever anyone singles him out and takes the trouble to discuss things with him. He never says much but he drinks it in.

"I respect the fact that you don't want to say much about it, and we've never pressed you, but I have a hunch that you've had a lot of losses and hard blows in your life."

Mark said nothing.

"You don't have to tell me what they were, now or ever, if you don't want to. But I want to share another thought of mine. Again, it's only a hunch. I could be wrong. But I believe you've been telling yourself a lot of bad things about yourself. Like you're not good enough. If you had been a better person, maybe your father would have paid more attention to you. And if you were a really adequate person, maybe you could have protected your mother from some of the stresses she's had. I don't know what happened with your stepfather but my guess is, you blame yourself for that too."

Mark listened. He made no comment but he did not deny what Anthony had said.

"You know, Mark, you're not to blame. A lot of things happened that you had no control over. But you do control what you tell yourself and how you treat yourself. You've done a lot for yourself since coming to Argus. You're becoming a responsible person. I'd like to see you go one step further and take these groups seriously. See what you can get out of them if you really get involved. We believe they'll help you learn to trust people who can be trusted, to set goals for yourself and achieve them. You'll learn that you're an okay guy, that you've got talent, that you can do what you want to do. And you'll stop *thinking* that you're not good enough. Because that's what you've been doing. You're downgrading yourself. And you know what? You don't deserve it. You wouldn't treat your mother or your best friend that way, would you? Well, you gotta stop treating yourself that way."

In the next group, the fourth, Mark was more involved. He gave every evidence of listening to what other group members were saying. He was following the arguments. He would lean forward, putting his elbows on his knee, tensed, waiting for the right moment to jump in but seeming not to find it. The discussion revolved around the ways some girls hide their true feelings and inclinations, dressing, putting on the type of makeup they think will appeal to boys and even pretending to think the way boys want them to think in order to be popular and get dates. One said, "If that's the way to get a fella, I'm all for it." There was a lot of arguing back and forth.

Suddenly Mark spoke. "How could you trust a girl who wouldn't let you know what she really thinks about things?"

After that Mark spoke up in the group. He began to connect. He took chances, jumped in, saying whatever was on his mind. He learned that he had a talent for telling people off when they talked trivia.

To speak up in group, to put forward an idea or a feeling and to stand up for it when you may be contradicted, criticized or even on occasion attacked, requires guts. For Mark it was an exercise in self-affirmation. He was taking chances and defending himself.

The Project Outlook groups (Positive Mental Attitude) were tremendously liberating for Mark. He developed a sense of what was important to him and of the power of words and ideas. He would jump in but never get carried away. He had to be sure that what he was putting out was "right." We wanted to see more spontaneity; we wanted Mark to give himself permission to make mistakes, to try out new things.

Bellevue, a large municipal hospital, chronically understaffed, asked Anthony in December for someone on a YEP line to assist in the print shop, where one man was going bananas turning out forms and printed matter for the entire hospital. They wanted someone who could learn quickly, who was consistent, reliable and steady, who could work with a minimal amount of supervision and would be capable, for brief periods, of taking charge of the print shop. Anthony told Mark that he thought he could handle the job. There would be the possibility of a line opening up for the right person.

Mark was stunned. "Can I do all of those things?"

"I think you can. And so does the rest of the staff. We talked it over in case conference. We all agree that you can do it. You won't know how to do everything the first day. Your boss's name is Carlos. He won't expect you to step into the job fully trained. He'll teach you."

Mark went for the interview, bolstered by good wishes and faith of the staff and the peers—and more importantly, by his burgeoning belief in himself. The administrator at Bellevue liked Mark. He got the job. Like Mark's counselor at Argus, Carlos, the head of the print shop, was a blond, blue-eyed Puerto Rican. He accepted Mark and let him know it. We didn't realize it then but being accepted by blond Puerto Rican males had a special significance for Mark. Anthony, a former brother in a religious order, said afterwards that Providence had arranged for two such persons to enter Mark's life at that particular time.

From the first day Carlos shared the responsibility with Mark. "You help me design this. I'll set the type." Carlos showed him how to operate the machines, took an interest in Mark and was a patient instructor. Eight weeks after Mark came to work, Carlos went on vacation and left Mark in charge.

"I'm handling myself okay," Mark told Anthony. "I'm happy here. And I haven't had any fights. Carlos is cool people. We're tight."

Mark prepared to take the high school equivalency exam again. He studied hard.

"Because if for some reason, like I was nervous that day or didn't study hard enough, I don't pass, I'll be ready to take the exam again as soon as they give it. And besides, I want to learn everything I can so I'll be able to do my job when it comes through." He passed the exam.

Bellevue planned to hire Mark on a nonsubsidized line but suffered a funding cut. He worked over the Christmas season at Altman's, a Manhattan department store, and later moved on to a job at Clearwater Publishing Company, where he has been for almost two years, doing well.

Mark and his mother finally found the confidence to tell us their story. It seems that the father was already married and had a family when he became involved with Mark's mother. Ruben Chalefont didn't tell Carmen about his wife until she was pregnant. Then he promised to get a divorce and marry her, but he didn't, leaving her to manage as best she could. Carmen lived with her cousin until the baby was born, then went back to the embroidery factory where she had worked before she became involved with the celebrated Bucks guard. Mark's grandmother disapproved of her daughter and refused to speak to the child or acknowledge his existence as long as Carmen was in the house but took care of him while his mother was at work. The grandmother died of heart failure and they struggled on their own. A neighborhood babysitter "took care" of Mark by tying him and another young child back to back in kitchen chairs. When the toddler made his mother understand this state of affairs Carmen fired the babysitter and placed Mark in a day-care center. An uncle and a cousin lavished affection upon Mark, bought him clothes and presents and made plans for his future. Both were killed when Mark was eight, one in a car accident, the other from asphyxiation by carbon monoxide.

Ruben Rios Chalefont had disappointed Mark's mother; he disappointed her son as well.

"He made so many promises," Carmen Tapia said. "It just about broke the boy's heart. He would call Mark and say he was coming. Mark would wait and his father wouldn't come. His father promised to buy Mark a basketball and teach him to play, but he never did. Once in a while he would drive Mark around in his Cadillac. The boy would wait in the car while his father did business with people in different parts of the Bronx. He only sent money if I ran behind him crying that we were desperate. I don't set myself up to judge, but I believe there's a special hot seat in hell for people who disappoint children. Mark stopped crying after a while.

"For years I didn't go out with a man or even look at one. But when so many of my family died and Mark and I were all alone I got panicky. Hector Tapia was the son of one of Mark's sitters. He used to beg me to go out with him. I finally said yes. We enjoyed each other's company for a couple of years. Then I let him move in with me. I thought it was for the best. Hector had a good job and was well liked in the neighborhood. But after he got involved in drugs he changed. His business failed. He wouldn't let me set foot in the street or even look out of the window for fear some man would see me and get interested. I tried to avoid fighting with him but it was either fight or be a doormat. Our quarrels ended with him beating me up. Once he laid my head open with a frying pan because he didn't like the way I had cooked the beans and rice. Mark was afraid his stepfather would kill me. So was I."

Mark lived with this fear. "If she died, I wanted to die with her," he said. "But my mother told me, no, stay alive and take care of your sister. So I decided that if she died I would keep her coffin in the apartment and look after Olinda."

The terror began when Mark was in the sixth grade, the year his grades dropped from excellent to zero, the year he started to roam the streets and take drugs. "I couldn't stand what was happening. I wanted to kill my stepfather but I couldn't, so I cancelled myself out with drugs."

The misery dragged on until Mark was sixteen. That year he dropped acid (LSD) for the first time, had a bad trip and became paranoid. He thought people were out to kill him. Mrs. Tapia took him to the hospital where he was placed on Thorazine. He was on this medication for several months after entering Argus. This accounted for his drowsiness and torpor.

The LSD episode, and her son's bizarre behavior, shocked Mrs. Tapia into action. She put the stepfather's belongings out of the apartment, had the lock changed and waited on the street. When he found himself out in the cold Hector beat Carmen up with a baseball bat. Eventually he moved to Puerto Rico. We learned that Mark's stepfather was a blond Puerto Rican and prejudiced against blacks. He never accepted Mark and probably never accepted his mother either. She was half black.

As Anthony says, "Maybe it's better that we never knew Mark's history. If we had known what he had been through and how he got all those negative messages into his head, we might have been afraid to push him so hard. He's had so much trouble and so many losses, we might have treated him as a basket case."

As it was, Mark learned with Positive Mental Attitude a new way to view himself and his history. And we helped him do it without knowing what that history was.

"How do you feel now, Mark?"

"I'm lookin ahead. Don't look back, you'll turn to stone." He sat for a moment, the moss green eyes resting on an African batik hanging above the couch in my office. "I feel like *that*," he said, pointing to the three Congo peacocks, long necked, high crested and gorgeous, in the batik. "That's my mother, my sister and me. How do I feel? I feel good. I'm *pro*gressing. I'm stepping. I'm flying. Flying so high. I don't ever have to come back to the low. Nothing can stop me. Nothing can ever put me back on Dump Street again."

"And your mother? What about her?"

"My mother's fine. She's a fantastic lady. I had the love all the time from my mother. She's what I call a miracle worker. She's found a job. She's the type of person, she could be out of work for twenty years and if a job comes up she could go back to work and make it. I'm proud she's my mother."

"She's proud that you are her son, Mark. I don't have to tell you that. You know it already."

"Hey, I still can't handle a compliment too well," Mark said. "But I'm learning." Then, "I got to go now. I'm taking a young lady out to lunch. And at three I have to pick up my sister, Olinda, at her school. My sister, she's the one that is going to be something after me."

13. WIDENING CIRCLES

*One of the crucial parts of it, in trying to get these kids
to change, is that we share our histories with them. They
have to feel that the model is not too high above them;
that the adults who are trying to help them are warm and
human, and have made mistakes like them.*

ARGUS STAFF MEMBER

Saint Augustine saw the nature of God as a circle whose center
is everywhere and whose circumference is nowhere. Our highest (and
our most earthly) task is to find our own center and to go out from
it, with God, if you like, but always with our fellow creatures and
toward that bondedness which is the full expression of our humanity.

The way of widening circles leads toward personal and social
growth, knowledge and competence (getting one's hands on the tools
and technology of society), a value system which incorporates mutual
aid and cooperation, appreciation of the uniqueness and beauty of
one's own culture and the ability to transcend—to cross over, to learn
about, to admire and partake of the uniqueness and beauty of the way
of life and qualities of others.

In our society, with its conflicting values and aims, some find
their way with circumvolutions into a generous, inclusive and happy
track of life. For others this can happen only during or after a time
of crisis when painful events make necessary a redrawing of the inner
maps, reevaluation of the goals handed down and internalized without question. War, holocaust, losses of one kind or another can bring
about a changed self-concept, new values and a view of the world from
a different perspective.

Sometimes an intervention by one person—a minister, a therapist, a friend—or by a group of persons, such as our staff at Argus,
can help an individual to re-form the self, the value system and the
world view. There are instances of a whole people being "reborn"
after devastating and dehumanizing experiences. This happened
when the Seneca Indian leader Handsome Lake, under the influence
of a vision which came to him after a severe illness, persuaded his

182

people to give up the alcoholism and demoralization into which they had fallen as their lands were wrested away by white men and to adopt a new ethic and a peaceful, agricultural way of life.[1] This may be one of the early American examples of self-help and group support and control under the guidance of an inspired individual. It led to a remarkable renaissance of the Seneca, who today, I am told by a member of the tribe, are sober and thriving.

A reemergence is taking place in the "Black Is Beautiful" movement and in the celebration of Soul or black vitality, generosity, sharing, history and tradition, flinging down the gauntlet to claims to white superiority.

For Mary Taylor there was a clear demarcation, a breaching of the wall she had built around herself, through which her earliest yearnings for bonding and for a peaceful and orderly existence found a way. For several years director of our group home program, a staff trainer for child-care programs, now director of the Haven, Argus's refuge for runaway and homeless adolescents, with a master's degree in social work, Mary used Argus as an anvil to hammer out a new life, and, at the same time, she put her mark upon the forge, shaping and heaping fuel on the white hot process whereby we transmute the human spirit. When she came to us in 1969 as a volunteer seeking an antidote to a sterile and unsatisfying job, she already had much to offer as an empathetic person, able to arouse a sense of identification in the lost, affection-hungry kids cast up at our doors.

In the mid-sixties, she had been on the streets, immersed in drug addiction. "Somewhere inside of me I knew the street life wasn't for me. I resisted a total commitment to it. I kept a little part of me back. To anybody observing from the outside, it looked like I was committed to it. But I wasn't. I wanted something different. I wanted to be somebody else. I wanted to reclaim my family. My mother was abused as a child, and she abused me in turn. I didn't understand it then. Now I know that she was a victim and she victimized me. My father took my brother and me away, gave us to a lady to take care of. We hardly ever saw him. He was shot when I was six, killed in a fight. After that my mother took us back, kept a home for us, part working, part on welfare. We were poor, but we didn't think about it too much. Everybody was poor. Working people. We didn't know middle-class people existed or how other people lived. We didn't have TV sets. But I saw my brother strugglin to get to college in spite of his poverty. He always cared about me. I guess it was that. My mother made me feel that to be female was a terrible fate. For me to go to college would have been unthinkable.

"As soon as I got my high school diploma I ran away to New York City. I went straight to Broadway and Forty-second Street and stared at the neon lights and the marquees. They were as gaudy and as crazy as my dreams. But the only job I could get was taking care of a white woman's children. When I lost that job I stole $60 to keep from starving, got caught and was sent to prison at Bedford Hills. There I got into real stealing and then into dope. But I always had this feeling that I didn't belong on the streets or in the House of Detention. I'd begun as a runaway and it all just happened to me somehow. At least that was how I saw it. I didn't feel I had any power, any will of my own.

"But I had a little spark. Just a teeny little spark. But it was there and kept telling me, 'I don't belong here. I belong somewhere else.' I used to talk to my little spark. 'Maybe someday,' I would say. 'Maybe someday.' But it was a fantasy. I couldn't put any reality to it. I couldn't plan with it. I couldn't say, 'Tomorrow I'll do this or that.'

"Then one day I was laying up in the Women's House of Detention, wantin some dope and dreading what I had to go through if I couldn't get it, and Father Egan walked in. The Junkie Priest. Energetic, white-haired, a big cross hangin around his neck. I said, 'Aw shit! Here I am wantin dope and he's gonna preach about the church. I don't wanna hear his bullshit. Damn!' I don't remember what he said but he made contact with that little spark. It was not the words he said, it was the contact. A very profound human contact. It was his presence. It was warm. It was love. I think he saw *me*. It wasn't the church. The way he touched me was beyond the church, beyond the priesthood, beyond me being an addict and layin there in jail. I can't remember what he said. He asked me to come to his shelter. I went there but I only stayed a few nights. I left and I went back to the old life for another year.

"But I never forgot him and those few days when I had been voluntarily clean. He had made the spark glow and grow until finally I went into Phoenix House, which helped me get my behavior together. But it was only after I came to Argus and got into staff development and into Dan Casriel's groups that I dealt with the pain. Until I did that, I couldn't keep my behavior together because so much encapsulated pain was in there, eating away, making me do things I didn't want to do. I dumped and dumped and finally I got rid of most of the historic pain. I've come to a place now when I can walk around feeling pleasure unless something really bad is happening.

"Two men were important to me. My brother and Father Egan who wanted me to change for *me*. There was nothin they wanted from me. They wanted me to change just for me. That must be love in its purest form."

Aubrey LaFrance is another Argus staff member who went through profound change. J. Allen Strother took Aubrey out of the Criminal Court and talked him into giving Argus a try. He was charged in several cases involving possession of a weapon and possession of dangerous drugs. When we first saw Aubrey, a floppy leather horseman's hat half-covered a wild afro that was like the other end of a mop. Despite his six feet four inches, he was wearing platform shoes and a multicolored jump suit. "Green was the predominant color. Green, flashing, pimp-style clothes. I was hung up on clothes. I tried to dress up my emptiness with clothes," Aubrey told me.

Yet he was never a pimp. "In all of that one of the things I didn't do was to pimp. I had many opportunities to pimp, but I never accepted a dime from a female. I learned later it was my feelings for my mother."

Aubrey came in from the streets because the D.A.s were on his tail. But court pressure was not the only reason. "I still had a lot of things left with people who didn't want me to get away from selling and organizing and making contacts. I knew everyone and who was doing what. They thought I might expose them, and they threatened to kill me. I dared them to do their worst. I didn't have sense enough to be properly frightened."

Aubrey's intelligent, finely chiseled features (Nilotic perhaps or a legacy from his French grandfather), his long straight limbs and his superb posture give him a certain majesty, although he is essentially modest—confident, entitled but not boastful or macho.

"I had no love or admiration or respect for myself or anyone in that area," he told us, meaning the drug world. "From using, I had fallen subtly into drug sales and into a whole area I couldn't handle. From being an experiment it had turned into a portion of survival. The one thing I feared was blood guilt. Yet killing was common. I knew many who killed and gave no thought to it. In war that happens regularly. But basically I had a lot of love in me—for people. Remember, I already had a wife and nine children at that time. As a child I had played the organ and sung in the choir in churches of all denominations. Later I became a Jehovah's Witness because I liked the balanced racial thing—brothers from Africa, India, Sweden, Holland, all parts of the world. I love that more than anything. When someone said brother it didn't mean we were sons of the same blood father but sons of the Father of Knowledge. Racial equality was a reality with us in the Jehovah's Witnesses.

"In selling dope I never dealt with children. But I knew I was part of something that was death dealing. That was why I could no longer see the sky or the grass or anything beautiful. I was no longer entitled to it. I knew drugs were costing me everything. I was killing myself. I was hurting other people. I was prepared to die. But I also was ready to make my mark if I did go. I was determined to take others with me."

About this time Aubrey went from heroin to amphetamine. He stayed awake for days. When he came off the amphetamine he felt only a deep fatigue. It was an easy way to come off heroin. He was a polyaddict: heroin, cocaine, LSD, mescaline, amphetamines. He used Seconal (a barbiturate) to try to balance himself out.

"I lost weight, developed splotches, my hair fell out, my teeth melted away. I smoked cigarettes only when I was locked up and I ate very little at any time. Mostly honey and water and maybe a little cheese.

"The Jehovah's Witnesses had left me with a basic method for being honest with myself, and although I wasn't affiliated with any church when I came to Argus and I still am not, I carried that imprint of what brotherhood and racial equality mean. Still, when people in Argus—Al and George Maldonado and others—asked me how I felt, I was incapable of expressing my feelings. I was full of confusion and pain, but my anger protected me from it just as the drugs had done. Drugs and anger. Those were the shells I crawled into."

Then as a sign of shedding the old life Aubrey voluntarily shaved his head. After that, oddly, he began to hear what was being said in the groups. The words began to take on meaning, to sink in.

"The more I listened, the more I tried to apply the information of being open and honest with my feelings and not worrying about what other people would think. I began to see that if I walked the walk and talked the talk a lot of superficial things would fall away. I began to realize that no matter what had happened to me in my coming-up, no matter what my parents had done or not done, no matter what I had been or had not been, there was no excuse for not living up to my potential. I began to get in touch with a desperate need to do *one thing* correctly. I studied the group leaders. I studied the tools they were using. I began to grasp the structure of the program. I began to get knowledge that I knew could benefit me out in the world. I felt good when I was praised for doing the right things. I knew it was real and I knew it was right. I began to tap all the resources. Everything that I had experienced and known—and I realized that it wasn't wasted, I could use it all.

"I had done a lot of other things in the world besides push dope.

I had driven a trailer truck, worked in a steel mill, helped my father in his moving business. But I had never been turned on by anything but my hobbies—painting, music, photography, building model planes and cars. Now for the first time I saw a way to make it all fit together: with all my strength and wits I worked toward learning the counselor's trade. I would carry out my old ideals from the Jehovah's Witness days, and I would make amends by helping others. At the same time I would be able to support my family, pass along what I had learned to them and pursue my painting and music.

"Did I succeed in passing it along to my kids? Well, you know the old saw about the shoemaker's children going without shoes and the barber's daughter needing a haircut. So I wasn't sure I could help my children. But I did. Especially when they saw—when I finally let them see—how scared and bad old man Superfly felt all that time, deep down inside."

Aubrey shares his art work with his children. He brought his son into the Argus program. "I grew firm in looking at those parental lines where you want to soften the blows—the harm you do your children when you don't keep a sound structure. I could sit alone and visualize for the first time as a parent. I could devise systems for my children, so my wife and I no longer rewarded bad behavior but instead reinforced good behavior."

Open anger, open love, concern and dedication to serving oneself and others—these are the pathways to self-reclamation for addicts and those who have lived outside the law. The actual history of such people is not of concern to us; *how* they experienced that history and how it affects them currently is of great concern, particularly when the person is on our staff. Addicts and criminals, unless they are psychotic or neurologically or organically impaired, are not very different from the rest of us. Once the overriding problem—the addiction itself—is out of the way, we find that alienation and negative attitudes constitute the main problem. Sometimes, after a person realizes that other people care and begins to return that caring, it may take five or six years of continual nurturance and reinforcement for the "conscience" to become strong enough to stand on its own.

Mary Fritz, nineteen, tall, elegant and sturdy as a young black oak when she joined our staff in 1975, came out of a different background. She grew up in Mobile, Alabama, and although she was a foster child and angry at her mother for giving her away, she considers that she had a fortunate childhood. She empathizes now with her natural mother, who bore her first child at thirteen and had four babies by the age of seventeen. "I understand why she gave me and my sister to her half sister who couldn't have any children of her own," Mary says. "I would have done the same, given her circumstances." Mary never saw her real father nor heard him mentioned. She never asked his whereabouts. Her foster mother did not approve of her real mother whom they visited from time to time. Mary felt confused, divided and anguished—and also angry at her foster parents. She rebelled and fought.

Still her foster parents made her feel loved. They were hardworking and upright and they demanded a great deal of her.

Mary feels she had a good adolescence. Her foster father lost the business he had owned but made good money driving a truck. Her foster mother was a beautician. Mary called them father and mother.

"If I had to choose a parent, I'd choose my father. He was impressed with me because I was outspoken. He talked all the time about segregation. He wouldn't permit us to use the separate restrooms, drinking fountains or other facilities they had in the South at the time. If we had to go to the bathroom when we were out driving, he took his gun and escorted us to the nonsegregated facilities. One thing was clear: my father insisted on respect from everybody.

"My mother was ill a lot. Always complaining. It was diabetes and later her heart. That influenced me to become a nurse. I had visions of taking care of her when she got old. It turned out though that I didn't like the practice of nursing. I liked the theory but I hated to see people dying."

Mary went to nursing school in New York City, and shortly after she got her certificate, married an African. In spite of her family's pleas, she stayed in the city. She didn't like hospital work. "I was an LPN, but even as an RN, I wouldn't have been happy. I had done per diem jobs at Abbott House, a residential program, and found that I enjoyed the teenagers. They related pretty well to me. The manager at the registry suggested that I apply for the job at Argus. I did and was accepted."

Mary felt confused at first. "The Argus group home was unstructured at the time, chaotic. We were trying to put a positive peer group together, and there had been a turnover in staff."

Before she had been at the group home a month a fourteen-year-old girl picked up a bottle off the sidewalk, broke off the neck, put it in Mary's face and threatened to cut her. Mary's handling of this incident of violence was remarkable. No one would have blamed her had she thrown in the sponge; particularly when the senior staff, instead of getting rid of Flavia, held a series of groups with the girl and the staff, including Mary. In the end, they both stayed, and Mary was influential in the girl's development (see Chapter 16).

Mary: "Argus became very significant. I had no experience but I knew the girls needed structure and warmth and I put my whole effort behind that. Mary Taylor was tough but she was warm. Gradually I came to understand what angry concern is and why we use it. I began to see how the expression of pure emotion could quickly open the door to deep insights and significant incidents and attitudes they didn't realize they had. The same thing happened to me. Mary Taylor confronted me a lot in the staff sessions. She told me to take the girls shopping, help them select their wardrobes. I said I was a nurse, that going to the hospital should be my priority. She said, 'My dear, you have to do everything here.' I saw that we didn't have the resources for staff to be compartmentalized. I took the girls to their medical appointments, I managed their medicines, *and* I woke them up in the morning and helped buy their clothes. I learned a lot about my own emotions. We walk around not being in touch with what drives us on.

"I needed so much, but if I tried to get it from the girls, I would cheat them. I had to get something for me so I would have something to give to them. That's not to say that I can't enjoy and get satisfaction from the girls. But some of us when we have leftover little-girl needs, we begin to feel desperate about the girls in the house. We try to make sure that they don't go without the way we did. We try to give them what we want ourselves. And it's too much. Adult behavior. *I* had to learn it myself before I could teach them. And I'm still learning it. We teach them to exercise maximum choice. I knew something about that, more than they did, because my foster parents taught me. But I needed to practice it, to really grow into it. And I realized, if I was going to ask the girls to work toward their full potential, I would have to do the same. I went back to school. I'm working toward my B.A. degree. I plan to go to graduate school. And I'm not doing it just to please—or to spite—someone out of my past. I'm doing it for me. I choose to do it because it's exciting and it brings me closer to my girls.

"To get there I had to lose my rigid concept of myself. I had to get in touch with my present feelings about what happened to me historically. My early experiences. My anger at my mother for giving me away, at my father for abandoning me. I had dumped that on my foster parents. They didn't deserve it. They gave me so much love. My real mother didn't deserve it either. She did the best she could with what she had.

"Being responsible for twenty-four girls and the staff of two houses is the hardest job I could ever imagine. But it's thrilling and exciting too. I get so worn-out and weary I think I'm going to die. Part of it is not knowing how to delegate. I'm learning that. We've just made Charlotte Bowman the assistant director. She's taking a load off of my shoulders." A laugh. "But we're starting a group residence for twenty-four homeless boys, so I'm taking on another load."

Elsie Lopez, senior counselor in the group home, works closely with School District 7 in her leisure time and is concerned about what is happening to children in the community. "The biggest problem is to teach them right from wrong. They've got to learn not to do wrong, not because they could get caught, but *because it is wrong and they know it in their hearts.* The only way I know to get that knowledge into someone's heart is to love them and get them to love you in return. And from that beginning, get them to believe that it is wrong to hurt themselves and other people."

Elsie is no bigger than a child herself (less than five feet tall), and her small flower face, with its tiny nose peaked like an elf's and the vertical scar folded between her brows, plus spontaneity and generosity, make her seem childlike. And this is in no way incongruent with an ample bosom, a soft woman's body, an ability to get to the bottom of matters, to come on strong when necessary, to protect and teach her three children as well as the girls she counsels. She and her children live in an apartment in the group home, lending stability to the program.

Elsie's life has been hard, but faith and purity (I can think of no other word) have shielded her with outstretched wings, and she has remained innocent of heart. The kids in the group home sense this. Her own children know it, for she has concealed nothing of her history from them. Their love, reaching her across long separations, healed and drew her into a new incarnation. They are aware of this, and proud and strong in the knowledge that they played a key role in their mother's rebirth.

Not long ago her daughter, Elizabeth, asked Elsie to tell her story to her class at Hunter College so that her professor and her fellow students could learn first hand what a human being can go through and still emerge as an immensely positive and vibrant person, with much to give to her family and the community. Elsie told them the following story:

I call myself Elsie López but my real name is Esperanza Colón. Esperanza means hope. The kids in Brooklyn couldn't pronounce it. They made fun of it. I changed it to Elsie. López is the name of my common-law husband. I didn't know it then but changing my name to

Elsie was a step in turning my back on my Puerto Rican identity.

I was born in Barranquitas, at the foot of the hill. The poorest part of what they would call a little hick town. We had latrines outside. I was the sixth child, the fifth girl born into the family. Two brothers came after me, José Antonio and Israel. My father did a little farming, raised chickens, pigs, and cows. My mother died when I was three—a tumor in her breast. I imagine it was cancer. I remember they watched her in the house. They was cryin and screamin. My father told us she was sleeping. I knew he was lying when they carried her away. They carried the coffin up the hill to the cemetery and buried her.

I was confused and scared. And it got worse when my father gave me to his oldest sister in Rio Piedras. She took me with her to New York. I never saw my father's farm again.

My father's family was fair-skinned, very, very, very white with blue eyes. My mother's family was darker. The two families didn't get along. My aunt had green eyes. She always said, "Your mother was a whore." My mother was black. "Your father ruined the family. He brought darkness into it." When I was twelve and thirteen I told my aunt I would marry the darkest man in the world.

We moved to the projects in Brooklyn. They didn't want me to be with black kids. To get back at them, that's all I associated with.

They made me do all the work. Clean, wash, iron. Aunt Juana did the cooking. Her daughters didn't do anything. I played the part of Cinderella in the school play and I cried. I was always lonely. There wasn't anybody there for me.

When I was thirteen, I asked could I make my communion. My aunt said yes, when I had the money to buy my own dress. I didn't have nice clothes so I was learning how to steal. I took clothes from Mays, A & S—all the department stores along Fulton Street. I took real nice blouses, real nice skirts. I liked—and I still like—flashing colors so that people would see I had on something real nice.

My aunt took me to court, told them I hung out with a bad crowd. She meant black kids. The very first time in court they asked me did I want to go back to my aunt's house. I told them I didn't. They said they would send me to P.R. I cried and said no, I couldn't go back to my father, I hadn't seen him since I was three.

They had Hudson then for the really bad kids. And they had St. Filomena's Training School for Girls, run by nuns. All types of kids was there. Girls that had run away, that was pregnant, that had stolen, truanted. They put me there and I went through hell. I was hostile, I was very nasty. I took out my hostility on anybody.

I had to fight at lot in St. Filomena's. I had real long silky hair. They stuck gum in my hair. They stuck my hair to the chair with thumb tacks. I was very pretty—very nice legs, pretty shape, long, straight brown hair. Brown eyes and fair skin. One nun, Sister Rita, gave me a lot of affection. She taught me in the sewing shop and she was real good to me. Most of what I got, I got from her. I still today don't like people that won't hold or pet you, that are cold.

When I was seventeen they released me to my aunt. I stayed one month, left and never went back.

I had learnt everything negative in that training school. I went across the park to Fulton. That's where the crime was, the drugs. I could sew good an I got a job in a factory but the money I was making didn't suit my taste. Bobbie, he was gay, educated me about the money I could make with old men. He rented his room out to girls to bring their men there. Oh, man, I used to make a lot of money. $200, $300 a night. It didn't seem risky.

I had been in love with Louie. I didn't want to mention that because it still hurts. He had conned me into giving up my virginity. Then he quit me. The next time I seen him he was with one of my girl friends. I was destroyed. Louie was the only man who ever left me. After that, I left them.

After I broke up with Louie, I met Bobbie. He said, "Hey, why bust your ass in a sweat shop? I got somethin really glamorous for you."

I never felt anything for those men. They were middle-aged, thirty, forty-five. Old to me. They gave me a lot of money. It might be three, four guys in a day. Bobbie knew guys that were making lots of money.

A lot of the prostitutes used drugs. That all goes together. But I didn't do it till I met Julio. He used heroin. I went out, brought back the heroin, he gave himself the shots. That was his entire occupation, to wait for me to come home with the dope so he could shoot up. But I had to have somebody. I didn't think he would leave me. He was good-looking, had a lot of friends. The strongest attraction was sexual.

The first time I used drugs I threw up for two days. I looked in the mirror. I thought my looks were ruined. I didn't touch it again for eighteen months.

I must have been depressed. I must have been feeling really bad when I put a needle in my arm that second time. I knew how it was.

"If it's that good, gimme some."

The drug dealers loved me. They give you the first ones free. When they get you strung out you have to be their customer.

In sixty-two when Liz was born I wasn't using. I wasn't dipping and dabbing. But I was in the streets and I was selling. My son Michael was born in sixty-three. It was after the kids that I got heavy into drugs. Michael was in my stomach when I was arrested. I told the judge, "Don't make me have my baby in prison." He let me go. It was a grand larceny charge—stealing from department stores.

When Michael was one and a half, I left his father. In 1965 I was arrested, sentenced and went upstate to Bedford prison. My aunt took my kids and put them in placement. She wanted to keep Michael because he was fair-skinned and put Lisa, who was dark-skinned, away. I told her if she didn't keep them both she couldn't have either one.

I was in Bedford thirteen months. When I got out and saw the kids, Michael didn't recognize me. The nuns had to take me out. I started screamin. I walked forty blocks straight to the dope man. He was more than willing to give me some. I was clean. It didn't take a lot. I got ossified.

I never went back to Julio. I started living with Raul López, an older man. I have one child by him. I didn't suffer from him. He didn't beat me. He was a money maker. He taught me to be a lady. I loved him. I could actually say I loved him. But he got four years for a burglary. That's too long to wait for anybody. Rita was his, born November 3, 1967. That's the kid that's not with me. I can't find her. I gave her to some people when I went up another time. The lady never brought her back.

Every holiday when Christmas comes, I get all choked up. I still get into a fit about it. I would like her to understand I didn't just leave.

I changed my name to López when Rita was born. The other three I gave the name Colón, my father's name.

It was 1975 when I finally left drugs alone. I was thirty-two. It was the biggest decision of my life. I had to change for my children's sake, not for mine. It was that frame of mind that led me to Project Return. For two painful years I dealt with my drug problem. My children had gone back into placement and someone had kidnapped my little Rita.

In the reentry phase from Project Return I went to work at Argus. Mary Taylor really educated me. I still hadn't dealt with my pain and my identity problem. I didn't know what or who I was. I worked with Dan Casriel himself. And recently at Dr. David Freundlich's workshop I finally was able to see what my father went through, what his life was like. I think I've forgiven him now. My son Michael and I visited him in P.R. and took him a nice Father's Day card. I want my children to know their grandfather. But before I take my girls I have to know whether he will accept them. They are black. I wouldn't let them be hurt by him.

Right now this is how I feel. I am Esperanza—Hope. I have white skin and long silky hair. I'm a sensitive, honest, sincere, strong Puerto Rican woman who works and takes care of teenage children at Argus. I'm not on the welfare line. No food stamps or Section 8 or any type of assistance that as a single parent I would be entitled to. My children are out of BCW. I take care of them. I do it all myself. I'm head of a household of four—except that I can't find my youngest; but I will. I pay taxes and I vote. My daughter Elizabeth is in Hunter College majoring in business. My son Michael went through the Argus program and got his G.E.D. He's doin good. Works with computers. He's coming back to Achievement Day at Argus this spring to speak to the kids about his experiences.

I'm black and I'm proud. I'm Puerto Rican and I'm proud. I'm white and I'm proud. My kids are black and Puerto Rican and white and I'm proud of them. My kids are proud of themselves because they know that they gave me the will and the strength to get out of the streets and lead a positive life.

I was lied to, cheated, betrayed, and given away. I was called all kinds of names. It hurt me then. Now nothing can hurt me. I'm strong. I know who I am.

I don't have to feel guilty, I don't have to pacify my children any more. I've got all that out of my system. If they want something I say, "Have you earned it?"

It hurts me when I look out the window and see people nodding out on drugs. Heroin is everywhere. Last week a man O.D.'ed in the doorway of the group home. Our girls saw him laying there dead. Young people throwing themselves away. I want to teach my people how to deal with their children, how to save them from doing what I did.

Each of the staff at the Learning for Living Center is a remarkable person and gives a great deal to the kids. The same can be said for the staff at the group home. I would dearly love to present all their histories, not because their lives and values are typical of the ghetto, for one finds as great variety and richness, as many starting points, as many trajectories in the ghetto as elsewhere. I would like to present their stories because they are fascinating and because each one sheds light in a different way on our task of moving kids and ourselves into upward spirals and widening circles.

14. MY OWN CIRCLES

I feel free at Argus to love people without bounds. I don't know why this is so and I realize that some of the reasons could be suspect. One is that I created this extended family and community to pour balm on my own sores.

ELIZABETH L. STURZ, *Journal*

Through the windows of my apartment in Manhattan I can hear the bells of St. Thomas More. They speak compellingly, and almost always as I listen my everyday life falls away; I find myself adrift on the river of forgetfulness where all souls are said to drink before they pass from some previous existence into this life. I know that the bells are telling me that this is my hour, that matched against the "tooth of time and the razor of oblivion," my chances are nil. The presentiment is clear; it is not new to me.

But the bells are not merely the tongue and throat of time, putting forth, flowering and devouring; they have more to tell if only I could understand. My marrow comprehends, but the prosy logic of my brain cannot make the translation. Then one day the message ripples clear, simple and profound: live your life as a blossoming and a fading away that is natural and gentle in the face of doom. Let it leave behind some trace of that sweet reverberance which is the only immunity to death.

My apartment, as attested to by the bells, is as sequestered as any living space can be in New York City where quiet and privacy are the quintessential luxuries—as indeed they are in most cities in this age of technological advancement where every step away from want, ignorance and isolation brings a fresh problem or pollution.

This quiet place then is my inner circle. I start with myself and the books in my room. They are an extension of me as are the dishes, pots and utensils piled on the shelves or hanging from the walls of my kitchen. I like food and I like cooking. These things help me to define myself, as do the children arriving at the nursery school outside my window, and at the end of the street, the joggers, the bicyclists, the

195

skaters, the riders on horseback, the strollers, the baby carriages and balloons, the sparkling water and the canopies of leaves along the trails in the park. To the north and west, beyond the reservoir, behind the tall buildings, my daughter spends her day in graduate school, a burgeoning anthropologist and a beautiful woman married to a scientist from the isle of Crete. Therefore, my circles now include a son-in-law and an extended family in Greece, as well as spiritual ancestors, gods and demigods who were masters of bull leaping and once held the clew of thread which leads out of the labyrinth. Ninety blocks and more to the south, at the heartbeat of the municipality, my husband is in his office overlooking City Hall and the two rivers. Based on twenty-five years of experience, I am reasonably certain to see him around dinner time. For I am a wife and my circles overlap his with surprising frequency considering that we are both consumed and subsumed by work that we love.

My circles go out beyond the city and backward in time, beyond the Hudson River, beyond Appalachia, beyond the Mississippi, into the Sun Belt, the Southwest, and the Hill Country to a yucca-studded realm of limestone, green rivers (yes, really green), live oak trees and small stone farm houses like the one where I was born. For I am a daughter, primal creation of my mother, brought to bed in a white-washed room with a fireplace where rattlesnakes have been known to invade. Our house, to which my father added one stone each afternoon after walking three miles from school, overlooks a rock fence, a corncrib, a cistern, a pear orchard, fields bordered with horehound, milkweed and wildflowers, and the most delicious creek in the universe. Delivered by a country doctor, I was welcomed into the bosom of an extended family with gifts, the recital of which strokes my self-conceit to this day: a gold ring with pearls, a silver spoon, a set of gold pins, four monogrammed crib sheets, a hand-embroidered sack, a hand-embroidered cap, a crocheted cap, a crib pillow and comforter, a dress trimmed with tatting, silk crocheted slippers, white kid bootees, a white piqué sack, a smocked dress, two pairs of silk hose, white felt shoes, a half-dozen nansook dresses, announcement cards, and a Baby Book. I inherited my mother's silver porringer. I was breast-fed, weaned after eight months, kept on a rigid schedule, and severely punished for manifesting the many forms of "wickedness" inherent in me, as in all of "God's children."

I was told that my father was a perfect gentleman and a scholar (he was a lawyer), an ideal son, brother, husband, father, that he was alive, that his whereabouts could not be disclosed and that it was better "just to tell people that he was dead." I learned not to mention his name because it gave my mother and my relatives a great deal of pain to talk about him.

So my circles included (and will always include) a phantom father and a mother who was bereaved and yet not bereaved, who was proud of her "aristocratic" family, was infinitely sad, competent in many ways, helpless in others, greatly desirous of winning approval and bringing up her children to be "refined" and "nice." Included also were a sister who was sensitive, wonderfully intelligent, angelic and ill and a brother who at times succeeded in acting as the "little man of the house," "taking his father's place" and "protecting his mother and sisters," and who at other times revolted savagely against this role. We lived among aunts, uncles and cousins who provided a dazzling array of designs for being and living, including Big Thicket frontier, gracious antebellum, sober professional, eccentric and outright lunatic.

My circles overlapped with those of the ministers of various faiths. I read Relevation, was cleansed of original sin through baptism and, when we moved to my mother's more refined milieu, pasted stars in my Sunday school picture book and stole sips of wine from the communion chalice. I was too numb to mourn for my father (although I studied the faces of strange men on street cars and trains, and hunted for him most of my life).

My favorite aunt died of a broken heart, they said, and my handsome adored older cousin was killed in a motorcycle accident in California, where he had gone to seek his fortune at eighteen. So I knew early about losses that can never quite be mourned away. By the time I was thirteen, religion had become a hard taskmaster that had to be overthrown. I believed that I had committed the Unpardonable Sin. It was either abolish God or annihilate my "black self" which seemed to be a very persistent part of me. Compared with my sister and most of my relatives, who appeared to fit easily into the mold of goodness and compliance, I was persistently "bad." I think I realized even then that I would never succeed in being good on their terms.

Certain books sneaked from the public library gave me a glimpse of a broader world and put me in touch with my sensuous soul, as the Greeks called one "part" of the psyche. Conflict overwhelmed me; I fell into despair and then into disease and was confined to bed and to the house for a year. The doctors said I had a lesion on my lung, and I suppose that this was true for the scar still shows up in the X rays. But my chief ailment, as I perceive it, was the fear of burning in hell's eternal flames. This fear was very real and graphic. It came up strongly at night and destroyed my sleep for about a year but it seemed like an eternity. There was no one that I could tell about it. My sister divined it and sympathized, which may have saved my life. It was a hell which finally subsided, leaving some of me intact and able to fight for survival. Gradually, over the succeeding years, the decimated part was rebuilt, to a degree.

My mother was affectionate, jolly, sociable, a good cook and a fair housekeeper. She made friends and kept them for life. When she had to punish my brother and me, as she sometimes did, she turned grim and white-faced and afterwards wept and complained. Putting children to bed without their supper, whipping and tying them to the bedpost was not proper work for a woman, she said, though in fact she was fairly adept at it. She liked to eat and was a bit overweight during the middle years. A husband was for protection, she thought, to take the burden off a wife's shoulders, to provide money, status, companionship and contact with the world. She had been trained in two professions—teacher and legal secretary—by her mother, an early feminist and herself a professional, and she shuttled between staying at home with her children and going out to work. She believed that marriages were made in heaven and that if she should take another husband the three of them would be seriously incommoded and embarrassed in the afterlife and that she would not know which one to choose as her celestial consort. I said, "Nonsense, Mama. There will probably be a lot of handsome, fine men in heaven. Maybe you would choose somebody altogether different—a third husband."

"Honey, you ought not to talk that way. It's sacrilegious," she would say, shaking her head but laughing too.

Physical manifestations, sexual matters, anatomy, sweating, passing wind, going to the bathroom, caused her to wrinkle her nose in disgust. Yet she allowed me to be a tomboy and encouraged me to think of the law as a career, "to carry on the family tradition." I believe she was gratified by my skating, swimming, diving, biking, tennis, horseback riding, and all the rest. "My goodness, honey, another scraped knee! Why, you'll hardly have any skin left! You'll be covered with scabs!" "I'll vow, child, you'll break your neck!" Her laughter was full and hearty, belying her ladylike airs. At times she laughed herself teary and breathless. Hysterical laughter perhaps but not like the wild, out-of-control whinny of the ever-loving, sweet and dutiful Lilabelle Tubman, her friend. My mother talked nonstop, to keep unwanted thoughts and feelings at bay, I surmise. Somehow, though she made many high-minded statements about marriage and what a sacred state it was, she never conveyed the sense of *what* it was. Nor did she tell me the "facts of life," as information about sex was called.

Never a word about menstruation. The little I knew I picked up at school, in the neighborhood, in the barnyards of various farms, from movies, books and magazines, mostly of the *True Confessions* stripe, and from our more down-to-earth and/or crazy aunts, and male cousins and uncles driven by incestuous lust.

There was no "latency period" in East Texas. I felt the pull of this earthiness (dished up with quite a lot of defiance and guilt) and, in contrast, the strong undertow of discomfort and anxiety, which passed by osmosis from my mother to me. Forbidden to fulfill her needs, or even to recognize their existence, she could not sublimate them either, as my Aunt Mary had so gracefully done. Below the level of her awareness, I think, she transmitted an altogether opposite message from the one she enunciated and tried to instill, the one she felt duty-bound to get across to her daughters. This below the surface message was: I am a hostage, an unhappy prisoner of the morals and customs of this time and place. Break the bonds, my daughter, by whatever means you can. Escape, escape! I don't have the courage. You must live for me as well as yourself. Be brave! Be free! Pleasure is not really evil. Discover it! Enjoy it! No matter what I *say*, I will revel in your enjoyment. Through you I will find a pathway to life."

My attempts to find freedom and pleasure are in part a response to her unconscious pleading, her unuttered cries which hung so heavy in the air. She who could not swim and blanched at the sight of a tall horse, delighted to see me ripple through the waves and gallop over the fields. Her little screams of fear and her outraged laughter urged me on. I went on my way, driven by her, though she never knew (or did she? Did she ever doubt her conventional rattlings?). Through a headstrong and sometimes antisocial adolescence I moved into my twenties and thirties with a fiery temperament, considerable joie de vivre, an undertow of self-doubt and self-denigration, sporadic outbursts of self-flagellation and less than perfect wisdom and judgment. It was only after setting up an honest-to-goodness two-way relationship with my husband that I became less defective in these areas. I think at last I have fully grieved for my mother—for her deprivations and mine, for her death. She was strong and loving in the best way she could be, and rather marvelous in her time. I grieved for my father this year for the first time, finally acknowledging that he is lost to me forever, and burying him in a ritual of mourning at David Freundlich's workshop.

What power do we have, really, to recall the past? When memories do bob up they tend to gather themselves under the banner of miseries lived through, of the unfairness of it all, of one's own imperfections, of regrets, of the sadness and futility of life. Of course, I have my long thoughts in the rainy nights, gentle, pleasing, entwined with sleep. And occasionally, quixotically, I lie in ecstasy while a procession of insights, images, prospects, plans pour through me, body and mind (I say body, not to separate the corporal state from the mind, but to emphasize how one and the same they are; for if at such times I cogitate—and I suppose I must—then surely it is as much with my toes, my womb and my fingertips, as with my brain).

Such a night came to me not long ago in Maine, after a day of shining grasses, leaves, fir trees rising out of the rocks, wet seaweed, ospreys and bald eagles flying over the nest, northwest winds gusting round to west and southwest, and sometimes to east, and wisps of spun clouds high in the sky, bringing soft rain, wet woods, and then that crystallized purity of weather—sunshine blown about in the blue heavens, in the dark waters, in the ospreys' nest, in people's homes. Perhaps it blew into me and I too crystallized, became pure and optimistic. Our friends Violet and Burke Marshall at North Haven Island had given us of their best and this in itself was moving. For once I felt that I deserved it. I do not love their island or Maine deep in my bones as I love the Hill Country of Texas or Italy. But I adored it that night because for me it became the center of the world. It was the center because I was there. I was important. After a long period of intermittent disbelief—in myself and in the powers that control the greening or the blasting of things—after hurt and bitterness and envy of those luckier or more capable or more laudable than myself, I saw with clarity that I was good and lovable and that others were also. I experienced those close to me as unique and precious treasures and delights.

I saw all my friends at Argus at the beginning and again at the end of the night, and in between I journeyed back into forgotten lanes and byways, weeping, laughing, burning and shivering with pain and pleasure as I relived the incidents of my infancy, childhood and young adulthood. Usually, forms and faces loom up, float before my eyes—aspects, angles, outlines, guises, colors, defining themselves, then shifting, blurring, fading, melting into dead yesterdays and unborn tomorrows. A peepshow, a burning glass. Mists before my eyes. A stone thrown into a pool. Terror. A poison spring: where? when? Beauty and deadly evil. Remnants of past torments, questions of days gone by, doubts. If my name had been given to me had I any right to it? Was it really mine? If not, then who might I be? Is a nameless one anyone at all? Who was it trembling there on the edge of becoming? A famous beauty or a milk cow? A joyous nymph or Niobe weeping endless tears? Was my soul a migrating bird or a naked, shivering tree? What fanged beasts were there? Riddle and unriddle and riddle again. That's how it often seemed to be. Yet this particular night I found a word, a key. I seemed able to see, to understand—and to care. Though I have hated them before and may hate them again, even the "monsters" were understood and loved.

If there were monsters, there were goddesses also. Two black women, Martha and Vera, old friends long lost to me, appeared again and again. Martha I had last seen in her open coffin in Bedford Stuyvesant, with the gladiolas banked around, and the choir singing "I came to the garden alone, while the dew was still on the roses. . . ." Death could not glaze over the warm velvet of her face. Martha spent a year with me once when I was ill and depressed. She was slender, slow-moving, patient, affectionate, and deeply sensitive. She brought me out of the prison of myself, not by talking about *me*, but by recounting, day after day, week after week, month after month, the story of *her* life as one of thirty-three children (born to two mothers or taken in by her parents) growing up on an East Texas farm. She talked and, as I gathered strength, I began to write it down. Martha was the twin sister of Mary, bound in the joys of a perfect union the like of which no nontwin could know and no twin could ever duplicate in later life. The second-born, with a cowl over her face, was thrown into the fireplace by the grannywoman who decided that even one more was too many in that house and that the second twin was not only an insult but a bad luck omen and a danger. Triumphantly reclaimed from the ashes by a father and mother who loved "childrens" and who could never get enough of them, their own or other people's (the grannywoman was driven from the door), Martha enjoyed a lifelong certainty of being wanted and affirmed in her value which racial prejudice and hardship could not destroy.

Like many black babies she and Mary, her twin, were held, cuddled, exclaimed over and passed from hand to hand and bosom to bosom when the members of the immediate family and their various relations gathered. Thus did she come to appreciate herself and her twin as truly wondrous and precious specimens of the human race. Thus did she experience her own body and those of others as pleasurable while her limbic centers grew big and rich with emotions and connectedness. Thus was she introduced from infancy onward to her network, a group of people who, as long as they lived and possessed a rag and a scrap of food, would share with her. This is not sentimentality. These babies were not welcomed only because of their rarity as twins. They were rejoiced in, as babies are in black families which have not been ripped apart by economic upheaval, migration, repressive religion and the welfare system. This may be a part of the African heritage. Fecundity was greatly appreciated in West Africa and along the Niger, where many of the peoples shared a common vision of the creation of "the world as an egg in two parts which were to procreate." The "egg of God" or the "placenta of the world" and other seeds, enfolded in a hibiscus seed, are often represented as an open flower with four petals sometimes called the "clavicles" of God. This egg contained one special pair of twins, one male, one female, the archetypes of human beings.

The story, as recounted by Germaine Dieterlin in "The Mande Creation Myth," is one of the most beautiful among the oral literatures which have been preserved for us. In this myth, human beings multiplied and diversified, giving rise to the Family of Man. Dieterlen reveals the myth as a charter for the far-flung lineages of the Mali Empire, evoking the theme of relatedness among African peoples. The Oyo and the Yoruba had myths of creation with similar features, as did other West African peoples. At the center of these myths is the Earth Goddess who represents fecundity. Islam, with its purely masculine concept of God and the world, has made little progress in uprooting this idea of basic harmony of peoples and principles or in substituting doctrines of exclusivity. Instead, Islam in Africa came to reflect the nature of the society and the ideals it found there.[1] African ideologies were rooted in the natural world and in harmony with it and consequently fostered fulfillment and happiness.[2] I believe that this partly accounts for the vitality and persistence of the black family in the face of extreme adversity and efforts literally to stamp it out, to make studs and broodmares of a people. More typical were people like Martha's parents, exuberantly raising children and opening their doors to orphans and displaced children.

Martha herself was not able to have children, but her twin sister "gave" her a few of the ten she bore. Martha fed, educated and watched over them all of her life.

Vera's story was much different. She too came every day for months, not to care for me (though she gave me a great deal, as it turned out) but in response to my desire to know about life among Southern blacks. Vera was one of the dolphins of this world, strong, well-fleshed, playful, and full of laughter. Her father had harnessed her to a plow when she was eleven, and she had worked hard all of her life. Love radiated from her center like the sun. Her pores were open to pain and pleasure. She deeply grieved for her man who was shot in a coal mine. What they had together was sexually and in every way so fulfilling that it was like the best recipe for homemade bread: once you taste it you never really want any other. Still, after he was gone she tried to find another man. There was something wrong with all of them: they drank or used drugs or played around or wouldn't work or tried to beat her. She didn't stay around for any of that; but she went on, fixing herself up as nice as she could, going out where "mens" were, trying to tempt somebody. Neither joy nor melancholy strained her, any more than a beautiful day or a storm strains the universe. Indeed, she herself was a piece of the sunshine, a part of the storm. She flashed lightning, when she sang it was an orgasm. When she fell into the sadness of life, well, this was an orgasm too in its way. The hurts, the losses, the deep misery, passed over her like dark clouds, wave after wave. She trembled, she sobbed. Tears rained down. Or she shook with laughter. Laughter welled up out of her every pore. She never turned up her nose at anything human. She said, "They hurt me, Chavella" (my nickname), and let the tears run down her face.

Well, Martha and Vera, as long as I live I will carry you within my flesh. Your message to me was, "Life is worth living. Pain hurts. To cry is okay. There is strength in anger. Pleasure is exquisite, hang on to it at any cost. Laughter is a great balm. Ecstasy comes when you least expect it. Breathing, just plain old breathing, is delicious." You were too ignorant to know that you don't impose your own history and miseries on a troubled one, that only the one seeking help is supposed to give forth. With your "untherapeutic" sharing of yourselves you did a great deal to heal and to nurture me, and to the degree that I am strong, you helped to make me so. I will do what I can to give you back to the world where you created such a harmony and a poetry of being.

In later years whatever else I was doing—getting married, getting divorced, having a child, searching for love, trying to be a good mother, finally making a solid marriage, working at things that interested me, reading, studying, travelling—there was always a part of me that stood aside, hurt, scared and lonely. An odyssey through the mazeways of psychoanalysis was one of my preoccupations, but although I enjoyed having first a beaming saintly aura seated behind the couch and later a warm, earthy, directive father figure who looked me full in the face and exchanged ideas with me, I never got disentangled; words weren't enough. Gradually I came to realize that traditional psychotherapy, with its insistence that all of the problems lie within, with its unashamed patriarchal and male chauvinist interpretations, and its admonition to adjust or remain a "cripple for life," was not a solution but part of the problem.

I never agreed with Freudian theories about women, which I considered (and still consider) to be a misreading of the facts. If I escaped wallowing in this particular slough, it is in part due to my mother's mother (she who had each of her daughters trained in two careers). No doors in society had been represented by the family as closed to me. The narrow horizons of the women captives of either doctrine—religious or Freudian—held no lure for me, nor did the theories behind them. Still, I had thought free association might lead me out of my pain. But it was not until 1968, at the Casriel Institute, that I was able to express my feelings full measure and clear away, over months, the swamp where I had been mired.

It was not entirely a childhood swamp, interestingly enough; the locus of much of my pain, anger and fear, I discovered, was in my everyday interpersonal relations and quite a bit of it was valid, simply a human response to unfair and intolerable situations and verdicts of society. I found a lamentable lack of confidence in myself, almost an abjectness. I had scanned the environment for signs of pessimism and failure and had incorporated them. It was my way of excoriating myself, amounting to self-persecution. Well, I've stopped it. And I've substituted life-and-pleasure-building messages instead. I take in love and I give it out. The Institute was also of help to others I knew who had sought in vain and had gone the disappointing rounds of traditional psychotherapy.

Growing up as a child in East Texas and Louisiana I heard about and witnessed acts of injustice, violence and murder against blacks and saw the white perpetrators upheld by the white community and in the courts. In one instance a teenage black whom I had known most of my life was sadistically and wantonly murdered by a white man on a drunken and deluded spree. My black playmate was forced into a car at gun point and after being threatened and tormented was shot in the head. The young man's body was then thrown from the car and the killer ran over it again and again while bystanders on the streets of the small town watched.

I knew the killer well. He was my half cousin; I had lived in his parents' house; I too had been tormented by him and knew what it felt like to be whipped by him or have his gun held against my head as we sped at ninety miles an hour on the black-topped roads in that cut-over and despoiled pine country. When the case came before a judge only one question, posed by a highly respected white lawyer and politician, was sufficient to clear my cousin, "Why would any Southern white gentleman kill a Negro man?" No details were asked for or given, no witnesses were called. The case was dismissed. But my cousin convicted and sentenced himself: he moved into the tiny one-room house in the backyard near the animals' stalls and cages, the same house where the murder victim had lived. His wife, whose "honor" he was supposed to have defended, left him and returned to her own family. There were no amenities in that tiny house, not even screens on the windows. The family's pleas were in vain. He lived there until he died, twenty years later.

Why had this boy, Teejay, for whom I felt a self-sameness, been killed while I was still walking around drinking up the light of day? As low ones in the pecking order, Teejay and I and the other children had been forced to venture into the bee-infested glade to gather honey from the felled oak. Teejay had told us that anyone molesting the bees would be stung to death. We were stung in a dozen places, but not to death though we were mad with fear. When they found and killed my pet turtle (in his secret lair near the bayou) Teejay yelled and fought beside me, in vain, and that afternoon was seduced as I was, by the delicious smells coming from the gumbo pot. We both ate the gumbo—and experienced an uneasiness never to be resolved by me. Teejay helped to drive the alligators from the Anacoco so that we could swim. He himself refused to enter the bayou for fear a catfish would enter his urethra and nibble away his insides. Teejay was petrified of ghosts, as was I.

But he showed me raccoons washing their food and mayflies hatching from their mother's body after her death. He said that if she feels like it a mayfly mother can airmail her eggs in the pond as she flies over it (giving birth on the wing—that is true exuberance). He said that "some mens gits a terrible venery sickness from layin up with alligators." Teejay kept an interested eye on egrets, high-diving ducklings, and other water creatures. His job was the care of the myriad wild animals and birds collected and kept in cages by my uncle. People called Teejay "simple." But in another time and place he might have lived and become an ethologist. One night I helped my cousins rig up a bucket above the door to Teejay's house so that when he opened it to go in (returning late from the movies) water showered down and the bucket fell (we had not anticipated this) and struck him on the head. He was more shaken than hurt and spent the night on the kitchen porch muttering and nursing his head. I had a nagging suspicion that I had betrayed my friend—and I know for sure now that I had.

It would be fakery to say that the lines were drawn, even on the clearest of nights, or that, for all my brain-racking and reading of books, I understood much of anything. I wandered into middle life unprepared in any direct way for what I was about to undertake. A year in Haiti; sojourns in Appalachia with people eking out a living in lonesome hollows, union men and women feuding, dynamiting, fighting it out with scabs and bosses; some acquaintance with black and white laborers on the plantations and farms South and North; more than a year learning and writing about the cane cutters and fisher people in a Spanish village; my years in antipoverty work in Trenton—this was the only preparation I had for stirring about in the ashes of the South Bronx. I was striving to reorder my life around deeply felt values, and in response to my sense of failure, frailty and mortality. My motives were and are far from selfless. I wanted closeness. I wanted to be of use. I wanted to leave a footprint somewhere, perhaps even a wingbeat.

Argus came about, in a very real sense, because my teenage daughter and I were not communicating. Nor was I able to get through to the adolescents who were under my supervision as a volunteer probation officer. The Neighborhood Youth Corps kids in the antipoverty agency where I worked were treated like boot camp recruits by some and like precious cargo by others. I could relate to them but they saw me as a stereotype—white, middle class, middle aged and incapable of comprehending who and what they were. Many a night I lay awake constructing variations on bridges that I fancied they—and I—might be able to cross over. I wanted to know them and I wanted them to know what I was. It came to me that I needed to start something of my own. I believed that if I could find persons willing to take a chance, I could experiment until I made it work. I looked at everything I could find—projects in the community, in halfway houses, behind the walls. An idea slowly formed itself.

Looking back at my journals from those early years I realize that our present project is not different in any essential element from my original conception. Communication and closeness were to be the keys. And the demand that people—kids and staff—do what they were supposed to do and do it right. Mistakes and failures would not only be tolerated, people would be praised for daring to fail and learning from their failure. We would teach kids that it's okay to fail but not okay to think of oneself as a failure. We would encourage them to risk falling on their faces, to pick themselves up, dust themselves off and try again. We would put them in touch with a spectrum of people, ideas and resources.

In 1968, I found a board of public-spirited citizens interested in doing something constructive in the South Bronx. Helen Buttenwieser, Schuyler Meyer, B. Pendleton Rogers, Susan Herter and Faith Schwarz were the most active among them. We shared a number of ideas. They called themselves Volunteer Opportunities, Inc. (VOI), and they hoped to utilize the great pool of energy, creativity and good will among middle- and upper middle-class volunteers to help out in the ghetto. I had been on the board of the Morrow Association on Correction in New Jersey, working closely with Millicent Fenwick and Nina Alexander, and had helped to develop projects of interest to the VOI board. They gave me three months' salary on condition that I design a project and get it funded during that time. I came up with four or five proposals, and by consensus we chose one which we called the Bronx Community Counseling Project. Because of the credibility of the VOI Board, the Taconic Foundation and the New York Foundation took a chance and gave us money to get started. I moved our operations from East 49th Street in Manhattan to East 161st Street and Third Avenue in the South Bronx, into the only space available near the court—two moldering and fly-specked rooms more suited to the hatching of crimes than to any redemptory purpose. Still, I set chairs in a circle and put a pot of water on to boil for coffee.

The Fund for the City of New York had ventured in with a grant of $125,000. This gave me breathing space to experiment with young adults sentenced by the Bronx Criminal Court and teenagers diverted from Family Court. I was stunned when 99 percent of the persons sent by judges turned out to be hard-core heroin addicts and polydrug users. I tried to hire graduates of the drug free therapeutic communities to help me cope with this drastic situation but was not successful. A Catholic priest on sabbatical signed on and the two of us tried to reinvent the wheel, making as many errors as it is possible to make. I remember leading a group for addicts just released from jail and after it was over, lending one woman $25 to pay the rent and another $10 to buy milk for her child. They both shot dope. I hired an ex-amphetamine freak from Haight-Ashbury to make the rounds of the therapeutic communities (T.C.'s), in an attempt to recruit staff. No go. We hired a number of splittees. Some were charismatic, they could spout jargon, but their behavior was only a hop and a skip ahead of that of the enrollees. Various among them stole, forged checks, used the kids to buy dope and perform other illegal acts, took kickbacks from staff members, ripped off our food budget, made crooked deals with merchants.

Our first "clinical psychologist," was a blind man who had come highly recommended from the Mayor's office, with forged degrees and certificates. He bamboozled us all and none of the bona fide psychologists or psychiatrists who met and worked with him at Argus questioned his credentials or his sometimes crazy antics. Since he worked round the clock, kept a hot-line for enrollees and staff and gave us the equivalent of $40,000 a year in volunteer time which we used as in-kind match for a federal grant, it was easy to overlook his foibles and discrepancies. He was conspiratorial and divisive, a great purveyor of gossip about his "patients," and nagged me to install equipment which would have enabled him and me to listen in on people's telephone conversations. His downgrading of the female staff amounted to misogyny; and he deliberately brought me on a collision course with my Board. Some of the staff were ensnared by his crazy pronouncements (he had them read their "diagnoses" from a psychology text book) and sank into self-denigration. Others resisted and confronted me for allowing him to promulgate such awful garbage.

Though vicious to the staff he was zealously devoted to the street addicts and criminals who came our way. They accepted his ministerings. Once or twice he moved into the house with families in crisis and worked with them round the clock for a week. But finally, his lies, malice, manipulations and divisiveness were such that I swore to get rid of him if it meant throwing him physically into the street, blind as he was, and even if we it meant losing a federal grant. It was at that juncture that the detectives appeared with the news that our Dr. Jekyll was really Mr. Hyde. He had served ten years of a twenty-year sentence for blowing up a building and had assumed the identity of a Columbia University-educated certified psychologist who had been living abroad for years.

A couple of months after our self-designated certified psychologist left us, a bomb was planted on our front steps. The block was cleared and the device dismantled by the bomb squad. Perhaps he thought I had got wind of his secret and betrayed him to the police. I later heard that the police were tipped off by a woman he had stolen from his closest prison buddy, had then spurned, and about whom he had written scurrilous letters.

It fell to me to explain to our funding sources the presence of this fiendish interloper in the social welfare field. Fortunately, our record in other respects was good. Independent evaluators, hired by the city, had studied our enrollees and followed them up in the NYSIS and city arrest records after they left the program. The findings were encouraging. We had done better than any other agency dealing with a similar population, except in one age group, the sixteen-year-old heroin addicts; nobody did well with them at the time.

By 1972 we were putting together a strong staff, learning from our errors. Group facilitators trained by Dan Casriel led our staff development effort. Mary Taylor, Aubrey LaFrance and I conducted training groups also. We had managed to establish fairly solid enrollee peer groups to help us run the program.

We had never had any "anti-drug" money, though we were dealing with hard-core "greasy street addicts" of a type most drug programs would not touch. In 1973, we showed our program to Graham Finney of the City's Addiction Services Agency. He liked what he saw and funds were forthcoming. When those funds ran out the state took us over, with monies coming from the State Division for Youth, the State Division of Substance Abuse Services, and the State Department of Social Services through Special Services for Children of the City of New York. Later, we acquired city Department of Employment funding.

One of my strengths is the ability to select talented people and develop them as staff members, to be firm in maintaining quality and to keep our fiscal noses clean. Aubrey LaFrance, Mary Taylor and I together developed and adapted concepts and treatment methods. My admiration for the local people, my belief in their talents and abilities and my affinity for the consensus model have been catalysts in the creative process. I am persistent (some call it stubborn) and I love certain kinds of adventure. But to know these kids—and this type of staff—is to love them. I am in awe of their ability to survive and overcome. I am in love with the particular squiggles and arabesques of their personalities. They are so deeply appreciative of anything you do for them. In fifteen years at Argus, although countless kids have knocked on my door and demanded a hearing for their grievances, I can honestly say that not one has said a rude word to me. Such is the attraction and the power of the environment our interethnically joined hands have created.

When I learn that a treatment approach Mary Taylor and I have cooked up has been successful, that the girl's suicide attempts have ceased; when I sit in a circle with these kids and they share their experiences, their dreams and their aspirations, I am transported and that is all there is to it. When a kid drops by my office and tells me that she regularly visits the Frick and the Metropolitan (never having been out of the South Bronx before coming to Argus), I am elated.

José Velez told me the other day that the single most important thing he learned in Argus was to "walk that extra mile." He works at Burger King to keep beans in the pot, and knowing it was an interim job he never took it seriously until he read Clement Stone's and

Napolean Hill's "little green book." "Now I see that what I do at Burger King is important for my future. It's the way it will fit into my later life. I walk that extra mile there too so I'll be in the habit of it. Then when I get the job I want it will be second nature to me." José wants to go into the food business.

So many have felt, as I did, like a stranger within our own society, alienated from God and the world by chaos, economic crisis, upheavals, wars and disasters. Technology, which promised plenty and expansion without end, has shown its darker side. Our waters and our soil are polluted. Our forests are being murdered. Our streets are choked with throwaway people. Our spiritual world has dissolved, leaving us walled off, adrift on the scarred bosom of nature. We are losing awareness that we have spiritual strivings, a need to give and to take, to dream and to share our dreams. We are losing the fullness and the ripeness of our humanity. We cultivate our working identity. We say that we fit in here or there as cogs in a wheel. We perform in this way or that at a particular point and it is said to be enough. But is it?

At the turn of the century people were required to be "nice" and "appropriate" in their adjustment to society's demands. When Freud gave us a method of getting in touch with what was under that "niceness," we—and he—mistook the furies which psychoanalysis uncovered as a suppressed part of human "nature." This was better than believing that evil resides outside ourselves as witches and devils who must be burned. But it is no more in the nature of humans to be perverse and antisocial than it is for bound heads or feet to be misshapen and dysfunctional. We have flip-flopped now and wear our erstwhile unmentionables on our sleeves. It is the "spiritual," the tender, affectionate, altruistic side of ourselves—the side that yearns to live and die in harmony, to be bonded, to believe that there is meaning and a reason for living—that is suppressed today.

What I and those joined with me in the "muck and rapturous essence" of this venture try to do is to uncover the altruism that lies buried in each of us. We succeed some of the time.

Not even Saint Thomas More has all the answers.

15. DIAGNOSTICS AND OTHER CONFUSIONS
Labeling and Mislabeling Children

I feel like nobody cares
I just sit there daydreaming my life away
That's just the way I feel
Feeling as if I'm going to be lonely
For the rest of my life

ARGUS ENROLLEE

There is no way around naming the ills which beset us. Diagnostic classifications are useful. They provide society with markers in what otherwise would be a trackless forest. Besides being a thoroughly human inclination, this zeal for taxonomy can set us on the road to other indispensable activities, such as describing the problems, their prevalence and the toll they take and encouraging a search for the best treatment under the state of the art. Without diagnostics we could not make sensible decisions about individual children, allocate funds, design, run or evaluate treatment programs.

These categories can be a blessing. But they are also a curse. There are so many of them. They overlap frequently, are used differently by diverse practitioners and observers who may or may not have the eye, the motivation and the time for accuracy or be possessed of the most up-to-date information. Also, some diagnostic labels are applied differently to different classes of people. For example, autism and mental retardation. About 40 percent of children with infantile autism have an IQ of less than 50 and only 30 percent have an IQ of 70 or above. Maternal rubella and phenylketonuria (a hereditary metabolic disorder) are thought to be implicated in some instances of both conditions. But doctors seem reluctant to assign well-to-do children to the mentally retarded category, even when their IQs are low, preferring instead to diagnose them as autistic. (*The Diagnostic and Statistical Manual of Mental Disorders* [DSM–III] recommends that when retardation is present, as well as autism, both diagnoses should be recorded.)[1] It has been speculated that this practice may be a factor in the overrepresentation of the well-to-do among the autistic. On the other hand, the borderline and mild retardation categories, where the

211

poor are overrepresented, may be a dumping ground for deprived persons whose low self-esteem, sense of hopelessness and unfamiliarity with and mistrust of tests and middle-class personnel and trappings affect their scores and interviews.

There are many disagreements among schools of medicine, psychiatry, psychotherapy, psychology and education, not to mention the philosophers, anthropologists and others who try to weave it all together in a coherent fabric. Also on the debit side is our seemingly ineluctable tendency to embalm our discoveries in their definitions, to get stuck on the flypaper of official nomenclature and ignore the advances made in various fields. William James expressed the situation eloquently when he wrote:

> When, then, we talk of "psychology as a natural science," we must not assume that that means a sort of psychology that stands at last on solid ground. It means just the reverse; it means a psychology particularly fragile, and into which the waters of metaphysical criticism leak at every joint . . . a string of raw facts, a little gossip and wrangle about opinions; a little classification and generalization on the more descriptive level; a strong prejudice that we have states of mind, and that our brain conditions them: but not a single law in the sense which physics shows us laws, not a single proposition from which any consequence can causally be deduced. . . . This is no science, it is only the hope of a science.[2]

At Argus we try to amend misdiagnoses. If a girl has been called a schizophrenic by a psychiatrist, and we disagree and believe that we can work with her, we take her to a psychiatrist whose definition of that disease is much narrower (properly so, we think) and replace the pejorative label.

Since federal, state and city programs do categorize clients, the participants are bound to know about it, even when the hands-on personnel is careful and plays down labels as we do. Labels are one more hurdle for the kids—and us—to leap over, *if we can.*

Must we affix labels to children? The answer is an emphatic no. But to accommodate society in its need for classifications *and* protect the children from further damage by the very people whose job it is to help them requires acuity, awareness and vigilance, plus the knowledge of how destructive a label can be. Even so it probably cannot be done. For no matter how careful we are there will always be a leak in the dike. One of our girls, before she came to us, broke into the locked files of the institution where she was placed, read about herself and some of the other inmates, passed along the descriptions she considered insulting and instigated a riot. It would behoove us all to watch our language in relation to adolescents and others, even on paper. When we ask for funds or report to monitoring agencies, we have no choice but to describe our children in terms of their deficits and disabilities.

But what if policy makers and legislators were to turn the nomenclatorial process around and give out funds for *developing strengths* in particular areas? What would be wrong about that? A lot could be right about it, particularly if we really mean it when we say we do not wish to run mere "holding tanks" for children. All people must learn to live with their particular weaknesses, to cope with them as best they can. We can't be namby-pamby or nice-nice about that or cover up the facts. It won't work. But a contiguous and far greater emphasis should always be placed on strengths (and we all have them). Strengths have to be uncovered and cultivated, given air and water and fertilizer.

Our present emphasis on disabilities and deficits encourages many to cultivate their weaknesses, to relate to them and to make a career of them. Why? Because that is the package the "help" comes in. As we label people we push them into identities and shape their self-concepts. It has never happened at Argus but I have nightmares about the children getting their hands on the reports we are required to write about them. It could be detrimental to their growth and their self-esteem to hear themselves described in terms of their "diseases." How would one of our children feel if he heard himself described as an epileptic? *He suffers from epilepsy. But he is not an epileptic.* And the others are not Delinquents, Persons in Need of Supervision, et cetera. They don't need signs around their necks saying, "I am Disadvantaged," "I am Emotionally Disturbed," "I am Brain Damaged," "I am Dyslectic," "I am Abused and Neglected," "I am Dependent," "I am Perceptually Defective," "I am Hyperactive," "I am Learning Disabled," "I am Personality Disordered," "I am a Drug Addict," "I am a Pseudoneurotic Schizophrenic," "I am an Adjustment Reaction to Adolescence," or "I am a COH Child" (Committee on the Handicapped).

Such labels can be internalized and become another link in a chain of denigrating self-messages caught from parents, teachers, living conditions and a string of failures. Everyone else seems to blame the kids; why shouldn't they blame themselves? Yet it may be that these negative messages are the chief stumbling block in the road they need to take, and which society desires them to take, toward independent living. We all know someone who has snuggled into an identity as a patient, using illness to evade responsibility, finding uniqueness and even a minor glory in being seen as a sick person.

Policy makers, as well as people in the helping professions, should rethink the system of pejorative labeling.

Numbers of poor children need special attention from professionals, both in and out of schools, institutions and community settings (such as ours) so that they can survive and, it is to be hoped, move toward full human growth and independence. Many of them did not receive adequate care during the prenatal period, during birth or as infants and preadolescents. Their problems often are associated with developmental neglect.

It can be crushing to have a label pinned on you; if it is the wrong label to boot then an element of terrible irony enters. Argus enrollees have been victimized by misdiagnosis more often than they should be, partly because of the widespread and awesome carelessness and waste inherent in every human endeavor but in some cases because of misconceptions and bad practices that can be corrected. I will discuss some of these presently. But first a bird's-eye view of some of the major diagnostic categories currently in use may be helpful. I will not discuss blindness, deafness and other physical handicaps which do not cause as much diagnostic confusion, although quite a number of children come our way whose sight and hearing problems have been overlooked altogether.

1. Failure to Thrive. This generally means abnormal shortness of stature and delayed sexual development brought on by malnutrition; lack of maternal or caretaker affection, touch and sensory stimulation; and genetic and/or other environmental factors. I have never kept a count of them, but I have the impression that an undue number of Argus children, both boys and girls, are small and that breast and genital development occurs rather later than it should in some. This is a diagnosis which might have applied to Marvin Manders and to Ramona Ruiz, though their medical evaluations did not mention it as a possibility.

2. Behavior Disorder. This category overlaps partially with what the New York City Board of Education has called the Socially Maladjusted and the Emotionally Disturbed, although I have never been able to obtain a precise definition of what is meant by the term "emotionally disturbed." Behavior Disorder may show itself in younger children as temper tantrums, shyness, exacerbated jealousy and fears, restless sleep, night terrors, nightmares, bed-wetting, fecal incontinence, intense separation anxiety, hyperactivity, school phobias, *absence of social bonds or inadequate or inappropriate social bonds,* lack of guilt and remorse, et cetera. As children grow older they may violate the rules, defy authority, run away, play truant, turn to alcohol and drug abuse, to lying, setting fires, stealing or to mugging, robbery, rape, assault and, occasionally, homicide.[3] This behavior is also known as Conduct Disorder, Character Disorder, Personality Disorder or, informally, as Acting Out.

There is no doubt that most of the Argus children have shown some of these patterns or committed some of the acts described, enough to qualify them for the diagnosis. Some have committed one or more of the serious offenses. A few have done most or all of these things. The trouble is that this diagnosis, because so few people know what to do about the problem, leads to institutions and places of confinement which replicate the deplorable conditions that give rise to it in the first place and add a further helping of anger and bitterness to the sufferers. It is extremely difficult to endure the acting out of those who are Conduct Disordered, for often they violate the rights of others. Their behavior is seriously maladaptive and must be changed. But the "remediation" society employs at present is harmful. Therefore, our conduct is worse than theirs. For the most maladaptive behavior of all is the prescription which not only fails to cure the "disease" but exacerbates it. This is wasteful and even wanton, for we possess the knowledge to do a great deal that is positive for these children if only we would apply it.

3. Learning Disorders. This encompasses a whole sea of troubles, known also as Neurological Impairment, Brain Damage, Brain Injury, Minimal Brain Damage, Minimal Brain Dysfunction, Attention Deficit Disorder, Hyperkinesis, Hyperactivity, Perceptual Defects, Dyslexia, Developmental Reading Disorder, Developmental Arithmetic Disorder, Developmental Language Disorder (Expressive Type), Developmental Language Disorder (Receptive Type), Developmental Articulation Disorder. These categories appear in the lexicons of various professionals—physicians, psychiatrists, neurologists, psychologists and educators. There seem to be as many etiologies as there are names in this potpourri of disorders, with no single cause assigned. The symptoms overlap and the diagnostic criteria vary and are imprecise. Up to five times more males than females are afflicted, suggesting a genetic etiology. It is estimated that 5 to 15 percent of U.S. school children (2.5 to 7.5 million) have some type of learning disorder.[4]

In one way or another these children are characterized by distortions in the development of the psychological functions (and perhaps of the equipment) required for normal language, social and motor skills, perception and reality assessment. These conditions may or may not be inherited or result from chromosome damage or irregularities, nutritional deficiencies, severe deprivation, toxic substances, poisons, disease, intrauterine, perinatal, neonatal, infant and childhood traumas. Positive neurological findings have been reported in about 85 percent of these learning disordered children, but since central nervous system disorders cannot be diagnosed directly except by surgical post mortem procedures and can only be inferred from behavior, the diagnosis of Learning Disorders must lean upon the skill and the experience of the clinician and can be quite mystifying. It is our experience that children in this category are often identified as behaviorally disordered, especially if they are poor, because their impulsiveness, their constant touching and handling of objects, emotional instability and hyperactivity are perceived as willfulness and disobedience by authority figures and educators who lack training in the field.

Many of our "learning disabled" youngsters, like Marvin Manders, have been tested and found to have no signs of neurological damage, but there are so many unknowns in this field. Fortunately, this is changing with the explosion of knowledge about the brain and nervous system which will no doubt accelerate in the future.

There are a number of behavioral and therapeutic techniques that can help Learning Disabled children, but the teaching of cognitive material per se for them, even in special education classes, is not radically different from the methods used with normal children. The big issues seem to be finding teachers and backup personnel who can work with the concomitant behavioral and emotional problems, resulting from frustration, sense of failure, being scapegoated and losing or not developing a positive self-concept. For this reason, the present policy of putting these children in classrooms with normal pupils would seem to be counterproductive. The resource room, where such learning disabled children are sent for part of the day offers some support, but calls attention to their differences and deficits. A recent study has shown that pupils exposed during the day to two systems—the "normal" classroom and the resource room—become confused and do not learn in either environment. I believe that these children would do better in separate schools with their peers. The schools should be staffed in part by people like themselves who can provide inspiration and strength by having transcended their own limitations and should be oriented toward discovering and building on strengths.

The diagnosis of Learning Disorders, as it is used, overlaps to some extent with the following:

4. Mental Retardation. This category consists of children with less than normal intellectual ability, resulting from a number of causes, 85 percent of which are unknown. The well-known chromosomal abnormalities, such as Down's, Edward's and Patau's syndromes, make up the bulk of the known causes. Hereditary diseases, perinatal complications, postnatal infections, poisonings, head traumas and malnutrition comprise the remaining known causes of mental retardation. It is believed by many scientists and medical men that malnutrition, coupled with maternal or nurturance deprivation (absence of the physical, emotional and cognitive support necessary for normal development), may well be the leading cause on a global scale of this condition. One significant finding is that the majority of retarded children are conceived during the hot months when pregnant women are prone to eat very little.[5] Sound nutrition is vital to fetal brain development, particularly during the first eight to twelve weeks. Malnutrition can be controlled if we set our sights in that direction, and it offers a challenge worthy of our noblest human aspirations and goals.

Argus accepts only the borderline and mildly retarded (IQ 84 to 50).[6] The "mildly retarded" (IQ 70 to 50) often have lovely social natures, can attain fourth- to sixth-grade level and can tolerate jobs in which people of a higher level of intellect may grow restless. A number of our youngsters in this category have become nurse's aides or aides to the elderly and are able to give help and affection to the sick and the old. There seems to be a kind of symbiotic exchange in this relationship. The kids, young and healthy, are thirsty for affection and have a deep, in-dwelling need to give to others. These groups seem not to threaten each other. Perhaps this type of relationship is worth exploring further, since the need on both sides is great, and society would benefit and rest easier for knowing that these positions, so hard to fill, are held by persons capable of being responsible, patient and caring.

5. *Abuse and Neglect.* Children in this category have sustained physical, emotional or sexual injuries or misuse from their parents, foster parents, caretakers or siblings or have not been given adequate food, shelter, clothing, health care or education. They may be children whose parents are depressed, schizophrenic or otherwise mentally or physically ill or involved in drug use or sales, alcoholism or crime. Or they may have been abused themselves as children.[7]

Many of the children we see at Argus fall under this category. A few have been designated by the court as abused and neglected but most suffer cruelties (of commission and omission) and deprivation without bringing themselves to the point of reporting their parents to the authorities. They may see their abusing parents as the only possible source of hoped for affection and care, the only chance for survival. The parents are nearly always overstressed, vulnerable and isolated from family networks and friends who might have lent support and helped in the crises they endure. Sometimes the parents are psychotic but even so the children cling to them and protect them. Often the children blame themselves when their parents injure them, citing their own irritating behavior, willfulness and disobedience. Their parents have a God-given right to punish them, they believe. Then, too, these children have witnessed and experienced physical and emotional abuse from their earliest years and tend to see it as inevitable. They may sympathize with the hardships their parents undergo, and even when they rebel, they seldom go so far as to notify the police or inform BCW.

By law Argus must report abuse and neglect cases; it is a class A misdemeanor for any social agency not to do so. But often when children complain of their family's mistreatment they refuse to follow through. Sabine, whose story is touched upon in Chapter 9 was one of the exceptions. Not infrequently children, neighbors or relatives make reports which are untrue for spite or revenge. BCW investigates as many cases as it can, thoroughly and fairly, in our experience. Children are not as reluctant to go after a stepparent who abuses them, but sexual assaults by blood relatives are much more frequent than most people suppose. Incest is common between fathers and daughters, with the mother often looking the other way for various reasons. Brothers, uncles, or grandfathers may be involved with one or more young girls in the house. Nor is incest confined to the poor; it occurs in middle- and upper-class homes also.

Alcoholism, drug abuse, chronic depression and schizophrenia are recurring themes in cases of abuse and neglect. Temporary or even permanent removal from the home by court petition may be the only solution. Our staff tries to work preventively with parents and children involved in abuse and neglect and we are seeking ways to expand this capability, for the problem is widespread. This category, used by courts, physicians and social welfare agencies, may overlap with Failure to Thrive, Behavior Disorder and Learning Disorders. It spills over also into the following categories.

6. PINS. PINS are defined by the New York State Family Court Act as boys or girls, under sixteen years of age, who are found to be habitually truant, incorrigible or out of lawful control. Formerly, a female child could be adjudicated as a PINS up to her eighteenth birthday; but in 1972 the New York Court of Appeals overturned this discriminatory law (in re Patricia A, 31 N.Y. 2nd, 83, 1972). Since then no girl after her sixteenth birthday may be brought up on a PINS petition. Prior to 1962, when the Family Court was established in New York as a statewide court, truants and "incorrigible" children were treated as delinquents. However, even after this separation was made, the courts continued to send PINS children to New York State training school facilities, where they were commingled with delinquent children until 1972. That year, as a result of a lawsuit (in re Ellery C., 32 N.Y. 2d, 588), the State's highest court forbade the practice, challenging the legislature and the public and private child-care agencies to set up appropriate residential care for PINS children.[8] Private agencies have generally rejected these children, who are regarded by judges, probation officers and others as the most difficult cases before the Family Court. PINS are described as having severe emotional and behavioral problems. They are generally considered harder to handle than all but a small number of hard-core, disturbed delinquents.[9] Argus has seen quite a number of PINS children over the years. Many are indeed hard to work with, in large part because they have been kicked from pillar to post in the system and do not have viable homes. Among them are an undetermined number of Abuse and Neglect cases, adjudicated as PINS because Abuse and Neglect petitions are difficult to prove. Children have remained in temporary placements and shelters for three years and more while Neglect and Abuse petitions are pending. Several of our PINS children have been in and out of Family Court on Juvenile Delinquency petitions for years. It is not unusual for Argus to take in PINS children who have been referred to nine or ten agencies and rejected, because they were "emotionally disturbed," suffering from "adjustment reaction of adolescence," "had a tendency to run away," were not "amenable to therapy," "needed long term placement," "lacked impulse control," "were too severely disturbed," or "required more structure." It is sometimes said about these children that they are "not willing to face their problems" and are "oppositional" because they cannot or will not talk freely to psychiatrists or traditionally oriented psychotherapists.

It is obvious then that the PINS category overlaps with Behavior Disorder and Abuse and Neglect and, more often than we care to acknowledge, with Delinquency. Family Court judges have such broad discretion that they can move neglected and abused children into the PINS category, stigmatizing them but getting them out of public shelters at least; on the other hand, they can allow delinquents to "plead" to PINS charges. It is not unusual to find PINS children with one form of "Learning Disorder" or another, and we have seen both situational and long-standing, ingrained depression and schizophrenia among PINS children.[10]

7. Depression. Sometimes called Depressive Neurosis (in its milder form) and Manic-Depressive Illness (in its severest form). Diane Moore, director of our PMA experiment at Argus, prefers the term Situational Depression for acute sadness brought on by losses and conflicts with families, such as we often see in our young clients, and Chronic Depression for the more serious, long-lasting type where internal dynamics or chemistry seems paramount. Many of our youngsters have feelings of dejection and disappointment that may hang on for months or even years but which they mask with marijuana, alcohol, sex or other acting out, either hostile, clownish or hyperactive. They brighten up between intense bouts of sadness or when something entertaining or exciting is going on. They are generally irritable and flare up at criticism or when things don't go their way. Some sleep for long hours; others wake up in the night and can't fall asleep again. There have been suicide attempts or "gestures" among young persons in placement and in detention, but rarely do actual suicides take place in detention. (The latter seem to be more prevalent among hispanic males).

To my knowledge none of our kids has ever been diagnosed as manic depressive nor have any of them manifested these symptoms, so for purposes of this discussion I will pass over this category, regarded by some as the end of a continuum which includes the milder depressions. From what I can gather, there seems to be a biochemical and/or neurotransmitter and perhaps a genetic involvement in deep chronic depression. Or maybe after an unknown amount of catastrophe and loss, the happy juices won't well up any more. Who knows? The mask of acting out which the Argus kids put on may very well protect them from the ultimate helplessness, sadness and hopelessness, but leads them into prisons and other infernos.

8. Schizophrenic Disorders. Also called Process Schizophrenia and Poor Prognosis Schizophrenia. This is diagnostic quicksand. For years one could hardly get a footing anywhere. Our knowledge of schizophrenia has increased but is still incomplete. What is known has not filtered down to some practitioners. E. Fuller Torrey, a Washington-based psychiatrist, is the first investigator, to my knowledge, to round up the worldwide epidemiological information on schizophrenia.[11]

The new knowledge may open the door to the solution of this tragic disease, which is so far incurable, not killing its victims but actually immunizing or protecting them in some fashion, it is thought, from other diseases so that often they must drag through a long life of agony or kill themselves, which some of the afflicted do. DSM–III states that the concept of schizophrenia is unclear; but the Manual, in its definition, excludes illnesses without overt psychotic features, referred to by some as Latent, Borderline or Simple Schizophrenia, listing conditions of this type under Personality Disorder with subheadings such as Schizotypal Personality Disorder. In order to qualify as schizophrenic in DSM–III, the illness must always involve "delusions, hallucinations, or certain disturbances in the form of thought," must show deterioration from a previous level of functioning and must have manifested continuous signs of its presence for at least six months, with an active phase of psychotic symptoms present for at least a portion of that time.[12] This definition limits the illness and differentiates it from other conditions, such as behavioral and personality disorders, a distinction that is not always made in American psychiatry or psychology. For example, some psychiatrists and clinical psychologists have stated that they would place our Argus enrollees in the diagnostic category of the schizophrenias. Needless to say, we did not engage these professionals as consultants.

Dr. Daniel Casriel, who has evaluated our youngsters and advised us for fifteen years, has a narrow definition of schizophrenia that is not dissimilar to that of DSM–III. He avoids most labels. "These names are not dynamic," he says. "They do not take us any place we want to go." Dr. Casriel evaluates people on their functional maturation levels (for instance, some people function as adults professionally but as adolescents or children emotionally), whether they are closed or open, are acceptors or rejectors, et cetera. He sees schizophrenia as a biochemical illness of unknown origin, the symptoms of which can be compensated for by the phenothiazines or related drugs, and for which there is no cure at present.

E. Fuller Torrey believes that the epidemiology of schizophrenia strongly supports an association between the disease and civilization and thinks it probable that this association is a causal one. "The most likely causes are biological," he writes. "Viruses in particular should be suspect as possible agents, although they probably interact with genetic predisposition and/or familial transmission in complex ways in the causation of the disease."[13] He believes that diet and environmental contaminants must be considered also. Torrey sees schizophrenia as a heterogenous disease with subgroups falling into various biological categories. "It is most unfortunate," Torrey writes, "that in the United States the term schizophrenia is used so broadly—often completely erroneously."[14]

It is important for those of us who are dealing with disturbed persons to become familiar with schizophrenia, to appreciate that the best research points to the fact that *it is a disease* or a biochemical breakdown of some sort, to recognize its symptoms, and above all, not to classify behavioral and emotional disorders as schizophrenia. If we do not sort this out we will continue to put our Medicaid and other treatment dollars in the wrong places, and to mete out inhuman "treatment" by drugging, labeling and stigmatizing people unnecessarily. Often young people who have behaved violently are placed on maintenance doses of chlorpromazine or other phenothiazines and/ or are placed in mental hospitals and called schizophrenic when there is not a valid diagnosis of the disease. We have taken these youngsters into our program, have asked that the drug be discontinued, and have worked with them successfully. In fact, Argus has recently been asked by SSC to confine its intake to adolescents on heavy tranquilizers and to remove them from the drugs. Disturbed behavior not arising from psychoses can be dealt with by other less harmful though more painstaking means, and these children can and should be spared this unnecessary damage. They can also be spared the outrage of being incarcerated in mental institutions.

One such boy, Ronald Birdsong, came to us at fifteen after six years in the schizophrenic ward of a state hospital. He had been "parked" there because nobody could think of anything else to do with him. As the years passed, Ronald's behavior mimicked that of the schizophrenics he lived among; attendants, nurses, psychiatrists came and went and his papers were lost, so that regardless of the original "diagnosis" or reason for placing him in the psychiatric ward, he was eventually regarded by all as psychotic. Finally, a relative turned up and with our help and that of a wise judge arranged for his release to Argus. When he came to us Ronald Birdsong had to learn how to live in the "normal" world without Thorazine. He had to be taught how to relate to nonschizophrenics and how to act like a nonschizophrenic, as well as acquire all of the other knowledge and competencies he had missed. After six months he made one friend among his peers. At the end of two years he had made substantial progress academically, was outgoing, friendly and eager to make something of himself but still felt a little hesitant about assuming too much independence. Donald Cole recommended that he try the armed forces, which he did. It was a happy choice, combining an institutionalized and sheltered life but providing challenge, further education, discipline and, for him, a launching pad for a career. Upon his release he got a job, married, and had children. At his last visit to Argus he was doing well and reported that he was very happy.

This young man was fortunate in that he did not suffer permanent side effects after being maintained for so long on antischizophrenic drugs. He had to undergo withdrawal and the frightening feeling of vulnerability that comes when a drug that has filtered out reality for so long is taken away—a little like a lobster who finds itself without a shell. At first Ronald juddered, skittered and tried to hide, but eventually he learned to trust himself and others and realized that he didn't need drugs as a defense or for any other purpose.

Though he spent six years in confinement among schizophrenics and suffered the deprivations and miseries that this entails, Ronald Birdsong was still fortunate compared to his fellow inmates: he did not hear eerie voices threatening him, fearful visions did not appear before his eyes. He was frightened of people, but he never knew the ultimate dread that schizophrenics feel when they have to relate to others. His thinking processes, his perceptions and the spectrum of his emotions remained within the "normal" range.

I have no way of knowing how many adolescents are placed on phenothiazines without having the disease for which that drug is specifically indicated, for the convenience of their caretakers. I do not know how many children are parked in mental hospitals and forgotten. We at Argus see enough of them to convince us that it is a serious problem and one which should be addressed by policy makers, who should put their weight behind a demand for accurate and careful diagnosis, restricted use of phenothiazines and other tranquilizers and the development of community-based programs with the capability of dealing with today's tough behavioral and emotional problems. I am convinced that counselors of backgrounds similar to those of the disturbed persons who are leading productive lives themselves are best suited for this work and that persons of this type should be selected and carefully trained for it.

Hospitals and other institutions place acting-out persons on heavy tranquilizers because they disrupt the routine of their programs and because the personnel are not trained or equipped to deal in any other manner with this behavior. So pervasive is the notion that a "really disturbed" youngster must be placed on Thorazine or one of the heavy tranquilizers that a program which has found other ways of dealing with disruptive persons may be accused of not admitting "disturbed" persons and penalized financially by the funding sources. This did in fact happen to us several years ago when Argus was told to take in twice as many children as we had been handling since the orderly atmosphere and the fact that we did not have to rely on tranquilizers seemed to belie the children's histories. Fortunately, after a thorough evaluation, this ruling was reversed; we were permitted to go back to the smaller numbers and were given more money. In 1978–79 the Board of Education told us we would have to certify our children as "severely emotionally disturbed" or face the loss of eight teachers. We fought tooth and nail against hanging this label on our youngsters, stigmatizing them possibly for life. This order too was reversed but not without our paying a heavy toll in terms of energy and time diverted from the main objective: running a program which meets the needs of youngsters.

What is "wrong" with the adolescents who arrive at our doors? Are they emotionally disturbed, seriously or otherwise? The answer once again depends upon who is choosing the classification. Our experience has been that for the practical purpose of deciding which youngsters our program can help and which ones would require another environment, we simply cannot depend upon the diagnostic classifications currently in use. A diagnosis of schizophrenia does not necessarily mean that youngsters are indeed schizophrenic according to the current definition. On the other hand, some children diagnosed as undergoing "Reaction of Adolescence" have been found to be hallucinating and displaying bizarre thought patterns. In this case, our next step is to decide whether the bizarre behavior is "true" schizophrenia or whether it is drug induced—by cocaine, amphetamines, LSD (no longer much used by our youngsters) or phencyclidine (PCP), known as angel dust.

All of these substances can produce "craziness" under certain conditions. Amphetamine psychosis, particularly the state induced after large amounts of the drug have been used over a period of several days, is unique in that it so closely resembles schizophrenia of the acute paranoid type that doctors may misdiagnose these persons as schizophrenics. It is the only drug-induced psychosis besides that brought on by cocaine where the *hallucinations are auditory.* The symptoms of amphetamine psychosis at one time were thought to be the result of sleep deprivation bringing to the fore a latent schizophrenia. Controlled research studies at Vanderbilt University and at New York University have shown that this is not the case: the schizophrenic-like symptoms are true drug effects.[15] It is interesting to note in this regard that in the long search for antidotes to amphetamine psychosis, the only effective drugs are our old friends, the phenothiazines and their close relatives. The barbiturates often used by addicts are not effective and sometimes make matters worse, whereas the phenothiazines "turn off" the amphetamine psychosis at once; and, conversely, when amphetamines are given to schizophrenics their condition worsens. These facts have led psychiatrists, biochemists and pharmacologists to study amphetamine psychosis intensively in the hope that this chemically produced model of schizophrenia would lead them to a hot trail in their search for the causes of the elusive disease.[16]

Any person displaying the symptoms of acute paranoid schizophrenia—auditory hallucinations and bizarre and delusional thinking occurring in a setting of clear consciousness—should be seen by a psychiatrist. *If the person has been taking amphetamines, cocaine or PCP, this information should be conveyed to the psychiatrist.* This is of utmost importance in helping a busy psychiatrist to prescribe the proper antidote. Once amphetamine users are stabilized, that is, after the psychotic effects of the drug have been neutralized with phenothiazines, we accept them and work with them, often with favorable results.

Cocaine psychosis also is of great interest to researchers since it too mimics schizophrenia. This psychosis usually occurs after massive doses have been taken over some weeks, when users begin to believe that they are being followed and threatened and that ordinary people in the streets are enemies, out to kill them. Voices are heard, lice, worms, mice or other creatures may be felt running over the body or digging under the skin. Although some psychiatrists claim that cocaine psychosis is easily distinguishable from schizophrenia, others point to the large number of cocaine addicts who are misdiagnosed as evidence that the two symptomatologies have much in common.[17] It is important for us, as program operators, to be aware of the cocaine psychosis and also of the lesser effects of cocaine, the drug of choice in the entertainment and musical worlds, as well as in the underworld, and therefore enjoying a certain prestige among young people who have adopted or are flirting with a negative identity or who are trying to straddle both worlds.

Both amphetamines and cocaine destroy tissue and bring on a chain of behavior which can seriously undermine the health. Although some people do not become addicted to these drugs, others do, and it is not unusual for cocaine users to escalate the dose required to produce euphoria to one hundred times the amount they begin with. We have seen people whose nostrils are no longer separated because the cocaine they sniffed has eaten away the tissue wall.

Angel dust, made cheaply and easily in fly-by-night neighborhood laboratories, has largely replaced LSD as a mind-altering drug in the ghetto. This deadly substance is also capable of producing psychotic effects—drifting euphoria, unpredictable outbursts of violence, stupor, paralysis, brain damage and convulsions which can be fatal. We have struggled with epidemics of angel dust use for several years. The year 1978–79, when we were forced to double our enrollment, was the worst, because the staff could not cope with the increased numbers of unprocessed youngsters who poured into our program. Some youngsters, when they come to us, have been on angel dust for a year or more. They often show signs of bizarre thinking and behavior. When we see violent behavior and extreme impulsiveness coupled with the use of angel dust, we have no choice but to make a referral to a psychiatric hospital, because the danger to the Argus family is too great. The users also may be in grave peril, for the effects of this horror-drug are unpredictable and can include self-destructive acts, though apparently homicide is more likely.

Since drugs are endemic to the South Bronx, we find it necessary to hire ex-addicts who are specialists in this area. They have a blood-houndlike ability to sniff out drug use and drug dealing. Those who have been through programs like Daytop, Synanon, Project Return and Phoenix House, as well as those who graduate from Argus, may have good training in encounter and behavior techniques and often make excellent candidates for further training and education, as well as good role models. Although some do go back on drugs, others, in our supportive environment, stay drug-free for years and are productive. Some have remained clean for ten to fifteen years, which we regard as a cure, belying the view, held by some authorities, that there is no cure for heroin addiction.

I try to interview any applicant suspected of being schizophrenic or of being in the grip of a drug-induced psychosis, and such a person is always seen by our human development specialist. We also talk with those who may be brain damaged or otherwise impaired, as well as with persons who are depressed. If we remain in doubt, we ask for a psychiatric evaluation from Dan Casriel, whose experience with all types of disorders, including drugs and various behavior disturbances, makes him, in our view, a psychiatrist uniquely qualified to make accurate judgments about the range of problems we confront.

Formerly, under a special program, medical students from Einstein University screened Argus enrollees and shepherded them through clinics and doctors' offices in an effort to take care of the many health problems these youngsters have. At present our enrollees are evaluated and treated at Segundo Belvis, a neighborhood health center. Soon after admission each enrollee undergoes a complete physical examination and, when necessary, a neurological and/or psychiatric evaluation.

In spite of these efforts we find ourselves in murky waters as we try to sort out possible psychobiological deficits of some of these

youngsters, especially those who are hyperactive, who have poor impulse control or who readily flare into violence for "no reason" or
because of stresses that others seem to weather without violent displays.

Fortunately, research is going forward on several fronts. Six
years ago the Ford Foundation initiated a series of studies to explore
possible causal factors of health and nutrition in disruptive behavior,
poor scholastic performance and high rates of juvenile delinquency
and crime.[18] These studies, carried out in several locations across the
country, have turned up increasing evidence that organic problems,
interacting adversely with conditions of poverty, are heavily implicated in juvenile antisocial behavior. One team of researchers at
Yale University found that violent delinquents, when compared with
nonviolent delinquents, showed more psychiatric symptoms, such as
paranoia, hallucinations and delusions, and that they suffered more
from neurological symptoms—blackouts, falling and other signs of
epilepsy. The more violent delinquents displayed the more serious
symptoms. They also had more serious medical histories and over-
whelmingly greater incidences of physical abuse in their backgrounds.
A greater percentage of the parents of the more violent youngsters
showed neurological symptoms of one kind or another. Dr. Dorothy
Otnow Lewis, clinical professor of psychiatry at Yale's Child Study
Center, and the other researchers, concluded that "programs designed to diminish violence which focus primarily on socioeconomic
and psychological factors are likely to be unsuccessful if they ignore
the medical problems that contribute so strongly to the expression of
violence."[19]

Although there is no proof yet that food additives are directly
responsible for hyperactivity, we do our best in the group home to
avoid serving foods that are prepared with colorings and chemical
flavorings. As for lunches at the Learning for Living Center, provided
by the Board of Education, we are not sure whether additives go into
some dishes or not. Hot dogs, processed cheese, margarine, cold cuts
and bacon we know contain nitrites, colorings and other additives,
and since these items turn up regularly in the menu, we are exploring
ways to change this or provide our kids with lunches and breakfasts
prepared by our own staff. We hope to effect this change in the near
future.

Dr. Richard Wurtman, director of the neuroendocrine laboratory at Massachusetts Institute of Technology, believes that research
into the influence of nutrients on the workings of the brain will uncover new ways to treat some mental illnesses and will further illumi-

nate the chemical process of the brain. Eating foods rich in lecithin (contained in soybeans, eggs, liver) can raise the choline in the brain. "This chemical is known to be involved with memory, sleep disturbances, REM sleep, and motor coordination . . . ," Dr. Wurtman says. "We know, too, that tyrosine, another amino acid found in protein foods, can enhance the formation of dopamine and norepinephrine in the brain. Both of these substances play a role in motor coordination as well as in the secretion of certain hormones, and in the perception of reality. . . ." As a consequence of these discoveries priority is being given in the United States and abroad to research on ways that diet can help patients suffering from clinical disorders. One finding has been that choline taken by mouth can help patients with tardive dyskinesia control the motor disturbances that afflict many persons maintained on antipsychotic drugs. There are implications for non-psychotic people as well in the capability that choline displays for improving memory and that tryptophan has for increasing serotonin, a sleep-inducing and pain-moderating substance in the brain.[20]

According to Dr. Wurtman this research may eventually "permit us to make informed decisions about what foods to eat or avoid—to maintain a bright eye by day, memorize the phone book, or after a long, tense day, fall asleep without pills."[21]

It is a hard fact that the task of translating this new knowledge into programs that work for people may be more thorny than the complex laboratory research which led to the discoveries in the first place. Still, if our purpose is to deal with the problem of troubled and troublesome youth—we must confront the implications and develop policies and practices based upon the full reality insofar as we are able to discern it.

16. WHAT IS THE MATTER WITH FLAVIA?

*This family and this community called Argus is set up in
such a way that despite the disappointments, losses, and
betrayals, which occur among us, as in all human
settings, someone is always there for the kids—and for the
staff. That's what a family network and a community give
—or should give—to the kinspeople and the
communicants.*

ELIZABETH L. STURZ, from her *Journal*

Donald Cole asked me to see Flavia. He and Mary Taylor had
already interviewed this fourteen-year-old girl. I found her slouched
in a chair in the intake area, taking no notice of anything in that sunlit
room. Everything about her seemed to droop and sag, the dejected
head, the half-closed eyes, the downcast mouth, the dangling arms
and hands.

"Flavia?"

The head came up, the lids lifted, and suddenly an enormous
pair of eyes stood out from the face, projecting a voiceless woe upon
the world. Underneath, something else was stirring: anger and, under
that, fear and pain.

Flavia was a big-boned girl, overweight by twenty-five or thirty
pounds, with dark skin and large, handsome features, framed in an
unkempt afro. She wore a sleazy skirt, a torn and dirty blouse and
rundown shoes.

The child-welfare worker had tried for six months to find a home
for Flavia but she had been rejected. Not surprisingly. Her last official
residence had been the psychiatric ward of a county hospital and she
was being maintained on Thorazine. None of her relatives would have
her.

A psychiatrist's report stated that Flavia was not psychotic, and
we were convinced, after a talk with her, that this was correct. Still,
something was the matter. A stench rose from her person, a purulent
odor which ordinary human excrescences, however stale, do not produce.

Flavia had been brought before the Family Court on a PINS

petition and had been remanded to the Commissioner of Social Services. The computerized printout referred cryptically to "School Behavior," "Home Behavior," and "Community Behavior," and said that parent and sur (short for surrogate) were unable to cope, with the parenthetical word "incompetent" by way of explanation.

A Department of Social Services report spoke of Flavia's "emotional problems and her parents' inability to cope with her."

There was one more report from a psychiatric outpatient program to which Flavia had been attached for a brief period, stating that she had behaved badly, was emotionally disturbed and that she had been returned to the hospital.

"It's the same old story," Don said. "The girl has been passed from agency to agency. The worker who brought her to Argus speaks in a very optimistic way about her chances of making an adjustment if she could just get placed somewhere. She's been living with her half sister's mother—that is, one of her father's former common-law wives —and that woman is very eager to get her out of the house. In fact, Flavia hasn't really been staying there. She's been in the streets most of these last few months."

"I find it surprising, if this mother of the half sister is so eager to get out from under, that she didn't clean the girl up a bit before sending her out for an interview," I said.

"You know I agree with you," Don said, with a pained laugh.

Asked whether she would like to come to live in the Argus group home, Flavia shrugged and mumbled, "I don't care."

Nothing in what Flavia said made us think that she was not in touch with reality. She was not retarded or brain-damaged, so far as we could tell. She had used drugs but was not addicted.

"According to the reports, this girl fights. She's big and strong. She'll give us trouble. I've hardly ever seen anyone so neglectful of her person. She's deliberately wallowing in filth. She'll be hard to work with" were Mary's observations.

"Well, shall we take her?" It was a rhetorical question.

"We may not be able to do much with her, but I think we should try" was Mary's response.

"Don, are you in favor?"

"Sure. If we don't take her in, the next step is a DFY training school."

"Okay. Now that we've decided to take Flavia in, what on earth shall we do with her?"

"Hum. Yes. That's a good question. What shall we do? Well, why don't we just say for starters that we'll take some soap and water and give her a good scrubbing?'' was Don's reply, echoing Mr. Dick in *David Copperfield.*

"Splendid."

"A shower bath though. Let's don't put her into a tub," said Mary. "And before she sleeps in one of our beds I think we should take her to a doctor."

"We definitely should. Though I find it strange, since she's been in and out of the hospital so much recently, that we should have to rush her off to a doctor."

"We'd better burn these clothes and get her some new ones," said Don. "I'll take her over to the group home now, introduce her to Mary Fritz and get the process started."

Flavia followed Don with the shuffling gait that was to become familiar to us over the next months. She moved like a zombie, mechanical, heavy, half dead.

As they started down the stairs, Flavia stumbled. Don reached out a hand to help her. She recoiled, her eyes full of venom.

"Keep your hand offa me, mother-fucker! I don't need no help!"

The medical examination revealed that Flavia was suffering from untreated gonorrhea, that she was infected with pubic lice and, for good measure, was two and one-half months pregnant (an abortion was performed for medical reasons at the first possible opportunity).

As they emerged from the clinic, Flavia picked up a bottle from the gutter, broke the top off of it, held it in Mary Fritz's face and said, "I'm gonna cut you, bitch!" She was angry because Mary had written her name on a hospital form. Flavia thought she should have been allowed to put her name on the paper herself. "Makin it look like I can't write."

Mary Fritz was only six years older than Flavia, pretty and gutsy. She looked Flavia in the eye. "Go ahead."

Flavia dropped the bottle, turned and ran back to Argus. She arrived screaming, tears pelting down her cheeks, and found Mary Taylor in front of the building, on her way out to lunch. I was there, with some visitors from DFY, who had just asked me if Argus took the "really acting-out kids."

"I'm gonna cut that bitch! I'm gonna cut her! Do you hear me?"

"I hear you." Mary Taylor put her arm around Flavia. "Let's go into my office."

Mary Fritz insisted that we get rid of the girl. She was new to our staff and the only training she had in dealing with girls like Flavia was at our weekly case conferences. She was afraid of Flavia and she wanted her punished. Most of the staff agreed with her. I couldn't blame them. We had several sessions in our soundproof room, with everyone getting his/her feelings off. Flavia was put on a ban. We hoped that things would work out. After all, she *had* dropped the bottle. I was surprised when Mary Fritz stayed on: with her young strength and skills she could have found a job elsewhere, but she had become interested in our process and curious to know whether something could be done for a girl like Flavia.

Mrs. Jackson was fourteen years old and living with her mother when her second child, Flavia, was born. Jimmy Jackson, Flavia's father, was nineteen, was residing with his parents and earning good money as a truck driver.

It was extremely difficult—impossible, in fact—to piece together Flavia's history. Parents, relatives and everyone connected with her had a different tale to tell. Jimmy Jackson denied that he had ever officially married Flavia's mother. Lillian Jackson maintained that they were married before Flavia's birth and that, although her first child had a different father, three of the children among her brood of six were Flavia's full brothers and sisters. Jimmy Jackson acknowledged Flavia but denied that any of the others were his.

Lillian Jackson stated that she had a hard time "getting Flavia into the world," more than with her other children. She said that Flavia was unusually large, that she ate like a pig, and was a pig for attention too. She said that Jimmy Jackson and his mother put pressure on her to let them take the infant into their care but that she refused to give her up. Both the father and the mother-in-law insisted that Flavia had come to live with them when she was two months old and that she lived most of her life in her grandmother's home, with her father (in residence when he was not living elsewhere with one of a series of common-law wives and children).

Flavia's mother at times stated that Flavia was shuttled back and forth between the two households at three-month intervals when the welfare worker made her visit so that Jimmy's mother could draw AFDC payments. The grandmother denied this, insisting that it was the mother who collected the welfare payments for Flavia.

Lillian Jackson reported that Flavia's dark skin had peeled off when she was a baby, leaving her white as a bar of Ivory soap, and that when this occurred Jimmy Jackson brought the child back, saying that she was not his but the child of some white man. These claims, and also Lillian Jackson's statement that Flavia was an extremely troublesome baby and was hospitalized with measles, pneumonia, and whooping cough, were denied emphatically by her father and her grandmother, who said flatly, "That woman is a liar. Flavia was a good baby. She lived with us and she was never in any hospital."

Flavia herself does not remember being with her mother or her father for any length of time. "I stayed mostly with my father's girl-friends. The only reason they treated me half right was they hoped by doin that my father would stay with them. All they done was tryin to find my love so he would stay with them."

The grandmother agreed that her son had taken Flavia from her to live with one woman after another, although at other times she insisted that she alone had raised Flavia.

Flavia said that the main thing she had against her father was not that he hit her repeatedly and had raped her and her half sister (there was a Family Court order forbidding Mr. Jackson to live under the same roof with his children), but that "he was strollin all over the place strewin children, getting babies with all kinds of women." What incensed her was that he refused to support any of his children except those of whatever women he was currently living with. Flavia said that her brothers and sisters, as well as her half brothers and half sisters were "all raggedy." One of her brothers was in a reformatory, and another was hyperactive with clear signs of perceptual and psycholog-ical disturbances. The adults in his life expressed their annoyance with his behavior by scolding and punishing him. The amphetamines prescribed for his condition seemed to aggravate it, and Jimmy Junior poured Drano on his testicles and had to be hospitalized. The whole family agreed on one point. that too often Jimmy Junior's playfulness and high spirits crossed the line into harassment and hurtfulness.

The grandmother accused Flavia's father of dragging the girl from one school to another. "I can't count the number of schools that child has been in. If they had left her with me she'd have gone right through and nothing could have happened."

Flavia reported that she hated school and that her mother en-couraged her to stay at home because she didn't have clothes for her. "She didn't want us teased by the other children." Her father, on the contrary, beat her if she skipped school or acted up in class.

It appears that very early Flavia developed a pattern of living first in one place and then another, running away or being asked to leave when conflicts heated up and taking refuge with some other relative.

School records show that Flavia was absent 102 days one year, 95 another. One guidance counselor described her as sullen and uncooperative, and on her recommendation Flavia was transferred to a SMED school (for the Socially Maladjusted and the Emotionally Disturbed).

A psychiatric social worker reported that Flavia fought with the siblings in all the homes where she had resided. Flavia claimed that her brothers and sisters hit her and then told her mother that she had hit them.

At the SMED school Flavia was described as keeping her head on her desk and refusing to speak or wandering the halls. Twice when she was thirteen Flavia swallowed all of her brother's pills in an attempt to kill herself, and according to her mother "went crazy," broke up the furniture and beat up her sister's baby. The psychiatrist at Bronx County Hospital described her as having "low frustration tolerance. She appears disheveled, ill-groomed, perplexed, and displays an apathetic immobility alternating with rage and other violent emotions. . . . School and family functioning are grossly impaired. . . ."

After her first suicide attempt Flavia was signed out of the hospital by her father. Flavia states that he took her to his home, smoked marijuana, drank whiskey and began to force himself on her half sister, who was ten years old. Flavia drew attention to herself by trying to save the younger girl. Her father then beat and raped them both, according to their stories, which were believed by Lillian Jackson and by the Family Court.

Although she assured us that she found the girls' account of the incident entirely credible, Lillian Jackson, when angry with Flavia, taunted her and insisted that she had lied about the rape. Flavia's grandmother stated categorically that her son would never have committed such an act and that the whole thing was one of Flavia's crazy lies. "Jimmy never should have taken her out of the Bronx State Hospital. That's where she belongs and everybody knows it."

Flavia's second attempt at suicide came a few days after her father's release from jail and the proceedings in Family Court, where Flavia and her half sister had given their statements. Again she swallowed her brother's pills, only this time she was quite ill. The psychiatrist who interviewed her stated that her answers to questions were "brief and unelaborated, showing a poverty of speech. Dysphoria is the prevalent mood, often taking the form of anger, anxiety and depression. Her case history reveals that these features had been present for more than six months prior to this crisis with her father. It appears that a change in personality occurred at puberty and that there has been an insidious downhill course since age 12. . . . Patient states that she would be better off dead. . . ." His diagnosis was Depressive Personality with Schizoid Features.

Another psychiatrist gave her the diagnosis of Explosive Personality Disorder.

Flavia remained in the hospital for three and a half months. In spite of the court order her father came and signed her out. No one seems to have objected. She refused to go home with him or to see her mother, taking refuge instead with one of Jimmy Jackson's ex-common-law wives, then fleeing from there when the usual fights and turmoil developed.

At the time she came to Argus, Flavia told us, she was sleeping with five bums. "One of them gave me the clap. If I knew which one it was, I would shoot him and then shoot myself."

About the rape Flavia said: "I don't look anything like my father. He always did think I was somebody else's child. Otherwise, he never would have bothered me that way. At the hospital they told my father he couldn't drink and smoke reefers at the same time. He always did it anyhow. Before that happened between him and me he used to hit my stepmother. He never hit me because I stay out of his way. The day he raped me he told me I better not tell anybody because they wasn't goin to believe me. Which was true."

Jimmy Jackson denied the rape at times. He said, "I told Flavia to clean the house. When I came back she had gone out. She knew I would beat her and she wanted to avoid it. That's why she made up that story. I don't like to whip my child but don't think it don't tear me up to see her wanderin the streets, sleepin with this dude and that, lookin like a tramp and a slut."

Flavia: "My little half sister, she wrote the same statement I did and we never had a chance to talk to each other since that happened. I didn't see her till we went to court. My mother, she was at court. I don't know what she told them because it was all behind closed doors. She must have said something because they let him out. She called me a liar in front of everybody."

Mother: "The judge transferred the case to Family Court. He said a man raping his daughter wasn't no crime. He said it was a family matter. 'Not no crime?' I said. 'Well, what in the world is a crime?' I can't believe it's no crime for a man to rape his daughter."

Grandmother: "Sure I went down and bailed him out. My son never would have done nothing like that."

Mother: "I believe he done it because when the police came he just sat there in the car with his head in his hands. When they asked him did he do it, he didn't answer.

Father: "I'll tell you one thing. Flavia didn't like it to be dull. That's a helluva weapon for a kid to carry around."

Later the father said: "That's a scar we'll both carry to the grave. The city say Flavia can't stay here any more. They say they'll send the police to my house if she does. By sayin that I abused her they took her from me. But now that she's gone from me she done got worse."

Flavia: "Nobody believes me. Nobody cares. I'll keep on tryin to kill myself cause I don't feel like livin any more."

In the group home and at the Argus Learning for Living Center, Flavia continued her well-established pattern, going from one person in authority to another, from teacher to counselor, from counselor to administrator, carrying tales of woe, making herself pitiful and evading the rules. When demands were placed on her, she growled and cursed. At intervals she ran away—back to whatever relative was most receptive at the moment. Several times she made the full circuit of mother, grandmother, father's ex-common-law wives and even her father, who gave her shelter, in spite of the court order forbidding him to do so. At the end of the cycle, which usually lasted about a week, she was back at Argus, again dirty and draggle-tailed, with some horrendous story on her lips.

We realized that Flavia was at Argus only because every other door was closed to her, not because she planned to avail herself of the help we offered or to make other than surface changes. But the fact that she moved into the group home and enrolled in the Argus Learning for Living Center we viewed as a moderately hopeful sign. She consented also to be treated at a clinic for gonococcal endocervicitis and endometritis. She may have become reinfected from time to time during the early period at Argus, for we were not able immediately to influence her choice of companions. For months after her arrival at the group home she slept in her clothes, resisted bathing, showering or using the washing machines. Fortunately the whole house had a stake in getting Flavia to take care of her health, to bathe and to wear clean clothes.

We knew that unless Flavia could be induced somehow to expose her hurts and deal with them she would leave our doors as she had entered them and might end up in a mental hospital, a jail or in the clutches of a pimp. Our treatment plan was (1) to get Flavia to relate to us, to trust the program enough to stay with it; (2) to restore her to physical health, to motivate her to clean herself up and to curb her behavior to a point where she was endurable and could begin to meet her own need for love and friendship; (3) to get her involved with the Learning for Living Center counselors and to provide her with successful classroom experiences; and finally (4) to get her to stop acting out and instead to feel the emotions that had been anesthetized by that behavior and to begin to act and live in a responsible manner as a pathway to emotional health and happiness.

Breaking through Flavia's shell (constructed of acting out behavior of all kinds, including sex and drugs) presented a major challenge. Conventional methods would not work. As Dan Casriel says, "Character-disordered persons actually go through years of one-to-one therapy (those who will relate to it at all) without making real progress. They'll talk about their symptoms, paint verbal pictures of their lives past and present, rationalize, defend, parry with the therapist. But rarely will their real feelings be touched."

There was enough in Flavia's history—inconsistency, lack of love, neglect, mistreatment, and the rape by her father—to provide copouts for a lifetime. We did not accept this history nor the fact that Flavia grew up poor and a victim as an excuse for irresponsible behavior. Nor did her present state of emotional upset provide an excuse. We let her know that we understood that she had been mistreated and that she felt miserable. We commiserated with her. But we made it plain from the first interview that we expected her to fulfill her obligations to herself and to the program *no matter what she had been through or how badly she felt.* We expected her to keep herself clean, to take care of her health, to work toward defined educational and vocational goals, to socialize with girls and boys who could have a positive influence on her life and in general to treat herself and other people with respect. Only in this way could her needs be met.

We had to go over this ground again and again. Work with Flavia spun itself out over five years. What follows is an excerpt from a house confrontation with Flavia. As she had been in the group home two years and was still acting out, this encounter gives us a hint of the painstaking, repetitive work we had to do to break through her shell of self-destructive, near suicidal behavior.

Taking part in the group were Cliff Rawlins, senior counselor, Shirley Branden, house manager, Mary Taylor, then director of the group home program, nine of the girls residing in Argus One: Flavia herself, who was being indicted; Chessie Washington, a peer leader who exerted a positive influence over the other girls but hadn't yet dared to face her own feelings; Marisol, a gregarious, affable girl whose mind was on clothes and boys, but who sympathized with Flavia and befriended her to a degree; Vida, fifteen, whose mother resided in a nursing home and was an alcoholic, and who covered her need with a tough stance and a focus on money and getting ahead, but was able to be sympathetic and helpful at times; Vera, Vida's older sister, who appeared younger because of her soft voice and childlike dependency and shyness; Linda, fourteen, a hyperactive little sprite, the trial and the pet of the house; Tracy, seventeen, a dark-skinned, beautiful girl who four years ago lost the only person who ever loved her—her mother—and had given up on loving or expecting to be loved, or trusting anyone; Cecile, who in spite of being house captain and hating Flavia's slovenly habits, took very little part in the confrontation; and Monique, a girl from Haiti, whose family totally cut her off when she gave birth to a child out of wedlock and who up to the end of this encounter was so severely dissociated that we despaired of getting through to her.

17. THE HORSE CONCEPT*

*If one person tells you you're a horse, ignore it. If two
people tell you you're a horse, it's probably a coincidence.
But if a whole room full of people tell you you're a horse,
either change or go out and buy a saddle.*

ENCOUNTER-GROUP APHORISM

Cliff Rawlins (*senior counselor*): Any indictments?

Several voices (*with enthusiasm*): Yes!

Chessie: I got somethin to say to Flavia. Flavia, can you tell us
what you did? Why you didn't come home this weekend?

Flavia: I didn't want to.

Chessie: Why you didn't want to?

Flavia: Friday I couldn't.

Chessie: You was high?

Flavia: No.

Vida: Flavia, why you act the way you do? Why? Do you know
why?

(*Flavia remains silent.*)

Vida: You not tellin us nothing. Where you been? I mean,
why you couldn't come home?

Flavia: I just told you why.

Vida: You didn't tell me *nothin.*

Flavia: Yes, I did.

Chessie: Well, let me tell you somethin, honey. You come and
go in this house when you get ready. I don't think you deserve
to be in this house.

Vera: What kinda condition you was in?

Flavia: What kinda condition?

*The dialogue in this chapter is transcribed from a tape recording of a girls' Monday
night encounter group.

239

Vera: Yeah.

Flavia: I was high.

Vera: High? Offa what?

Flavia: Liquor.

Chessie: So you were drunk?

Linda: So where did you stay?

Flavia (blankly): Where did I stay?

Linda: Yeah, where did you stay?

Flavia: In my aunt's house.

Linda: So how come you didn't have your aunt call to let us know where you was an that you wasn't comin home?

Vida: Yeah, we worried about you. We was all here wonderin where you was an you didn't call.

Flavia: My aunt wasn't home that night.

Linda: Yeah? An why didn't you call?

Flavia: I wasn't thinkin about it.

Vida: You *thought* about it. I know damn well you thought about it.

Marisol: Could I say somethin? Flavia, you would have been better off if you had called, because see we was worryin bout you. We was sittin up here in this house worryin bout when was you goin to come home an stuff. I know you *thought* bout it. Cause you been here longer than that. You been on bans for that too.

Shirley: Flavia, on Friday night, when you called me, where were you?

Flavia: In Soundview. At my aunt's house.

Shirley: What aunt?

Flavia: My Aunt Jennifer.

Shirley: That's another aunt?

Flavia: I got a lotta aunts. An cousins.

Chessie: You don't have permission to go to aunts an cousins that we don't know.

Shirley: Why didn't your aunt call me that night the way I asked her to?

Flavia: She wasn't home. I done tole you.

Shirley: Why didn't your cousin call?

Flavia: You was gonna take her word before mine? I done tole you when I telephoned where I was. My aunt didn't want to call. I couldn't make her call.

Mary T: That was Friday night. What about Saturday?

Flavia: Saturday my aunt did call here. She talked to Mrs. Billie Jean Bunting.

Marisol: How did all of this come about? How did you get drunk?

Flavia: We was—

Cliff: What *we* are you talkin about?

Flavia: Me an my cousins an some friends of mine. I don't have to tell you their names.

Cliff: What's wrong with tellin us their names?

Vida (forcefully): Can I tell you somethin, Flavia? This happened Friday an you was supposed to be home Friday? How dumb can you git? What time did you leave here Friday?

Flavia: At nine o'clock.

Vida: You was planning to be back here at 2 o'clock, right? So how can you get drunk—I mean, I know you felt it comin on. But how come you kept on drinkin when you knew you had to come back in this house?

Chessie: Flavia, can I tell you somethin? You left this house at nine o'clock. You knew you had to be back here at 2:00 A.M. You drinkin an everythin. You know that liquor smells on your breath, your eyes get red.

Flavia: No. I went to sleep

Vida (incredulous): You went to sleep?

Cliff: You wasn't *thinkin* bout comin back in this house, was you? Before you drunk the liquor you said, "Well, I'm gonna stay out." Because if you knew you was comin back you wouldn't have got drunk.

Mary T: He's got a good point. Somewhere along the line you said, "Fuck the group home."

Flavia: You tellin me I said that?

Vida: I know you said that. You said, "Fuck that fuckin house, I'm gonna go ahead an do what I have to do."

Linda: Flavia, you know that reefer don't even put that much effect in you unless you smoke a whole lot of it. I know damn well that liquor done turned your ass off an get you where you be stabbed an all that bullshit. You knew you had to come back in this house. You said, "Fuck the house!" Cause if you was thinkin bout gettin back here safe, honey, you wouldn't a touched that shit.

Cliff: You think you can do anything you wanna do an get back in this fuckin house.

Chessie: That's true, Flavia.

Flavia: I didn't care if I came back or not!

(Indignant cries of "Bullshit")

Tracy: How come you came to Mary Taylor's office Monday morning? Didn't nobody put no gun up to your head. Cause you knew you can get back in, that's why you *went!*

Flavia: No, I didn't.

Linda: You came *here,* why you do that if you didn't want back in?

Flavia: Cause Mary T. told me to.

(Jeers and outcries)

Chessie: That's bullshit and you know it!

Flavia: I wasn't plannin to come here. I was planning to go to my father's. Then [to Mary T] I heard you talkin' to him on the phone. I knew you was tellin him things.

Mary T: Flavia, you know you can't go to your father's house.

Flavia: I know the court says I can't but I do it anyway.

Chessie: Do you wanna get your father arrested?

Mary T: You were at your father's house when we spoke on the telephone. I told you to come to my office. You didn't have to come. Nobody forced you to.

Flavia: I don't care, I still don't haveta come back.

Chessie: Flavia, you're *here.* If you don't wanna come back what you doin here? Why don't you go back out in the street?

Tracy: Yeah! Why don't you?

Marisol: That's *bull*shit.

Chessie: Yeah! We're the ones that don't want you back here.

Cliff: You always tell us, "Fuck y'all, I'll go wid my mother or my father or some other relatives."

Tracy: We gotta sit here an take that bullshit?

Cliff: Back an forth, here an there. An when it doesn't work out wid your mother it's "Fuck you, Mama, I'll go back and stay at the group home."

(Everyone talks at once, shrilly, upbraiding and scolding Flavia, who defies them, while tears stream down her face.)

Cliff: Hold it! Hold it! Hey listen! We're not even going to relate to that shit that you don't want back in this house. Flavia, are you going to stop lyin an tell us what was goin on with you? If you weren't thinkin about the group home while you were out there, what were you thinkin about?

Flavia: I don't know.

Chessie: I don't buy that bullshit. If you have a place to go to an you don't need the group home, what the hell is you doin here *now?*

Flavia: Did you hear me say "Fuck the group home"?

Vida: It's the same thing. You say you wasn't *thinkin* about the group home. You could have came back late Friday night but you didn't call or return. You didn't even give us a damn call.

Linda: So why is you here if you don't care, Flavia?

Mary T: We're here to decide whether you will stay here or not, Flavia. It's *our* decision and it's *your* decision.

Flavia: Can I tell you somethin, Mary Taylor? You didn't have to bring me from Soundview to decide whether I can stay in the house. I could have stayed at my father's house an you could have decided then.

(An outcry from the girls, protesting Flavia's insincerity.)

Mary T: If you insist on going to your father's house, Flavia, I can't stop you, but I can't sanction your being in your father's house. I guess one of the reasons that I wanted you back here is so that you can start makin a decision about your life. The girls who are in this room, and the staff too, have something to say about it. The girls live here too. The staff work here. This is their house too. What you're saying when you won't answer or when you say "I don't know" is "Fuck you!" Or "I'm not gonna share nothin with you."

Marisol: You know what the answer is: keep your ass out of the house.

Rebecca: You the only girl in this house that ain't doin shit for yourself. You need to be out at Rikers Island where they stick damn brooms up your ass.

Linda: You know your shit, Flavia. Why don't you do somethin with your shit? In two years you'll be eighteen. *Shit!*

Marisol: Not even that—a year an a half. Laying up in the bed with a different boy every weekend.

(Chorus of "Yeah!" "That's right!" "Dig that, Flavia!")

Flavia: I ain't laying up with boys. Don't none of em care anything about me.

Cecile: Flavia, look at your *character!* Can't you see why they feel that way?

Vera: You haven't changed one bit, Flavia.

Flavia: Linda's sittin here saying I'm doin the same things I did last time an that's not even true.

Linda: You made a commitment to us to change, Flavia. An you still pulling the same shit.

Flavia: That was a long time ago. I ain't made no commitment recently.

Cliff: The commitment you made at that time still runs true, Flavia. You can't say, "I made that commitment ten weeks ago and that don't count any more."

Flavia: I'm not stupid.

Cliff: Then what do you mean, that was then and this is now?

Flavia: I didn't say that.

Cliff: You made a commitment when you came back in this house to number one, stop disrespecting the counselors; number two, to try and do something about yourself and your personal hygiene, your obligation to do your room upstairs. You are the only girl that ever came here that when they leave within a day or two everything they learned goes straight down the tube. Leaving here and coming back three or four days later with the same fuckin clothes on. You don't even *think* about it. Where are you goin? What are you doin with your life? You don't ask yourself shit. An you're not accomplishing anything. And you know what? You really don't have any place to go when you leave here.

Flavia: I do.

Cecile: Shit! If you do, speak up. Maybe we can arrange for you to go there.

Tracy: If you really had any place to go you would have stayed your fuckin ass out there then.

Cliff: Anything that you arrange is totally fucked up for you.

Chessie: You can't stay any place a damn week.

Mary T: Flavia, why is that so, that you can't stay any place a week?

(No answer. Mary T repeats question.)

Flavia: I don't know. I mean, what place you talking bout?

Mary T: Any place you go. Uncles, aunts, parents, cousins, why is it you can't stay in those places?

Flavia: Cause I don't like it.

Mary T: Why not?

Flavia: Same reason I don't like it here neither.

Mary T: Why do you keep runnin there? Flavia, the places that you go, are you really wanted there?

Flavia: Ask them.

Mary T: I have asked. They say you can't stay there.

Flavia: You don't know my whole family.

Mary T: That's true, I don't. But the ones I do know, they really don't want you.

Chessie: The fact is, Flavia, ain't *nobody* can put up with your shit, just like we can't. We can just guess what happened tween you an your mother by what goes on around here. Your mother couldn't take your shit, that's all.

Flavia: I do what I want when I'm at my mother's house.

(Outcries of "Bullshit!")

Cliff: I know that's not true. We sat there and talked with your mother from 10:30 in the mornin until 3:30 in the afternoon and she tole me how it is with you.

Flavia: If my mother said she didn't want me, she lied.

Girls (shouting): Flavia! Flavia! Flavia!

Marisol: Your mother gets on you about your shit just like we do here. You have a two o'clock curfew on the weekend there just like you do here. Your mother tries to make you do your chores at home just like we do here.

Chessie: Flavia, I wanna tell you somethin. You lie to your mother like you lie to us here in the group.

Linda: Just face the facts, Flavia. You ain't got an education, you ain't got a job. You ain't got a husband. You ain't got nobody that wants you because nobody can put up with your bullshit.

Cecile: When you got back to this house, Flavia, you were smelling. I swear, so bad. I couldn't get close to you. I ask the nurse why she didn't take your ass to the hospital. Because it's no need for your ass to be stinkin the way it does.

(Flavia begins to cry.)

Linda: You gonna sit up there an cry, right?

Flavia (scornfully): Cry? You think I'm crying?

Vida: What's that rolling down your goddam face if not tears?

(Everyone yells at once.)

Marisol: Flavia, you got sense enough to go out there an get down with a man, so why ain't you got sense enough to wash your *behind.* There ain't no damned tears in it. That's bullshit.

Chessie: You need somebody who can really deal with your ass. This place is too fuckin easy for you.

Mary T: Hey wait a minute. Hold it! Flavia, put your hands down from your face. Look at us. Don't you feel you owe us an explanation? You know, if you want to stay here, your reasons for comin and goin the way you do?

Flavia: I ain't sayin nothin.

Vera: Do you know how to git down with a dude?

Flavia: Yeah.

Vera: Then why the hell can't you answer our questions, Flavia?

Flavia: Cause I don't want to.

Chessie: Then your fuckin' ass should be kicked out!

Flavia: I don't care. You can put me out if you feel like it.

Mary T: Where could you go, Flavia? Where you going? Who can you stay with?

Flavia (weeps): With bums.

Mary T: Who can you stay with? Where are you goin to be?

Flavia: I'll find a place.

Mary T: Okay. But I still have an administrative responsibility for you. Where can I say on the papers that you will be goin?

Flavia (weeping): Just out in the street.

Mary T: Just out in the street?

Cliff: Is that what you want? The street?

Cliff: Can you be honest, Flavia?

Flavia: I won't tell Mary Taylor nothin.

Cliff: Why? Here we all are trying to resolve somethin about you an your feelins, to help you get a little reality, a little understanding of your life and you talk about you don't want to talk to Mary Taylor. Why not?

Flavia: I don't know.

Cliff: I'll tell you why. Because if you talk to people you love and who love you, you are going to have to tell the truth.

Mary T: Why are you crying, Flavia?

Flavia: I'm not sheddin no tears.

Linda: What's that slidin down your cheeks?

Vera: Be honest now.

Chessie: That's what makes us angry, Flavia. We see right through you. All you have to do is to be honest an say what's happenin with you.

Mary T: You're not the only one in here that makes mistakes. If we indict you over an over again it's because you don't want to be honest. You don't want to show other people the real Flavia. What are you afraid of?

(Flavia cries.)

Mary T: It's okay to cry, Flavia. There's nothin wrong with cryin.

Flavia: I don't feel like cryin. Just cause my eyes are waterin don't mean I'm cryin.

Shirley: If I thought I had to do what you do to get affection and was going through the changes you're going through, I would cry. You know your mother didn't want you. Your family don't want to be bothered. They never try to find out how you're doin. Think about it. How many times have they called to speak to Flavia, or us? Not once. Okay, your grandmother has called but it was to say, "I don't want Flavia back here at my house."

(Flavia snickers.)

Cecile: It's not funny. Ain't a damn thing funny about that.

Cliff: You need love and affection so bad that you'll do most anything to get it—if you feel it's coming from somewhere other than this house. We give you a lot of affection and care here, but you don't trust it. You feel that up to a point we've *got* to do that here. But any time anyone from the outside, specially any old bum-ass dude, comes up an shows you any type of affection or gives you a possible outlet to receive love other than from this quarter right here, you will jump on it. You've got no standards that you set about yourself at all. Listen, you might as well admit that you are love starved, that you do need love. Last week in an exercise everybody in here admitted that. We held hands and everybody said how much they needed love, with the exception of Monique. An you were a part of that. You better start lookin at that an being honest about it. Admit that you need love honestly and what you'll go through to get it. You'll destroy yourself in order to get any type of affection from anybody, specially if they are from the opposite sex, because you don't have anybody else.

Mary T: Is any of that true, Flavia?

Flavia: No.

Shirley: How can you sit here an say that, Flavia? Is it true?

Flavia (weeps): Some of it.

Shirley: What part of it is true?

Mary T: Why is it so hard to you to talk to us?

Flavia: What?

Cliff: It seems hard to you to hold your head up and look around this room and look people in the eye.

Sonia: Why didn't you give us the explanation, Flavia?

Patricia: Don't you think we deserve some kind of explanation?

Flavia: I'm not answering no more questions.

Shirley: Come on now. Is it the pain that stops you from talkin? You know, Flavia, the only way you can get rid of that pain is to share it with people who care about you. You reacted to all that pain by gettin down in the gutter. An you'll stay there until you let in some people who really care about you and can share your pain.

Flavia: I don't have to speak on it to nobody else.

Cliff: Well, since you're so eager to stay where you are, tell us what it's like. Maybe some of us would want to go down there with you. Tell us, what's down there?

Linda: Misery, sorrow, loneliness—all that junk, that's what's down there.

Marisol: Flavia, if you would stop bein so doggone stubborn and begin to face up to how you been treated and what you been doin to yourself an how much it hurt—

Patricia: Flavia, before you can understand your mother and how she acted to you and why she won't have you, you got to understand yourself an what you're doin.

Flavia: I understand myself.

Patricia: Then tell us so we will understand too.

Flavia: Do I have to?

Mary T: Please share with us. I think we're entitled to that.

Chessie: She shouldn't expect to *be* here if she can't give us a good explanation of why she left. An it's not the first time she's done it. She gets dealt with, she gets put on a ban, *an nothin.* She turns right around and does it again.

Flavia: You're stupid!

Vida: Somebody ought to knock some sense in your head.

Cecile: That ain't going do no good. She'll do what she wanna do. You better listen to what we're tellin you, Flavia.

Marisol: If you don't, you're in the wrong fuckin place.

Linda: You seen them people beggin in the street? That's the way you going to be if you keep this up.

Vera: You gonna end up bein a drunk.

Rebecca: You've got good friends here now willin to help you before it's too late.

Shirley: Flavia, do you hear what they're trying to tell you?

Flavia (sullen): I don't know. I don't know.

Linda: Don't close your ears.

Flavia: My ears ain't closed.

Cliff: All she do is run around, mess with older men. You haven't been confronted about being that way since you was a little girl? Now wait, don't cut me with those dagger eyes!

Flavia: That's bullshit! I wasn't doing that with my eyes! I know I wasn't.

Cliff: Are you sure of that? Or are you just answering out of anger, trying to be smart. Be real. That's what this is about. Cause, Flavia, you cannot grow unless you start to be honest with yourself.

Flavia: I don't want to grow.

Cliff: You don't want to grow because in order to do that you're going to have to face your shit. When people deal with their shit it's very painful for them. You don't want to grow because you know if you grow you'll have to have higher standards, you got to be a better person, you got to function on a better level. You know, it's easy to be *nothin*. Where you are right now, an imbecile could do that. You have to be somebody to face your shit and learn how to really start growin. Maybe you ought to talk to Chessy because she's learnin. And so are some of the other girls. All that shit is painful for them, but they're facing it. You might as well start to face it too.

Flavia: I do.

Cliff (skeptically): How do you face it? Will you tell us how you feel about yourself?

Mary T: Are you afraid to talk to us, Flavia?

Flavia: Yeah.

Linda: Are you afraid you might get rejected?

Flavia: That's the last thing on my mind, Linda.

(Cries of derision)

Mary T: Flavia, Flavia, what do you mean, that's the last thing on your mind? Here are eleven girls that you've been livin with, some of 'em for a long time.

Flavia: I got a big family, too. I'm not worried about it.

Cliff: You know what, I was just sitten here thinkin, I wish we had a playback of this session. You are slick, Flavia. You manipulate very good. You come in here, you know everything you're supposed to be saying. You come in here an you test everybody out. If you get beat up in groups you say to yourself, "Hey, they really do want me. They care enough to beat me up." That's one of your fuckin reasons for bein quiet, so we'll go after you.

Flavia (defiantly): I don't want to speak. It ain't none of your business what I do with myself.

Cliff: Hey, you know what? It is my business as long as you're *here!* We're just tryin to help you to *be* somethin, to be *somebody* instead of nobody.

Flavia: I ain't goin to be nothin.

Cliff: You may not never be shit but we're going to make sure we put out a good effort to make you somethin. If you just learn how to do your personal hygiene for the rest of your life and be clean, then we'll do that. Even if we can't make you raise to the standards of the rest of the girls here. We're gonna put it to you. Cause we can't *make* you do anything. But as long as you stay here you are goin to have to abide by our rules an regulations. You are going to have to respect people, and you are going to have to act in a manner that they can respect you. And you are going to have respect for these groups. Even if you *don't* have respect for *yourself,* these things you are going to have to respect. Now if you want to *learn* somethin and start to grow up—*do* you?

(Flavia does not answer.)

Cliff: You don't want to do nothin for yourself?

Sabine: You can be a slut for the rest of your life.

Flavia: Don't you call me a slut.
(Flavia jumps up and starts toward Sabine, hand raised to hit her.)

Everyone: Sit down, Flavia! Sit down!

Mary T: You can't hit people in this group, you know that, Flavia.

Flavia: Sabine called me a slut.

Sabine: You should hear it. Because that's how everybody is going to name you if you don't change. A damn slut!

Cliff: How do you feel, Flavia? Here was a whole room full of people reachin out for you and now by your stubbornness they done got to the point where they say, "Fuck her! She ain't nothin but a slut!" One of the most caring people in here was Chessy. Now she's just lookin and sayin, "Fuck it! We can't get anywhere with Flavia." Where would you be without people to care about you? Where will you be if you drive them all away?

Flavia: Alone. Where I'd like to be now.

Chessie: Liar!

Flavia: If nobody don't talk to me it don't make me no difference.

Chessie: I think you'd better take your words back, right quick, honey. Right quick. Cause you remember in that group where we told you we wasn't going to talk to you an you said, "All right, I don't care!" Well the next day at school you told me *an* Marisol *an* Sonia—

Vera (interrupting): An me!

Chessie: *An* Vera. You said, "Ooh, I can't stand not talkin to you. Would you talk to me now?"

Cliff: In fact, you were the first one to speak up, Flavia, when I told Tracy she was on a speakin ban. You said that's too hard to take.

Flavia: I know it!

Cliff: Then you have to acknowledge the fact that you want to be a part of these girls?

Girls: Do you? Do you, Flavia?

Flavia: Naw.

(An outcry of anger from the girls.)

Mary T: Wait a minute! Flavia, why?

Flavia: Because I can't.

Mary T: You want to be a part of this group, part of this house?

Flavia: Half of me do.

Mary T: Half of you does an half of you doesn't. Why doesn't that half?

Flavia: I dunno.

Mary T: Well, I'm addressin myself to the half that does. Why? Why? Come on, Flavia, we've been talking to you a long time.

Flavia: I don't know.

Mary T: Why does that half want to remain?

Flavia: I don't know, I guess I wanna be here. I don't know why.

Mary T: But why you want to be here?

Flavia: I just like it here.

Mary T: Because—

Flavia: I don't know bout no because. I just—

Marisol: You don't know why you like it here?

Flavia: I'll be thinkin bout that.

Chessie: Holy shit!

Flavia: I think I knew from the beginning I had to like it cause there wasn't any place else for me to go.

Chessie: Well, you better think up some other reasons. You try to make us feel sorry for you. Well, your bullshit done played out here.

Tracy: You run the same bullshit every time, Flavia.

Vida: That's why people in this house have given up on you, Flavia, cause you won't be honest.

Flavia: I don't care. If it ever did bother me what you think it ain't botherin me now.

Chessie (disgustedly): Shut up!

Marisol: You member when you left here cause you thought we didn't care? Remember? You thought we didn't care about you?

Shirley: You remember what you did? How you cried an everybody reached out for you? They told you how they felt about you?

Flavia: Uh-uh.

Shirley: What did you do?

Flavia: I dunno.

Marisol: I'll tell you what you did. You cried.

Flavia: I don't know. I don't feel like it.

Marisol: You don't remember crying an us reaching out an huggin you an tellin you we did not want you to leave?

Shirley: Don't you remember that, Flavia? Why did you cry?

(No answer.)

Chessie: Flavia, is you there?

Mary T: Did it hurt?

Flavia: No.

Marisol: Git out of here! You was crying a whole fuckin river of tears!

Mary T: Do you know why it hurt?

Flavia: I don't remember that.

Vidu: You forgot it cause it hurt too much.

Chessie: That's a hell of an experience—to think no one wanted you an then to find out that quite a few people did.

Shirley: When people tell you they love you, Flavia, an you have reason to think it's for real, you get all fucked up because you're not used to it. You can deal with a whole lot of garbage but you can't deal with somebody lovin you in a way that really makes a difference, with people who really want to take care of you an help you grow up to be somebody.

Flavia: I don't want no help.

Shirley: Do you feel that we really want to help you?

Flavia: Naw. *I* don't want it.

Shirley: When did you start to feel this way?

Flavia: Always.

Shirley: It's been like that?

Flavia: I only do things that I *want* to do.

Sonia: No. You do things that you're *used* to doin an don't do things that you're afraid of—

Shirley: Like reachin out and trusting people. You have asked for help before, Flavia.

Mary T: Come on, Flavia. Talk to us.

Flavia: What is there to say? It go in one ear an out the other.

(There is a general outcry.)

Mary T: Wait a minute, give her another chance.

Chessie: Flavia, you shouldn't have come back here if you haven't got nothin to say to us.

Vida: You better take that shit back outside, Flavia!

Tracy: What do you think this is, a revolving door?

Chessie: This is not no hotel. When things are not right out there you run back here.

Vida: I don't understand you, Flavia.

Mary T: What do you think we should do about you, Flavia?

Vida: If you treat us this way, Flavia, you're gonna get treated the same way yourself.

Marisol: Shit, she don't even want to be here.

Chessie: Let's kick her ass out of here.

Flavia: Try it, why don't you? Anybody who don't want me in here please raise their hand.

(The girls all raise their hands, except for Monique.)

Vida: Well, we've voted you out of here, Flavia. Go back to the street since you won't relate to the rules of this house.

Flavia: Don't worry, I'm goin.

Monique: That's too hard. To put somebody out. She might not make it. No! No!
(Her voice rises to a scream. A smile appears on Flavia's face. Monique falls to the floor and begins to thrash. She continues to cry "No! No!" in an agony.)

Cliff: It's okay, Monique. Cry. Let that out.

Vida: You've kept that inside too long. Let it out.

Chessie (who can never express her own pain): Tell us that you hurt. Go on. Say "I hurt."

Monique (screams): I hurt! I hurt!

Chessie: Yes you do. Let that out. You'll feel better after you let it out.

(Flavia stands to one side, a little awkwardly, then slides to the floor, reaches out and takes Monique's hand.)

Cecile (to Flavia): You're safe for now. But we haven't finished with your ass.

Chessie: You gonna have to write your own program to get back in this house. If we decide to let you in.

Cecile: Go upstairs, Flavia, and get a box of Kleenex. Make yourself useful.

Flavia: Thanks, Cecile. I will. *(She half rises, then collapses on the floor, bawling.)*

Cecile: Flavia, get up. Do what I tell you. Can't you let anyone else have anything?

Vida: Go on, Flavia. Git outta here. Do what Cecile tells you. We're dealing with Monique now.

(Flavia gets to her feet, pouting, and goes for the tissues.)

18. PULLING OUT AN EMOTIONAL SPEAR

*Hold on to somebody and let the pain out. It's very hard
to let in pleasure when you have a spear in your belly.
You have an emotional spear. Pull it out.*

DAN CASRIEL, speaking to Flavia in the workshop

The girls in the group home decided that Flavia must choose her
own penalty for having acted irresponsibly. She put herself on a
two-week ban, which meant that she lost all her privileges and, except
for attendance at the Learning for Living Center, had to remain in the
house.

She was in her room, slumped in a chair by the window, when
the call came from Mary Taylor. Flavia told us later that she had been
thinking about the latest of her bummy boyfriends, a drug addict who
beat her and demanded that she hit the street and hustle for him.

"Flavia, how would you like to go to a workshop with me? You
remember, I've talked to you about Dan Casriel? Well, he's having a
workshop today. I'm going to be in it and I'd like you to be in it with
me, if you'd like to."

"I don't know nothin bout no workshop, Mary Taylor, but I'm
tired of staying in this group home. Whatever it is I'll go with you."

"Good. Now listen, Flavia. I want you take a shower, wash your
hair and put on clean dungarees—or any slacks will do—and a clean
shirt, okay? Be at the Learning for Living Center at noon. I'll drive
you down."

"Okay, Mary Taylor."

When Flavia appeared at the Center she had on a dingy green
sweater and pants with strings hanging from them. Her clothes had
been washed but didn't look it. Flavia herself had not been washed.
Mary sent her back and told Mary Fritz, "Scrub her, wash her hair, put
clothes on her that are clean and that look clean, deodorize her and
send her back by 2 o'clock."

Two hours later Flavia was back, "Do I look good enough now
for your workshop?" she demanded in a sneering, hectoring tone.

256

"You look fine. Wait outside, Flavia. I'll be with you in five minutes."

In the anteroom the receptionist asked Flavia whether she was off her ban. Flavia turned on her with a ferocious bellow, followed by a prolonged and abusive denunciation of the Argus staff. Cliff Rawlins, who was standing nearby, took Flavia into the intake area, which was deserted at the moment, and blew her away. She was passive and gentle as a lamb when she drove off with Mary half an hour later.

It was a watershed in our work with Flavia. Her credit in the group home had run out; the girls were restive. If Flavia continued to act out, she could turn the whole house around. Our positive peer group, the most valuable tool we had—forged with time and the sweat of our brows—worth diamonds and pearls and rubies in therapeutic coin, was threatened. Even the girls who had brought their behavior under control and were living more or less up to their potential were still not fully incorporated into our process. They were, after all, teenagers, and shaky teenagers at that. They could fall back easily if they got the idea that the structure was not sound. Not one of them had reached the point where they could rely upon inner restraints to curb their hostile and self-destructive tendencies. Cecile, for example, the girl who was most angry at Flavia, was disciplined and correct on the outside. But inside she was a boiling volcano. Cecile could scarcely tolerate the thought of Flavia, who so flamboyantly lived out her anxieties and aggressions and thereby focused everybody's attention on herself when she least deserved it. Cecile was ready to blow and we knew it. Her mother had cast her off totally.

"How could you let Flavia come back into this house?" she demanded of Mary Taylor. "It makes me want to walk out of here and never come back."

"You let her back in yourself," Mary replied. "You girls made the decision."

"Yeah, but you would have let her back in no matter what we said."

"We're all trying to help her. No one is perfect, Cecile. You've done wonders for yourself; I can't praise you enough; yet even you had to have an abortion recently. No one tied you up and threw you on the carpet. You went with that boy of your own accord. Some people might have rejected you but we don't. The truth is, you reject yourself, Cecile. You're too strict on yourself. Sometimes that leads you to be too hard on other people. Flavia is a person. She has feelings. We've all told her that she's doing harm to herself. Maybe it would help if you talked to her, as one girl to another. You set a good example for the house, Cecile. Flavia needs an older sister she can look up to, someone who will give her advice."

"I hate her when she talks about the way her father raped her. I wish she would shut up about that."

"I know how you feel, Cecile. And maybe Flavia does talk about it too much. She uses it to get people's attention and to dramatize herself. But you know, in some ways that's better than burying it out of sight. If you could share what happened to you, Cecile, you would find out that no one will despise you for it. You're human, and your mother is human, too, no matter what. If you could bring it out, if you could get really angry at her and at yourself and feel all the pain behind it, maybe you could forgive her and forgive yourself. You might feel a lot better. It's really yourself you haven't forgiven, Cecile. Do you know that?"

"Okay. I'll think about it. But I still wish Flavia was out of this house."

Dan had a private session with Flavia before the workshop, to ascertain whether she was a proper candidate for New Identity Group Process Therapy and, if so, to map a course for her.

Flavia went into the workshop wearing her mask of truculence. But she liked Dan and she listened to what he had to say, straining to understand. She was strong, and in spite of the psychologist's report, she was intelligent. She had formed bonds with Argus, and she had made a promise to her peers in the group home. Flavia was different from the other girls in one important respect: most of them had been institutionalized before coming to Argus. Many had been the rounds of group homes and institutions. They had finally accepted the fact that they didn't have a home intact enough to go back to. Although Flavia had been shunted from relative to relative, this was her first placement away from family. She was still hoping somehow to get back to her mother and that by a miracle her mother would accept her and love her no matter what she did and prefer her to all the other children.

That first afternoon in group Flavia sat like a block of granite. Then, after supper, when Mary Taylor began to work on her own feelings and told her mother goodbye for the thousandth time, Flavia, who was listening intently, fell to pieces. Leah Stein, a volunteer at Argus, saw the state she was in and put her on the mat. Flavia's pain erupted in long ululations. She screamed for five minutes, then cried out in terror, "Let me up from here, I'm dying!"

Group members helped her onto a chair. Leah and Myron, a

former district attorney, knelt on the floor in front of her, holding her knees. She screamed again. Mary, on the mat, forgot herself, tuned in to Flavia's screaming, got up and came to her. Leah and Myron were giving her plenty of sympathy, but they didn't know what to do since they were new to the process.

Mary said, "Flavia, tell us that you hurt. Say, 'I hurt.' Come on. Tell us."

Flavia repeated, "I hurt!" several times. It became a long scream from a deep level of pain. She continued to scream for fifteen minutes or more while tears gushed from her like water from a gargoyle.

"Oh fuck! Oh fuck! Ah-h-h-h! Wah-h-h-h! Wah-h-h-h! Wah-h-h-h-h-h!"

It sounded at first like she was under the surgeon's knife, then the sound became that of an infant crying in vain to be fed, to be picked up and held, to be relieved of its fears.

Mary said, "Flavia, tell us you hurt. Say, 'I hurt.' Come on, say, 'I hurt.' "

"I hur-r-r-r-t!"

The sounds rose from deep in Flavia's belly and gradually took on an assertive tone. She had gone quite a way back and had become a helpless infant; now she was belting out her pain in a gargantuan roar

The workshop was galvanized. Everyone stopped to listen to Flavia. Six or seven people began to scream out their pain. Cries of "I hurt too! I hurt too!" filled the air.

"Push it out, Flavia! Let it go!"

Flavia: "I hurt! I hur-r-r-r-t! Oh God, help me! Help-p-p-p! Help me!"

Mary. "More! Come on! Say, 'I hurt!' Come on! Don't stop!"

Flavia: "I hurt! I hurt! Help me! Help me! Help me! Uh uh uh!"

At one point Flavia flopped back, exhausted. But in a short while she started up again in her whining voice, back on the squally, puling, helpless level, then slowly gathered force again, working her way upward and out, toward strength and assertiveness.

Mary: "Say, 'Ah!' "

Flavia: "Ah-h-h-h!"

Mary: "Get all that shit out of your belly. That's what's making you unhappy, making you act the way you do."

Flavia: "He-l-l-l-l-l-l-l-lp me! Ah-h-h-h-h! Help me! Help me!"

Her cries of "Help me" were ear splitting, almost unbearable. Her pain hit everyone straight in the belly. She lay back tired out, gasping for air. Slowly she began taking in love from Mary, Leah,

Myron and others who had gathered around her.

Mary: "Flavia, look at us. Don't hide. Show us your feelings. Come on, open your eyes."

Flavia opened her eyes. Everything that she had fought so hard to conceal lay exposed in her gaze: her vulnerability, the tender center of herself. Pain. Love. There had been no balmy island on her map of the world, no garden soil worthy of receiving the precious seed. So she had buried it in a secret place, put out signals denying that it was there, had herself forgotten that the longing, the softness, the need existed. Now she had found a key, had unlocked this part of herself. Throughout the evening she continued to dump pain. She dumped, took in love, dumped some more.

At midnight Mary took Flavia to a steakhouse. They ate ravenously, had a long talk. Mary explained the process. Flavia said that she wanted to go to as many workshops as she could.

The next day Flavia found that she was the heroine of the workshop. A superstar. "Poor little kid from the ghetto." People said they had never heard such screams coming out of anyone, and later, when I heard the tape, I agreed. The quality of Flavia's pain, it seemed to me, was on a level with that of a woman in one of our workshops who had undergone repeated surgery for cancer and kept screaming, "Don't cut me up! I don't want to die!" I had been in workshops with this woman and had never forgotten it. It was a whole other world from "neurotic" pain, which of itself can be quite unbearable.

That Saturday Flavia seemed to go crazy with people's approbation. She messed with her fellow group members. Whenever she saw an opportunity to be cruel she seized it. She told one woman that she looked old and ugly, told a man he was a faggot, teased any man who came near her, playing "Catch me, fuck me," rolling her eyes seductively, then rounding on them in a punitive way. She tried her tricks with Eddie, an attractive black teenager from AREBA (Dan's therapeutic community), and got back as good as she gave. Members of the workshop pointed out to them both that they were trying to use each other, that it was a cruel game with little pleasure to be squeezed from it. Dan made Flavia say to Eddie, "Play straight with me." This brought up pain and she let Eddie see and hear how she felt.

"Don't use me!" she screamed, letting out the pain. Afterwards she felt light and free and had no further need for the moment to hurt anyone. Eddie said he felt better about Flavia. They had carried their game to the point of slipping out of the workshop, necking and hanging out in the lobby. Mary, busy with someone else, had feared that Flavia would abscond with Eddie. She might have, if he had asked her, for all of her dependent, hostile feelings about males had come to the fore. As soon as she was free, Mary made her work on her feeling of being used. After lots of angry concern from Mary and other group members she opened up on this theme, got to a lot of feelings and was able to look at what she was doing.

The group told Flavia that the teasing and tantalizing that she engaged in made enemies of males even as they desired her.

Flavia was told that she was playing a bitchy slimy game. She had to look at it and to admit that she had been too frightened to play straight with Eddie or any of her boyfriends.

"Pick out a good man and let him see how you need him. He'll like that and he'll respect you for it. He won't want to gnaw on you like a bone and toss you away. He'll stay with you because your needs are beautiful."

Getting in touch with her need brought up more pain. Flavia continued to dump feelings throughout the weekend. When the workshop ended she signed up for a weekly group and attended regularly. Five other girls followed in her footsteps. Flavia was pleased that she was the first, but she didn't make a big thing of it with the girls, as she would have done in the past, vaunting her superiority. She had begun to overcome the code blindness which had made it impossible for her to make friends among her peers. More and more, she found herself able to share instead of snapping like a starving cur for attention and affection. Now that Flavia was able to express her feelings full measure she demonstrated less need to act them out. She didn't exactly turn into a ministering angel; she grumbled and muttered, but she attended to business, abided by the rules and became tolerable. She was like a hailstorm that had turned into a pelting rain. Not always comfortable but there was a certain steadiness and warmth. One sensed that a blossoming could follow but no one could say when it might occur or precisely what shape it would take. On the other hand it was not out of the question that Flavia would revert to her old life as a mudlark, at least once or twice more.

Note: Flavia Jackson has been working for four years as a nurse's aide, supporting herself and remaining drug- and alcohol-free. She lives with a man who works and treats her well. From time to time she returns to the group home for counseling or for warmth and affection from the staff.

19. MINING THE LOCAL GOLD
Staff Development

When we were doing goal setting, an enrollee asked me,
"What is your goal and what are you doing to achieve
it?" I had to be prepared to answer the question.

ARGUS STAFF

While tools are important, the people who wield them are more
so. Our foremost strategy, therefore, is finding and training staff who
share a similar background and have been through some of the same
experiences as the enrollees—and helping them develop in order to
do the job.

Certainly, a key aim is that a substantial number of the staff for
a program aspiring to be more than a "holding tank" be recruited
from the local community and include persons with backgrounds
similar to those of the program clientele, people who are poor (or
have known poverty) and are black, hispanic or of whatever ethnicity
is appropriate. Ex-addicts and ex-offenders can bring special knowledge in dealing with drug abuse and antisocial and manipulative behavior and can make outstanding contributions in program and administration.

Each prospective staff member must be carefully screened. We
ask at least three or four of the Argus senior staff to interview an
applicant individually, and if there is a difference of opinion, we may
conduct a group interview. People sometimes reveal other aspects of
themselves in a group.

We generally do not give standardized tests for intelligence or
aptitude to job applicants. These are not accurate and are irrelevant
to the kind of productivity we need from staff. However, an applicant
may be asked to write a sample report to the court or a treatment plan.
To screen out those who have serious problems I try to get people
to "race their motors." If they are led into a subject which is meaningful to them, they will often let their guards down and reveal their real
attitudes and feelings. The topic may or may not be connected with
the work we do. But almost always, in addition, I lay out a problem

experienced by Argus enrollees and ask applicants what they believe caused the problem and how they would attempt to handle it. In their answers I look for sensitivity to life and environmental stresses and the importance of interpersonal relations. We avoid taking on a professional who emphasizes psychodynamic process while showing little awareness of other aspects of our clients' lives. The interviewer, of course, has to know the difference between blaming the victim and holding people accountable and demanding responsible behavior.

In our experience many people out of social work school, as well as other professionals, have been trained not to make demands or set boundaries, are overly permissive and think in terms of seeing clients only at set hours. Such mind sets do not bode well for productive work with our clientele. It is important to realize that professional training per se is no guarantee that the person can relate warmly and sensitively to other people. We look for this ability in all applicants, as well as a flexibility and a willingness to fit into our setting and learn our methods; when we hire people with these qualities we often learn from them, thereby acquiring new tools for our kits. Social and personal sensitivity, flexibility and openness, warmth, stamina, generosity, belief in our clients, assertiveness and sound judgment are the qualities we look for or hope can be developed in the people we select.

To test judgment we might ask applicants to tell us what they would do to defuse an angry confrontation building up between two persons in a crowded recreation room or classroom. The most sensible answer is to do nothing until all counselors have been called to the scene, determine whether either party has a weapon, call 911 for police help if the person is unwilling to give up a gun or knife, ask all bystanders ("the audience") to leave the area but request perhaps that two or three responsible peers stay and assist the most respected counselors as they try to talk the situation down and separate the angry persons.

We do not expect applicants to know the particular procedures we have developed for dealing with violence. However, street people often suggest sound interventions of their own, while professionals rarely know anything beyond calling the police, expelling the antagonists or sending them to a psychiatrist, which is understandable given their education. But we are interested in their reactions to our way of handling such episodes and whether they can accommodate to our setting, which works to deescalate violence and to render offense and defense unnecessary.

We might pose the problem of a girl who won't get out of bed or refuses to eat, to go to school or to do lessons. What would the applicant do? The answer can give a fair indication of whether there is empathy, insight, resourcefulness and assertiveness and can reveal something of how applicants view the possible cause of the problem and the outlook for a solution. Can they think of anything to do beyond lecturing, nagging or threatening to take away privileges? Would they sit down with a kid and ask what is happening in his or her life and how he or she feels? Or would they demand instant compliance and obedience? You can't expect people who haven't done this kind of work to know all the answers, but you can form some notion from their responses about whether they would be comfortable with the kids and whether they are the kind of people who can see choices and alternatives.

It is necessary to screen out those who are withdrawn, rigid, autocratic or paranoid and those who can't function well in the give and take of human interchange or under fire. Nor can we accept staff who themselves have serious behavioral or emotional problems. We look for people who have stamina, an interest and belief in our clientele, who can be assertive and can enforce the rules without bullying or being punitive and who are warm and vital—or who we think have a chance of developing such qualities. We hire everyone on a three-month and occasionally on a six-month trial basis, because you never really know people until you deal with them every day.

One mechanism for screening staff was our on-the-job counselor training program. Salaries for the trainees came through CETA, and for about six years the Wildcat Service Corporation, the State Communities Aid Association and other agencies provided us with carefully screened adults who acted as counselor trainees. At Argus they assisted our regular staff while learning to be counselors and to develop good work habits. Because of the rigorous training we gave them many were able to move into staff positions with Argus, and I have been informed by Amy Betanzos, director of Wildcat, that Wildcatters trained at Argus were almost always able to find nonsubsidized employment elsewhere. We usually had from six to ten persons in training as counselors and the trainees provided valuable services.

The selection process for "squares" is as rigorous as it is for those who have been in the streets or on welfare. Here the object is to find professionals who are flexible, warm and inventive and who believe in our clientele. They also are subject to the three-month trial period and participate in staff development and training.

Whatever their backgrounds, all new staff sign an agreement to become seriously involved in staff development and Positive Mental Attitude training sessions (each an hour and a half weekly), and whatever other training we can provide. Some of the staff attend groups or workshops at the Casriel Institute or with David Freundlich, a psychiatrist at the Center for the Whole Person.

Not only counselors are involved in staff development. The entire organization—switchboard operators, maintenance people, secretaries, intake workers, program developers, coordinators, assistant directors and the director of the agency—are drawn from their duties to take part in the Friday staff development sessions, to sit in a circle of hats-off people who try to relate honestly and get in touch with their feelings and with those of the other group members. The same pattern holds in the group home program. Some may say that this is impractical and a waste of time. But what if the maintenance man is a pot smoker? What if the switchboard operator throws out a tactless word and precipitates a fight? What if the cook doesn't grasp the therapeutic importance of the kitchen? What a horror if she or he shoves the food at the kids half-frozen and yells at them as they try to eat? These staff members must be role models also. Their input is just as important as anyone's in maintaining a therapeutic environment.

And if the higher-ups are not there, tuned to the experiences and feelings of the staff, then they are denied a whole level of feedback which is vital to decision making. Just as the front-line staff needs to know how the higher-ups feel and think and what *their* problems and limitations are. Without this interchange administrators cannot know the real and harrowing problems faced by front-line staff and may very well make decisions which harm rather than help. They will not know how to lend proper support. Front-line staff, on the other hand, need to know that administrators are human, that they don't have it within their power to solve every problem; and they need to know how valuable their input is in helping administrators solve the solvable problems.

But beyond the need for an exchange of information, a mutual appreciation of the difficulties and strengths all around and the improved morale that can result, there is the need to have everyone in sync. For to make our program work we must all be united in upholding a clear, visible, unambiguous value system and structure. This is no easy task, for though some staff remain for years, others flow in and out. Thus, we are forever creating and recreating a fabric, holding it up to view, reweaving the torn threads, changing and strengthening the design. Furthermore, the trust and affection that grow up in the staff development groups provide the culture medium in which both ideas and practice can flourish. Without a way to encourage these human bonds our staff would be less cohesive, less dedicated. Fewer among them, whatever their potential, would be able to embrace our value system with sincerity or stick to a task fraught with frustrations and perils. Although our staff grows weary and feels fed to the teeth and explosive at times, the groups allow expression of these feelings, and in consequence, there is more control on the floor, almost no backbiting or bad rapping, and burnout is rare.

It all boils down to this: we provide for the staff a climate that resembles what we provide for our enrollees, except that, as staff members and adults, we are required to be more responsible and to go about our task with more consistency than the enrollees.

Don't misunderstand me. We do not run a nursing home for staff. They are basically strong, adult persons. Still, they are human beings with human needs. The job they are asked to do is gruelling, may seem thankless or hopeless at times and can be dangerous. They too need a safe place to express their feelings; they need nurturing; they need to understand themselves, to improve their self-concepts; and they need encouragement to grow to their full potential. They need to be heard. They need to be told explicitly that they are entitled, valuable people. They need to know that they belong, that they have the support of an organization and that their efforts are appreciated. They need to be bonded to one another, to be confident that they can rely upon one another. And they need to grope for and find solutions to knotty problems and situations.

What happens in group homes, schools and institutions where the staff does not get this kind of support and development, where training does not take place or training of a didactic type is given to the on-hands staff only, without the participation of the administration?

First, the policy and decision makers may never fully comprehend how complicated, frustrating and dangerous it can be for those staff members who confront and interact with teenagers all day—and in residences all night. Even if administrators are humane and empathetic, they cannot know enough of the detailed problems faced by child-care workers to give them proper support, make the right decisions or inspire and foment until creative approaches are spawned. This takes the input of the entire staff. Such brainstorming sessions produce the best results when many perspectives and levels of experience are represented.

Second, in the absence of this top-to-bottom model of staff training, the kids get conflicting messages. They find that the person on duty in the morning has one set of rules, while the afternoon person has another and the night person may not care one way or the other. They learn to play one set of rules and values and one staff member off against another. They realize that the staff does not operate as a team, that their lines of communication are weak, that they may be at odds with one another and that the higher-ups don't know what is going on. It is easy, in this climate, for staff members to misbehave on the job—drinking, smoking marijuana, stealing, ripping off the program and the kids—and not be held accountable. Staff may behave sadistically to those who cannot defend themselves or may allow children to bully, scapegoat and abuse each other. In that milieu, even staff who would like to be helpful realize that they can do nothing. They don't know one another very well, and the higher-ups are far off and inaccessible. They have no confidence that they would be listened to or believed, even if they reported what is going on. For the same reasons, the better kids among the enrollees feel helpless and trapped. They see that the staff is corrupt or powerless, that there is no support from the administration, so they fall into line behind negative peer leaders. Negative peer leaders make contracts with negative staff members. Before you can turn around and ask what has happened street values and street behavior have taken over the program. Staff turn their faces, look on or actually participate in bullying, scapegoating, drug use, assaults and rapes—the gamut of appalling and scandalous behavior which characterizes some programs consuming large sums of money each year. Even in long established charitable institutions, those with religious affiliations and the highest motives, this kind of snake pit can flourish and may be spoken of as unavoidable and tragic. The higher-ups may not be aware; the middle-level staff feel they *ought* to take action but don't know how; and the hands-on staff ask themselves how long they can stand the job and whether they will get hurt. Some do get hurt. Many leave. Staff turnover is a major problem in the child-care business. Those who stay "cool out" the "incorrigible" kids, bending every effort to fob them off on other agencies. They tell themselves and everyone else that the kids are to blame. The kids are difficult, but they are not to blame. They can be worked with; the key is developing the staff, teaching them how to operate as a team and how to do the kind of job that will make them feel competent and proud.

Merely to keep the streets out and build a safe program requires teamwork and high morale from everyone in the agency. Every staff member must know the philosophy of the program and how it translates into action and interaction. This is not a body of facts that can be stuffed into people in a lecture or a crash course. They have to absorb it—on the job as they model themselves after skilled, experienced staff and in the staff development workshops, week after week, where they learn to speak frankly to their fellow workers and to accept valid criticism, as well as support and praise of their own efforts. This can happen only in a climate of trust, where it is safe to let people know how you really feel and what you think. If people are coming in late, failing to keep the log, refusing to get involved, they are going to hear about it from the group. If they are doing a good job, they will hear about that too. If they are having a hard time and need help, they'll get it.

We want staff to be more than simple custodians, and we want them to move kids and transmit values. To make this happen, what kinds of things do they need to know?

1. They need to appreciate the importance of their role as change and growth agents. This is so momentous that it is awesome. They must be made aware that they are engaged in a noble and serious undertaking, of grave consequence to the young persons in their charge. If they ask, does society care? The answer should be that sooner or later society will care and that meanwhile they are beating a path through the wilderness for others to follow.

2. The staff must be able to abide by the rules and live within the value system of the program. This is not easy since they are on the edge of poverty themselves and are confronted by serious personal and family problems and with vice and corruption on all sides.

3. The staff must be flexible enough to transcend some of their earlier conditioning—attitudes about corporal punishment, "ratting" on other people and ethnic, racial and sexual prejudice are among the tough ones. Some males need to stretch out beyond machismo, find new paths to self-esteem and more cooperative patterns with females. Some females have to reach beyond flattery, seduction and manipulation and find more honest ways to relate to males and to be genuinely self-assertive and female. Staff need to push beyond the "It's us against them" attitude in sex or race and find a "We've got a problem, let's solve it together" approach.

4. The staff need to become aware of themselves as people. Though they are adults, their need to be appreciated, validated and loved is not that far from the need of their young clients. Though as adults they have stabilized and toughened, they are still vulnerable; they can be hurt; they can be overwhelmed; they can get fed up and angry. Like the kids, they have their breaking point. Like the kids, they are growing and changing; they are struggling with life problems,

trying to cope with a world that is less than perfect. They too are looking toward the future, wondering what it holds and whether they will be able to realize their aspirations. They too build images and defenses and feel threatened when faced with openness, intimacy and affection. Only through coming to know themselves—including their child and adolescent selves—can they move toward knowing the tee-nagers, and toward interactions of a helpful kind.

Some of what the staff need to know can be absorbed "on the floor," as they go about their daily business. But some of it can only be learned in groups where staff bring problems that they have ex-perienced with kids, with co-workers, with the administration or in their personal lives. And inevitably people take ideas from the groups and try them out in their working relationships or in their home life.

One of our maintenance workers, Vincent Hamilton, was ap-prenticed while still a boy to a carpenter who was a stern taskmaster. Vincent is well liked by the staff, but tends to be impatient with the Argus kids. He sees them as bad-mouthing young hellions who could do with a beating. By dint of working full time for Argus and holding down a second job in the evening, Vincent is able to meet the pay-ments on a house, drive a car and travel during his vacations. Vincent is physically powerful, tough and energetic, and rules his family with a strong hand, refusing to let his wife work outside the home and brooking no nonsense from his children.

We had tried to apprentice Argus enrollees to Vincent, but their lack of discipline and their vagaries drove him wild. Not being allowed to give them the back of his hand, and not knowing any other way of dealing with them, Vincent felt unmanned and helpless. He de-manded the absolute obedience and acquiescence which had been imposed upon him as a boy, which he equates with respect and which had become an ironclad part of his personality. But there was another side to Vincent. He had difficulty standing up to peers and bosses and sometimes he missed out on what was rightfully his and smoldered, and sometimes he misunderstood what was going on.

A staff member, Horatio Raines, proposed some changes in procedures that he thought would make Argus more efficient. He pointed out that the maintenance men were going to the vendors in person and were wasting half a day waiting for their orders to be filled. No names were mentioned and no blame implied. Vincent was not present at the meeting (he was at the vendors') but someone told him about it, distorting the sense of what was said and leaving the impres-sion that Vincent was being accused of goofing off. He went into a state that I can only describe as swollen to bursting. Horatio spoke to him next day about a casual matter and Vincent "broke." The power of his emotion was such that he was reduced to incoherence; garbled sounds poured from him like lava and hot ashes. The only fragments that could be distinguished were "Black mother-fuckers can't never be trusted."

We called a meeting of the senior staff, with Horatio present. Vincent was asked to explain what was going on with him. He began to yell, again incoherently, and did not stop for half an hour. Tears streamed down his face. Finally it came out that he had admired Horatio, had been fond of him and believed that Horatio had sold him down the river. I asked Vincent if he thought he could remain calm and take in what some of the rest of us had to say about the incident in yesterday's meeting. "We've been working together a long time, Vincent," I said. "We've been through a lot. I trust you. I hope you feel you can trust me."

"Yes, Lisybeth," he said, "I trust you."

"Well, look, Vince," I said. "I'm glad you felt you could come in here and tell Horatio to his face what you are feeling and what you *thought* happened. But it didn't happen that way. I was at the meeting and I heard everything that Horatio said. I know you regard Horatio as a friend. I can assure you that he said nothing against you. He was talking about changing a procedure that would help you and help the rest of us."

The others present assured Vincent that this was true and recounted what they heard at the meeting. "Whoever told you that Horatio said anything against you either misunderstood or was trying to stir up trouble."

Horatio said, "Hey, Vince, I like you a lot. If I had something to say about you I'd say it to your face."

We explained the new procedure in detail. Vincent was convinced. He apologized to Horatio. Then we went into the matter of not being able to trust black mother-fuckers. We asked Vincent how he felt when he said that. He replied that he had been very angry and that if he'd had a weapon he might have used it on Horatio. We told him, "Man, you *did* have a weapon. A weapon that you've been hit with yourself. It's called racial prejudice. It was lying there like a club and because you were hurt and angry you picked it up and used it to bash away at Horatio."

Vincent said, "Yeah, that's what I did. I'm sorry, Horatio."

"Yeah. Well, I accept your apology, man," Horatio said. "I understand how you felt. You had been manipulated. But you are going to have to explain it to the kids who were there because they don't understand. I'll talk to them with you and we can explain it together." They walked out of the meeting with their arms around one another's shoulders, planning what they would say to the kids.

Vincent apologized to the kids. He blew his top several more times after that, always in connection with a misunderstanding, when he didn't feel entitled to say what was on his mind, but he never again employed racial epithets. Though he said little in groups he did absorb the atmosphere of trust and acceptance. His devotion and his dependability and skill have meant a great deal to the Argus family, of which he feels a part. And gradually, he has become more able to assert himself in relation to his co-workers and bosses. At the same time, he seems more tolerant of the shortcomings of the Argus kids. When his own boy got in trouble, Vincent's notions about authoritarianism and punishment were shaken. He had not mourned when his father died and for years hated the stern and punitive image of him, which he carried around like a rock in his breast. Then one day in group he got in touch with how much he wanted and needed a loving and kind father and burst into wild sobs. In the calm that followed he decided to visit his father's grave in Jamaica and lay flowers on it.

He realizes that street peer group pressures, drug pushers and other elements out of his control had preyed upon his son, and that the Argus kids, many of them, suffer the same fate. "It's made me believe in Argus more than ever," he says. He has not developed the patience which would enable him to work directly with kids, instructing them in carpentry while pulling them in to new ways of behaving and thinking. He may never do so. But he is now able to count to ten and hold his rage when baited, and he is not walking around like a time bomb because he no longer lets people trample all over him. If he thinks someone is stepping on his toes he can say so in a more or less "normal" tone, without going completely beside himself, and can assert his right to better treatment. It's a relaxing of the old strictures and it has come through group interaction, through the working out of problems as they arise on the floor and through the various mediating procedures that we have created. It is difficult to get skilled and reliable journeymen to work consistently anywhere today, and it is particularly hard in the South Bronx. In our buildings and storefronts something is always breaking down, always in need of repair. Vincent turns out the work and is dependable and honest. He has been with us eleven years and whatever we have put into him has been well worth the trouble.

It is hard to deal with certain problems in the staff development groups or within the organization. If a staff member is drinking heavily, using drugs, going out with an enrollee or otherwise violating the personnel practices, that person will generally not bring it up for fear of being fired. The interactions and behavior of such persons in staff development groups may give the first clue that something very serious is the matter. Heavy drinking and drug abuse can scarcely be hidden from a street-wise staff and are dealt with in various ways, sometimes in the group, sometimes in smaller senior staff groups called especially for the purpose. Depending on the gravity of the problem, the staff member may be placed on probation and directed to AA or to intensive therapy in one of Dan Casriel's groups; or he or she may be asked to resign and go into a live-in therapeutic community, with perhaps the chance to resume the job at a later date when the problem is taken care of.

Staff members who date enrollees or become sexually involved with them are terminated. There are no extenuating circumstances and no exceptions. To be attracted to young girls or young men in the program is human; to act out these feelings is unprofessional, harmful to those who depend upon us as adult and parental substitutes, confirms enrollees in their suspicion that everyone is out to use and rip them off when they need to incorporate concepts of trust, basic human worth and altruistic love. Only five times in fifteen years have we had to let people go for this offense, and in each case the staff member had serious personality problems, including a compulsive need to prove his manhood by continual sexual conquests.

It is crucial to their growth for our kids to learn that they are valuable as human beings, particularly the girls who, like most females in our culture, pick up the message that they are not able to offer much of value beyond sexual and reproductive roles. The boys tend to place an undue emphasis on sexual prowess and making girls pregnant, as well as on toughness and combativeness, so that we must make a special effort to let them know that they are valuable and can achieve respect in other arenas. Needless to say, staff members who are Don Juans do not promote these aims, so we draw a clear firm line.

Not long ago a girl transferred to Argus One from another group home where she had caused a great deal of trouble. A counselor in that home was having an affair with her, followed her to our premises and assumed as a matter of course that he would be accepted as her "boyfriend." No one at the previous institution had questioned their relationship. We discovered that he was married and drank heavily. We informed the girl's mother, who forbade her to see him. He was not permitted to take the girl out or visit her at Argus One. After kicking up an awesome fuss and driving our staff up the wall, the girl turned her attention to a more appropriate young man and is doing well. Her displaced boyfriend did not acquiesce without threatening our staff in a variety of ways and trying to force his way into Argus One. Fortunately, we had male staff who sent him packing and a strong director who resisted his more slimy maneuvers.

Some ex-addicts, hired fresh from a therapeutic community, go through a difficult period of adjustment. Decent living quarters are almost nonexistent at prices they can afford. They may be in debt, possess no furniture and few clothes and have as friends only ex-addicts who, like themselves, are trying to stay clean and make it in a world that sometimes seems bent on sending them back to the cooker. They feel insecure with "squares" and shaky about their ability to hold down a job. Many struggle through this rocky period and make decent lives for themselves. But a couple of years ago, for what reason we do not know, two talented staff members, who were doing good work, were lost to us and for a time to themselves because they couldn't stand up to the pressures.

Afterwards, we found ourselves focusing more on those group members who had had a drug problem in the past. Two other staff members, hired out of a therapeutic community, came in for a lot of attention. We felt determined not to let them fall. They were open and willing to share their feelings and experiences, and we were able to be helpful. But as the months went by we noticed a change in one of them, Derrick McVay. Derrick, usually open and honest in groups, had become extremely gloomy and turned inward. He was drinking too much on weekends and made a couple of bad decisions (about his roommate and his living quarters) that filled him with anxiety. He got through these crises somehow, but continued to be very, very down. The director of operations had a couple of talks with him in private and he agreed to confide in the group.

That Friday, as soon as we were gathered in a circle, Derrick announced that he had something to say. He was slumped in his seat, heavy with gloom, but as he talked he straightened up and his former vitality and self-respect returned. He confessed that he had put a needle in his arm.

From what Derrick told us he sounded more like a person with an overly bothersome conscience, who persecuted and punished himself so relentlessly that he had taken to the cooker to try and get some surcease. Various group members told him so. Michele Berdy said she had a hunch that the urge to punish himself filled some kind of need and suggested that he try to figure out what it was. All of us told

Derrick how much we cared about him and how happy we were to see him get that load off his belly.

The senior staff mulled over how to deal with Derrick in terms of the cardinal rules and the effects on the program. We didn't see that it would serve any purpose to fire him or reduce his rank. His fall had been brief. He had owned up to the lapse of his own free will. It was obvious that he had suffered. The community as a whole didn't know that he had shot dope, and though he had been depressed and guilty, he had not been walking around the building high. We advised him to get some additional help on the outside, in a group or individual setting where he could be open and could free himself from the bondage of self-persecution and low self-esteem. His task is to take full responsibility for himself, stop blaming other people and circumstances and appreciate himself for the many fine qualities and talents he possesses.

One Friday Rachel Weill arrived at the staff development group in a white heat, determined to let us know what was bothering her, yet reluctant to get into it.

As soon as we were seated in our customary circle, Rachel pounced. "I'm sick and tired of the way the male staff around here treat the girls, eyeing them up and down, telling them they look good enough to eat, that they're pretty, that they're foxy, that they're sexy. I'm so angry about it I just couldn't wait to come in here and tell you about it."

Her outburst was greeted with shocked silence. The male staff ducked sheepishly, grimaced. We asked her to be more specific and to name names. She refused at first, then blurted out, "Okay, I will. I'm talking to you, Lennie. And you, Jimmy. And Derrick, I've heard you do it too."

"Now come on, Rachel," Lennie countered, with his most winning smile. "I may have been a little loose in one instance today with Shawn Gannoway, but hey, it's not the way I treat my girls, day in and day out." His eyes swept the circle for approval, sure of getting it as he usually does.

"What in the hell is wrong with telling a girl that she is pretty?" Jimmy demanded, his face reddening with indignation. "You think she's gonna die of it or something?"

"Listen to this. This is unendurable," Rachel cried. "How could you be so insensitive? Don't you see what you're doing? A girl like Shawn Gannoway is pretty, sure. But she's also intelligent, she's got a good personality, she's strong, she's writing some wonderful poetry in the workshop and has turned out a good piece on child abuse for the newspaper. How do you think it makes her feel to have just one quality singled out for attention all day long? Gee, Shawn, you're sure foxy. You're sure sexy. You sure turn me on. How do you think that makes her feel?"

"Well, I would think it would make her feel terrific," Lennie said. "I know how good I feel when some girl tells me I'm sexy."

"It might very well make Shawn or anyone else feel good to be told they're sexy," Michele said. "But what else? What are some of the other things a female might feel if that was what she mainly heard from males and if she heard it a lot?"

"She might feel like a piece of meat," Lennie said, relenting suddenly.

"That's right! A piece of meat! That's it exactly!" came from the chorus of female staff around the circle.

Aubrey suggested that the staff try to imagine how they would feel if their daughters were whistled at in the streets and told that they were foxy and sexy. They admitted that the thought wasn't pleasant. We talked about the fact that so much of our culture is out of our awareness and how hard it is to realize the meaning of a lot of the patterns that we simply fall into and never think about. Michael Shimkin suggested that if the staff wanted to raise self-esteem among the girls, it might be more effective to compliment them on their achievements and their personalities, their punctuality, neatness. "Or just tell them how lovable they are generally. Girls who are seen as less attractive may desperately need attention and compliments. Try to find positive things to say about them, not necessarily sexual, but things that indicate that they are attractive human beings." The male counselors seemed able to accept this idea, since it came from Michael, whom they admire and trust.

Rachel had denied that her strong feelings about the male counselors' behavior sprang from anything personal. Michele ventured a guess that the incident had set off resonances within Rachel and suggested that she try to get in touch with whatever it might be.

Rachel then told the group that she herself felt insecure about her own basic human value, especially when she was singled out as a sex object and her other qualities were overlooked. "That's why I got so angry about it," she said.

"You might find males more open to your ideas, Rachel, if you approach them from some other place besides your anger," Michele said.

"That's right," I said. "But let's get this clear too. Your anger is a natural human response to a painful and unfair lot of crap. You're entitled to your anger, Rachel. Feel it and decide what you want to do with it. You may decide that dumping it on males isn't the most effective way to deal with it."

"I was angry," Rachel said. "And I am angry. But I'm not angry at you, Lennie, or you, Jimmy, or you, Derrick. Not anymore. I just want you to be more sensitive to the way I feel and the way the girls here might feel. I can see Shawn has already fallen into the trap of believing that sexual attractiveness is the only thing she's got. And I don't want that to happen to her. She's got a lot and she needs to be made to feel valuable as a human being, apart from sex."

It was a very productive session. Lennie and some of the other males were able to get a new slant on the way females feel. Jimmy took a small step in that direction, although he was going through some heavy stuff of his own and was not as open. The point was made that each enrollee has to be looked at in terms of individual needs, and that everything a counselor—or any Argus staff member—does is significant.

Many of the members of this group were experienced and very aware, but we all had a lot to learn. There was a general feeling that Rachel had been gutsy to bring her objections to the group. She took a risk and we admired her for it. Rachel's strong statement of the issue, although it made the males uncomfortable and defensive at first and put us all a bit on edge, had a salutary effect since she was forthright and honest, acknowledging finally that she had personal feelings about their behavior as well as concern for the girls.

I don't know what the group members carried away from that encounter. People generally resist change; nothing is ever resolved in a day. But by the end of the group there was a lot of good feeling and a sense of heightened awareness. It became plain to us all that what we've thought of as harmless pleasantries may take on other dimensions and colorations and, given our special relationship to the kids, can be harmful. The group ended with the men resolving to be more sensitive and with a lot of hugging and affectionate exchanges.

What does it feel like to be thrown into the Argus waters and told to sink or swim? Here is the reaction of Lena Hernandez, a twenty-three-year-old Puerto Rican woman sent to Argus by Wildcat. She had street experience, had been a skin popper, had been in jail on a shoplifting charge, never had held a job for more than two or three weeks at a time (in department stores where she had a pattern of stealing, messing up the inventory and getting fired). When she was assigned to the counselor training program at Argus she had detoxed and was determined to make a new life for herself but was by no means sure that she could succeed.

"I told my supervisor I wanted to be a counselor because I like working with children. She said, 'Well, they have this opening at Argus, but it might scare you. You won't be working with little kids, you'll be working with adult children.' She brought me over here and I seen how they reacted and I was scared. I said, 'Oh my goodness, I'll probably be fighting with one of them in two days!' But they put me on the switchboard for six weeks so I could watch and see how the program works. The staff development group, it scared me, you know. Because everybody was meditating, and I'm sitting there looking and everybody is going to sleep. And I'm saying, 'What's happening?' But they told me, 'After a couple of times you'll understand how it's done.' But I said, 'Maybe I don't belong here. I don't know nothing about this.'

"Then Aubrey told me I had been on the switchboard long enough. My time had come to get out there among the kids. I said, 'Oh no!' The kids were disrespectful. The new ones. Getting high on the premises, cutting out constantly. How was I supposed to deal with that? I followed Connie Phillips [a more experienced counselor] around, stuck to her like a burr, watching to see what she would do. One day Connie was called away. Me and Barbara [another counselor trainee] were left alone. It was about five o'clock and we had just dismissed the group. Renata Wells started cursing in the hallway, calling Flavia Jackson all kinds of a mother-fucker. 'You bastard mother-fucker, I'll kill you!' I didn't know what was going on. I'm trying to hold Renata and 20 million kids are standing there, looking at me. I bumped my head and hurt my hand. I was all alone just hanging on to that girl. I said, 'I'm about ready to quit.'

"But then I got mad myself. I was furious. I was fuming. I really walked on the kids. I said, 'You better straighten out, or *I'm* going to be the next one to break here.' And you know what? Their reaction taught me something. They said, 'Lena is mad! Lena is mad!' They freaked out, you know. It turned out they had a lot of respect for me.

"In the staff development group they told me that the reason the kids like me is because I like them and show them concern. And I do. I care for the kids. They make me angry but they *know* when someone really cares for them. In the group they made me understand how much power there is in *caring*. And I realized I really do have something to give the kids. They like you to be tough and make demands. It makes them feel like they count, they're worth battling over. I can

do that. I've got the drive and the energy. Maybe because I had to
scramble so hard to survive. With me they know they have to toe the
line. Sure, I play with them. I'm not always strict. I'm not as rigid as
some of the counselors. But they know they can't get around me
where it matters.

"You learn how to let out your feelings in the staff development
group. They tell you to hold your gut on the floor. It's easier to do
once you know you've got people you can talk to about whatever's
bothering you. It's okay to let them see that you're angry at times, but
you can't *react* to them. It's not like on the street where if she cussed
me out, I can cuss her back. Like when they need somebody to cuss
out it may not have anything to do with the counselor. It's probably
about something else altogether. So instead of cussing them back, I
give them a little hug, a little pat, and I say, 'Let's go for a walk. Let's
have a little talk. Maybe you'll tell me what's bothering you.' I know
now that I can do it, I can get through to them. My gut hardly kicks
up any more. And if I give them enough space to get their bad feelings
out, they don't need to cuss as much. It really works."

Constance Phillips had a different background. Tall, black, serious and distinguished, she also came through Wildcat, but not as an
ex-street person. Connie was an AFDC mother with teenage children
of her own, an ailing mother to take care of and no steady man. She
had worked only intermittently outside the home and had never been
trained for any job. I marveled that anyone as thin as Connie could
be strong and full of such abundant energy. I thought she would kill
herself running up and down our five flights of iron stairs, and though
she was not overly talkative, her voice box opened without inhibition
or effort—and without offense—releasing sounds that carried the
message of entitlement, assertion and personal power. Until they
heard that voice the kids took her for one of their own. She looked
so young. But there was a resigned set to her full mouth and a sadness
in the depths of her eye. To escape her mother's home, where she had
been the chief baby-sitter and housekeeper, she had become a teenage mother. Now her ambition was to get off welfare and make something of herself.

"The kids relate well to me, a lot of them, boys *and* girls,"
Connie told the staff development group. "I guess I feel I've got
something special for the girls. When I tell them to put off having a
baby they can *hear* me. They know that I know what I'm talking about.
A lot of them are just where I was fifteen years ago—trying to get out
from under their mama's thumb."

Connie told how Cynthia, a very large girl, went after another girl who had incited her friends, telling them, "Get her, get the bitch, kick her ass!" But when they saw Big Cynthia, one of them snatched up a chair. Connie and another trainee tried to intervene, got in the way and were hit and scratched, though the blows were not meant for them. An experienced peer ran and got Aubrey LaFrance. The instant he and other male counselors appeared there were loud "Pssts!" and "Shhs!" The antagonists froze.

"Okay, that's more like it," Aubrey said. "Now we'll sit down and talk this out. Let's form ourselves in a circle so we can look one another in the face. Find chairs and sit down."

In the course of the group it came out that the immediate dispute arose out of rivalry over a man on the block, but behind that was prejudice. Cynthia was "Spanish." The other girl who was black had said, "All Puerto Ricans are the same. You can't trust no Puerto Rican."

"You can't classify all Puerto Ricans as the same because they're not the same," a hispanic girl had argued.

"If someone is after your man you're ready and willing to say anything about them," another girl countered.

Aubrey took them through their attitudes and feelings and got them to take the first steps along the road to understanding and dealing with the hydra-head of racial prejudice. Connie studied Aubrey in action, sharpening her tools.

When her eighteen months with Wildcat were up Connie was taken on the Argus staff. At that time she told the group, "I'll be frank with you. Coming from not knowing anything at all, I'm proud to tell people I'm a counselor. I'm a counselor of kids. I'm proud to say that. It's like a status symbol for me. It is. Plus it has helped me personally. I have learned how to deal with kids so now I manage my own kids better. We have a house meeting—a group—at home every Saturday to fill each other in on what we're all doing, to set goals for ourselves and see whether we're getting somewhere. We've learned to put our feelings right out on the table. We yell at each other sometimes and we cry but we work it out. We're in contact. We do more hugging and kissing than we used to. You wouldn't believe the change in my kids. They're all doing well, all going someplace.

"One thing: I give them a lot more time and attention than I did. I don't think I *could* before. I was too worried and harassed. But now that I don't have to hassle with the welfare and have a halfway decent salary, I'm a new person. And I know now that my kids are starved for attention just like the kids here at Argus. I need too. And I know that

I can't expect the kids to fill all my needs. It's a priority for me to find a really reliable man. That's hard. But I'm working on it." Incidentally, Connie did find her reliable man and they are very happy. His name is Aubrey LaFrance.

We believe that the recognition of stress and rage and facilitating ways for the staff to deal with these feelings in a safe environment (where they can trust enough to let it out and will be protected from hurting themselves or anyone else) is a key to preventing staff burnout. Once people can acknowledge their rage and realize that they are not "bad" for feeling it, and once they know that they have a safety valve in the groups, and the support of their fellow group members, they will probably not be in danger of acting out on it (losing their temper, performing poorly, blaming the clients for their plight, backbiting, bad rapping, drinking) and they will be able to distance themselves from it.

One way to remove emotional blocks and gain access to a person's rage or other feelings is by role playing rather than merely telling about it. We have often done this in staff development groups but it is always wise to have experienced staff present who know what to do with the acute and copious feelings that may rush to the surface. Staff members need not have formal credentials in order to utilize this technique creatively and avoid harmful consequences, but they must have first class training and be warm, empathetic and responsible. Group leaders who are well meaning but don't know what to do may leave a person in an unresolved state; and I have seen a few group leaders with credentials, as well as self-styled therapists, pursue their own agendas (unconsciously), inflicting wounds on people made vulnerable by playing out a deeply felt conflict. When handled responsibly, however, the approach is very effective indeed.

Both Mary Taylor and I, in our groups, have asked staff members to "go back" and play themselves as adolescents, choosing a group member to act as the other party (perhaps a parent or a sibling) in both a painful and a pleasurable situation and then to reverse roles. Almost invariably deeply buried feelings surface, followed by insights and understanding of both themselves and the adolescents in their care.

One of the most important features of the staff development groups is that they facilitate human contact and bonding in a society which tends to alienate people. Although all of the staff development objectives discussed in the opening of this chapter are vital to the success of a program such as ours, the knowledge that your co-workers are human, that they can be trusted and relied upon and that they share many of the doubts and fears, as well as the joys and satisfactions in personal life and in the task at hand must be written in letters of gold, for without this knowledge high quality, productive interactions with the kids can scarcely be generated.

We have been taught to hide our feelings, to value control and to regard the expression of emotion as a loss of face and a weakness. In the beginning staff members (like the young persons we work with) deny their feelings or talk about them in an abstract, intellectualized or disparaging manner. In the subculture of the streets and in our society in general playing it cool is admirable. Inexpressiveness is pervasive in the character-disordered society, where the common defense against loneliness and alienation is to shut down and go numb. In the ghetto and on Park Avenue people seek to cloak their loneliness and their longing for intimacy in possessions, money, accomplishments, fame and acting out or to medicate their pain with work, television, ever stronger doses of thrills and sensations, alcohol and narcotics.

Healthy human beings when life is treating them halfway decently should be in high spirits a good part of the time, and I have seen it happen over and over again when people drop their masks, share their feelings and those of the group and become bonded. When loss and anxiety strike, as they inevitably must, the blows are more easily borne and recovery is speedier when the balm of human intimacy, sharing and caring is laid on rather than chemicals, which may bring temporary relief but carry a high price tag in side effects, and the exacerbated woes and complications of addiction.

Severe personal problems and family crises beset the Argus staff. Many cannot find apartments in the better areas of the city at prices they can afford. The awareness that landlords shut them out because of color and ethnicity is a sore that is rubbed raw whenever they even think about searching for a place to live. Most are forced to settle in neighborhoods where vice flourishes and every form of deadly panacea is available for a price. At times even the strongest feel like throwing in the sponge. Frances Foye, who entered Argus as a welfare mother trainee and is now our director of operations, told the group members for months about her frustration as she hunted for a decent apartment. When she finally found one and moved in she discovered that the roof leaked, and for the next six months she shared the agonies of wrangling with the landlord and registering complaints with city agencies, while she moved her furniture out of the way and placed buckets under the leaks whenever it rained. So many of our staff have been crime victims that I long ago lost count. A mental patient released to "community treatment" held Aubrey's ex-wife up at gun point and tried to rip the cast off her broken arm, convinced that money was hidden in it. Aubrey tracked down the perpetrator and made a citizen arrest because the police were busy with other matters. Within the last two years the husband of Aubrey's niece was shot and killed in his store by robbers, and his nephew's wife, a lovely young woman of twenty-two, was strangled, stabbed and thrown from a sixth-story window. Aubrey's daughter was threatened with rape at gunpoint on her way to school. Anthony Davarese's cousin, who had just passed the bar examination, was gunned down in a store in the course of a robbery and died a week later. One of Larry Gordon's twin sisters was robbed and murdered in 1980, and in 1982 the remaining twin suffered the same fate. People need a place to express the agony, the turmoil and the fear evoked by such tragic events. In staff development groups people listen, sympathize and lend support. They proffer advice and give assistance when they can.

It helps to get good and angry once in a while at the daily grind —the noise, the filth, the bums. The zoo that is the subway. The feeling that any attempt to reap justice is futile. The worry about the kids and the old people. Trying to make everyone come in by eight o'clock at night and stay in where it's a little safer.

Staff members survive in this inferno, and that's a tribute to their ingenuity and tenacity. They keep decent homes, raise their children, move ahead by dint of unremitting struggle. Many attend college, pursuing advanced degrees. The quality of their work at Argus is gaining recognition. I am happy for them. They deserve to be appreciated. They deserve the Purple Heart.

To the extent that our counselors—and our staff in general— learn how to recognize and express their own feelings, to listen, to understand, to empathize to communicate, to share with others and to take control of and develop their own lives, they will be able to steer our young charges toward similar ends. To the extent that they can weather their own bad patches without numbing themselves, they will be in a position to help young people do likewise. To the extent that they can achieve high spirits and find pleasure and ecstasy without drugs, they will pass these attainments along. It isn't a drill, it isn't a grind. It can't be pulled out of a textbook or stuffed into a person like forcemeat into a piece of tripe. It is more like a contagion. We catch it from one another. It's a warm energy that flows from hand to hand, from body to body, from brain to brain. We are all born with it. We just have to find it again, to overcome our dismal conditioning, to learn how to turn it on.

And true affection, as we measure it, includes getting people to behave responsibly. "Confronting someone's negative behavior is a piece of love," is the way Mary Taylor puts it. "When you care enough to put yourself in front of all that hostility and abuse and say, 'You've got to change,' and stick to it, that's real love." This applies to the staff as well as the kids. "Staff have to be confronted, just like kids do. I have trained staff—or *tried* to train them—in a number of agencies where confrontation did not take place. The staff had bought into a system of 'Chill out, don't criticize me. If you care about me you'll let me do anything I want to do and you won't say anything. Don't confront me and I won't confront you. We'll sweep everything under the carpet.' The same old patterns go right on, for the staff and the kids. The only way to break out of it is for the administration and the entire agency to sit down and confront the fact that they have this problem, that the program is not working, and decide to do something about it."

In order to be effective a staff has to get from an agency the very same things the clients need in order to grow—safety, nurturance, belonging, love, self-esteem, and self-actualization. To the degree that they get those they can give them to the kids.

For this reason staff development cannot be ignored, curtailed or done in a prefunctory manner but must be deep, ongoing and must include the entire agency.

20. THE CONSENSUS MODEL
Minimizing Differences and Distances

. . . a dispute between the Squatters (settlers on the land)
was like those sores you get in Africa, and which they call
veldt-sores: they heal on the surface if you let them, and
go on festering and running underneath until you dig
them up to the bottom and have them cleaned all through.

ISAK DINESEN, *Out of Africa*

For over fourteen years a staff composed of blacks, hispanics, caucasians and some orientals have committed themselves to the Argus program. Many remain on the staff for long periods of time. Our client population is roughly half black and half hispanic; each half regards the other with some hostility which surfaces when conflict arises. Yet there has never been a major ethnic or racial confrontation within Argus. By and large, our staff is harmonious and morale is generally high. There is little tension or friction, a high degree of cooperation and not a lot of staff burnout. Morale is maintained amid the daily drudgery, the slow, often imperceptible advances, as well as the backsliding of our young charges, which seems like our own failure (as indeed it is at times), and the investment of ourselves that we put into the kids.

Something keeps us traveling down the same road, relatively free of cliques, bad rapping and backbiting. That something is the decision and policy-formulating processes that have evolved at Argus, the kind and degree of staff participation in these processes; and the level of interdependence among staff members. In searching for ways to weld together an effective staff, inspire commitment, maintain morale and give life to the concept of role model, we have reinvented for ourselves a tried and tested formula: the consensus method.

At Argus we use the consensus method for building self-esteem and as a part of staff training. It is the key process in organizing and structuring our program. We have come to rely upon consensus to keep destructive conflict in check and to provide the ground for the esprit and trust which are the bread, wine and medicaments of people on the firing line.

284

Consensus differs from democratic or authoritarian modes of decision making and conflict resolution, although it can coexist and overlap with either. Webster defines consensus as group solidarity in sentiment and belief, a general agreement, unanimity. Some would say that there is no such thing as collective opinion. For us consensus is not a thing which exists ready made; it has to be hatched and kept alive in a context of vigorous and honest communication. It can be developed within a hierarchy, as in the moot and similar group processes widespread in sub-Saharan Africa. In West African societies, state or tribal, hierarchy and rank did not impede consensual decision making. The fact that these societies were small-scale and interdependent and that political authority overlapped with kinship fostered the process.[1]

Anna Chairetakis, a student of Italian villagers transplanted to the New World, observes: "The Italian Trentini, former Alpine Valley farmers and cattle raisers, now an ethnic enclave in the United States, provide an instance of consensus from a Euro-American setting. While they see their social world as riven by jealousies, frictions, and unregenerate individualism, they in fact go everywhere in a body, congregate in groups, consult with one another and take no decision without something close to unanimity."[2]

In a democratic setting the majority prevails through the vote which is mobilized by select committees of power brokers. The consensual process takes more time than the democratic way and more again than the authoritarian. It involves a continuous getting together, sorting out of facts and acknowledging and considering all viewpoints. However irrelevant some of the input is, it could be the burgeoning of self-assertion, the whir of new wings being tried, the calling card of the hitherto inconversable. Quite a lot of indirect education takes place in the course of reaching consensus. On the heels of "incongruities" and "irrelevancies" a problem may be viewed in a new light, a connection made, intense feelings may emerge; conflicts and contradictions become easier to get at. A creative and unexpected solution may be forthcoming.

How did this idea take hold at Argus? I am not really sure. Some of the staff seem to have it in their bones, as a legacy from Africa, and perhaps as a New World survival tool. Our staff takes to consensus as though it had been laid down in their genes. I may have picked up the lineaments of it in the South, in Haiti, from talks with Africans, and from my reading about African stateless societies. Just as courts are agencies of politically developed states, so moots (called Gotlas in Botswana, Kyamas in Kenya and by other names in various parts of sub-Saharan Africa) are a mode of the community. This method of dispute resolution by the community, sometimes referred to as a "tribal court," flourishes in present-day Africa side by side with the state court system. It usually is held in the open air, with the elders seated in a circle and the villagers and disputants gathered around. The complainant speaks first, at whatever length he wishes, and then the accused is heard. After this anyone who has anything to say about the pros and cons of the case, the habits and lifestyles of the contending parties, their characters and histories is free to speak. Everything is admissible—that this one has fleas in her mattress or that one stole a cow ten years ago. It is what Edward T. Hall would call a high context situation,[3] and its essence is compromise with an eye to long-term peace in the community. The elders listen to it all. When everything has been said the most junior judge gives his opinion, then the next and the next in seniority, until the chief elder is reached. Having had the benefit of everyone's input the senior elder then delivers his opinion, which is binding and is generally abided by. If either party is not satisfied, the argument can be extended or the case may be taken to the state court. Contenders will sometimes resort to the threat of the state court; but most Africans deem hailing one's kinspeople before a state court a breach of tribal mores.[4] Women have sat as elders. Isak Dinesen was a high-ranking judge in the Kyamas in her village in Kenya.[5]

Although certain cases today are restricted to the state courts, there is a wide range of complaints and disputes which may be brought before the moot, including civil and criminal matters. I talked to no one in Africa, including hard-bitten ex-colonial whites, who was not an admirer of the moot as a system for settling disputes, relieving the state courts of a burden and keeping the peace. Everyone seemed to believe that the moot works efficiently and fairly and that it could serve as a model for use in places, such as the United States, where the courts are overwhelmed.

At Argus we have in place an informal moot. Its activities consume a fair amount of time but not nearly so much as a festering quarrel would. If ever we fail to hear all points of view, if we brush disputes under the carpet in the hope that they will go away, we pay the price. Whenever ill-will has erupted within our ranks, there have been rumblings beforehand that had been ignored.

The case of a young black staff member, Malaba, illustrates this point: tall, stork-legged, proud as a Masai warrior, clothed in dashikis made by the women of his household, he gave the impression of a man whose hurts were so grievous and so deeply overgrown that neither he nor anyone else had access to them. Malaba grew up as Sheldon Warren in a middle-class family, attended the Bronx High School of the Arts, won a scholarship to Yale, graduated with honors, embarked on a career as a sculptor and supported his wife and children by teaching. He came to Argus in the early years when we hired our own teachers and later was taken on the Board of Education payroll when they decided to outstation teachers in our agency. Malaba was a devotee of black history and culture, and even before a trip to Ghana, which moved him profoundly, he had taken his African name.

The troubles which arose with Malaba are complicated. He was an excellent teacher and charismatic but focused primarily on art and on his activities in the community, and his commitment to the Muslim sect of which he was a member. Despite his professed admiration for Argus and its unique atmosphere, he used the program and the staff as a forum for his own ideas, which emphasized racial differences and conflict, rather than the mutual interest, acceptance and cooperation we were trying to foster. He told staff members that no white could understand or feel black history and sufferings and that blacks were superior, should distrust what the whites said and should distance themselves. At staff meetings he made "brilliant" speeches and waved his arms.

I told him that his behavior was contrary to Argus methods and philosophy and that if he continued in this way, he would not be able to stay with us. He replied that I had been misinformed, that someone was out to get him, that I had misunderstood his remarks or denied that he had ever made them.

"Nor is it acceptable that you leave every afternoon at three o'clock," I said. "We work until five."

"I am a teacher. Teachers quit work at three o'clock."

"But you are on our payroll. You work for us nine to five. You are supposed to help us develop our education program, as well as teach."

"But what about my career as an artist? And my work for the community? I don't think I should be subjected to the same rules as the rest of the people here."

"If you can't follow our rules, you should work elsewhere."

"Are you firing me?"

"No. I am simply telling you that you will have to follow the personnel practices and the Argus rules, which you put your signature to. It is only possible to work at Argus under these terms."

Malaba continued to leave early and stepped up his remarks to whites and about them. I called him in at the end of two weeks and told him to look for work elsewhere.

To me the case was open and shut, but Malaba seemed not to comprehend why he had been asked to leave. He went around to the staff and told them that he had been fired for no reason. Since I had talked it over with only two or three top staff and had not included anyone else in the final decision or at the meeting where Malaba was told to go, most people believed him.

On the day of our staff development group I was delayed by a telephone call and when I got to the group I walked into a thunderstorm. Many of the staff, including some of the whites, told me that I had no business firing Malaba. I tried to explain but was interrupted constantly. I let the storm take its course (I had no choice). When finally there was a lull, I asked if they would listen to what I had to say. There were cries of "No, we want Malaba reinstated." I said that I would sooner close down the place than see everything destroyed. And I stuck to my guns. The group ended with the staff still angry and insistent. I did not know how to win them to my point of view since they would not permit me to complete a sentence and lit into me every time I opened my mouth. But nothing they said changed my mind.

Aldo Reyes expressed the opinion that Malaba really and truly did not understand that he had done anything wrong.

"If he doesn't then we are better off without him," I replied. I was smoking mad.

It was Friday and we went to our weekend sore and unsatisfied. On Saturday Aldo called me at home and told me that he had just come from a long talk with Malaba.

"He is very unhappy. He wants to come back, Elizabeth. He loves Argus and he will do whatever he has to do to stay with us. He likes you and the other whites on the staff, especially some of those he's gone after the hardest. It's a very complicated situation emotionally, Elizabeth. I wish we could find a way to get him together with you. The funny thing is, in spite of all that stuff he's been putting out he's really heartbroken."

"I'd like to believe it." I had called Malaba a lot of names in my head, among them "grandiose," "histrionic," and "narcissistic." It's called trotting out the old psychiatric lexicon and beating your adversary over the head with it.

"I'll see him on Monday. And if he will agree to abide by our rules and stop testing whites on the racial issue and stop being divisive, well, anything can happen," I told Aldo.

On Monday Malaba and I had a talk. He said that he realized he had been harmful to Argus and to the kids. He promised to stop it and to put in a full work day. I asked him to make his commitment to the senior staff. He did so. We embraced.

The outcome was a surprise to me, particularly in view of the way I had bungled the situation by acting unilaterally in the beginning. Everyone was pleased. Most astonishing of all was Malaba's subsequent, changed behavior. And he taught me a lesson: I had to consult at every step of the way. I needed culturally sensitive mediators, such as Aldo, who understood the feelings and interests of all parties.

Malaba left us several years later, along with another excellent black teacher, when Board of Education provisionals were let go in the financial crunch. He went to a career in New England. For my part, I hated to see him go.

Since that time the Argus senior staff have taken all major decisions in concert, after whatever discussions and meetings were necessary to allow everyone to be heard and to expose us to as many points of view and as much information as possible.

Sometimes before going into a meeting I weigh the problem and jot down various possible solutions. Invariably, as a result of the consensual process, the group comes up with a different solution— usually a better one, since more information is supplied, more perspectives are brought into play. Brainstorming is an especially powerful tool with us since many of our staff have not been stifled by a traditional education.

In a specially convened group, one of the counselors, Earl Richards, was taking Chessie Washington to task. "I got a call from the college. You haven't been there all week, and I think I know why. You're up to your old tricks, messing around out there in the streets. Furthermore, you've been smoking a lot of marijuana."

All eyes in the group were on Chessie to see how she would respond to this confrontation. Chessie treated Earl to her most withering stare, mixed, however, with a touch of coquettishness for he was big, black, athletic, good-looking and, as she was well aware, by no means immune to the female sex. "You can't prove that I've been smoking pot, Earl Richards."

"This isn't a court of law, Chessie. This is a group of your peers. We're not out to *prove* anything. We deduce from the way you carry yourself, from the pupils of your eyes and from your skin color that you've been smoking heavily."

"You can't weasel out of this, Chessie," Flavia said. "You asked me to go outside yesterday and you offered me a roach."

Chessie turned to Mary Taylor, who was sitting next to her, and rolled up her eyes like a dying calf. "How come you allow a staff member to confront me about pot smoking when he's doing the same thing himself?" Her powerful voice rang with indignation.

"Hold on, Chessie, you're just trying to turn the game on me. Mary, as a counselor, do I have to listen to this shit?"

"He is smoking, Mary, and heavily. I can prove it!" Chessie sprang from her chair.

"Sit down, Chessie!" Mary commanded.

"Yeah, sit down, what's the matter with you?"

"Sit down!"

"Sit down!"

"I'm not sitting down until Earl shows us his hands. Go ahead, Earl! Hold up your hand and let's see the stains on your fingers! Look at that! He doesn't smoke tobacco. That's from holding roaches! How can he ask me not to do something when he's doing it himself?"

"Are those marijuana stains on your fingers, Earl?"

Earl denied it. Then he said, "It's true. I have been smoking. I feel very tense. It helps me to relax."

"Well now, ain't that the livin end," Flavia grunted. "He's just like my father, trying to make *me* into a angel when he's smoking an drinking till he don't know where he's at half the time."

"*Relax!* Well, *we* need to relax as much as you! What you trying to tell us, Earl, that you can break the cardinal rules around here and we can't?" Chessie demanded.

"She's right, Earl," Mary said.

A special staff meeting was called. It was pretty open and shut, no major disagreement among the staff. Earl had broken his contract with Argus and had ruined his credibility with the girls in the group home and the enrollees at 170 Brown Place. He admitted that he was smoking. We suggested that he spend six months working at something else and that he get some help with his problem of rigidity and the fear that tied him in knots. He promised to do so.

Six months later Earl came back, looking more than ever clean-cut, athletic and upstanding. He swore to us that he was now drug free and said that he was seeing a psychotherapist. He asked for a job as a caseworker. "I believe I'll be less tense doing the paperwork."

We gave him the job with a long probation period and he did fairly well for some months. Then Teresa Torres, a girl at the Learning for Living Center, accused Earl of asking her for a date and, when she refused, of coming to her apartment uninvited and offering cocaine to her and her sister. Teresa said they spurned the drug and that he then snorted in front of them and when Teresa refused to go out with him, approached her sister and badgered her. Teresa said that she then tried to call her boyfriend and was prevented from doing so by Earl. At that moment her boyfriend showed up (he had come to help her move some furniture), and Earl excused himself and left. The staff questioned Teresa at length and took notes.

They then questioned Earl alone. He said that Teresa had asked *him* for a date and that he had refused, reminding her that as a staff member he was not at liberty to take out girls in the program even if he wanted to. He said that Teresa had become angry and had evidently concocted this story out of spite, to hang him. We asked Earl to tell us when and where this conversation with Teresa took place, and again we made careful notes.

Teresa and Earl were then asked to confront each other in a senior staff group. Teresa accused Earl forthrightly. He was equally strong in his defense and in his charge that she had approached him and that he had turned her down. He maintained that he had never been in her apartment. They both sounded convincing. We agreed that we needed more facts.

We went on gathering evidence. Earl swore that on the evening in question he had been with Cesar Colon, a trainee who had recently been promoted to a counselor line. When questioned, Cesar backed Earl in his story. They had spent the evening together, he said. But now a second girl, Adele Hampton, came forward and said that Cesar was having an affair with Fatima, one of the girls he was counseling, that he had broken up his marriage and had moved in with her. Adele also said that Cesar and his new girlfriend both knew that Earl was interested in Teresa and had urged Teresa to go out with him.

When we asked Adele why she came forward with this information she said, "I've been here long enough to know the rules, I should have said something before. I felt guilty, knowing all that and not telling anyone. The counselors are not supposed to go out with the girls. There's a good reason for that. But I knew if I said anything it would cost Cesar his job. Then when I heard the lies that Earl was telling on Teresa and I saw that the staff was having all these meetings, I said, oh oh, I better tell what I know cause they are going to find it out anyway."

The staff questioned Fatima. She denied any involvement with Cesar. Cesar said that Adele had a grudge against him and was trying to do him as much damage as she could.

There were disbelief and dismay among the senior staff. Cesar had come a long way with us. We were proud of him and we relied upon him. The idea of probing into his life caused us much unhappiness. We put Cesar's case aside temporarily, hoping that if Earl were exonerated, Cesar too would be shown to be in the clear. But Cesar's name kept cropping up.

Teresa backed Adele's story in part. She did not know whether Cesar and Fatima were having an affair or living together, but she had seen them walking down the street holding hands in Cesar's neighborhood which was where her uncle lived. She said that Fatima had urged her to go out with Earl, saying that as a counselor, he would be a good catch. "Not if he loses his job, he won't," she described herself as having replied.

The staff was divided. Some thought that Teresa and Adele had formed an alliance against the two counselors out of pique. But others, I among them, thought that a commonsense view of the situation probably did not support such a notion. Considering Earl's history and his insecurity, it was possible that he might indeed be taking cocaine. Teresa and Adele were credible witnesses or seemed to be. They did not falter or trip over themselves or each other. They were both doing well in the program, about to get their G. E. D. diplomas and graduate from secretarial training. Teresa had always seemed somewhat stable; Adele had made spectacular progress at Argus, changing from a gaudily clothed, wild-haired chick, hung with plastic necklaces and bracelets, into a neat and conservatively dressed young lady who was ready for the business world. She and Teresa both had boyfriends of their own age, more or less, and were looking forward to getting good jobs.

Fatima was another matter. She had been doing well, but a recent drop in her attendance made us wonder what was going on in her life. Cesar was her counselor; he said he hadn't been able to win her confidence.

We interviewed Teresa's boyfriend. He confirmed that he had come by to move Teresa's furniture and had found Earl in the apartment with the two girls. Earl had departed immediately. The boyfriend had not seen any cocaine but had been told of it by the girls. He thought Earl was high on something.

Confronted with this witness Earl again denied that he was at the apartment, claiming that Teresa's boyfriend was lying and was out to get him.

"Why would I be out to get you, man? I was there. I can tell you what you had on and what kina car you was drivin. I watched you from the window." He gave details which were very convincing.

One or two staff members suggested that Teresa might have given him a description of the car, although others thought that they weren't likely to have gotten together on so many small items, such as, "I noticed your car before I even came upstairs because you had one of them white wooly dogs hangin from a string in front of the windshield. It had red eyes."

We had noted down the details as to time of day, where people were situated in the room, what they said and did, what they were wearing, et cetera. Without giving Teresa and her sister a chance to confer, we now interviewed the sister. Her story corroborated in every respect what Teresa and her boyfriend had reported. We figured that even if the sisters were in collusion, they wouldn't have been able to foresee or invent such a detailed story without being at variance in some particulars.

Confronted with the sister Earl changed his story. He now admitted that he had been there but said that Teresa had asked him to come and help her move some furniture.

"In that case," Aubrey said, "you should have spoken to your supervisor or to Mary Fritz, your director, to let them know of this request and what you intended to do about it. Did you do that?"

"No, I did not."

"Why not? Those are our rules. Were you aware of the rule that says you may not visit an enrollee's home without discussing the visit in advance with your superior?"

The staff asked Earl to excuse us so that we could consult in private. We were now unanimous in believing that Earl was not telling the truth about his visit to Teresa's apartment. We called Earl back and told him that we didn't believe his story, "But even if you weren't using cocaine as the girls claim, you yourself have admitted to a serious infringement of the rules. You visited Teresa at her apartment without informing your supervisor," Aubrey said. "What do you think we should do about it?"

"You don't have any choice but to fire me," Earl replied. Then, perhaps to clear his conscience, or maybe in the hope of being given another chance if we saw that he was willing to be honest, Earl admitted that everything the girls had said was true. "I did ask Teresa out and she refused. I have been snorting cocaine. I can't help it. It gives me a bigger bang than anything else I do. I can't seem to feel much of anything without it."

Earl also told us that Cesar and Fatima had been with him on several occasions, though he did not know, he said, whether they were living together or not.

When confronted with Earl, Cesar said, "You're lying. You're trying to pull me down with you."

But in the meanwhile a top staff member had seen Fatima and Cesar together in the front seat of his automobile on 149th Street and Willis Avenue.

At this point we asked ourselves whether Cesar was trying to get himself fired in order to go on unemployment insurance. Some people lead their lives that way, working long enough to get the insurance, then goofing off for six months to a year. We never knew because Cesar would not cop to a thing. He was very bitter and sarcastic. With heavy hearts the staff recommended unanimously that he be let go. That same afternoon someone hurled a chunk of conglomerate through the window of my car. Fortunately, Vincent heard the crash, brought the car around to the front and taped heavy plastic over the gaping hole. Cesar asked for and was granted two interviews in which he maintained that he had been framed by people who had it in for him.

Both Earl and Cesar exercised their right to ask me to reverse the decision of the senior staff. But I was not able to help either of them. We had spent a great deal of time and effort digging into the situation, weighing the facts. Everyone had his say. We made a decision that was consensual and unanimous.

Our next task was to hold a general meeting and answer the questions of a very anxious and restive staff and enrollees. We kept nothing back, and we encouraged them to express what they felt. The staff were disturbed that Cesar had been fired, scared that it might happen to them.

"Follow the rules and you'll have nothing to worry about," Mary Fritz told them. "We don't fire people, especially not valuable people like Cesar, unless there is an overriding reason. Play by the rules, do your jobs and you'll be okay."

We talked once again about the rationale behind our ban on counselors socializing with clients, except on special occasions, in the company of other staff and with the permission and knowledge of the staff.

The advantage of conducting such investigations with the participation of the senior staff is that when a large number of people are present and know what has gone on, the truth can be more widely and credibly disseminated. Rumors and misconceptions cannot take hold as easily. The atmosphere is less likely to become poisoned. If wild rumors are circulated, there will nearly always be some responsible person present to refute them. Firings—and even resignations—in a place like Argus, where the name of the game is people and there is a good deal of intimacy, are touchy affairs.

Almost as touchy are some of the program decisions that have to be made.

We thought that readmitting Pamela Harte to the program would be a simple matter. She had been on three-month compulsory leave from the Learning for Living Center for disruptive behavior *in extremis.* There had been agreement that a leave of absence, during which she would be tutored at the group home and would be helped to understand and overcome her behavior, was necessary. But though everyone had a different and very decided idea about how and under what conditions to readmit her, people didn't really want to hold a meeting—perhaps because there had been full agreement concerning the previous decision and it did seem like a straightforward matter to take her back into the program.

We had three phases at the time. Each phase leader had a different idea about which of the phases Pamela should be readmitted to. Aubrey LaFrance and I were approached separately by each leader and pressed to make a decision in favor of his or her approach. Although Pamela had progressed to Phase Three before she left, the Phase One people advanced a strong case for requiring that she start again from the beginning, as an example to the other enrollees and to drive home the lessons she had learned. Sandie Eno, who had tutored Pamela during her absence, thought the girl had made great progress and that it would be demeaning as well as superfluous to insist that she start again in Phase One. Sandie was afraid that close association with those just starting the program might cause Pamela to fall back when she should be consolidating her hard-won growth. Sandie pushed for reentry at her same level, and Connie Phillips, head of Phase Three, had no objection. Aubrey and others were afraid that the enrollees would see a return to Phase Three as a weakening of the structure.

"They would see it as rewarding bad behavior," Aubrey said. "I can just hear them. 'Man, these phases don't mean a thing. Look at Pamela, in Phase Three after she almost caused a riot around here. I ain't gonna work my butt off followin the rules if they don't mean nothing nohow.'"

Mary Fritz, administrator of the group home where Pamela lived, acknowledged that the girl had made progress. "But I'm not sure her growth is solid. She wants to come back to the Learning for Living Center and she'll say or do anything right now to get back. But I wonder if she could sustain that good behavior, especially if she goes right back among her old pals in Phase Three. Phase One would be too humiliating and Phase Three would be asking her to live up to a level she can't sustain. Why not let her reenter in Phase Two and work her way back up?"

My own thought at first was that Pamela had paid the heavy price of banishment. "I don't think we should penalize her further by putting her back. It would take the heart out of her," I said. However, I found myself agreeing with each of the viewpoints presented. Each one seemed to make sense.

We called the meeting. We had spent more time talking in pairs and three and foursomes than if we had called a meeting in the first place. I thought that the phase leaders were anxious and sitting on a lot of anger. Some of them had just moved into decision-making positions and were new to the senior staff.

Everyone presented his or her view of what ought to be done. I thought it would be hot and heavy, but as we talked and listened the tension lifted: there wasn't going to be any ideal solution. Then someone had a splendid idea. "Pamela has been 'visiting' the Learning for Living Center for three days, waiting to get back in. Let's send for the counselors and see if they have observed anything about her that might help us."

The counselors told us that Pamela's behavior had been less than acceptable in terms of Phase Three and in fact not good enough to land her in Phase Two. She had been acting in a high-handed and arrogant fashion, and it was thought she might be up to some of her old tricks. This threw an entirely new light on the situation. Unanimously we concluded that Pamela must start over again in Phase One. This would jolt her into reality. At the same time, we would save her self-esteem and allow her to work her way into Phase Two within two weeks and, if her behavior was good, to move into Phase Three after only a month. We were all quite pleased with the solution. The phase leaders felt that their opinion had been listened to and that things had been settled pretty much as they hoped.

Pamela was invited into the meeting and told us that she was eager to return. She got some feedback about that and about her most recent behavior. She protested that our shilly-shallying had made her very frustrated. We told her that we understood how she felt, that we had indeed taken a long time, but that it was important for her growth to work on tolerating situations which did not immediately give her what she wanted. She was willing to begin again at Phase One and promised to work hard at getting back to Phase Three. She received praise for a paper she had written while on leave on the history of her family, how she came to be in placement and how hurt and abandoned and angry it made her feel. Everyone welcomed her return to the

Learning for Living Center. She shed quite a few tears but left us in a joyful mood.

The difference between democratic and consensual decision making is that democracy tends to polarize viewpoints (and actions). The lever at the voting booth can only register a yes or a no. Most people feel that no one has heard their view. And indeed they haven't been allowed to tell how and why and what reservations they may have. Consensus can absorb all shades of opinion, and no decision is taken until a working agreement has been reached by all parties. The result is a feeling of participation, dignity and satisfaction unlike any other. We consistently find that this nonadversarial, high context method of investigation and decision making enables people who are at fault to admit it, pay the price and regain the respect of themselves and of the community. Whether they continue at Argus, return after an enforced leave or move on somewhere else, the fact that they have made their peace protects them from that special paranoia that can creep over all parties when ambiguity and uncertainty prevail.

We came to consensus through trial and error, as a result of my belief in the "task force" approach, which enabled us to change roles and areas of endeavor frequently. It was also a natural outgrowth of the group work which is always going on at Argus and of a culturally conditioned predilection among many staff members. I was drawn to consensus partly out of an embarrassment I felt as a white, middle-class woman administering a multi ethnic program and "telling" people who were members of disadvantaged minorities how to run their lives. I tried to keep in the background, encouraging them to make the decisions. What developed was beautiful. They insisted on my input, saying that it was important to them. I stopped apologizing and began to take pleasure in the power which we all shared. My delight in the process grows greater every year for experience has taught us beyond a doubt that decisions taken together are much better tailored to the situation and are more apt to stick. In consensus we use all available talents and all powers, and the variety and richness of it, the sheer creativity, as well as the harmony which ensues, are more than worth the effort we put into it.

And the process is fascinating of itself. It is one of the games we teach people to play for keeps.

21. THE PAPER BOA CONSTRICTOR
What Bureaucracies Do

Each time the victim breathes out, the boa tightens its coils until the animal dies of suffocation.

MAURICE AND ROBERT BURTON, *The Animal Kingdom*

It would be futile for me to take up my cat-o'-nine-tails and deliver another forty lashes to bureaucracy. The Old Monster, which has been around since ancient times, is excoriated daily by politicians, business persons, social scientists and consumers who rail against its inefficiency, wastefulness, irrelevancy and irrationality, as well as its self-serving and self-perpetuating qualities. But bureaucracy, as we know it, is on its last legs—not because so many of us have ardently wished for its demise but because it is outmoded. Its methods, well-suited to rising industrialism, are being sidestepped because they cannot respond to the varied and unpredictable needs of the postindustrial society. In contrast, a less hierarchical, task force approach enables interdisciplinary teams put together on an ad hoc basis to zero in on problems demanding immediate responses and specific kinds of technical knowledge that may not be relevant to the next day's problems. Toffler calls this new mode, becoming prevalent in both business and government, Ad-hocracy.[1]

I employed the task force approach at Argus from the beginning, but met with sabotage from within our own ranks by starchy inheritors of British colonialism from the West Indies, by hispanics with a strong sense of position for its own sake, and by others who have a love affair with rank, exclusiveness and the art of embalming processes on paper. I expected resistance from the bureaucrats who fund and monitor our program; it was forthcoming. Government agencies are threatened by any system different from their own, although they are being pushed into adopting some variant of Ad-hocracy themselves.

Argus simply cannot keep its head above water if we hang days, weeks or even months while requests creep up the chain of command and decisions filter down again. Often the person at the top of the pyramid has little expertise, is too far removed from the problem,

298

doesn't have enough facts to make wise decisions—or the situation may have changed radically one day after the toilsome process was initiated.

Typical of the general unworkability of the bureaucratic and hierarchical system is the swamp we got mired in when Argus had to create office space for a new program in 1978. The funds were available. Everyone agreed that the offices were necessary, that the project personnel had to have a place to operate from. The boa got us by the throat because the funding agency did not know whose permission would be needed or what portion of the budget could be spent for renovations of space.

We were launching a one-year research project. The start-up date was October. Guidelines permitting the renovations would not be forthcoming from the agency until the following May. The only sensible thing was to go ahead with the renovation, which we did, quickly and inexpensively. We created five offices and a waiting room in three weeks for $3,000, using our own labor. The staff moved in and had been occupying the offices and running the project for eight months when permission came for us to go ahead and create the needed space.

Although we had informed the contract manager in writing of our reasons for jumping the gun and she had given us verbal permission, she had not put it in a letter; we, caught up in other matters, neglected to press for one. She now took the position that permission had not been granted and that we could not be reimbursed for the renovation. We challenged this and eventually the case wended its irksome way to the top. The commissioner and his chief financial officer reviewed the evidence, heard our story and decided in our favor. The contract manager, who did not agree with the decision, dragged her heels for a year and a half.

The research project was laid to rest and another contract with the same agency was pending before the Board of Estimate when, out of the mire of papers, the old chimera of $3,000 owed us arose transmogrified as money owed by Argus to the funding agency. We were described as being in default and the Board of Estimate refused to pass our new contract. Fortunately, we had proof that not only did we not owe the money but that the shoe was on the other foot. Quick action by a key person of diplomacy and goodwill saved the day. The new contracts went through. The $3,000 was paid to us in 1980—one year after the project ended, two years after we laid the money out. Nevertheless, in 1982 the agency again billed us for the same $3,000.

This may strike the reader as a petty affair. But continuous scrimmaging of this kind tears the tendons, jars the nerves, slams at the vital organs and harrows the soul. For the first few years I looked upon these entanglements as a challenge, a game to be played hard and won if possible; if not, take your licks and smile. But in about the fifth year the game turned grim. The rules are set in such a way that with the best will in the world you are forced into an adversarial position. Of course, there are always, within any bureaucracy, individuals who will put your papers on the top of the pile and push them along expeditiously and will do anything in their power to help. They are decent, conscientious persons, and they deserve much praise. I have found generally that commissioners and people at the top are intelligent and understanding. But one compulsive neurotic or one sadist can play Russian roulette with kids' lives and set our administrative department boiling, hissing and thumping its lid.

One of the problems we face nowadays is not that bureaucracies don't change, but that they change too quickly and too often. Officials seem to have a different title, phone number and office every time you talk to them. They can scarcely remember you, and they often don't know who has taken over the management of your contract or what the guidelines currently are. After several meetings and much negotiation, terms are agreed upon, then just as the plan is to become final it is scrapped. The old guidelines have been discarded; the former negotiators are no longer on the scene: and the whole laborious business has to be started again from scratch.

The people in my finance department are especially dear to me. They work behind the scenes, seldom reaping any credit or praise. I do not know how they endure all the squeezing and suffocating they get from the bureaucracies, public and private.

Sudhir Patel, our fiscal officer, is especially easy to get along with. He has a high-pitched contagious giggle which is permitted to Hindu men. His manliness is of a tender, emotional stamp. He and his colleague, Ru Mei Wang, who is from Taiwan and with whom we communicated for a time only in the lingua franca of ledgers and balance sheets, keep our books in enviable order. Sudhir neutralizes bureaucrats by perfuming and bathing them in great gushes of reason, complaint, and cajolery.

But even the limber Sudhir has been subject to the coils of the boa. On more than one occasion a Project Operating Plan, known as a POP, has managed to get him by the throat. The POP is a twenty-one-page form in which we are required to present a breakdown of any given youth employment project in terms of administrative costs, fringe benefits, direct costs, indirect costs and contractual costs in dollar amounts and in percentages of the total budget. In addition, we must provide a breakdown of dollar amounts and percentages charged to administration, training, services, participant benefits, wages and allowances. Next, we must figure out the budget in each of the categories in quarterly and in accumulative terms. The figures change for each quarter as the budget is spent. For each staff person in a project we must figure out the hourly wage rate, the number of hours to be worked each week and the number of weeks to be worked in the year. Then for each staff person we must figure the time split between the administrative, training and service areas. Employee benefits and all other budget categories must be broken down in similar fashion among these three areas. Every category has its base ratio. Telephones and utilities are broken down by number of square feet used by the program; supplies are broken down by the number of participants, et cetera.

"Normal" individuals require three days to prepare a POP. Because of his exceptional agility and long experience, Sudhir can complete a POP in a day. Sudhir seldom makes mistakes, but he cannot defend himself against changes in the guidelines.

One April day Sudhir came into my office in the last stages of dissolution. "I must be reaping the results of several lifetimes of bad actions," he groaned. "That man [the contract manager] is a torturer. Each time I prepare the POP he changes his mind about some detail and I have to do it all over again from beginning to end. Here is a list of the thirteen different ways I had to prepare the POP, all because he kept changing his mind."

I looked at the list. The contract manager had required that Sudhir: (1) prepare the POP for one year at a 7 percent cost of living increase; (2) redo the POP based on a different budget amount; (3) prepare it for a six-month period; (4) prepare it for six months with a reduction in staff; (5) prepare it for six months with no cost of living increase; (6) redo it without participants' wages included; (7) redo it again without equipment; (8) put some of the equipment back in; (9) prepare it with work site supplies; (10) take out work site supplies; (11) prepare the POP with a four decimal point breakdown in salaries and fringe; (12) prepare the figures to the penny; (13) round off the figures.

Each reworking of the POP required one day of Sudhir's time. Six copies had to be made each time, three for the funding agency, three for Argus. That makes seventy-eight copies. Each copy contained 21 pages, adding up to 1,638 pages. That comes to $245 and change for the copying machine alone. Meanwhile the bureaucracy was haggling endlessly over smaller sums in the budget under the rubric of saving money.

"This contract manager deserves to be reborn as a goat," I said. "Or perhaps as a donkey. But no, that would be too good for him. He should be condemned to come back as a hookworm in the entrails of a pig." I knew that Sudhir would not give the man any kind of a curse, even if he had tried to kill him, because he believes that Yoga power could be turned against him; but I suspected he wouldn't mind if I did it for him. And indeed, he seemed to derive gratification from it and gave me a smile.

Lord Swaminarayan—Lord Krishna incarnated—once paid a visit to the home of Sudhir's great-great-grandfather, a consummate honor. The family sprinkled the sole of the god's foot with Kum-Kum (the powder young married women use to mark their foreheads) and caused Lord Swaminarayan to step on a sheet of blank paper, leaving his footprint. This footprint of the god is the most cherished possession of the Patel family. An elder brother has it now in Vidayanagar, a town of 36,000 founded by Sudhir's grandfather. The footprint of the god figures in the family worship, and although Sudhir is now many thousands of miles away in America, he is conscious of the distinction it bestows upon his line.

Sudhir believes that bureaucrats will get their comeuppance. "Whatever you do, you get," he says. "You eat onions, your breath will smell of onions. We had a cow, sometimes she ate onions. Her milk tasted like onions. If you do a good thing for society, you will get extra breaths of life. A bonus. God keeps the account for everybody. He keeps the balance sheet for the bureaucrats. God has no name and no shape, but anywhere you go, God is there. Anything you do, don't think that nobody is watching. Someday the bureaucrats will get it."

Beatrice Frank is a trim, disciplined person with iron-gray wavy hair, a humane face, large, eloquent brown eyes and a radiant smile. As our finance assistant since 1969 (when she returned to the work-place after bringing up her sons) Bea puts in five hours a day paying bills, preparing the payroll, disbursing petty cash and seeing to it that not a penny of our money is out of place. At two o'clock she walks to the subway and spends anywhere from forty-five minutes to an hour and a half, depending on the service, getting back to Pelham Park. Once in her apartment she devotes herself to housewifely tasks with religious zeal. Were it not for Bea we would not—quite literally, I think—be in existence. Few women would have the courage to come into our neighborhood by public transportation, seldom missing a day, except for vacations and the Jewish holidays, all these years. "If

I didn't feel so involved I wouldn't be here at Argus all these years. I suppress my fears. I have learned to be aware. I enjoy. I agree with the work being done here."

Part of her job has been to badger Con Edison and the New York Telephone Company, bureaucracies every bit as erratic and remorseless as any government agency. Years ago when the IRS was investigating the tax-exempt status of the telephone company, the organizations it serves came under investigation also. The telephone company has a special department for the tax-exempt agencies and we fell in for our share of interrogation. The IRS decided that we were not exempt from the excise tax. Bea has corresponded with them for years on this subject. They are demanding that we pay the excise tax but we cannot comply because no one has ever decided how much the tax should be.

Water, sewage and real estate taxes on the properties we own are a source of much aggravation. We have applied for and have received tax exemption for each of our buildings, yet the status of one or another of them is constantly under question. No one at the office of the Tax Commission seems able to locate the documents. We will suddenly receive a bill for back taxes with interest and penalties. Setting the record straight may require Sisyphean labor.

Once Bea Frank discovered that for several years Con Edison had been charging us for electricity on a meter which was not in use during that time. Bea's negotiations, carried on indomitably over several years, and after the most protean resistance, resulted in a recovery of the overpayment.

In 1976 we moved our headquarters from a totally burned out and ravaged area to a "neighborhood in transition," where mixed housing, including low income projects, made the long-term prospects for survival of the neighborhood seem brighter. Our former buildings had been wired against intruders, but the funding agencies decided that no such protection was needed after our move. We had as always a certain number of fairly new enrollees with one foot in crime, and they and others in the area quickly became aware of our vulnerability. The building was broken into and our administrative offices and classrooms were robbed nightly for over a month while we wrangled with bureaucrats who considered it a waste of money to install a burglar alarm system. Finally, after all our typewriters, calculators and teaching machines and much more had been taken, we were given the green light and the system was installed.

The protection service we employed at the time is a bureaucracy of itself. The alarms, electronic eyes and response systems by and large kept thieves and vandals at bay. But its employees range from indifferent to alienated. What are we to conclude about the employee who came to Argus at 2:00 A.M. on the Friday of a long holiday weekend, ascertained that the alarm had been set off by water pouring down from a fourth-floor bathroom and left without alerting any of the staff members whose telephone numbers were available to be called in emergencies? His explanation, offered the following Tuesday, after $30,000 worth of flood damage had been done, was that it was his duty to report burglaries and nothing else.

Bea Frank: "It is my experience that people in bureaucracies are taught not to make waves, not to make decisions and not to do anything that is not strictly within their job descriptions. No one can make a decision because no one can take the responsibility for it. Nobody seems to know what they are doing. And you know, they are very unhappy people. They are held down and they can't express anything. That all adds up to a lot of things that don't turn out well and that don't work."

The most desperate encounters between our fiscal people and bureaucrats are when government funding grinds to a halt (which we hope will be temporary) as the legislature tries to get its act together, and we experience a cash flow lag. During these periods we have to borrow from the bank to meet our payrolls. Bea casts some sort of spell over Con Edison, the telephone company and the vendors, which deters them from shutting down the services. Con Edison is the toughest customer, threatening us almost daily, but Bea has always managed to stave them off. Now they are familiar with her; they see that she is there, year after year, and that in time we do pay.

From each bureaucracy we get a lot of paper, enough to make up a fat book. But none of it tells us how to teach kids to help themselves. Much of it impedes our efforts. Still, the money that we receive adds up to a lot of resources and a generous amount of confidence reposed in Argus. We do not wish to seem ungrateful. Yet no matter how hard we try to synthesize these slivers of government funding into a program capable of treating the whole person, we remain essentially fragmented and disjointed.

One impelling need is for general support—unrestricted funds which can be used flexibly and without red tape to fill the gaps in government programs. But since the Tax Reform Act of 1969 foundations have tended to act like mini-government funding agencies, earmarking their grants for specific purposes and eliciting proposals which purport to carry out some innovative experiment or develop a program which can be replicated or can effect systemic change. In fact, both the public and private sector encourage charitable agencies to throw themselves out of shape year after year by going after one- to three-year funding for "research" and "knowledge development" projects when what they really need are operating funds.

A game is played, with operators attempting to manipulate and squeeze their needs out of the "research," while their "adversaries," the funding agencies, tighten the controls in order to see that the "research" and nothing else gets done. One official told us, "We are interested only in research. Quite frankly, we do not care whether you have a program or not."

Many of today's "research" programs are a desperate casting about for quick, paste-up solutions to problems which cry out for major social engineering after a reordering of priorities. Our young clients are labeled "socially maladjusted," "emotionally disturbed," "handicapped," "drug addicted," "delinquent," and "incorrigible," and slivers of programs are devised to correct their various defects and deficits, when at the root of the matter is their inability to cope with schools that do not respond, streets that bombard them with drugs and crime opportunities and their own low self-esteem and unpreparedness for a job market that is prejudiced against them.

Bureaucracies by and large are lined up squarely on the side of the status quo. They are mandated to be so. This is demonstrated in their willingness to underwrite liberal rent payments to commercial landlords of deplorable buildings in the South Bronx and elsewhere. Argus began by leasing space but found itself operating in buildings where the leaking roof was not fixed from one year to the next, the faucets ran red muck and where we froze solid on Mondays and Fridays and thawed out only slightly on Tuesdays, Wednesdays and Thursdays. Two different landlords told us when we complained, "Don't make too many waves. I can abandon these buildings at any time. Or a fire could break out." They weren't joking. At that time I regularly counted up to seventeen fires as I drove home each evening. But the rent was in the budget and had to be paid. There was no recourse and not even a quiver of interest in our dilemma from any quarter.

Argus severed these unhappy connections and bought its own buildings. We were confident that by acting as our own landlord we would be able to provide and enjoy nonleaking roofs, warmth in winter, pipes that spout clear water, walls that are properly plastered and painted, doors that lock, doorknobs that turn, windows that open and shut, toilets that flush. We planned to provide these amenities, to make swift repairs, to meet the building, fire and licensing codes and to spend less money than before. And indeed we achieved these ends. The worm in the apple is that none of our funding sources will pay for space costs. They were willing to pay a private landlord substantial sums of money to give disgracefully little, but we as nonprofit owners of our premises are not eligible or are not *considered* eligible for space use payments.

We are willing to take less than commercial building owners, to commit ourselves to a high standard of upkeep and to enter into a legal arrangement whereby all monies in excess of repairs and maintenance would be plowed back into the program. We so desperately need flexible dollars to glue the patchwork together and make it respond in a coherent way to the needs of the children that a modest rental payment would be very welcome indeed. But we are not even allowed to accrue funds for the emergency repairs needed when, for example, thieves made away with the copper flashing on our roof and a flood wreaked havoc with the entire west side of our building. We lived with water seeping in at the roofline and in a state of mildewed and peeling decay on one side of our building for two years until we could raise money to repair the damage. We get modest depreciation payments from one source, and two agencies allow out-of-pocket maintenance costs and minor repairs. But we are left flapping about distractedly when it comes to major repairs. As for the pressing programmatic need to make the surroundings inviting and attractive by redecorating and revamping, forget it. Only if someone can find the time and energy to mount a fund-raising campaign. Meanwhile we chip away on both fronts, trying to make the bureaucracy reconsider and raising what money we can.

Nothing that bureaucracies do is quite so out of order and so corrosive, however, as their demand that we write up short- and long-range treatment plans and keep elaborate folders which purport to record what happens in each interaction with our enrollees. There is simply not enough *time* both to interact and to write it down. Argus is not alone in its adverse reaction to these requirements, which have been greatly stepped up in the last two years as the medical model, coming down from Washington, has pushed other approaches aside. Many programs and clinics find themselves overburdened. A friend of mine resigned from Montefiore Hospital because she could not do the paperwork *and* give proper attention to the treatment of persons on her psychotherapeutic caseload.

Although we have always kept demographic and program records these were organized along simpler lines. In addition to the basic intake data, we have always collected information about the attendance, the movement of persons through the program, the length of stay, the goals achieved, the number of terminations and the reasons why people left. We keep track of academic and vocational gains, of changes in behavior and attitude, measured by objective yardsticks (such as involvement in drugs or the criminal justice system, getting a G.E.D., entering college or employment) or other outcomes, favorable, neutral (moved out of the area, for example), or unfavorable (drugs, prostitution, prison, welfare). Counselor, teacher, parent and peer impressions of personal and social growth are considered of interest in assessing outcomes and are noted down. These records we regard as indispensable to the process of assessing our own effectiveness, curtailing certain activities, expanding or devising new compoments. But even this much record keeping strains our slender resources.

The record-keeping schemata which we and other agencies are required to follow is no doubt intended as a means of detecting and cutting back on waste and fraud. We applaud the motive but deplore the fact that agencies such as Argus, which have developed methods appropriate to today's egregious problems, should be pressed into a program and record-keeping mode suitable to an outdistanced age when social workers and counselors had contact with clients once or twice a week for an hour or two and had time to write down their impressions of the interview. How can we create, sustain and continuously modify and amend an entire environment, act as an extended family, incorporate kids into a structure and a value system and in addition find the time to record our every interaction?

This is not to say that staff members of the kind that Argus employs (ex-welfare mothers, ex-addicts, ex-criminals) are not capable of mastering the intricacies of bureaucratic record keeping. Substantial numbers of our staff over the years have learned to perform these tasks, some with unusual proficiency and even flair. But they cannot fill out forms, write case histories and treatment plans, et cetera, *and* meet the needs of the youngsters. It is the latter task which they ought to be performing because that is what the funds were intended for, that is what the taxpayers want and that is what we must do unless we want young persons preying upon us like a pack of lions upon the herd, or parasites leeching us of our life substance.

The bureaucracies are dying as the dinosaurs died, because the cold climate of the postindustrial society is getting to them. Their blood is too sluggish to reach their up-in-the-clouds heads or their overburdened limbs.

The New York City Board of Education, and the school system

at large, is seen by many as dysfunctional in terms of today's needs. Argus, which provides a site and the pupils for a cluster school staffed by special education teachers, has gone through good times and bad with the Board of Education. A great deal depends upon leadership: a principal can make or break a school—but so can those in charge at the headquarters of the board. For six years after inviting board teachers onto our premises we were protected from one principal who was a bigot and very punitive and another who was weak and sentimental by the vigilant persons at headquarters who had a vivid appreciation of what we were doing and wanted us to continue. They visited us frequently and gave instructions that since the young persons at Argus were moving ahead at an accelerated pace in their studies, teachers and board personnel should fall in with our program, even though it required that teachers adopt nontraditional methods. The third principal assigned to us was fairminded, appreciative of the results we were getting but remote and looking toward his retirement, which soon took place. He was followed by a man who seemed to thrive on divisiveness. After two demoralizing years we were given a new head with a positive outlook.

During our early years with the board, teachers participated in groups and case conferences, and all on site Board of Education personnel, including administrators, met with the Argus staff once a month, oftener if necessary, to work out problems, share experiences and make plans in concert. We were allowed to participate in the selection process when new teachers were assigned to Argus. Our policy was to give every teacher a chance to work with us and for the most part they have been able to do so. Over the years, eight teachers have shown themselves unsuitable to work with attention-hungry and highly volatile minority adolescents. Four moved on to other assignments, while the other four hung on tenaciously. Most of the classrooms are orderly and real teaching can take place, since the pupils have been made receptive by our environment.

We have had teachers who literally ate, smoked, read the newspapers and slept in the classroom, presented themselves under the influence of alcohol, demeaned the kids, and behaved provocatively (which is extremely dangerous, given our population), but these teachers were not removed. The excuse was that it is almost impossible, under the union contract and the cumbersome procedures mandated, to remove a teacher. None of our principals have made the effort.

Under the United Federation of Teachers contract just about all that is required of teachers beyond formal credentials is that they bring their bodies to the classrooms. The principals are seldom on our premises, having other cluster (institutional) schools to supervise; and teachers seem to know when to expect them and to behave accordingly. Consequently, so we are told, the proper documentation for transferral cannot be assembled. It seems that an atom bomb is required to dislodge a public school teacher.

In the most flourishing schools, principals work vigorously to find good teachers and get rid of bad ones. Fortunately for us, nonproductive teachers assigned to Argus are in the minority. Most of our teachers work cooperatively with us, and six or seven are inspired and dedicated. All the teachers attend case conferences, though a few have not participated productively. From 1978 to 1980 we went through our lowest period with the Board of Education. But since then we have had a principal and an on-site administrator who are very cooperative and who have put an end to the divisiveness, backbiting and chaos prevalent before they came. Under their leadership and with the help of their new supervising principal and others at headquarters, the atmosphere improved so dramatically as to be almost unrecognizable.

We have had nine good years out of eleven with the Board of Education—an exceptional record. We are not ungrateful. Still, we know that some new disaster may be visited upon us at the whim of administrators too far removed to know the quality of our work and what it demands.

Even during the best of times with the Board of Education we find ourselves in very frustrating situations. Some teachers assigned to us don't use good teaching materials, don't make adequate lesson plans. We cannot persuade any of them to give homework, even though middle-class students tell me that in order to maintain even a C average they must do at least two hours of homework each night. These teachers are set in their ways; they do what they were doing twenty-five years ago, and resist change. Few care to rock the boat. Staying comfortable and going for the pension seems to be the pervasive goal. A program such as Argus, which must engage in a great deal of remediation, socially, emotionally, vocationally and academically, really cannot function at its optimum without an innovative accelerated academic program and devoted teachers. Our program would be more effective were we able to select our teachers. The same is true for the public education system generally. Until we make up our minds to hold teachers and administrators accountable and write such accountability into their contracts we will have no real hope of rescuing our educational system. Productivity and good working conditions for teachers are not incompatible.

At Argus we have done our best work by sidestepping and evading those bureaucratic requirements that would have forced us into the traditional social-work mold. This has been particularly true in our group home program, where we have persistently done it our way while keeping the required papers flowing. We have taken in PINS, assaultive, suicidal, abusive and other hard-to-work-with adolescents and have been able to incorporate them into an orderly, productive and loving environment. Only 5 of our girls out of 149 are now on welfare. The rest are in college, advanced training or nonsubsidized jobs, have been returned to their parents or are still in high school. We have no information on 9 who went AWOL and/or disappeared from view, so the number on welfare may be higher; but so may the number supporting themselves and paying taxes. The administration at Human Resources Administration (HRA) has been impressed with these results, and we are presently expanding our group home program to include boys. In recent years there have been repeated charges by the City Comptroller's office, by watchdog groups and by the office of the President of the City Council that the child-care agencies, public and private, including those operated by the major religious charities, have been providing poor care for homeless, neglected, abused and abandoned children, while receiving generous sums of money for the purpose (payments per day per child in 1983 was $54.60 for intensive care and $58.95 for extraordinary care). These agencies have been accused of not feeding or clothing the children adequately, of not planning for them, of keeping children in foster care when adoption was more appropriate in order to collect the money for their care, of deliberately misclassifying children as disturbed and troublesome in order to obtain higher rates of reimbursement, of padding their expenditures, of entering into "sweetheart" arrangements with landlords, taking kickbacks, et cetera. City officials were said to be allied with the powerful charitable groups and, with an eye to employment in private agencies after they left the administration, were not demanding accountability or performance. I am not in a position to evaluate these charges, but enough information comes to us in our dealings with children and agencies to know that the quality of care generally is not good. I was told by an evaluator for the Citizens Committee for Children who visited many of the group homes in the city that she did not find a single one which she could rate as passable.

Board members and administrators from other group homes are now beginning to look at our methods. We are eager to share with them, but we know that unless they really want to change and unless an entire agency, from top to bottom, is incorporated into the process, the graft will not "take."

Bureaucracies reject change from the outside. Yet they are changing from within. The New York State Division for Substance Abuse Services (DSAS) has made radical changes in the last several years, sloughing off programs which did not work and reorganizing around the most hopeful and productive of those programs that had evolved essentially out of the genius of street people: the drug-free programs. So far, in spite of the catastrophic results, neither the Congress nor the federal and state agencies have been willing to say goodbye to methadone maintenance. Every generation has tried to fight the plague of drug addiction with its own pet drug of the era, just as addictive and destructive as the one it purported to cure. Dr. Robert Dupont, an early methadone advocate, recently expressed disillusionment with methadone, and support for the drug-free model. DSAS is actively encouraging drug-free programs and has hired Julio Martinez, an ex-addict and former executive director of a drug-free therapeutic community, as director of their state-wide effort.

It may be that the most fragmented, divisive and contradictory system we deal with is the Family Court. Mandated to treat children as children, to act in their best interests, and deal with them in a context other than that of crime and punishment, the Family Court was set up in such a way that its process hardens adversarial relations between parents and children, saddles children with labels and negative identities and exposes them to case-hardened criminals, immorality and corruption. The concept of children's rights was scarcely recognized until Gerald Francis Gault, a minor appellant, and his parents, brought his case to the Supreme Court of the United States in 1967. Gerald was fifteen years old. He had been sentenced to six years for an offense which at eighteen would have brought him a $5 to $50 fine and two months in jail. The opinion of the Supreme Court was delivered by the late Justice Abe Fortas in a landmark decision, reversing the Supreme Court of Arizona and establishing the right of children to due process.

Before Gault, children were regularly imprisoned for conduct which in an adult would not be considered appropriate for court action. Since Gault, children, by and large, have had representation in court. However, the discretionary powers of Family Court judges are extremely broad, calendars are usually glutted and there is still a plethora of problems. Instead of being rehabilitative and helpful to children, the Family Court as constituted is often punitive and stigmatizing. Runaways, rebellious children and truants, often reacting to intolerable conditions at home, on the streets and in school, are treated as burgeoning criminals.

Most children who appear in Family Court in our experience (and we maintained personnel there for several years) have committed very trifling offenses. Speaking recently before the Justice Ministry Task Force of the Council of Churches, Judge Edith Miller of the Family Court stated that only about 10 percent of the young persons before the Family Court have committed serious offenses. Unfortunately this small group of hard-core offenders have been singled out by the media to such an extent that the public completely misreads the problem. Judge Miller spoke of poor education, inadequate health care (which may impede educational development) and lack of support systems for single parents as among the glaring crimes that the social order inflicts on children.

For several years the issue of whether to take status offenders (PINS in New York) out of the jurisdiction of the Family Court has been of great concern in many states. These noncriminals are often punished more severely than young persons who have committed serious offenses. I believe that status offenders should be removed from the jurisdiction of the courts for several reasons: (1) their "offenses"—just as in the case of drunkenness, homosexuality and consensual sex acts, vagrancy, gambling and prostitution—are relatively harmless and clog the courts, making it difficult to identify, prosecute and convict dangerous young criminals who are a serious threat to society; (2) processing status offenders in the juvenile justice system benefits no one and indeed is harmful; (3) court appearance and "placement," which all too often adds up to imprisonment, is unjust and is out of keeping with the kind of harm perpetrated by the children, which is noncriminal in nature; and (4) it has in no way been established that truants and "incorrigibles" who are wards of the state become better educated or better behaved than those who remain on the street.

It is argued that if the Family Court does not handle these cases no one else will. In our observation, it is precisely because the court does handle these cases that other agencies do not. Parents and agencies rely upon the courts to perform a function which is essentially one of socialization and humanization. The courts are in no way equipped to do this job and unruly, disobedient and out of control children do not get their needs met as a result of being haled into court. What happens is that parents and children are set against one another when what they in fact need is mediation, along with effective help and support outside the courts. Some argue that we must wait until other services are in place before we take PINS out of the court. I contend, with many others, that as long as the court gives the *illusion* of providing services, real services in the community are not likely to be developed.

In our experience, it is more difficult to reconcile children and parents who have been pitted against each other in adversary proceedings in court. The bulk of PINS ordered removed from the home are placed in juvenile justice facilities, albeit special and separate ones for status offenders. Children are not capable of making such fine distinctions (I find it difficult myself) and are apt to see themselves as sentenced criminals.

The situation is even more confusing because many of these children come into court on delinquency petitions and their cases are bargained down to PINS charges, a fact well known to the youngsters, inviting the conclusion that the PINS category is not distinct from that of delinquency. The fact that many PINS petitions are brought by parents who ought themselves to be before the court on charges of abuse and neglect adds to the confusion and bitterness of children who perceive that they are being scapegoated for their parents' shortcomings.

The National Council on Crime and Delinquency, the Institute of Judicial Administration/American Bar Association Joint Commission on Juvenile Justice Standards and numerous other organizations have concluded that years of experience with the PINS mechanism has demonstrated that it is ineffective and inappropriate, that it creates the illusion of services where none exist and leaves families without the assistance they need. Moreover, PINS procedures distract the court from other critical matters. As long ago as 1967 the President's Commission on Law Enforcement and Administration of Justice called for eliminating the PINS jurisdiction.[2]

The Vera Institute *Family Court Disposition Study* (1980) found that 41 percent of PINS cases had been before the court previously, coming back to clog the system at a time when concentration on serious and violent offenders is urgently needed.[3]

In contrast, the PINS Mediation Project of the Children's Aid Society, targeting those cases which were referred on petition and diverting children and families into mediation, found that only 8 percent of those they worked with returned to the court on new PINS petitions. In its work the PINS Mediation Project, directed by Margaret Shaw, an attorney with an excellent understanding of the problem, focuses on conflict as a family matter, rather than singling out the child as being at fault and emphasizes the power that lies within families to deal with and ameliorate their own conflicts.[4]

Courts have not been and never will be able to settle family conflicts. Legislatures in several states have amended the code by eliminating or seriously curtailing the status offense jurisdiction. The State of Washington in 1979 made parents responsible for keeping their children in school, rather than the truanting children who had formerly been haled before the court. Colorado abolished its CINS category (similar to PINS) and enacted a "child needing oversight" category, giving the courts control over children "whose behavior or condition is such as to endanger his or others' welfare" and removing truancy and runaway behavior to the neglected category—a step in the right direction, although the language is vague. Delaware in 1978 amended its code to eliminate the status offender jurisdiction and adding truancy to the neglect and dependent category. Pennsylvania in 1978 removed "habitual disobedience" from the delinquency category (formerly children could be confined in state training schools for this offense, along with delinquents).

Serious juvenile criminality, a most threatening aspect of crime in our country, cries out to be dealt with expeditiously and forcefully. A Family Court clogged with PINS and minor delinquency cases cannot address itself adequately to the serious juvenile crimes that are causing us so much concern. A major reorganization of the Family Court is called for in New York and other states, particularly those with large cities. Legislatures, assisted by the federal government, should make provision for dealing with PINS and lesser delinquency cases in the community in programs like Argus that can socialize and promote the growth of these young persons and prepare them to become productive adults and taxpayers. We must acknowledge that our dream of the juvenile court as a surrogate family and rehabilitative force has never worked and replace it with a realistic effort.

The Family Court and many other social service organizations and bureaucracies are not able to do the job in today's world. We must provide them with the direction and resources for retooling. We have no other viable choice.

22. WHERE DO WE GO FROM HERE?

One day I said grandma
What do you think America
Will be when I get 53?
Will it be like a big ugly
Tree or a pretty little butterfly
Sitting on my knee?
She said "Baby I cannot say,
But if I had my way
I would surely try and make it
A better day."

ARGUS ENROLLEE at age 14

It is ironic that in the South Bronx I have a cheerful tale to tell. I have chosen to focus upon the vitality and fecundity of a people rather than upon incendiarism and devastation and our indifference to it.

When nature goes on the rampage, we take up the challenge. But we sit Lazarus-like on our chronic, man-made sores—perhaps because we secretly believe that we are being punished for our sins, which in a way we are. And we hide behind rhetoric and unkept promises.

The nation's inner cities can be reclaimed. Argus, created by ghetto residents, staffed by them, managed by them, with help from the outside, teaches children how to heal their pain, reach for a broader world and live in it. Their achievement can be a reference point for efforts on a larger scale.

However, the notion that a program utilizing x, y and z techniques can be replicated by lifting out the formula and applying it elsewhere is misleading. Methods are important, certainly, but the key elements are the human beings who do the work of socialization—and the concept of the extended family and the mini-society, as well as the principle of self-help, fostered in the youths themselves. Without teamwork and the understanding and cooperation of an entire agency, such an environment cannot be created.

In the coming year we hope to launch, with help from Special Services for Children and private foundations, a Training Institute

315

and Resource Center for Child-Care Agencies, where voluntary organizations can receive training in the development of this type of
community for adolescents. We welcome the Institute as a training
vehicle for our own staff and have assurance that other voluntary and
public agencies will participate as well. Training would bring all levels
of staff together. They would be immersed in sufficient numbers to
return and "naturalize" the concepts within their own agencies.

The Institute would address long-standing problems in the
child-care system. In New York City, 19,800 children are in care
with sixty-eight child-care agencies. Although more than $200 mil-
lion of the $230 million budget comes from public sources, 90 per-
cent of the children are cared for by voluntary agencies, some of
which have existed for 150 years—before public monies became
available.[1] Applying oversight and standards to this loose and varie-
gated "system" has been difficult for city and state agencies. Most
voluntary agencies set up their methods and staffing patterns in an
era when children in placement were very different. Today's placements include more adolescents, more minorities and more tough,
alienated inner city youths with whom the voluntary agencies are
not equipped to deal.

The reluctance—and at times the refusal—of voluntary child-
care agencies to accept into placement adolescents defined in terms
of emotional, mental and behavioral problems burdens public facilities, closes the door to growth and positive outcomes for many of
these children and paves the way for their further harm.

Attention has been given to this problem by the media and by
politicians. Charges have been levelled, and the voluntary agencies
have come up with explanations which must be given serious consideration. In most cases, the voluntary agencies are not, in fact, rejecting behaviorally disturbed children because they are unresponsive or
irresponsible (they are, after all, providing the bulk of residential care
for needy children) but because they do not possess the concepts, the
tools and the assurance to create a safe environment where they can
deal effectively with these children. Yet these concepts and tools exist
and can be made available to those in the field, enabling agencies to
devote a reasonable portion of their resources to the care of such
troublesome children and to upgrade and make more creative their
response to the children they already take into care.

For the problem is not merely that of difficult children who are
turned away and the agencies' inability to cope with them. It is also
the need to improve the quality and the effectiveness of child care
generally, to acquaint agency staff at all levels with new approaches

which can enable them to accomplish more with children, to derive more satisfaction from their work and to take pride in it, as well as meet public goals.

As we conceive it, the Institute would be a place where agency personnel from top to bottom could learn new approaches and pass them along to their agencies. Institute staff trainers, where necessary, would also assist agencies in meeting the requirements of the New York State Child Welfare Reform Act, such as keeping uniform case records. Internships would permit trainees to be immersed in the everyday routines and interactions of selected agencies which have developed successful environmental and growth situations for hard-to-place children. Since the learning that can be incorporated from a handbook or seminar is limited, this experiential learning would be given priority. The Institute would develop curricula and a handbook for practitioners and for use in social work schools.

A condition of training would be that board members and top level staff, as well as child-care workers, social workers and counselors, devote substantial time to become immersed in the Institute and its approaches. Getting one's hands on the proper tools and learning how to use them can build confidence, but if the issues are not grasped by administrative and support personnel, the child-care staff can't do the job. The results of the two-year experimental training program conducted by Huntington Associates for the New York State Division of Youth at Argus and thirty-two other agencies in the city have shown that staff development, to be effective, must be understood and supported at all levels of an organization. Agency policies and concepts, as well as child-care workers, need to change if we are to develop the child-care network needed for the protection and growth of our children.[8]

In working with hard-to-place children we have moved beyond the concept of counseling or therapy as a discrete activity conducted by professionals at set times within an office. In order to work effectively with behaviorally and emotionally disturbed adolescents every interaction throughout the day—and perhaps the night as well—must be utilized therapeutically; that is, must be understood, responded to and interpreted in light of the youngsters' needs and goals. Child-care workers must be more than fixtures on the scene or mere custodians who cook, keep the place clean and perform the children's chores because they dare not make demands on their charges. Since child-care workers are with the youngsters day in and day out, it is their imprint which will be decisive.

The objectives of the Training Institute would be:

1. to enhance the capability of child-care agencies to provide care for hard-to-place adolescents

2. to ease the burden on public agencies which, with a few exceptions, must provide care for PINS and other difficult adolescents

3. to help agencies identify and develop their special training needs and assist them in meeting those needs

4. to improve the quality of child-care services by making state of the art knowledge available to service providers and to those in policy-making and administrative positions

5. to enable agencies to create an environment in which nurturing, values, structure, growth-promoting and goal-oriented interactions, positive peer support and control, as well as staff teamwork and bonding, are woven together to make the load lighter and the results meaningful

In seminars, workshops and groups at the Institute and in an internship program at Argus and selected programs, trainees would learn how to construct a residential program with the following features:

1. a value system espoused and carried out by staff and residents and thoroughly understood and supported by board members, consisting of a commitment to take responsibility for oneself and others, to keep the environment safe, to uphold the structure, to live up to one's potential as a human being and to ask others to do the same. In short, to look after one another as an extended family.

2. a structure, consisting of rules and regulations, a daily and weekly routine and the defining and realization of short and long term goals that are constantly in focus and in process of being achieved.

3. an environment that is, by and large, safe and free from antisocial behavior and violence. This would include learning how to head off or deal with disruptive behavior by new residents, how to abort, defuse or deal with violence, threats of violence and incursions from the streets and drug and alcohol abuse by residents and staff.

4. a positive peer group of residents that can pull in and inspire other residents, help enforce the rules, deal with street and maladaptive behavior and make the climate tolerable and enjoyable for everyone.

5. a staff selected for warmth, strength, firmness, consistency and assertiveness or the willingness and ability to develop these qualities. This staff would participate wholeheartedly in the program, work as a team, confront and make demands on the participants and on one

another and uphold the value system and the structure while bonding with the kids and giving them lots of support and love.

6. a child-care and administrative staff—and board—who can communicate, appreciate each other's capabilities, problems and limitations and, far from feeling alienated and hostile, are able to trust, to give mutual aid and to bond with each other.

This may seem Utopian but the know-how is available and this kind of environment can be achieved by any agency not burdened with the civil service or inflexible union regulations, with guts and determination and the willingness to set high goals and try new approaches.

Other areas in which, based on our experience, the public interest would be served by change and development and which could help troublesome adolescents achieve alternative lifestyles involve the public school system, the Family Court, youth employment programs and the creation of an enlarged and better coordinated network of prevention services.

The number-one problem in our schools is the alienation of students and antisocial behavior, truancy and high dropout rate. In inner-city schools this alienation is largely due to the practice of placing youngsters in grades according to chronology without regard to achievement level, and passing them along whether they have mastered the work or not. The Gates program, where children are held over in the seventh grade, is not a remedy. The system should be reorganized so that children are placed in tracks according to their achievement level, and are passed to higher tracks only after mastering the work. Whipping the system and excoriating teachers is a popular, if useless, sport. As long as the system remains as it is, with youngsters sitting in classrooms where they cannot comprehend what is being taught, we will continue to have failure and chaos. In many cases, leadership could be more vigorous, imaginative and demanding, and in schools where this type of leadership has been brought in, improvement has been remarkable.[3] Administrators often become discouraged, however, because union contracts make it virtually impossible to enforce standards and get rid of teachers who cannot or will not function. Yardsticks for measuring effective teaching should be written into all contracts.

In schools where classrooms are dominated by disruptive and dangerous youngsters, administrators and teachers need help, not opprobrium. Teachers are not trained to deal with this type of behavior, and indeed, teachers should teach, not act as disciplinarians and police persons. But unless a way is found to keep order, the classroom becomes a circus and an arena for antisocial activity. Teachers and pupils suffer; children do not learn; and we taxpayers throw good money after bad.

Here are a few quotes from Argus kids who had dropped out of the public school.

Like I know kids who don't know how to read at all and they pass. Every year they pass grade. Kids, when that happens, they feel like nobody cares.

The kids was horrible in my school. They jumped around, threw papers, pulled your hair, called you all kinds of names. They hit the teachers and teachers hit them back.

I have yelled it out in front of the class: "I can't read! I can't read!" I have stood up and said it in front of twenty-five or thirty people, "Look at me! I can't read! I can't read! I want you to teach me something!"

I would like to stand up and read but I don't know how.

The New York City school system is bringing truants back to school, with the help of the police, and have tightened security. But these measures do not address the root cause of truancy; the alienation of students assigned to levels of classroom work above their heads. In those schools still earmarked as unsafe by New York City school teachers (and there are quite a number of them), programs like Argus can make a difference. The Board of Education teachers assigned to our program sum up their experiences before and after being at Argus.

Where I taught before, youngsters wandered in and out of the classroom, taunted their teachers, threw books and erasers, jumped on and off desks, broke up equipment, smoked marijuana, sniffed cocaine, sold drugs, and abused other children and school personnel both verbally and physically. They threatened to beat up teachers that tried to discipline them, and they did it often enough to keep us in terror.

I've been teaching for ten years and I've been at Argus six months. I simply can't believe it. When I announce that the period is over, these kids hear me. They gather up their stuff, get up and go to the next class, making room for the succeeding group.

The kids have to know that you care about them before you can teach them anything. You can be a master teacher and be a total failure.

Teachers and counselors work together. Teachers couldn't do it alone. And the counselors need us. We both give something very real to the kids.

These teachers' experiences show that a great deal can be accomplished, even with the so-called unteachables. We need to go back to the "Three Rs"—make our schools Responsive, Responsible and Relevant. Teaching kids on their own academic level would go a long way toward making schools responsive and relevant and would remove a major motive for acting out. The Argus approach of streamlined accelerated academics, assigning each student to a track according to achievement level, works well. Teachers like it because they get results. This approach could be adapted to the larger classroom settings of the public schools, and "paras" (community people now employed in more menial ways) could be trained as classroom assistants and tutors, affording more individual instruction. Paras could also be trained as counselors and could prevent or resolve behavioral problems.

We want to investigate in more detail how our young people view themselves and their histories of economic and social deprivation. We also want to find out under what conditions counselors and child-care workers resort to blaming the people they are supposed to be helping. Michelle Fine recently conducted a study of counselors in twelve child-care agencies in the New York City area, six of them public and six private. Her findings suggest that this population is more likely to blame *themselves* rather than their neighborhoods or their poverty for their problems. Dr. Fine also found that child-care workers who feel *powerless* and do not believe that anyone at their agency listens to them are apt to agree that the children in their charge are to blame for their problems.[4]

We want to investigate this in greater depth, for the implications of this self-blame by children, reinforced by counselors and teachers, are enormous. We hope to produce some studies on the subject and to generate, in addition to our package of materials for introducing Positive Mental Attitude to youngsters of the Argus "type," a training manual for counselors, teachers and administrative staff in child-caring agencies.

Above all, we should bring positive peer groups inside the schools. Most schools have tried to shut out or disperse peer groups, since they are generally negative. But shutting out or discouraging peer groups, which are so vital a part of adolescent behavior, particularly in ghetto and blue-collar areas, casts the institution in an adversary role and drives young people, especially young males, into the streets for gratification of this real need for bonding and affiliation. Schools should take steps to coopt the peer group, to utilize it creatively. This cannot be done overnight; it would be hard work but worth it.

We should select community people with street backgrounds to act as tutors, counselors and liaisons, with these titles. We should screen and supervise them, give them status and training and let them form a nucleus in every school. Committees of such paras and positive peers could deal with disruptive behavior and truants who are returned to school by the police. To dignify such positions, we should abandon the term "paraprofessional." It is démeaning. Their contribution would be to free teachers to teach and help keep classrooms, halls, stairwells, rest rooms, lunchrooms and recreation areas free of drugs and crime, as well as defusing violence and keeping order. They can achieve through toughness, rewards, leadership, magnetism and bonding what purely get-tough methods or school guards will never achieve.

Our experience has taught us that art can play a part in opening doors to learning for many who can't find words to express their feelings. To remove the stigma of "sissiness," the art instructor needs to be someone with a background similar to that of the kids.

Most young persons who are disruptive and antisocial can be worked with in programs such as Argus. For the most part, their bad behavior represents the only response they know to the general disregard shown them. The main evidence of this disregard is the joblessness that they experience personally and see on every hand in the ghetto.

Argus youngsters who go on to serve in the Job Corps or the armed services have for the most part returned clean cut, better educated and disciplined and with more to offer employers. But many ghetto youths cannot qualify for the armed services and the Job Corps is too small to accommodate the numbers who could benefit from such an experience. Although the Job Corps is an effective organization (it has been rigorously evaluated),[5] it is our belief that ghetto youth would be better served by taking part in a service which could respond to the idealism and the desire to serve inherent in young people in all walks of life.

The answer to this problem, in a low-employment economy,

should be some form of work program or national service which would match the needs of young people of all classes with the needs of children, the elderly, the handicapped, the sick and the environment (also sick and in need of remediation). The duration of service could be for one year or more. To respond to the need for challenge and the desire to serve inherent in all young people of whatever class or caste, and to the vast needs of our society, the service should be universal.[6]

Government-funded youth employment and vocational training programs should be overhauled, made more realistic and expanded, and Positive Mental Attitude motivational and attitudinal training, as described in Chapters 11 and 12, should be utilized widely in the newly constituted program. Youths who are not job ready and at risk need special help of the type Argus provides, but the Department of Labor programs, as presently constituted, make no provision for responding to this need. Argus makes good use of youth employment funds but only by planning carefully for the special needs of our high-risk youth and by marshalling additional resources from the public and private sectors to meet them.

An adequate staff of specially trained persons is essential both to bring high-risk youth to the point where they can offer employers responsible conduct and a willing attitude—and to persuade employers to take a chance on these young persons. We suggest that the Positive Mental Attitude Job Horizons model at Argus, which pulls in private businesses to assist in the training of youths, as well as to provide employment and funds, has something to offer as a blueprint for a national youth employment and training program for high-risk youth. Supportive services are a necessity if these youngsters are to overcome the turmoil of their life situations, their behavioral and attitudinal difficulties, their deficiencies in basic education, their low self-esteem and their belief that nothing they can do would cause employers to open doors to jobs. Positive Mental Attitude can be a valuable tool in this effort.

We should discontinue the practice of paying teenagers in subsidized employment the minimum wage. Argus finds that although our youngsters desperately need money, they work as well or better for modest stipends, and they work eagerly toward the day when they are ready and deserve to earn minimum wages in nonsubsidized jobs. Teenagers, as well as adults, know the difference between being paid for work well done and a government handout. They resent the handout. It decreases their already low self-esteem. It is one more proof that they are good only for the welfare system or prison. And parents, particularly working parents barely able to keep the pot boiling, resent their kids who don't know how to do a day's work coming home with the minimum wage when they must undertake arduous toil for little more, and sometimes in sweatshops for less.

Youngsters involved in programs such as Argus learn that they have a future in the job market. They will work to earn an allowance while preparing themselves and will feel lucky to get it. Kids who are unaffiliated, hostile and without a belief in the future sneer at the minimum wage as "chump change," goof off, rip off and engage in hustles. They regard the whole transaction as income transfer, a disguised way of paying them off and keeping them cool.

The key is bonding—being incorporated into society, first at the program level and then into the larger community. Another key is self-esteem. These are the essential ingredients, missing in the lives of high-risk youth and youths at all levels.

Four hundred thousand black teenagers are out of work. Federal funds have been drastically cut. American technology is advancing and changing. Black and minority teenagers are scarcely advancing at all. Young people who are not taught how to function effectively are a threat in a democratic society. They are a time bomb. We experience the fallout every day.[7] In New York City crime and the fear of walking the streets is perceived as the number one problem, outranking all others.

Daisy Pizarro, a former Argus enrollee, puts it this way: "By all means let's make this economy of ours better. But how and at whose expense? The poor? What can you take away from someone who does not have much to begin with?"

NOTES

Introduction
1. Bernard Lefkowitz, "Training the Troubled Ones," *Psychology Today,* September 1982, p. 14.

Chapter 2. A SAFE PLACE
1. E. Fuller Torrey, M.D., *Schizophrenia and Civilization* (New York: Jason Aronson, 1980), pp. 172–74.

Chapter 4. PHASE TWO: Jobs and the Youth Crime Connection
1. Argus Yearly Report and Statistics: 1979–1980, Xerox.
2. Ted Morgan, "They Say, 'I Can Kill Because I'm 14,' " *New York Times Magazine,* Jan. 19, 1975, p. 10. For a discussion of the "leveling-off" of violent crime in the mid- and late 1970s, and how much these statistics may mean given the fact that the United States is two to ten times more violent than any country in Western Europe, see Philip M. Bpffeu, *New York Times,* Feb. 2, 1982, p. C-1.
3. Thorsten Sellin, "Maturing Out of Crime: Recidivism and Maturation," *National Probation and Parole Association Journal* 4 (1958): 241–50.
4. Patricia Huntington, *Youth at Risk and Work: A Working Paper* (New York: Huntington Associates, 1982), Xerox, p. 13 and passim.
5. Study by the Bureau of Social Research, Washington, D.C., cited in the *New York Times,* Jan. 3, 1982.
6. For further discussion of these matters, see W. Thompson et al., *Employment and Crime: A Review of Theories and Research* (New York: Vera Institute of Justice, 1981).
7. Edward I. Koch, *Mayor's Criminal Justice Legislative Program, 1982* (New York: Office of the Mayor, 1982), Xerox, pp. 10–11, and Criminal Justice Coordinating Council of the City of New York, "Plan for 1980" (New York: 1980), Xerox, pp. 23–28.

Chapter 6. The Eyes of the Peacock
1. See, for example, Daniel Casriel, *A Scream Away from Happiness* (New York: Grosset and Dunlap, 1972), and Lionel Tiger, *Men in Groups* (New York: Random House, 1969).
2. Herbert J. Gans, *The Urban Villagers* (New York: The Free Press, 1962), chap. 4.
3. Casriel, op. cit., passim.
4. Michelle Fine et al., "Final Report and Evaluation of Training in Child Care Agencies" (New York: Huntington Associates, 1981), Xerox.

Chapter 7. Group Home Structure

1. See Vera Institute of Justice, "Protection of Children in Foster Family Care: A Guide for Social Workers" (New York, March 1982), Xerox; Citizens' Committee for Children of New York, Inc., *Foster Care in New York City* (New York: Foster Care Report no. 3, July 1982), Xerox; Community Council of Greater New York, *Planning for Children and Families in New York City* (New York: October 1979), Xerox; Division of Criminal Justice Services, *Resource Assessment Panel: Final Report* (New York: June 1982); and Michael Fabricant, *Juvenile Injustice: Dilemmas of the Family Court System* (New York: Community Service Society, September 1981), Xerox.

Chapter 8. The Hungry Cow Syndrome

1. Interview with Jody Adams Weisbrod, May 1982.
2. Conversation with Mitchell Rosenthal, M.D., Psychiatric Director of Phoenix House, 1980.

Chapter 9. Using the Language of Touch and Emotion

1. Ashley Montagu, *Touching: The Human Significance of the Skin* (New York: Harper & Row, 1978).

Chapter 10. Understanding the Process

1. Virginia Adams, "Consensus Is Reached: Psychotherapy Works," *New York Times*, July 10, 1979, section C.
2. Hans H. Strupp, "Psychotherapy," *Annual Review of Psychology* 13 (1962): 460–71.
3. Dorothy Tennov, *Psychotherapy: The Hazardous Cure* (New York: Abelard Schuman, 1975), p. 15.
4. Daniel Casriel, *A Scream Away from Happiness* (New York: Grosset and Dunlap, 1972), p. 135.
5. Ibid, p. 119.
6. Ibid., p. 95.
7. Ibid., p. 56.
8. Carl Rogers, *On Encounter Groups* (New York: Harper & Row, 1973), p. 7.
9. Diane Moore et al., "Report on the Positive Mental Attitude Experiment at Argus Community, Inc." (Bronx, N.Y.: Argus Community, 1982), Xerox.
10. Daniel Casriel, *So Fair a House: The Story of Synanon* (Englewood Cliffs, N.J.: Prentice-Hall, 1966).
11. Elery L. Phillips et al., "Behavior Shaping Works for Delinquents," *Psychology Today*, June 1973, pp. 75–79.

Chapter 11. The Sleeping Giant: Positive Mental Attitude

1. Napolean Hill and W. Clement Stone, *Success Through a Positive Mental Attitude* (New York: Pocket Books, 1977), p. xviii.
2. Ibid., passim.
3. James S. Coleman, *Equality of Educational Opportunity* (Washington, D.C.:

Department of Health, Education and Welfare, Documents Catalogue
no. 5.238:38001, 1966).

4. John U. Ogbu, *Minority Education and Caste: The American System in Cross-
Cultural Perspective* (New York: Academic Press, 1978), p. 43.

5. Susan Stodolsky and Gerald Lesser, "Learning Patterns in the Disadvantaged," *Harvard Educational Review,* reprint series no. 5 (Cambridge,
Mass.: 1971), pp. 22–69.

6. Patricia Cayo Sexton, "Schools: Broken Ladder to Success," in Frances
Cordasco and Eugene Bucchiono, eds., *The Puerto Rican Community and
Its Children on the Mainland: A Sourcebook for Teachers, Social Workers and
Other Professionals* (Metuchen, N.J.: Scarecrow Press, 1972).

7. New York City, Board of Education, *The Puerto Rican Study, 1953–1957*
(New York: Orioe Education, 1972).

8. Coleman, op. cit., and Ogbu, op. cit., p. 222 and passim.

9. Ogbu, op. cit., pp. 40–65.

10. Ibid., p. 51.

11. Ibid., p. 54.

12. Caroline Hodges Persell, *Education and Inequality* (New York: The Free
Press, 1977), p. 134.

13. Ogbu, op. cit., pp. 87–95.

14. *The Persistence of Preschool Effects,* a study by twelve research groups for the
Education Commission of the States and the Administration for Children, Youth and Families for the U.S. Department of Health, Education
and Welfare (Washington, D.C.: U.S. Government Printing Office,
Stock No. 017 000 00202 3, 1977), p. 107.

15. Quoted in Hill and Stone, op. cit., pp. 52–54.

16. See discussion of the neo-Freudians in J. A. C. Brown, *Freud and the
Post-Freudians* (Baltimore: Penguin, 1961), pp. 161–216.

17. M. E. P. Seligman, "Depression and Learned Helplessness," in R. J.
Friedman and M. M. Katz, eds., *The Psychology of Depression: Contemporary
Theory and Research* (Washington, Winston-Wiley, 1974).

18. Aaron T. Beck, M.D., *Cognitive Therapy and the Emotional Disorders* (New
York, London: Meridian Books, 1979), pp. 24–46.

19. Diane Moore et al., "Report on the Positive Mental Attitude Experiment
at Argus Community, Inc." (Bronx, N.Y.: Argus Community, 1982),
Xerox.

Chapter 13. Widening Circles

1. Anthony C. Wallace, *The Death and Rebirth of the Seneca* (New York: Random
House, 1972).

Chapter 14. My Own Circles

1. Germaine Dieterlen, "The Mande Creation Myth," in Elliott P. Skinner,
ed., *Peoples and Cultures of Africa* (Garden City, N.Y.: Natural History
Press, 1973), pp. 634–53.

2. Elliott P. Skinner, ed., *Peoples and Cultures of Africa* (Garden City, N.Y.: Natural History Press, 1973), pp. 631–33. Also see Paul Bohannan and Philip Curtin, "African Families," in *Africa and Africans* (Garden City, N.Y.: The Natural History Press, 1971), pp. 101–18.

Chapter 15. Diagnostics and Other Confusions

1. American Psychiatric Association, *DSM-III* (Washington, D.C., 1980), pp. 37ff.
2. William James, *Psychology: Briefer Course* (New York: Holt, 1892; Crowell-Collier Paperback, 1962).
3. American Psychiatric Association, op. cit., pp. 45–50.
4. *The Merck Manual of Diagnosis and Therapy,* 3d ed. (Rahway, N.J., 1977), pp. 1058–59.
5. Ashley Montagu, *Life Before Birth* (New York: New American Library, 1965), p. 198.
6. *Merck Manual,* pp. 1062–63.
7. Brandt F. Steele and C. B. Pollock, quoted in Ashley Montagu, *Touching: The Human Significance of the Skin* (New York: Harper & Row, 1978), p. 177.
8. National Council on Crime and Delinquency, *Status Offenders and the Juvenile Justice System* (Hackensack, N.J.: 1978), pp. 61, 65, and passim.
9. Daniel R. Young and Stephen Finch, *The Voluntary Child Care System in New York: Sectoral Trends and Agency Operations* (S.U.N.Y. Stonybrook: The Institute for Public Policy Alternatives, 1975), Xerox.
10. American Psychiatric Association, op. cit., pp. 181–93.
11. E. Fuller Torrey, M.D., *Schizophrenia and Civilization* (New York: Jason Aronson, 1980), p. 187.
12. American Psychiatric Association, op. cit., pp. 181–84.
13. Torrey, op. cit., p. 4.
14. Ibid., pp. 4–10 and passim.
15. Solomon Snyder, M.D., *Madness and the Brain* (New York: McGraw-Hill, 1974), pp. 205–8.
16. Ibid., pp. 210–14.
17. Ibid., pp. 179–80.
18. Virginia Adams, "Studies Relate Physical Causes to Delinquency," *New York Times,* June 26, 1979, section C.
19. Dorothy Otnow Lewis, "Treatment Programs for Delinquent Children: Implications of the Psychobiological Vulnerabilities to Delinquency," in Lewis, ed., *Vulnerabilities to Delinquency* (New York: Spectrum Publications, 1981), p. 318.
20. Richard Wurtman, "Brain Muffins," *Psychology Today,* October 1978, p. 140.
21. Ibid.

Chapter 20. The Consensus Model

1. Paul Bohannan and Philip Curtin, *Africa and Africans* (New York: Natural History Press, 1971), pp. 135–54.

2. From a discussion with Anna L. Chairetakis, spring 1980.
3. Edward T. Hall, *Beyond Culture* (Garden City, N.Y.: Doubleday, 1977), p. 39 and passim.
4. Bohannan and Curtin, op. cit., pp. 147–54.
5. Isak Dinesen, *Out of Africa* (New York: Vintage, 1972), pp. 99ff.

Chapter 21. The Paper Boa Constrictor

1. Alvin Toffler, *Future Shock* (New York: Bantam Books, 1970), p. 113 and passim.
2. National Council on Crime and Delinquency, *Status Offenders and the Juvenile Justice System* (Hackensack, N.J., 1978), pp. 3–5. President's Commission on Law Enforcement and Administration of Justice, *The Challenge of Crime in a Free Society* (Washington, D.C.: U.S. Government Printing Office, 1967).
3. Jody Adams Weisbrod, *Family Court Disposition Study* (New York: Vera Institute of Justice, March 1980), Xerox, p. 440.
4. The Children's Aid Society, "The PINS Mediation Project" (New York: March 1982), Xerox.

Chapter 22. Where Do We Go from Here?

1. Speech by Gail Kong, Assistant Commissioner of Special Services for Children, Human Resources Administration of New York City, 1982.
2. Michelle Fine et al., "Final Report and Evaluation of Training in Child Care Agencies" (New York: Huntington Associates, 1981), Xerox.
3. Interview with Marian Schwarz, Special Assistant for Education, Office of the Mayor, New York City (1982).
4. Fine et al., op. cit.
5. Charles Mallor et al., *Evaluation of the Economic Impact of the Job Corps* (Princeton, N.J.: Mathematica Policy Research, April 1980).
6. Committee for the Study of National Service, *Youth and the Needs of the Nation* (Washington, D.C.: The Potomac Institute, January 1979).
7. Edward I. Koch, *Mayor's Criminal Justice Legislative Program* (New York: Office of the Mayor, 1982), Xerox, p. 10.

GLOSSARY

break	let go emotionally or in dance; become wild or enraged
chiba	marijuana, especially a finer variety grown in Colombia
chill out	cool it
cop	buy drugs
cop out	evade responsibility
cooker	bottlecap for heating dope before shooting up
death	adjective meaning terrific, smashing
fly	exciting, fantastic clothing, hairdo, shoes
flying	high on drugs
foxy	sexy, attractive
ice	kill
jam	a disco with improvisations, often held in the street
the joint	a highly congenial place to be; a permissive, enjoyable place
Locator Test	a quick reading and math level assessment, useful at intake
mean vines	gorgeous clothes
off	kill
Panthers	Black Panthers
playpen	a place to enjoy oneself, especially in the street, partying, smoking pot, etc.
Project Foothold	Argus' CETA Youth Employment Program.
Section 8	federal program for rent subsidy for new construction, now defunded
skag	heroin
smoking	angry
speedballing	Injecting a mixture of cocaine and heroin to achieve a "bang" or "rush" and a mood elevation and to relieve the excessive agitation produced by pure cocaine use.
superfly	more fly than fly
take a chill pill	calm oneself, cool it
vines	threads, clothes

ACRONYMS AND ABBREVIATIONS

AA   Alcoholics Anonymous

ACD   Adjournment in Contemplation of Dismissal

ADC   Aid to Dependent Children

AFDC   Aid to Families of Dependent Children

BCW   Bureau of Child Welfare (City of New York)

CAT   California Achievement Test

CETA   Comprehensive Employment and Training Act

CJCC   Criminal Justice Coordinating Council (City of New York)

CRU   Children's Rights Unit of SSC

C.S.W.   Certified Social Worker

CWIS   Child Welfare Information Service

DOE   Department of Employment (City of New York)

DFY   Division for Youth (State of New York)

DOL   Department of Labor (U.S.A.)

DSAS   Division of Substance Abuse Services (State of New York)

DSS   Department of Social Services

G.E.D.   General Educational Development, a federal program offering, among other things, a high school equivalency diploma

HRA   Human Resources Administration (City of New York)

J.D.   Juvenile delinquent

LPN   Licensed Practical Nurse

LSD   D-lysergic acid diethylamide—a mind-distorting synthetic drug

M.S.W.   Master of Social Work

NYSIIS   New York State Intelligence and Information System

OD   Overdose—death commonly attributed to heroin but probably due to a combination of heroin with alcohol and/or the quinine used to "cut" the drug

PCP   Phencyclidine, known as angel dust. An animal tranquillizer used as a street drug.

PINS   Person in Need of Supervision

POP   Project Operational Plan

333

SMED   Socially Maladjusted and Emotionally Disturbed
SSC   Special Services for Children (City of New York)
            CIU of SSC—Confidential Investigations Unit of SSC
SSI   Supplementary Security Income
T.C.   Therapeutic Community
ULURP   Urban Land Use Review Procedure
W.I.S.C.R. Wechsler Intelligence Scale for Children
YEP   Youth Employment Program, a work experience program
            funded by the U.S. Department of Labor.
YETP   Youth Employment and Training Program, a training and
            employment program funded by the U.S. Department of
            Labor